THE MAKING OF MODERN
IRISH HISTORY

This book is about the writing of modern Irish history: how it has been influenced both by the changes in professional historical methods in the last half-century, and by the involvement of history with political ideologies.

The book is arranged so that the reader is guided through the main topics in Irish history since the eighteenth century. Each chapter offers a review and an analysis of major work published on a particular event or issue, together with a discussion of the historical controversies involved. Each contributor then offers their own interpretation of the subject and an analysis of how interpretations have changed over the last thirty years. In this way the book makes a substantive contribution to key issues in modern Irish history as well as contributing to the debate on revisionism.

The editors have written a comprehensive introduction which outlines the history of the revisionist controversy and places Ireland within a historical and contemporary context. The combination of synthesis and original analysis make this book ideal for both students and historians alike.

D. George Boyce is Professor of Politics and Head of Department at the University of Wales, Swansea. His most recent publications include *Ireland 1828–1923* (1992) and *The Irish Question in British Politics* (1988). **Alan O'Day** teaches at the University of North London and holds the title of Professor at Concordia University, Montreal. He is the author of *The English Face of Irish Nationalism* (1994) and *Parnell and the First Home Rule Episode* (1986).

THE MAKING OF MODERN IRISH HISTORY

Revisionism and the revisionist controversy

Edited by
D. George Boyce and Alan O'Day

POPLTAN

London and New York

First published 1996
by Routledge
11 New Fetter Lane, London EC4P 4EE

Simultaneously published in the USA and Canada
by Routledge
29 West 35th Street, New York, NY 10001

Routledge is an International Thomson Publishing company

© 1996 selection and editorial matter, D. George Boyce and Alan O'Day.
© Individual contributors, their contributions

Typeset in Palatino by LaserScript Ltd, Mitcham, Surrey
Printed and bound in Great Britain by
Richard Clay Ltd, Bungay, Suffolk.

British Library Cataloguing in Publication Data
A catalogue record for this book is available from the British Library

Library of Congress Cataloging in Publication Data
A catalogue record for this book as been requested

ISBN 0-415-09819-X (hbk)
ISBN 0-415-12171-X (pbk)

CONTENTS

NOTES ON CONTRIBUTORS

Paul Bew is Professor of Irish Politics at the Queen's University of Belfast. He is author and co-author of eleven books including *Ideology and the Irish Question* (Oxford, 1994) and *Northern Ireland, 1921–1994* (Serif, 1994). He is currently working on the Ireland volume in the Oxford History of Modern Europe series, under the general editorship of Lord Bullock and Sir F.W. Deakin.

D. George Boyce is Professor in the Department of Politics, University of Wales, Swansea. He has published in the field of modern British and Irish political history. His *Nationalism in Ireland* is now in its third edition (Routledge, 1995) and his most recent book is *Political Ideas in Ireland Since the Seventeenth Century*, co-edited with R. Eccleshall and V. Geoghegan (Routledge, 1993).

S.J. Connolly is Reader in History at the University of Ulster at Coleraine. He has written *Priests and People in Pre-Famine Ireland 1780–1845* (Dublin, 1982), *Religion and Society in Nineteenth-Century Ireland* (Dundalk, 1985), and *Religion, Law and Power: The making of Protestant Ireland* (Oxford, 1992). He is currently editing the *Oxford Companion to Irish History*.

Mary E. Daly is Associate Professor of Modern Irish History at University College Dublin and joint editor of the journal *Irish Economic and Social History*. Her publications include, *Dublin: The Deposed Capital, 1860–1914. A Social and Economic History,* (Cork, 1984); *The Famine in Ireland* (Dublin, 1986) and *Industrial Development and Irish National Identity, 1922–39* (Dublin, 1992).

John Hutchinson is Senior Lecturer in the Faculty of Humanities at Griffith University, Brisbane. He studied History at the University of Edinburgh and took a doctorate in Sociology at the London School of Economics. He is the author of *The Dynamics of Cultural Nationalism: The*

Gaelic revival and the creation of the Irish nation-state (London, 1987) and *Modern Nationalism* (London, 1994), and has co-edited (with Anthony D. Smith) *Nationalism* (Oxford University Press, 1994) for the Oxford Readers series. He is presently working on the subject of nations in world historical perspective.

Alvin Jackson is Lecturer in Modern History at the Queen's University of Belfast. He is the author of *The Ulster Party: Irish Unionists in the House of Commons, 1884–1911*; he has also written *Sir Edward Carson*, and *Colonel Edward Saunderson: Land and loyalty in Victorian Ireland*. He has been a Post-doctoral Fellow of the British Academy and Lecturer in Modern Irish History at University College Dublin.

David S. Johnson is Senior Lecturer in Economic and Social History at the Queen's University of Belfast. He has published widely on nineteenth- and twentieth-century Irish economic history and is the author of *The Interwar Economy in Ireland* (Dublin, 1985).

Liam Kennedy is reader in Economic and Social History at the Queen's University of Belfast, co-editor of *An Economic History of Ulster, 1820–1939* (Manchester, 1985) and author of *The Modern Industrialisation of Ireland, 1940–1988* (Dublin, 1989).

Alan O'Day is Senior Lecturer in History at the University of North London and Professor of History at Concordia University, Montreal. His publications include *The English Face of Irish Nationalism* (London, 1977; reprinted 1994), *Parnell and the First Home Rule Episode* (Dublin, 1986) and with D. George Boyce he edited *Parnell in Perspective* (London, 1991).

1

INTRODUCTION

'Revisionism' and the 'revisionist' controversy

D. George Boyce and Alan O'Day

What is the popular image of historical revisionism today? A retelling of Irish history which seeks to show that British rule of Ireland was not, as we have believed a *bad* thing, but a mixture of necessity, good intentions and bungling; and that Irish resistance to it was not as we have believed, a *good* thing, but a mixture of wrong-headed idealism and unnecessary, often cruel violence. The underlying message is that our relations with Britain on the Irish question the Irish have been very much at fault. This is the popular image of historical revisionism.

Desmond Fennell[1]

REVISING HISTORY

Revising national history is perilous, especially if cherished legends are debunked or heroes pushed off their pedestals. History is viewed as having the functions of inculcation of the young with a sense of their own national past and of recounting a public morality tale legitimising the state, nation or community. It can give self-respect to a diaspora suffering from disorientation, alienation or a sense of inferiority. One commentator notes of Britain's Irish community

the Irish have often found solace in reminding themselves of their victimised past. The past is where a small nation was colonised and crushed by a ruthless oppressor. In their own lives they may well be ridiculed at work for being Irish. Since the re-emergence of the 'troubles' twenty years ago, the abuse has sometimes been more than verbal (particularly if the IRA campaign comes across the water). A reading of traditional Irish nationalist history helps to place their experiences in context. It gives people pride in their past, and thus national self-respect. The classes are dominated by first and second generation Irish and the climate is one of uncritical

1

nationalism. To introduce 'revisionist' history into such classes would be to take away a major reason why people have attended.[2]

Anything which questions national or nationalist priorities is suspect for history above all is the property of those who control the political apparatus or, in the case of certain of the disaffected diaspora, of a patriotic tradition. Liberal societies no less than authoritarian regimes are zealous in detecting historical heresy. Indeed, contemporary historical heterodoxy is comparable to religious heresy and inspires much the same suspicion and hatred from those who feel threatened by it. Like the priest of old, the historian's standing in society depends on how well he or she satisfies the psychological wants of the community. To challenge its presumptions is to invite disdain, rejection and possibly humiliation. Democratic nations, it is alleged, even sponsor the establishment of a Marxist historiography that allows for the expression of a harmless counter-state version of the past while effectively affirming the integrity of the existing society.[3] Certain of Northern Ireland's so-called 'Orange' Marxists have been put in the dock as a state-sponsored Trojan Horse. Relatively new nations or those that have experienced a recent revolution jealously guard their 'approved' history, for the state or its current political leadership lacks the legitimacy of a lengthy pedigree. New national states, most lacking an ancient territory, frequently possessing antagonistic ethnic or religious groups, and often lacking a consensus on the existence of the political structure, employ an approved public history as substitute for antiquity.

The nature of 'revisionism' and responses to it vary between communities and over time. Whether it is called 'revisionism' or by some other name the new history is often identified with efforts by some historians to propagate a different political agenda. 'Present-mindedness', in some contexts an innocent historical perspective, has none-the-less become a coded phrase for history with a purpose, a political purpose meant to change, not uphold, currently existing ideologies or institutions. Probably historians can never be divorced from their own experiences and concerns but it is worth recalling S.R. Gardiner's dictum: 'He who studies the society of the past will be of greater service to the society of the present in proportion as he leaves it out of account.'[4] There is revisionism and 'revisionism' and historians everywhere have found it easier to adopt the first but to deny the validity of the second.

New writings that disturb approved traditions are always a quicksand but they have had an exceptional place in German historiography that holds pride of place as the storm centre of 'revisionism'. Perhaps it is fitting that the culture that pioneered 'scientific history', systematic archival research and the academic doctorate should be at the forefront of the present intellectual controversy over the function of history. Revival of nationalist historiography in Germany raises fears transcending the ivory towers of academe. Containment of Germany has been the foundation stone of the Cold War and instigated elaborate constructs of alliances, a problem now made even more urgent in the face of the collapse of the Eastern bloc, the reunification of Germany and a resurgence of virulent German nationalism. One British scholar anxiously dismisses the whole revisionist debate in Germany as having 'little to offer anyone with a serious scholarly interest in the German past' while another, less severely perhaps, declares that 'at any rate the *historikerstreit* has resulted in no new and lasting insights into a deeper understanding of the Third Reich'.[5] The problem that these and other historians identified is that revisionism of the Nazi era advances, not a genuine challenge to scholarship, but a moral and political discourse, though one conducted through the medium of leading historians, about how far contemporary Germans can cope with this past. Since this was at heart a political debate, the expertise of these historians offers 'no great advantage or special privilege'.[6] In the eyes of its critics this revisionism had 'nothing to do with the internal demands of historical scholarship'.[7] Arguments about German history are not purely or even primarily confined to Germans. Germany's history is a preoccupation of historians from many cultures. It is much too serious a business to be left to Germans. Yet, the controversy raises one of the long-standing and still germane issues about the practice of history. What, if any, part should an academic historian play in the political uses of the past? Is the historian not a citizen as well as an observer? Can the modern historian in the emergent global village continue to be bound by the limits of national allegiance? And, how does the historian respond to the demand by the state for a new version of the past when the old no longer seems entirely convenient? The Coroner of Sligo when commenting on the murder of Lord Mountbatten gave voice to the need for a new version of history, noting:

> I believe it is necessary to stress again the great responsibility that parents and teachers of any nation have in the way they interpret history and pass it on to the youth of their country. I believe that if history could be taught in such a fashion that it would help to create harmony among people rather than division and hatred, it would serve this nation and all other nations better.[8]

British historiography, too, has experienced a plethora of 'revisionism' but to a great extent this has been carried on within the universities or the pages of relatively low circulation periodicals beloved by the literati. Participation in these disputes, like German studies, is an activity without national boundaries. The battle for the soul of history, in contrast, is fought over techniques and ideological issues of interest to the academics but lacks a dynamic capable of rousing popular sentiment. 'Revisionism' then has a wide impact only when it is perceived to affect the community in a significant way.

Trends in historiography elsewhere made it inevitable that Irish history would experience a 'revisionism' of its own. Southern Ireland's recent 'liberation' and the continued division of the historic territory insured that 'revisionism' when it arrived would replicate public contention as in Germany. Northern Unionists also were sensitive to any tampering with their 'history'. Desmond Fennell's sharp rebuke of 'revisionists' aptly draws attention to the passions roused by the new history in a society where the past has been the handmaiden to a political present. Yet, it is vital to note that there is an important distinction between 'revisionism' of Irish history and the new history of Germany, for instance, in that in the former case the impulses are liberal and pluralistic whereas in Germany it is associated with the resurgence of the extreme right. But what is 'revisionism' in the Irish context? What are its origins and progression? Has this historiography had any meaningful impact? Should anyone outside Ireland bother giving the controversy more than passing notice?

There has been remarkably little coherence to the debate on Irish 'revisionism'. A clear definition of 'revisionism' remains absent from the discussion. Partly as a consequence there is not an agreed list of who is and is not a 'revisionist'. As Hugh Kearney observes, the same individual historians are cited with approval by 'revisionists' and 'anti-revisionists' alike.[9] Also, there is no universally accepted date for the beginnings of 'revisionism' or for its influences. Most public participants have been impelled by its effect (or virtue) in enervating the principles of modern Irish republicanism, as the corrupter a generation of politicians, civil servants, teachers and leading figures in the media, though it seems more probable that these influences have done more to 'corrupt' the historians than *vice versa*. Echoes of 'anti-revisionism' are present in Unionist circles as well. Yet other antagonists disclaim any influence for this historiographic movement. Seldom has a major dispute within the intelligentsia been so lacking in agreement on what the issues are. However, certain features do offer common ground. First, disputants assume that history is an important political tool. This is a crucial intellectual assumption, even arrogance, for historians in many societies are painfully aware of their impotence in public life, of their enforced exile from forums where decision-making takes place. As J.J. Lee notes, the New Ireland Forum in 1983–4 did its work largely without the benefit of the historians' expertise. 'If the Forum was a "gigantic academic session, a 'teach-in' on the national question", the historians were conspicuously ignored'.[10] To the extent that the intelligentsia plays some part in governance, it is most frequently economists, sociologists or political scientists who find themselves enlisted to aid political establishments as was the case in the New Ireland Forum. Yet, it is refreshing, if somewhat surprising, to have one Irish commentator declaring in a paper delivered in the United States, that historians do not live only in the ivory tower. It is incontestable that some wider social role is performed by the historian: as textbook-writer for schools, as advisors to government and educational bodies, to publishers and the providers of historical resources for learning, as contributors to popular newspapers, to radio and tele-vision programmes.[11]

This certainly set an unrealistic expectation, for few in the audience would ever be called upon in a significant public capacity to comment on Irish affairs. Opportunities for Irish historians to play a public role out-side Ireland, 'revisionists' or otherwise, are slight indeed and as Lee suggests their place even in Ireland is insecure. Second, it is a char-acteristic of Irish 'revisionism' that though the writing of Ireland's history is international in origin, including 'revisionist' studies, the controversy about 'revisionism' is intensely parochial. Contributions to the debate on both sides have taken place mainly among the Irish themselves con-ducted principally in periodicals and a media that receives little notice outside Ireland. T.W. Moody, F.S.L. Lyons, Roy Foster, Ronan Fanning, Brendan Bradshaw and Desmond Fennell are at one in seeing Irish history as *our* history.[12] Lee is a partial exception to the extent that he acknowledges an outside dimension to historical writing on Ireland. This insularity is especially curious as a supposed impetus for 'revisionism' is the international and European impact on Ireland since the 1960s. Because it is *our* history, the participants in the dispute have been conscious of the local context for the shift in historiographic tendencies and, in the cases of Fennell and Bradshaw, critical of those who have by omission or design eroded nationalist traditions of suffering and resist-ance to oppression. While it might be arguable that historians in Ireland owe a duty to their community not to be derogatory about the country's patriots or undermine public self-esteem, scholars outside Ireland have no such obligation. Patrick O'Farrell denies any intention of writing out of any 'filo-pietism'.[13] Whether many participants in the 'revisionism' controversy have much sense of this global dimension is unclear. Third, 'revisionists' and 'anti-revisionists' largely agree on an agenda that takes a less Anglocentric view of the past. Roy Foster is upbraided for failing to achieve his aim of a less Anglocentric interpretation of modern Ireland.[14] Such a project would be truly 'revisionist' for the country's relationship with Britain is unquestionably a fundamental reality of Ireland's past, something implicit in the 'anti-revisionist' demand for traditional nationalist history. Neither 'revisionist' nor 'anti-revisionist' Unionist writing suffers from this affliction.

'Revisionism' has been dated variously to a revulsion from the officially propagated histories of the post-1922 Irish Free State and of Northern Ireland culminating in the founding of *Irish Historical Studies* in the late 1930s, to disillusionment with the failure of the Republic to deliver the promised economic and cultural goods by the 1960s generation of Irish who looked to America and swinging London as their talismans, to the 'troubles' in Northern Ireland that laid claim to a tradition of Republican violence, and to the whole island's entry into the European Union, a decision nullifying fundamental tenets of nationalism and Unionism. Extreme Republicanism and militant Unionists have been at one in rejecting the island's integration into the European Community. Brendan Bradshaw, who gives effective form to the 'anti-revisionist' case, identifies two crucial stages in the progression of 'revisionism'. He notes the impact of the 1930s generation of graduate students, largely trained in London, who sought – misguidedly in his estimation – to impose 'value-free' history in Ireland. He argues that this attempt has led to a selectivity that omits inconvenient aspects of the country's past thereby laying the foundations of an interpretation unsympathetic to the suffering, struggle, heroism and sacrifice of those who liberated the nation. Similarly, he expresses concern about the impact of this 'value-free' approach on unionist history though this is incidental to his theme. Because of a ruthlessly austere methodology, he contends, the works emanating from this 'value-free' school are clinical and sanitised. A second stage, in Bradshaw's estimation, was reached by the generation of students of the 1960s and 1970s, also mainly trained in British universities, who added to the earlier 'value-free' approach a deliberate iconoclasm, a practised irony that juxtaposes incidents and phrases in ways calculated to convey an ultra-scepticism, even cynicism, about the national tradition. His critique gives academic credentials to 'anti-revisionism' popularised by Fennell and is a beacon to others who have reservations about the work of the now dominant generation of historians. Both 'revisionists' and 'anti-revisionists' agree that the movement originated outside Ireland and was slow to reach an apogee. Similarly, they concur that revisionism had its take-off into unrestrained growth in the later 1960s and 1970s.

Bradshaw's chronology and critique of the often-forced iconoclasm of contemporary historians commands attention though, of course, this is not necessarily a feature of 'revisionism'. Whether 'anti-revisionists' would be content with a history that reaches the same conclusions without iconoclasm is a moot point. Some of Brendan Bradshaw's comments suggest otherwise. Both sides in the debate, though, err in attributing excessive importance to the academic pioneers centred around the founding of *Irish Historical Studies* in the late 1930s. While these historians made a considerable contribution to the field and to academic history in Ireland, their work, methodology and inspiration was derivative, their influence on historians of Ireland elsewhere (the majority) remained slight. To the present day it remains the case that few overseas graduate students of Ireland's history are drawn to Irish universities but prefer those of their own respective countries or migrate to one of the international universities in Great Britain. Because the numbers of historians produced by the Irish universities has been modest, they have not flooded into institutions abroad thereby influencing succeeding generations of historians. It is difficult to visualise historical scholarship in Ireland having much presence in contemporary global scholarship without replacing the polemical approach with a 'scientific' or 'skills-based' methodology.

Though the 'new' learning in Ireland has a part in the 'revisionist' saga, Germanic historical methods are of much greater significance. Perusal of manuals widely used by students and tutors abroad in courses on the 'practice of history' have copious references to German, American, French and British pioneers in the profession but seldom mention Irish historiography at all. Had the historians of the 1930s not adopted an English transmitted version of these techniques, the serious writing of Ireland's history would have fallen almost entirely into the hands of historians from elsewhere. While the founders of the modern school of Irish historiography attempted to establish an agenda for the study of the country's past, as Lee notes the greater number of practitioners began their research without reverence for, sometimes even knowledge of these priorities.[15] Application of social science methodology in history and of 'history from below' are instances where the motivation for their use for study of the Irish past owes nothing of consequence to scholarship in Ireland. Richard Cobb, Maurice Cowling, Oscar Handlin, Eric Hobsbawm, E.P. Thompson and latterly Mirslav Hroch and Ernest Gellner along with British demographers, all working outside the framework of Irish influences, have had a profound effect on Ireland's historiography. In short, what the current debate on 'revisionism' often lacks is some sense of the extent that Irish history has been pushed rather than has led. It is difficult to identify any aspect of historical writing in Ireland of specifically Irish provenance.

Bradshaw's charge of iconoclasm is less easily dismissed. Again, it reached Ireland through a multiplicity of avenues, many owing nothing to scholarly trends in Ireland. To note that it is extra-Irish in origin, however, does not vitiate the objection. Critics of the new history elsewhere have been unhappy with the tendency to sanitise the past, to treat it as a metaphorical game in which historians rival one another for the cleverest means to disprove previously accepted truths or, if evidence fails to do the job, to frame language in ways to achieve the intended effect anyway. Iconoclasm is not an integral element of 'revisionism' and the vast majority of publications that might be labelled 'revisionist' have no trace of it. However, Bradshaw poses once more the dilemma of the function of academic history. Is it merely a game between academics having no particular relevance to the wider public or do historians have a wider responsibility? Some of the misunderstanding arises from the hazy distinction made by many between history as it actually happened and history as a collective representation of what happened.[16] What has been in the Irish setting a largely parochial argument has a wider frame of reference. Irish 'revisionism' usefully illuminates this bigger question and contributes to wider considerations of contemporary historical methodology.

REVISING NATIONALISM AND UNIONISM

The case against Revisionism centres on the question of nationalism in Ireland. This is in itself a revealing controversy. 'Revisionism' of the role of unionism, or the British connection, are seen in the light of their reflection on Irish Nationalism, and so Ireland's history cannot be said to have moved much further on since J.C. Beckett remarked in 1965 that there was an obsessive concentration on the nationalist tradition. Beckett quotes Michael Tierney to illustrate his point, that 'thus construed and invoked, it makes nonsense of a great part of our history; for in this rigid form it is a product of the late eighteenth century and was first popularly preached only a little more than a hundred years ago.'[17] One of Bradshaw's objections to the work of Stephen Ellis is the contention that English rule in Ireland was not exceptional but part of a pattern and also that he fails to give due weight to popular, sometimes individual, resistance to foreign oppression, something expressed, for instance, in Gaelic folk culture.[18]

This is not to say that nationalism should be relegated to a less central role in Ireland's history. Rather, it is to urge that nationalist writing that simplifies the tradition, ignores its variety, sets aside its own internal disputes and contradictions, can hardly be said to amount to historical thinking at all. Indeed, the prominence of nationalism raises the question of what is 'historical thinking'? Is it the past 'as it actually happened' or a version of earlier events that are germane to the present? An example of the latter can be found in Patrick Pearse who saw Theobald Wolfe Tone, the United Irishman, and Thomas Davis, the Young Irelander, as part of a unified whole. But Davis would have had no time for Tone's eighteenth-century rational thought, his concept of citizenship as something endowed by the state; and Tone would have detested Davis's search for a cultural identity, based on Irish history and language, without which no Irish state was worth having. Indeed, Tone's words on hearing of an Irish Harpists' Festival to be held in Belfast in 1792, 'strum, strum and be hanged' speak for themselves.[19] Parnell, who was incorporated into the

Republican myth was, unlike his sponsors, the men of 1916, notoriously indifferent to cultural aspirations.

Moreover, since Irish nationalism was engaged with both its enemies, the Protestants of Ireland and its dominating power, the British Kingdom, it was necessarily shaped and influenced by these forces. Unionism in the British Isles in the nineteenth century was a powerful force; it would not surrender the pass easily. The British government was the arbiter of Ireland's political and economic destiny; its reaction to nationalism was crucial. Nationalists had to come to the British Parliament to make their case; they were working in an environment in Ireland where Anglicisation was making a greater impact on Irish society and in which government policy was transforming that society, or the rural part of it, into a conservative peasant proprietorship. The British government and the Irish nationalists were struggling for the support of the most powerful institution in nineteenth-century Ireland, the Catholic Church. This again modified nationalist political activity, as did the assumption, truly held until 1919–21, and still tenable in some degree even then, that Britain could not be driven out of Ireland by military force. Unionism, for its part, was a political ideology with no meaning outside the maintenance of the British connection: an obvious point, but one often overlooked even by some unionists, and certainly by all nationalists. As the British Parliament began to look like conceding home rule, in 1912–14, then unionism too began to change, from its Westminster-centred political role to populist opposition in Ulster, and a growing split between Ulster and Southern Irish Unionists.

The difficulty of being at once a professional historian, engaged with these issues, and a political polemicist, deeply committed to a special interpretation of the past, can be illustrated again by Brendan Bradshaw's dual role, as nationalist and Catholic polemicist, and as professional Cambridge historian. As the former, Bradshaw has gone so far as to insist that the popular perception of Irish history constituted a 'beneficent legacy – its wrongness notwithstanding', and even to demand the re-instatement of 'the popular perception of Irish history as a struggle for the liberation of "faith and fatherland" from the oppression of the Protestant English'.[20] As to the latter, his work on the Irish Reformation has been contrasted with that of R. Dudley Edwards. Dudley Edwards's *Church and State in Tudor Ireland* (1935) displayed 'strong links with earlier less scholarly writing', particularly in its 'use of emotional rhetoric to explain the Reformation's failure'.[21] Edwards, a Catholic writer, stood in the nationalist tradition, and explained the failure of the Reformation in Ireland in terms of 'an unambiguous, heroic and characteristically Irish resistance to the imposition of a foreign ideology by a foreign power'. But 'the study of the Reformation came of age with the appearance, beginning in 1966, of the pioneering work of Brendan Bradshaw, who breathed fresh life into the subject by developing a new conceptual framework and chronology for the failure of the Reformation'.[22] Bradshaw's own chronological location, in the 1960s, placed him firmly in the first wave of 'revisionist' historians of Ireland, alongside Patrick Buckland (on Irish Unionism) and L.P. Curtis, Jr (Conservative policy). And this reinforces the point that the most exciting innovations in Irish historical scholarship have been in areas untouched by the whole 'revisionist' *political* controversy. Or, if touched off by them, then not directly involved in that controversy. The simplicities of the 'revisionist' controversy are thus seen for what they are: an attempt to reduce complexity to simplicity; a search for a political rather than a genuinely historical pluralism on the one hand; or for a political and clearly unhistorical national field dressing on the other.

There is a Russian saying that 'the past is always changing, but the present always stays the same'. This could be applied to Ireland, where the political disagreements of the North, couched in the language of nationalism versus Unionism, are in danger of reinsuring that the present in Ulster always stays the same; and the sameness of the present is what provokes politically minded controversialists to demand that history does not change, but should stay the same as well. Desmond Fennell called for a kind of history writing that would bond and sustain the nation by representing its men, women and movements as essentially right-minded, even heroic, and criticising the 'counter-revolutionary' movement in Dublin for using the IRA campaign as an opportunity to turn its back on this kind of history.[23] *Famine Diary: Journey to a New World*, published in Dublin in July 1991 and launched on a tide of media publicity, conformed to the heroic genre of Irish writing; it was swiftly and easily exposed by Jim Jackson in the *Irish Review* as a piece of historical fiction.[24] This farce, aided and abetted by (among others) the *Irish Times* and RTE radio, might be taken as marking the final collapse of the 'anti-revisionist' case – that is, if that case had ever been based on rational argument.

The 'anti-revisionist' campaign has been orchestrated and given a (much-needed) intellectual underpinning in Brendan Bradshaw's article 'Nationalism and Historical Scholarship in Modern Ireland' first published in *Irish Historical Studies* (1989). Bradshaw calls to his side the eminent Oxford historian and philosopher R.G. Collingwood who, Bradshaw notes, conceives of history as the 're-enactment of the past'. Building upon this, Bradshaw urges the historian to empathise with the past, and thus to reconstruct not only nationalist but Unionist history: but to reconstruct it with empathy, which he sometimes equates with sympathy, and the abandonment of a critical dimension. Indeed, he assumes that Collingwood, because he describes what historians do as re-enacting the past, meant that the historian abandoned his position as a present observer, and enters wholly into the ideas of the past. This is to reduce Collingwood's rather complex writings on history to a simplistic and misleading account. Collingwood's historical thought demands more extended exposition than can be undertaken here, but a few corrections of how Bradshaw interprets him should be made.

The application of the expression 'empathetic understanding' to Collingwood's thought implies that history is a kind of intuition, even a 'slide into the thought of the past'. But, as John P. Hogan points out in his *Collingwood and Theological Hermeneutics*, Collingwood argues that history builds on evidence, and is a process of question and answer, which calls forth the past from the present.[25] An historian can reconstruct the thought behind an historical event, but the present presuppositions of the historian are not ignored. The historian thus enters into a dialogue with the unfamiliar. But he or she does not merely reproduce feelings or emotions. As Collingwood himself puts it:

> This re-enactment . . . is not a passive surrender to the spell of another's mind; it is a labour of active and therefore critical thinking. The historian not only re-enacts past thought, he re-enacts it in the context of his own knowledge and therefore, in re-enacting it, criticises it, forms his own judgement of its value, corrects whatever errors he can discern in it. This criticism of the thought whose history he traces is not something secondary to tracing the history of it. It is an indispensable condition of the historical knowledge itself.[26]

Thus, 'all thinking is critical thinking; the thought which re-enacts past thoughts, therefore criticises them in re-enacting them'.[27]

Bradshaw's misinterpretation of Collingwood's historical thought falls down on his misunderstanding of what 'empathy' means. As Rex Martin explains,

> the investigator does not take, in his imagination, the role of the agent in order to find out facts about him. Empathy is not a kind of research; accordingly, it is not an alternative to inductive inquiry. The investigator's use of empathetic imagination is not a substitute for the interpretation of evidence.

Empathy cannot, therefore, be employed as a way of disclosing something that cannot be got at through evidence. Thus,

> insofar as our question bears on the acquisition of information, Collingwood's answer is clear; the investigator utilises evidence, records and reports of what the agent did and said and presumably, thought. To regard empathy as a way of discovering peculiarly inaccessible facts or as a method of self-certifying verification is a categorical mistake; it confuses the dimension in which empathy

11

does operate, that of explanatory deliberation, with the logically distinct state of investigation and reconstruction from evidence.

Moreover, Collingwood's account of empathy is not that the investigator imagines reasons for a course of action; 'rather it is to imagine alternative courses of action and to measure these against the reasons which the agent presumably had, as indicated by the evidence'.[28] Evidence is, and remains, the basis of the discipline of history; empathy cannot substitute for that, as a well-trained historian such as Brendan Bradshaw knows and, in fact, reveals in his own professional research.

Collingwood therefore can offer no escape route for the professional historian who seeks to give respectable intellectual underpinning to what is patently a political point of view. What Collingwood claims is no new theory of history, but rather to describe what it is that historians do: they must get inside human action through a question and answer process, based firmly on the evidence, and they criticise these past thoughts as they 're-enact' them: they stand, at one and the same time, inside and yet outside the past. The re-enactment of past thought is no guarantee of the veracity of the account given. For Collingwood, history is an empirical discipline, and testing the validity of a given account, from Caesar's decision to invade Britain to the present day, is an essential part of its method. However sympathetic the historian may be to a particular tradition, he or she cannot duck that responsibility.

But at least the brief introduction of Collingwood into the debate gives it a genuinely historical dimension, even if the motives for introducing his historical thinking were in the end as much connected with nationalist ideology as the desire to advance historical understanding. This raises what was the most unsatisfactory aspect of the controversy: that it did not move historical scholarship forward at all. It is a product, not a cause, of the real revisionism that is an essential aspect of a subject that is in no way 'scientific' (in the sense that the physical sciences are) but at the same time is not simply a 'matter of opinion', or merely an aspect of political traditions or ideologies; it did not encourage a debate about the historians' method, but rather sought to prevent historians talking to each other about their method, inviting them instead to take refuge in their 'own' primordial loyalties – perhaps even threatening them if they did not thus take refuge. This is to stand Collingwood on his head: his plea that the historian develop a self-consciousness about what he or she is engaged in – the actuality of being an historian – is now reduced to a demand that the historian settle for a more comfortable and one-dimensional role. But history is a pluralist discipline, deeply influenced by varying techniques and perspectives. Indeed, insofar as the Irish debate on 'revisionism' has achieved anything, it is in displaying precisely the protean nature of what is all too often taken for granted as a single-methoddiscipline.

Although the present volume concentrates on Ireland and thereby forms a contribution to the on-going debate on 'revisionism' in Irish history, its ambition is to link that discussion to the methodology and perspective of historical interpretation. Contributors are drawn from a range of backgrounds, live in several countries and are in some instances specialists in other disciplines. It is these cross-currents as well as the actual topics that give the work breadth though, of course, the contributions are the work of individuals, not of a committee. There is not a pre-ordained 'opinion' binding the individual chapters together. What underpins the book is a common thread whereby each author examines 'revisionism' within the framework of a specific problem like the penal laws, the effects of the Union, and nationalism in order to assess both the received version of a particular historic event or movement that came into existence and how this has changed under the impact of modern scholarship. There is no agreed conclusion and a reading of the whole collection suggests substantial variations in the pace and character of 'revisionism' and of individuals' views about these changes. Overall, the collection confirms that historical interpretation has been more subtle and complex but also increasingly fragmented. Some of the certainty of an Irish history organised around the polarity of nationalism and opposition to it is removed, not infrequently to the discomfiture of those who prefer the older model. Contrary to common belief that political topics have been at the forefront of 'revisionism', it has had as large or greater impact on social and economic questions. Analysis of home rule, a defining objective of nationalists for long generations, demonstrates the relative stagnation in writings on the Irish section of the story. Similarly, the historiography of the diaspora reveals the parallel development of non-Irish scholarship working outside a political and polemical environment. Yet careful scrutiny of the literature on several themes shows that several interpretative traditions exist concurrently. Overall, the volume has three primary objectives – to augment the growing interest in how historical writings and ideas are shaped and transmitted, to advance the understanding of 'revisionism', and also to serve as a practical guide to students and tutors on the writings about particular themes. To some extent it cannot escape being a state-of-the-art product but it comes when the hard thrust of 'revisionism' has taken place and a counter-attack mounted: it also falls at a moment when the scale of historical scholarship has peaked due to reductions in funding and availability of university teaching appointments. Although the individual pieces note areas for further research, this is not an attempt at agenda-making but merely an effort to discover why, where and how historical interpretation has moved during the past decades.

NOTES

1 Desmond Fennell, 'Against Revisionism' in Ciaran Brady (ed.), *Interpreting Irish History: The Debate on Historical Revisionism* (Dublin, 1994), pp. 184–5.
2 Jonathan Moore, 'Historical Revisionism and the Irish in Britain', *Linen Hall Review*, Autumn 1988, p. 15.
3 Anthony Coughlan, 'Ireland's Marxist Historians' in Brady (ed.), *op. cit.*, pp. 300–5.
4 Quoted in Arthur Marwick, *The Nature of History* (3rd edn, Basingstoke and London, 1989), p. 57.
5 See Ian Kershaw, *The Nazi Dictatorship: Problems, Perspectives and Interpretation* (2nd edn, London, 1989), p. 170; Also P. Pulzer, G. Smith *et al.*, *Developments in German Politics* (London, 1992); and Charles S. Maier, *The Unmistakable Past: History, Holocaust and German National Identity* (Cambridge, MA and London, 1988).
6 Kershaw, *ibid.*, p. 184.
7 *Ibid.*, pp. 184–5, 187.
8 Quoted in John Tosh, *The Pursuit of History: Aims, Methods and New Directions in the Study of Modern History* (2nd edn, London and New York, 1991), p. 3.
9 Hugh Kearney, 'The Irish and Their History' in Brady (ed.), *op. cit.*, pp. 246–52.
10 J.J. Lee, *Ireland 1912–1985: Politics and Society* (Cambridge, 1989), p. 596.
11 M.A.G. Ó Tuathaigh, 'Irish Historical "Revisionism": State of the Art or Ideological Project?' in Brady (ed.), *op. cit.*, p. 323.
12 See the reprints of their respective views in Brady (ed.), *op. cit.*
13 Patrick O'Farrell, 'Writing the Irish of Irish-Australia' in Oliver MacDonagh and W.F. Mandle (eds), *Ireland and Irish-Australia: Studies in Cultural and Political History* (London, Sydney and Wolfeboro, NH, 1986), p. 219.
14 Kevin O'Neill, 'Revisionist Milestone', in Brady (ed.), *op. cit.*, pp. 217–21.
15 Lee, *op. cit.*, pp. 623–32.
16 Tosh, *op. cit.*, p. 22.
17 J.C. Beckett, *Confrontations: Studies in Irish History* (London, 1972), p. 16.
18 Brendan Bradshaw, 'Nationalism and Historical Scholarship in Modern Ireland', in Brady (ed.), *op. cit.*, pp. 191–9.
19 For Wolfe Tone's attitude to cultural themes see, Marianne Elliott, *Wolfe Tone: Prophet of Irish Independence* (New Haven, CT and London, 1989), p. 173.
20 Bradshaw, *op. cit.*, pp. 205–16.
21 James Murray, 'The Church of Ireland: A Critical Bibliography, 1536–1992: Part I, 1536–1603' *Irish Historical Studies*, xxviii, November 1993, pp. 346–7.
22 *Ibid.*
23 Fennell, *op. cit.*, pp. 183–90.
24 Jim Jackson, 'The Making of a Best-Seller', *Irish Review*, 11, winter 1991–2, pp. 1–8.
25 John P. Hogan, *Collingwood and Theological Hermeneutics* (London, 1989), ch. 6.
26 *Ibid.*, p. 64.
27 *Ibid.*, p. 159.
28 Rex Martin, *Historical Explanation: Re-enactment and Practical Inference* (Ithaca, 1977), pp. 52–3.

2

EIGHTEENTH-CENTURY IRELAND

Colony or *ancien régime*?

S.J. Connolly

John Bull's other island, anglicized Ireland, was the most colonial part of Britain, being bullied and bled by a frequently absentee Protestant landlord class. Landlords' incomes trebled during the century, largely at the expense of the indigenous Catholic peasantry, and by 1750 three quarters of a million pounds in rent was leaving Ireland annually. . . . In peacetime the largest concentration of the British army had to be stationed in Ireland. Catholics, though the vast majority, suffered legal disabilities, including disfranchisement. Furthermore Irish industry was sacrificed to English manufacturers, export of Irish wool and cloth being banned from 1698, except to England. By mid-century Ulster was already showing its industrial edge over the pastoral south, which was suffering worsening subsistence crises.[1]

These are the words, not of a specialist in Irish history, but of a contributor to the generally well-regarded *Pelican Social History of Britain*. The writer in question, otherwise careful to decorate his text with references to the most recent literature, clearly felt that no such effort was necessary for his brief remarks on Ireland: his one citation is of a work first published in 1936. But his comments are nevertheless of value. What they do is to preserve, embedded like a pterodactyl claw in fossil slate, the lineaments of one particular image of eighteenth-century Ireland, a former orthodoxy now very largely set aside. For anyone interested in the general processes behind what has come to be called 'revisionism', the story of that orthodoxy, its rise and fall, provides a particularly instructive case study.

I

The portrayal of eighteenth-century Ireland summed up in the extract just quoted had three main elements. The first was the complete political subordination of Ireland to British government and interests. In part this depended on the power of the British parliament to pass laws binding on Ireland and the ability of the English privy council to amend or veto the enactments of the Dublin parliament. In part it reflected the willingness of the small circle of propertied Protestants represented in that parliament to acquiesce in the measures of an English-appointed executive in exchange for the thinly disguised bribery of pensions, sinecures and other forms of patronage. In 1782 a surge of Protestant patriotism, taking advantage of the American crisis, temporarily liberated the Irish parliament from London's control. But the legislative independence thus achieved was snuffed out eighteen years later by the Act of Union.

Second there was the belief that eighteenth-century Ireland was an economically underdeveloped and desperately poor society. Poverty was in part the result of political subordination. British government excluded Ireland from full participation in the most profitable branches of colonial commerce; it intervened directly to cut off lines of economic development – such as the export of livestock, wool or glass – that threatened British interests; and it deployed its influence in the Irish parliament to ensure that no compensatory action was taken to build up local enterprises or protect them against British competition. Poverty was also the result of an exploitative land system, in which the peasantry, sucked dry by parasitic landlords, were left with neither the means nor the incentive to farm by anything other than the most primitive methods.

The third major feature of the traditional interpretation of eighteenth-century Irish society was the existence of a deep antagonism, rooted in a past history of conquest and plantation and the continuing reality of economic oppression and religious discrimination, between a ruling landed elite and an impoverished peasantry. The image of a uniquely polarised society found its classic expression in Daniel Corkery's *The Hidden Ireland* (1924). For Corkery, eighteenth-century Ireland contained two societies. One was Protestant and English-speaking, the Ireland of the towns and the Big Houses dotted throughout the countryside. It was the world of 'the wine-flushed revelry of the alien gentry, the hunting, the dancing, the drinking, the gambling, the duelling', and of the Dublin parliament, 'that noisy side show, so bizarre in its lineaments and so tragi-comic in its fate'. The other Ireland was Gaelic and Catholic, 'a peasant nation, harried and poverty stricken, with the cottier's smoky cabin for stronghold', but nevertheless possessed of a rich and independent culture. These two societies were physically close, even overlapping, but they remained culturally, psychologically and politically wholly separate. Gaelic Ireland was quietly but deeply resentful of foreign government and the rule of a Protestant planter class. The three great themes of its poetry were 'nationality, religion, rebellion'. The culture of the gentry, on the other hand, was one of 'wealth without refinement and power without responsibility', its outlook dominated by 'the first article in an Ascendancy's creed . . . that the natives are a lesser breed'.[2]

A composite portrait of the ideas put forward by a range of writers across a period of fifty years or more must inevitably involve some simplification. There were differences of emphasis between individual writers, which only a detailed bibliographical and historiographical survey could properly bring out. Nor, as will be seen later in the case of the penal laws, did ideas remain wholly fixed over time.[3] But in general it is fair to say that the views outlined above continued for several decades to be taken for granted at all levels of historical writing. To take just one example, K.H. Connell's *The Population of Ireland 1750–1845* was rightly hailed on its publication in 1950 as bringing a new sophistication to Irish demographic history. Yet the results of its innovative statistical analysis were set in the context virtually unchanged from that defined by Corkery and George O'Brien: a society characterised by economic stagnation, a rapacious landlord class and an impoverished peasantry whose behaviour was conditioned by the absence of any realistic prospect of bettering its circumstances.[4]

II

The links between this general depiction of eighteenth-century Ireland and the political background against which it took shape hardly need elaboration. A heightened historical awareness, with an emphasis on past oppression and injustice, was part of the developing Nationalist ideology of the late nineteenth and early twentieth centuries. More specifically there was the special status that nationalist thinking accorded to the year 1782. Successive political leaders, from O'Connell onwards, defined their ideal of self-government in terms of the legislative independence achieved under 'Grattan's parliament'.[5] One consequence was that the political history of the eighteenth century as a whole was assessed by the standards of Grattanite patriot virtue. A second was that the economic history of the period was seen in terms of a short interlude of prosperity under an independent parliament, punctuating long eras of poverty and stagnation. Thus George O'Brien, whose economic history, published in 1918, remained the standard text for more than fifty years, went out of his way to refute James Connolly's suggestion that the economic advances of the 1780s and 1790s had had nothing to do with Grattan's parliament, a claim that threatened to 'deprive the Irish nation of one great argument in favour of the restoration of its parliamentary liberty'.[6]

There were other interest groups whose cause was furthered by the depiction of eighteenth-century Ireland offered by O'Brien and others. For the Catholic clergy the remembered injustices of the penal laws were a useful weapon in denominational polemic, while the image of priests

17

and people united in the face of poverty and persecution helped to divert attention from the reality of a church ascending to new heights of material prosperity and political influence. The tradition of a parasitic and remorselessly exploitative landlord class had an obvious appeal at a time when landlord–tenant relations had become a bitterly contested political issue. The suggestion of an unbridgeable cultural gulf between the 'alien gentry' and the common people they exploited reflected the same social and political hostilities, as well as the new concern with language as the key to national identity.

All this is clear enough. At the same time it would be wrong to see the traditional picture of eighteenth-century Ireland solely as a reflection of the concerns of late nineteenth- and twentieth-century Nationalism. In the first place we must acknowledge the enduring influence on perceptions of eighteenth-century Ireland of two major works of Victorian scholarship, J.A. Froude's *The English in Ireland in the Eighteenth Century* (1872–4) and W.E.H. Lecky's *History of Ireland in the Eighteenth Century* (1892). Both Froude and Lecky wrote from a Unionist perspective, concerned, though with very different emphasis, to explain the long-term failure to assimilate Ireland into the British political system. Froude's thesis that England had failed to discharge its historic mission of civilising Ireland by firm paternalistic rule, with its assumption of inherent Irish inferiority, caused outrage; but his portrayal of the ruinous effects of short-sighted commercial restrictions and irresponsible landlordism was nevertheless influential.[7] Lecky's more moderate tone, and his detailed refutation of Froude's wilder attacks on the Irish character, made him more acceptable to majority opinion in Ireland, while his acknowledgement of the negative consequences of past religious, economic and political strategies could be taken over, with little modification, by those who did not share the underlying Unionist premises of his work. The long-term influence of both men was further assured when the bulk of the records on which they had drawn were destroyed with the rest of Ireland's national archives in 1922.

Even where the traditional picture was the work of writers of Nationalist sympathies, furthermore, it is important not to oversimplify or caricature. Daniel Corkery, for example, was indeed an enthusiastic supporter of the cultural revival. However a recent study reveals, not a narrow and parochial propagandist, but a sophisticated cultural theorist. Corkery's idealisation of a lost Gaelic world, for example, owed something to his early interest in the romantic socialist antiquarianism of Robert Blatchford and *Merrie England*. In 1915 he recommended Turgenev as a model for writers seeking to portray the realities of rural Irish society, while his own works included not just *The Hidden Ireland* but a play about a farmer whose obsession with an exalted Gaelic ancestry leads his family into economic ruin.[8] George O'Brien, meanwhile, may have been explicitly concerned to refute Connolly's politically inexpedient downgrading of the economic achievement of Grattan's parliament. But the moderate constitutional Nationalism he had acquired at Belvedere College, after an early upbringing in a Catholic Unionist household, was intellectual rather than emotional in character. According to his own account:

> None of my immediate relations had been agricultural tenants, and I was unaware of the bitterness engendered by the Land War. There were no tales of evictions in my family legends. Far from disliking the gentry I admired them at a distance for their style and elegance. My ideals in architecture and art were all based upon my admiration for the classical models of the eighteenth century which I associated in my mind with the landed aristocracy. Georgian Dublin was my spiritual home.

In later life O'Brien was to express his gratitude that he had been born early enough to escape the 'frustration and waste of energy' involved in compulsory Irish teaching in schools.[9]

Such examples make clear that the ideological background to what became for many decades the standard interpretation of eighteenth-century Ireland is more complex than might at first sight appear. Moreover there are other reasons, quite apart from political influences of any kind, why that interpretation took the form it did, and why it endured largely unquestioned for so long. In the first place the picture of eighteenth-century Ireland presented by George O'Brien, and by subsequent writers such as Constantia Maxwell,[10] did not involve any distortion or misrepresentation of the evidence on which these authors drew. On the contrary, contemporary pamphlets and the published accounts of such visitors as Arthur Young, dealt extensively with the perceived problems of poverty and economic underdevelopment, the baneful effects of English commercial restrictions and the deficiencies of Irish landlordism. Secondly we must acknowledge the plausibility of the interpretation that such sources suggested. The eighteenth century had, after all, ended in appalling violence. The rapid spread of popular disaffection during the 1790s, the willingness of the authorities to resort to increasingly vicious and indiscriminate counter measures, the re-emergence of bitter sectarian antagonisms, all culminating in the bloodbath of 1798, seemed fully to justify an emphasis on the depth and continuity of political, religious and social antagonisms across the century as a whole. In the same way the Famine of 1845–50 cast a powerful retrospective light on discussion of long-term economic development. The Ireland of Swift's *Modest Proposal* (1729) seemed so immediately recognisable as the Ireland of 1847 that it was easy to assume that nothing had changed in the intervening century and a quarter.[11]

A third reason why the traditional interpretation of eighteenth-century Irish history lasted so long is provided by the state of the Irish historical profession. In the years after 1922 academic life, in independent Ireland in particular, was severely underfunded, even by the standards of the day. Nor were universities immune from the culture of patronage that characterised other areas of Irish public life. Irish historians, in consequence, were relatively few in number, and not all of that number engaged in a great deal of research or writing. The result was a climate more favourable to the transmission of received ideas than to their critical exploration. Even those individuals who did break new ground – like Connell in his demographic work – had little choice but to fit their findings into a received context that was in many respects largely static. It is of course true that the 1930s and 1940s are seen as the period when Irish historical writing was given new professional standards of accuracy, thoroughness and objectivity. But this was a revolution that took place along a very narrow front, in constitutional, administrative and political history. New intellectual currents, among them the developments taking place elsewhere in the fields of economic history, social history and the study of popular politics, were largely ignored. In this sense the criticism that could be offered of Irish historical writing in the middle of the twentieth century was not so much that it was contaminated by Nationalist political prejudice as that it was rather old-fashioned. By the same token the dramatic rethinking of the whole character of eighteenth-century Ireland that began in the 1960s can be attributed less to a changing political climate than to the economic expansion that allowed the study of history, in common with other parts of Irish academic life, to broaden its professional and intellectual base.

III

What did that rethinking consist of? Its earliest and most far-reaching manifestations came in the area of economic development. In a series of publications beginning in the mid-1960s L.M. Cullen demonstrated that the traditional image of a society characterised by chronic poverty and underdevelopment concealed what had in fact been a long wave of spectacular economic expansion, commencing in the 1740s and continuing into the second decade of the nineteenth century.[12] During this period agricultural output rose rapidly to meet demand, first from British and French colonies in the West Indies and the rising volume of Atlantic shipping, then from the growing urban population of Great Britain. Linen manufacture also expanded, bringing prosperity to rural households not just in Ulster but in large parts of the other three provinces. Wool, cotton, glass making, brewing and luxury goods further contributed to a healthy and expanding manufacturing sector. Indeed the growing scale of industrial enterprises, and the increased use of water and steam power in textiles, milling and other trades led Cullen to insist that 'the Industrial Revolution affected Ireland strongly in the eighteenth century'.[13] Further evidence of economic growth was provided in the development of banking and transport, the growth of towns, the novel scale and magnificence of public and private building made possible by unprecedented prosperity, the laying down of road networks and field systems. Indeed it was from the 1740s onwards that 'the man made features of the Irish landscape, urban and rural, were created within little more than a century'.[14]

This dramatic reinterpretation of the economic lineaments of the century was made possible partly by a more critical use of evidence. In particular Cullen demonstrated how perceptions of the eighteenth-century economy had been distorted by reliance on a contemporary pamphlet literature that disproportionately reflected the particular concerns of years of depression or crisis, and in which economic analysis often took second place to the elaboration of constitutional grievances. As for the Gaelic sources that had formed the basis of Corkery's apparently corroborating portrayal of the poverty and apartness of the 'hidden Ireland', these were even more treacherous. What Corkery had taken as the voice of a whole people Cullen was able to present instead as the jaundiced outlook of a particular interest group, the Gaelic poets, lamenting the overthrow of a social order in which their profession had enjoyed privileged status. In addition, a careful reading of the same texts, discounting the rhetoric of oppression and alienation, allowed Cullen to bring out a wealth of incidental social detail which made clear that the lifestyle depicted there was not that of the rural poor but of a Gaelic elite of comfortable farmers and lesser gentry.[15]

The first major element in Cullen's revisionism, then, was to insist that economic questions be discussed in economic terms, separate both from the perceived injustices of the seventeenth-century confiscations and the constitutional grievances of the eighteenth-century Protestant establishment. This could be done partly by reading the contemporary printed sources more critically; partly, as in Cullen's pioneering study of Anglo-Irish trade,[16] by going beyond contemporary opinion to the actual records of economic activity. A second crucial element in Cullen's reinterpretation was a new awareness of the complex and varied structure of rural society. Earlier writers had assumed a single, undifferentiated peasant class. Cullen emphasised the regional variations created by differences in land quality, patterns of settlement, the extent to which agriculture had become commercialised, the presence or absence of domestic industry. He also noted the social gradations that existed within the rural population: 'a varied, complex pattern of tenant farmers, large and small, dairymen, in many areas artisans or domestic workers, and cottiers and cottier labourers, constituting in the aggregate for most of the eighteenth century a fairly well-balanced distribution of social and economic function'.[17] It was only from the end of the century that accelerating population growth, swelling the ranks of the rural poor, began to un-balance the social structure of rural Ireland, laying the foundations for the crisis of the pre-Famine decades and the disaster of the 1840s. This new perspective on eighteenth-century economic development also implied a reassessment of those who, in the traditional account, had been cast as the agents of Ireland's misfortunes. The idea that British government had pursued a coherent mercantilist policy towards Ireland came under critical scrutiny as early as 1959, and subsequent studies confirmed that there had been no concerted strategy for the management of Ireland's economy to England's advantage.[18] Where commercial restrictions had been imposed, moreover, it was now argued that their effects were less drastic than earlier assumed. Irish enterprise and resources were not crushed, but rather channelled into other directions, from wool to linen, from livestock exports to Great Britain to provisions for the Atlantic trade.[19] By the same token the supposedly novel strategies of economic improvement adopted by the Irish parliament after 1782 were now seen as a continuation of earlier practice, and the general prosperity of the 1780s and 1790s as a reflection of generally favourable economic condi-tions, rather than a testimony to the regenerative effects of legislative independence.[20]

A similar reassessment took place in the case of the other villain of the traditional story, the landlord. Cullen's critique of Corkery undermined the assumption that landlord and tenant lived in a relationship of per-manent conflict. A more systematic reappraisal began with the work of W.H. Crawford and Peter Roebuck, who drew on the records of indi-vidual landed estates to argue that the relationship between proprietor and tenant was more nuanced, and less heavily weighted in favour of the landlord, than had been assumed.[21] Both writers dealt exclusively with Ulster. However David Dickson, drawing on Munster evidence, came to broadly similar conclusions regarding the limited control that landlords in practice enjoyed over the terms on which they let their land.[22] Earlier Dickson had effectively demythologised another part of the eighteenth-century land system in a study showing that middlemen were a more varied and less uniformly parasitic group than had been suggested.[23]

Assessments of landlord–tenant relations were also affected by new work on agrarian protest.[24] The sudden popularity of this topic during the 1970s and early 1980s can be attributed to the belated arrival in Ireland of an awareness of the new social history typified by the work of George Rudé, Eric Hobsbawm and E.P. Thompson. It soon became clear, moreover, that the Whiteboys, Rightboys and other movements of the Irish countryside could be fitted without difficulty into the framework suggested by this literature. Like popular movements elsewhere in the pre-industrialised era, Irish agrarian protest was regional and episodic, arising in response to immediate grievances. The outlook of those involved was conservative and defensive, concerned to fend off unwelcome change rather than to challenge the social or political order. Indeed the Whiteboys of the early 1760s explicitly proclaimed their loyalty to King George III (as well as to the mythological Gaelic deity Queen Sive), a gesture that takes us a long way from Corkery's hidden Ireland resolutely unreconciled to the Hanoverian state. The use of violence remained, up to the 1790s, selective and restrained. By 1983 Thomas Bartlett could suggest applying E.P. Thompson's concept of a 'moral economy' to describe the tacit understanding, based on a sense of 'mutual obligation and shared responsibility', linking rulers and ruled, landlord and tenant.[25]

What of the other major element in the image of a society split into deeply antagonistic strata, the penal laws that protected the privileged Protestant minority at the expense of the Catholic majority? Here too there have been important changes in interpretation; but the chronology is very different. Indeed it is a creditable reflection on those involved – and a further refutation of facile links between 'revisionism' and a changing political climate – that the most important new ideas regarding the impact of the penal laws first took shape in the 1940s and 1950s, at a time when the ideology of Catholic nationalism was at its most influential. Where earlier writers had argued that the legislation concerned had been the instrument of a determined attempt to suppress the practice of Catholicism, new work emphasised the failure of government to make more than token gestures towards enforcement, and the consequent practical freedom of movement enjoyed even in the early part of the century by the great majority of Catholic clergymen.[26] Over the next few years J.G. Simms's careful and dispassionate studies of the Williamite confiscation and of the means by which individual penal statutes were enacted further highlighted the divided counsels, uncertainty of purpose and uneven implementation that characterised official religious policy.[27] Meanwhile Maureen Wall rejected the assumption that religious disabilities had reduced the Catholic population as a whole to poverty. Confiscation and penal legislation had all but destroyed the Catholic landed class; but neither anti-Catholic legislation nor the relief acts of the late eighteenth century had any real relevance to the condition of the rural poor. Moreover Wall emphasised the development by the later eighteenth century of a large, prosperous Catholic middle class of traders and manufacturers, whose commercial success was if anything enhanced by laws that prevented them diverting resources into politics or land.[28]

The work that has been done since the mid-1960s has mainly served to qualify and reinforce, rather than dramatically to extend, these earlier reassessments of the nature and impact of the penal laws.[29] The main exceptions are Thomas Bartlett's authoritative account of the politics of the Catholic question across the whole period up to 1829, and very recent work by T.C. Barnard which has brought a new sophistication to discussion of the political, religious and cultural attitudes out of which the penal laws were born.[30] Wall's thesis of a rising Catholic urban middle class has been modified by David Dickson, who has shown that despite an undoubted absolute growth in Catholic commercial wealth, reflecting general economic expansion, 'the commanding heights of the mercantile economy remained firmly in Protestant hands'.[31] On the other hand the general argument that the Catholic population cannot be conceived of as a uniformly oppressed peasantry has been confirmed and reinforced by studies of rural social structure, by Dickson and others, that have highlighted the existence of a continued Catholic landed interest of middlemen and leaseholders, as well as an emerging class of substantial tenant farmers.[32]

We come finally to the reconstruction of the political life of eighteenth-century Ireland. The centrality of political, constitutional and administrative history in the concerns of the Irish historical profession ensured that this field was never wholly neglected. The 1940s and 1950s, for example, saw important contributions from R.B. McDowell and J.L. McCracken, joined in 1963 by E.M. Johnston.[33] Simply by adding detail and substance to earlier outlines, their research inevitably created a more nuanced picture. The same is true of the much wider body of work that appeared from the mid-1960s onwards. But progress was more gradual and incremental, or from another point of view less 'disruptive',[34] than in the case of economic and social history.

In two areas, however, it is possible to point to a conscious revision of traditional assumptions. The first is in the treatment of Grattan's parliament. In 1964 J.C. Beckett questioned the significance accorded to the constitutional changes of 1782. He pointed first to the sparing use which British government, long before that date, had been accustomed to make of its theoretical power to interfere with Irish legislation, and secondly to the very substantial degree of control that remained in London's hands after 'legislative independence' had been achieved.[35] The following year Maurice O'Connell, in a major study, focused attention on the limitations of the radicalism of the patriot movement, highlighting both the middle-class character of the Volunteers and the shiftiness of their leaders on the question of Catholic rights.[36] It was left to Joseph Lee, in 1973, to complete the progression to out-and-out iconoclasm. For Lee legislative independence, in the absence both of parliamentary reform and of Catholic emancipation, served only to create a small Protestant elite responsible to no one but itself. As a result Grattan's parliament became 'little more than a gigantic relief scheme for the nobility and their relatives'. It was also – as the body that presided over the events of 1798 – 'the bloodiest repressive institution in modern Irish history'.[37]

These early revisions to the accepted picture of late eighteenth-century constitutional development have since been built on by more specialised studies.[38] By contrast the other major break with traditional orthodoxy, A.P.W. Malcomson's studies of electoral and parliamentary politics, stand largely alone.[39] Yet their implications are if anything more far-reaching. Earlier accounts had emphasised the mercenary and oligarchic character of eighteenth-century politics. Malcomson drew attention instead to the practical talents required to achieve significant office within the Irish executive, to the limitations of patronage as a political cement, and to the complexity of the relationships between executive, parliament and public opinion. Where previous writers had focused on the economic coercion that allowed landlords to dispose of the votes of their tenants, Malcomson demonstrated that electoral politics were in fact a complex business, governed by well-defined notions of legitimacy and requiring careful attention to local interests and to the maintenance of at least some element of reciprocity between borough proprietor and constituents. Even something as crude as the purchase of seats in closed boroughs turned out on closer examination to display an 'odd mixture of lucre and honour'.[40] Malcomson's arguments, supported by a formidable mastery of the sources, find an immediate echo in the parallel work of K.T. Hoppen on early and mid-Victorian Ireland.[41] Yet historians of the eighteenth century have been remarkably slow to follow them up, or even to take their implications fully into account.

IV

A survey of thirty years' writing thus lends little support to the claim of an all-embracing revisionism among historians of the eighteenth century. Interpretations of economic development and social structure, and of the relationships associated with these, did indeed change radically. But this was the result of the commencement of serious work on a subject that had previously been very largely neglected. By contrast the perception of religion and politics has changed slowly and incrementally across a longer period. The one exception, the radical reassessment of Grattan and the Volunteers, contrasts with the failure to build on Malcomson's equally challenging reassessment of electoral and parliamentary politics. Even today, it would seem, the opportunity to debunk the claims of the Protestant elite to represent any form of patriotic principle remains more attractive than the challenge of reconstructing from within the values and attitudes that shaped its world.

If, then, there is no revisionist consensus, what alternative summary can be offered of the outcome of three decades or more of increasingly detailed research? To some extent it is possible to detect in the work currently being done two broad approaches to the study of eighteenth-century Irish society. On the one hand there are those that set out to construct their analysis in the same terms – paternalism and deference, the dominance of landed property, traditional ideas of privilege and hierarchy – that are used by historians of other eighteenth-century societies. Bartlett, as already mentioned, has argued for extending to Ireland E.P. Thompson's model of a 'moral economy'. Malcomson similarly concludes that 'the local politics of the Anglo-Irish Ascendancy were not so very remote from their English counterpart.'[42] Others have turned instead to parallels with the continental Europe of the *ancien régime*, a term which might or might not be taken to extend also to contemporary England.[43] At the opposite end of the interpretative scale there are those who continue to see eighteenth-century Ireland as given a distinctive character by its recent history of conquest and expropriation. The concept of a society shaped by unique cultural, political and religious divisions between rulers and ruled has been invoked to account for features as different as the prevalence in upper-class circles of habits of drinking and duelling, the conservative character of Anglican theology, and the absence of a more impressive musical tradition.[44] The same assumptions lie behind much analysis of the literature of the period.[45] For many writers, indeed, the real parallels for the structure of eighteenth-century Irish society are to be found in the colonial world, with Irish Protestants occupying a position comparable to the white settlers of Barbados or the Spanish and Portuguese colonists of Peru and Brazil.[46]

The distinction between these two images of eighteenth-century Irish society is for the most part an implicit one. There is no question of self-consciously opposite schools. On the contrary some of the leading writers in the field could not be convincingly assigned to either of the two categories suggested.[47] Nor should references to two possible models – a society riven by the tensions of colonialism versus a recognisable part of the European *ancien régime* – suggest that these must be mutually exclusive. On the contrary, it could be argued that the key feature of eighteenth-century Ireland was in fact its ambiguous status: too physically close and too similar to Great Britain to be treated as a colony, but too separate and too different to be a region of the metropolitan centre; inheriting an undoubted division between settler and native, yet without the racial distinctions that could make these absolute.[48]

Having said this, the ability of writers on eighteenth-century Ireland to put forward such radically different models of the society with which they are dealing remains striking. In part the divergence arises from lack of information. The absence of substantial evidence on popular attitudes prior to the troubles of the 1790s, for example, makes it impossible to say with any certainty how plebeian Catholics felt about the established church or the landlord class. Nor can we do much more than speculate about how far these Catholics regarded the largely theoretical restrictions imposed on them by the penal laws as a serious grievance, before they were taught to do so by two generations of middle-class-led agitation. In other cases the problem is one of selection of evidence and the context in which it is placed. The small body of surviving assizes records, for example, indicates that the courts for the most part made only sparing use of the death penalty and in fact acquitted a high proportion of defendants.[49] But how is this information to be weighed against those notorious cases in which the criminal law was used for blatantly partisan purposes?[50] How far should one emphasise the willingness of groups like the Whiteboys to enforce their own concepts of legitimacy in defiance of the law of the land, as against the regional character and limited aims of all such protests? If the penal laws are to be distinguished from other instances of confessional discrimination, in France or the Habsburg lands, by being directed against a majority rather than a minority, how far is it legitimate to qualify this by appealing to the standards of an age in which numbers were not yet the touchstone of political legitimacy? In general it is noticeable that an emphasis on the divided character of Irish society is more marked among historians concerned with cultural and intellectual development than among those concerned with the practical workings of the economy, the land system or the criminal law.[51] This could be taken as further evidence of the dangers of too heavy a reliance on the literary imagination; alternatively it reveals the ability of cultural studies to expose the tensions hidden beneath a superficially placid surface.

The question of the most suitable terms in which to discuss eighteenth-century Irish society is further complicated by the outcome of recent work in the one area of eighteenth-century studies that has not yet been discussed here: the crisis of the 1790s. In the very substantial body of work in this area published over the past fifteen years or so, three points in particular stand out. First there is the closer attention that has been paid to the deepening sectarian conflict of the 1780s and 1790s. Other recent work on the eighteenth century may point towards a less conflict-ridden model of social relations. But the strength and viciousness of the response to what were initially fairly minor threats to Protestant privilege in the late 1780s and early 1790s provides powerful support for the view that intractable sectarian animosities were in fact built into the very fabric of society and politics.[52] Secondly, there was a perceptible trend in the 1960s and 1970s towards a less critical treatment of the role of government and the landed gentry in the developing crisis of the 1790s. R.B. McDowell, for example, saw official policy in the aftermath of the rebellion as representing 'a policy of measured severity'.[53] More recent writers, however, have once again begun to emphasise the part played in the final explosion by reckless and partisan official violence.[54]

Finally, and most important, the new interest in popular collective action has extended to the rank and file of the revolutionary movement.[55]

The Defenders, long seen simply as a shadowy peasant rank and file behind the more clear-cut figures of the United Irish leaders, are now recognised as a popular underground conspiracy with a wholly independent existence, and their own crude but coherent political ideology. In this, new ideas absorbed from America, from France, and from middle-class Irish radicalism blended confusingly with older and more deeply rooted elements: resentment of Protestant dominance, some broad ideal of an Ireland independent of English rule, and cloudy aspirations to the recovery of lost rights and possessions. The speed with which these local animosities overwhelmed the orthodox secular and cosmopolitan radicalism of the United Irishmen has obvious implications for any assessment of popular mentality prior to the crisis of the late eighteenth century. On one reading of the evidence Corkery's hidden Ireland, with its keynotes of nationality, religion and rebellion, has been expelled through one door only to reappear by another.

The grim events of the 1790s can hardly fail to have a powerful influence on the way in which the history of the whole eighteenth century is approached. Yet to read history backwards has obvious dangers. One thinks of the way in which the Famine of 1845–50 was allowed to distort interpretations of the economic history of the whole preceding century and a half. It is also important to recognise that long-term perspectives can work forwards as well as back. If the events of the bloody summer of 1798 may be seen as casting a retrospective light on earlier decades, revealing deep structural conflicts beneath an apparently tranquil surface, those events must in turn be set in the context of later developments. In the quarter century following the Union, Irish political life once again became a contest for control between rival landed interests, each deploying its compliant army of tenant voters. Even after the rise of O'Connellite politics from the 1820s, deference and proprietorial interest were to remain a real force in Irish political life for half a century more.[56] From this point of view it becomes possible to ask whether it is not the events of the 1790s that should be seen as exceptional, the local reflection of an unprecedented international crisis rather than the defining moment in Irish eighteenth-century history.

NOTES

1 Roy Porter, *English Society in the Eighteenth Century* (Harmondsworth, 1982), p. 49.
2 Daniel Corkery, *The Hidden Ireland: A Study of Gaelic Munster in the Eighteenth Century* (Dublin, 1967), pp. 8–9, 25, 40–1.
3 See below, p. 23.
4 K.H. Connell, *The Population of Ireland 1750–1845* (Oxford, 1950).
5 See Joseph Lee, 'Grattan's Parliament', in Brian Farrell (ed.), *The Irish Parliamentary Tradition* (Dublin, 1973), p. 149; Gerard O'Brien, 'The Grattan Mystique', *Eighteenth-Century Ireland*, i (1986).

6 George O'Brien, *An Economic History of Ireland in the Eighteenth Century* (London and Dublin, 1918), pp. 2–3, 437. For Connolly's brusque dismissal of the supposed achievements of 'Grattan's parliament', along with his denunciation of the former Catholic landed class as 'a collection of land thieves and their lackeys', see *Labour in Irish History* (Dublin, 1910), pp. 14, 16, 41–4, a text that should dispose once and for all of the suggestion that criticism of nationalist historical orthodoxy must necessarily be allied to the cause of political reaction.

7 Froude's influence on subsequent writing is given particular emphasis in L.M. Cullen, 'Economic Development 1691–1750' in T.W. Moody and W.E. Vaughan (eds), *A New History of Ireland*, Volume IV: *Eighteenth-Century Ireland 1691–1800* (Oxford, 1986), pp. 123–9. See also Donal McCartney, 'James Anthony Froude and Ireland: A Historiographical Controversy of the Nineteenth Century', in T.D. Williams (ed.), *Historical Studies*, viii (Dublin, 1971).

8 Patrick Maume, 'Daniel Corkery: A Reassessment', *Studia Hibernica*, 26 (1992).

9 James Meenan, *George O'Brien: A Biographical Memoir* (Dublin, 1980), pp. 26, 11. There remains the question of how far O'Brien adapted his work to the prevailing political climate. *An Economic History of Ireland in the Eighteenth Century* was written in a matter of months, with the conscious intention of equipping its author for an academic career at University College, Dublin (which O'Brien's family had earlier chosen for him in the belief that it would be a safer bet than Trinity College in the Nationalist-dominated Ireland they saw as imminent). O'Brien's defence of his failure to publish substantially once he had achieved his ambition of an academic post ('I had shown that I have the capacity to write bulky learned volumes if I wanted to do so, and there was no necessity to continue repeating the demonstration') reinforces the impression of pragmatic careerism rather than deep involvement, either intellectual or ideological, in his chosen field of study. *Ibid.*, pp. 141–3, 71, 13, 212.

10 Constantia Maxwell, *Dublin under the Georges* (London, 1936); *Country and Town in Ireland under the Georges* (London, 1940).

11 See for example Maureen Wall, 'The Age of the Penal Laws 1691–1778', in T.W. Moody and F.X. Martin (eds), *The Course of Irish History* (Cork, 1967), p. 221.

12 Cullen's views were first set out in 'The Value of Contemporary Printed Sources for Irish Economic History in the Eighteenth Century', *Irish Historical Studies*, xiv, 54 (1964); 'Problems in the Interpretation and Revision of Eighteenth-century Irish Economic History', *Transactions of the Royal Historical Society*, ser. 5, 17 (1967); and in Chapters 1 and 9 of L.M. Cullen (ed.), *The Formation of the Irish Economy* (Cork, 1969). They received more systematic exposition in *An Economic History of Ireland since 1660* (London, 1972).

13 Cullen, *Economic History*, p. 90.

14 Cullen, 'Economic Development 1691–1750', in Moody and Vaughan (eds), *New History of Ireland*, iv, 130.

15 L.M. Cullen, 'The Hidden Ireland: Reassessment of a Concept', *Studia Hibernica*, 9 (1969).

16 L.M. Cullen, *Anglo-Irish Trade 1660–1800* (Manchester, 1968).

17 L.M. Cullen, 'Irish History without the Potato', *Past & Present*, 40 (1968), 80; reprinted in C.H.E. Philpin (ed.), *Nationalism and Popular Protest in Ireland* (Cambridge, 1987), p. 135.

18 H.F. Kearney, 'The Political Background to English Mercantilism, 1695–1700', *Economic History Review*, xi (1959); Patrick Kelly, 'The Irish Woollen Export Prohibition Act of 1699: Kearney Revisited', *Irish Economic & Social History*, vii

(1980); C.A. Edie, 'The Irish Cattle Bills: A Study in Restoration Politics', *Transactions of the American Philosophical Society*, lx, 2 (1970).

19 Apart from the works by Cullen already cited, current thinking is most usefully summarised in T.M. Devine, 'The English Connection and Irish and Scottish Development in the Eighteenth Century', in T.M. Devine and David Dickson (eds), *Ireland and Scotland 1600–1850: Parallels and Contrasts in Economic and Social Development* (Edinburgh, 1983).

20 On this point see Lee, 'Grattan's Parliament', pp. 151–3; Cullen, *Economic History*, pp. 96–7.

21 W.H. Crawford, 'Landlord-Tenant Relations in Ulster 1609–1820', *Irish Economic & Social History*, ii (1975); Crawford, 'The Significance of Landed Estates in Ulster 1600–1820', *ibid.*, xvii (1990); Peter Roebuck, 'Rent Movement, Proprietorial Incomes and Agricultural Development', in Peter Roebuck (ed.), *Plantation to Partition* (Belfast, 1981); Roebuck, 'Landlord Indebtedness in Ulster in the Seventeenth and Eighteenth Centuries', in J.M. Goldstrom and L.A. Clarkson (eds), *Irish Population, Economy and Society* (Oxford, 1981).

22 David Dickson, 'Property and Social Structure in Eighteenth-Century South Munster', in L.M. Cullen and F. Furet (eds), *Ireland and France: 17th–20th Centuries* (Paris, 1980).

23 David Dickson, 'Middlemen', in Thomas Bartlett and D.W. Hayton (eds), *Penal Era and Golden Age: Essays in Irish History (1690–1800)* (Belfast, 1979).

24 Maureen Wall, 'The Whiteboys', in T.D. Williams (ed.), *Secret Societies in Ireland* (Dublin, 1973); J.S. Donnelly, Jr, 'The Whiteboy Movement 1761–5', *Irish Historical Studies*, xxi, 81 (1978); Donnelly, 'The Rightboy Movement 1785–8', *Studia Hibernica*, 17/18 (1977–8); Donnelly, 'Hearts of Oak, Hearts of Steel', *Studia Hibernica*, 21 (1981); 'Irish Agrarian Rebellion: The Whiteboys of 1769–76', *Royal Irish Academy Proceedings*, sect. c, lxxxiii, 12 (1983); S.J. Connolly, 'The Houghers: Agrarian Protest in Early Eighteenth-Century Connacht', in Philpin (ed.), *Nationalism and Popular Protest*; M.J. Bric, 'The Rightboy Protest in County Cork 1785–1788', *Past & Present*, 100 (1983), reprinted in the same volume.

25 Bartlett, 'An End to Moral Economy: The Irish Militia Disturbances of 1793', *Past & Present*, 99 (1983), 42–44; reprinted in Philpin (ed.), *Nationalism and Popular Protest*.

26 Kevin McGrath, 'John Garzia, a Noted Priest Catcher and his Activities 1717–23', *Irish Ecclesiastical Record*, lxxii (1949). For a general review of the literature see R.E. Burns, 'The Irish Penal Code and Some of its Historians', *Review of Politics*, xxi (1959), 297–9. See also Maureen Wall, *The Penal Laws 1691–1760* (Dundalk, 1961), which firmly rejects 'the picture of the Mass-rock, with the watchers on the hill-top waiting to warn the priest of approaching soldiery' as 'a rather fanciful one for the eighteenth century' (p. 59).

27 J.G. Simms, *The Williamite Confiscation in Ireland 1690–1703* (London, 1956). Simms's articles, published between 1951 and 1979, are collected in David Hayton and Gerard O'Brien (eds), *War and Politics in Ireland 1649–1730* (London, 1986).

28 Maureen Wall, 'The Rise of a Catholic Middle Class in Eighteenth-century Ireland', *Irish Historical Studies*, xi (1958); Wall, 'Catholics in Economic Life', in Cullen (ed.), *Formation of the Irish Economy*; Wall, 'The Age of the Penal Laws', pp. 220–1.

29 For example, Tomás Ó Fiaich, 'The Registration of the Clergy in 1704', *Seanchas Ardmhacha*, 6 (1971); Patrick Kelly, 'Lord Galway and the Penal Laws', in C.E.J. Caldicott *et al.* (eds), *The Huguenots and Ireland* (Dublin, 1987); W.N. Osborough, 'Catholics, Land and the Popery Acts of Anne', in Thomas Power

and Kevin Whelan (eds), *Endurance and Emergence: Catholics in Ireland in the Eighteenth Century* (Dublin, 1990). There is also the work of D.W. Hayton, essential to any understanding of the political background to penal legislation: see *Ireland after the Glorious Revolution 1692–1715* (Belfast, 1979); 'The Crisis in Ireland and the Disintegration of Queen Anne's last Ministry', *Irish Historical Studies*, xxii (1981).

30 Thomas Bartlett, *The Fall and Rise of the Irish Nation* (Dublin, 1992); T.C. Barnard, 'The Uses of October 23 1641 and Irish Protestant Celebrations', *English Historical Review*, CVI (1991); 'Reforming Irish Manners: The Religious Societies in Dublin during the 1690s', *Historical Journal*, xxxv, 4 (1992); 'Protestants and the Irish Language c. 1675–1725', *Journal of Ecclesiastical History*, xliv, 2 (1993).

31 David Dickson, 'Catholics and Trade in Eighteenth-century Ireland: An Old Debate Revisited', in Power and Whelan (eds), *Endurance and Emergence*, p. 90.

32 Dickson, 'Middlemen'; L.M. Cullen, 'Catholics under the Penal Laws', *Eighteenth-century Ireland*, i (1986); Cullen, 'Catholic Social Classes under the Penal Laws', in Power and Whelan (eds), *Endurance and Emergence*. The development of a rural Catholic propertied class below the level of the landlord is also a central theme in the work of Kevin Whelan: 'The Catholic Community in Eighteenth-century County Wexford', in *ibid.*; 'The Catholic Church in County Tipperary 1700–1900', in William Nolan and T.G. McGrath (eds), *Tipperary: History and Society* (Dublin, 1985).

33 R.B. McDowell, *Irish Public Opinion 1750–1800* (London, 1944); J.L. McCracken, 'The Struggle between the Irish Administration and Parliament 1753–6', *Irish Historical Studies*, iii (1942); 'Irish Parliamentary Elections 1727–68', *Irish Historical Studies*, v (1947); 'The Irish Viceroyalty 1760–3', in H.A. Cronne *et al.* (eds), *Essays in British and Irish History* (London, 1949); E.M. Johnston, *Great Britain and Ireland 1760–1800* (Edinburgh, 1963).

34 The term applied disapprovingly by Herbert Butterfield to Cullen's first assaults on the accepted picture of eighteenth-century development: T.W. Moody (ed.), *Irish Historiography 1936–70* (Dublin, 1971), pp. 59–60.

35 J.C. Beckett, 'Anglo-Irish Constitutional Relations in the Later Eighteenth Century', *Irish Historical Studies*, xiv (1964), reprinted in Beckett, *Confrontations: Studies in Irish History* (London, 1972).

36 M.R. O'Connell, *Irish Politics and Social Conflict in the Age of the American Revolution* (Philadelphia, 1965).

37 Lee, 'Grattan's Parliament', pp. 150, 159.

38 See in particular R.B. McDowell, *Ireland in the Age of Imperialism and Revolution 1760–1801* (Oxford, 1979); Gerard O'Brien, *Anglo-Irish Politics in the Age of Grattan and Pitt* (Dublin, 1987); James Kelly, *Prelude to Union: Anglo-Irish Politics in the 1780s* (Dublin, 1992).

39 A.P.W. Malcomson, 'Election Politics in the Borough of Antrim 1750–1800', *Irish Historical Studies*, xvii (1970); 'The Politics of "Natural Right": The Abercorn Family and Strabane Borough 1692–1800', in G.A. Hayes-McCoy (ed.), *Historical Studies*, x (1976); *John Foster: The Politics of the Anglo-Irish Ascendancy* (Oxford, 1978).

40 A.P.W. Malcomson, '"The Parliamentary Traffic of this Country"', in Bartlett and Hayton (eds), *Penal Era and Golden Age*, p. 156.

41 K.T. Hoppen, *Elections, Politics and Society in Ireland 1832–1885* (Oxford, 1984).

42 Malcomson, *John Foster*, pp. xxvi–xxvii.

43 J.R. Hill, 'The Civic Tradition in Scotland and Ireland in the Mid-eighteenth Century', in S.J. Connolly, R. Houston and R.J. Morris (eds), *Conflict, Identity and Economic Development in Ireland and Scotland* (Preston, 1995); S.J. Connolly,

Religion, Law and Power: The Making of Protestant Ireland 1660–1760 (Oxford, 1992), p. 2; C.D.A. Leighton, *Catholicism in a Protestant Kingdom: A Study of the Irish Ancien Regime* (Dublin, 1994). For the wider issues connected with the use of the term *ancien régime* see the exchange between Jonathan Clark and Joanna Innes in *Past & Present* (1987), p. 115.

44 V.G. Kiernan, *The Duel in European History* (Oxford, 1988), pp. 106–8; David Berman, 'The Culmination and Causation of Irish Philosophy', *Archiv für Geschichte der Philosophie*, lxiv, 3 (1982); Harry White, 'Carolan and the Dislocation of Music in Ireland', *Eighteenth-Century Ireland*, iv (1989).

45 For example, Seamus Deane, *A Short History of Irish Literature* (London, 1986), ch. 2.

46 For a particularly effective example of sustained comparison, focusing on Latin America, see D.N. Doyle, *Ireland, Irishmen and Revolutionary America 1760–1820* (Dublin and Cork, 1981), p. 13. See also Nicholas Canny, 'Identity Formation in Ireland: The Emergence of the Anglo-Irish', in N. Canny and Anthony Pagden (eds), *Colonial Identity in the Atlantic World 1500–1800* (Princeton, 1987).

47 Thus Cullen's insistence on a more positive picture of economic conditions and relationships may be set against his emphasis elsewhere on the continuity of ethnic and religious rivalries, and his characterisation of Ireland's relationship with Great Britain as 'colonial'. See *The Emergence of Modern Ireland 1600–1900* (London, 1981), p. 35 and chs 9–10, as well as the work on the 1790s in n. 52 below. In the same way Bartlett's application of the 'moral economy' thesis (n. 25) contrasts with the emphasis on long term religious animosities in *The Fall and Rise of the Irish Nation*.

48 This point is made in more detail in Connolly, *Religion, Law and Power*, pp. 103–14; Connolly, 'Late Eighteenth-century Irish Politics', *Parliamentary History*, XIII, 2 (1996).

49 Connolly, *Religion, Law and Power*, pp. 227–35.

50 The best-known such case is the trial of Father Nicholas Sheehy and other prominent County Tipperary Catholics alleged to have been involved in the Whiteboy movement of the mid-1760s. The fullest modern account is M.J. Bric, 'The Whiteboy Movement in Tipperary 1760–80', in William Nolan and T.G. McGrath (eds), *Tipperary: History and Society* (Dublin, 1985), pp. 158–60. For the rather different case of Sir James Cotter in 1720 see Connolly, *Religion, Law and Power*, pp. 229–30.

51 For example three valuable recent studies have shown how attempts to achieve an agreed synthesis of the country's history, comparable to that developed by Scottish enlightenment intellectuals, were crippled by religious differences: Joseph Liechty, 'Testing the Depth of Catholic/Protestant Conflict: The Case of Thomas Leland's "History of Ireland" 1773', *Archivium Hibernicum*, xlii (1987); J.R. Hill, 'Popery and Protestantism, Civil and Religious Liberty: The Disputed Lessons of Irish History 1690–1812', *Past & Present*, 118 (1988); Clare O'Halloran, '"The Island of Saints and Scholars": Views of the Early Church and Sectarian Politics in Late Eighteenth-century Ireland', *Eighteenth-century Ireland*, v (1990).

52 For example, James Kelly, 'The Genesis of the "Protestant Ascendancy"', in Gerard O'Brien (ed.), *Parliament, Politics and People* (Dublin, 1989); Bartlett, *Fall and Rise of the Irish Nation*; L.M. Cullen, 'The 1798 Rebellion in Its Eighteenth-Century Context', in P.J. Corish (ed.), *Radicals, Rebels and Establishments* (Belfast, 1985); Cullen, 'The 1798 Rebellion in Wexford: United Irishman Organisation, Membership, Leadership', in Kevin Whelan (ed.), *Wexford: History and Society* (Dublin, 1987); Kevin Whelan, 'The Religious

Factor in the 1798 Rebellion in County Wexford', in P. Flanagan *et al.* (eds), *Rural Ireland 1600–1900: Modernisation and Change* (Cork, 1987).

53 McDowell, *Ireland*, p. 677. See also H. Senior, *Orangeism in Ireland and Britain 1795–1836* (London, 1966) which largely acquits government of the charge of deliberately promoting sectarian animosities for its own purposes.

54 See in particular Bartlett, *Fall and Rise of the Irish Nation*, p. 231, which suggests that Dublin Castle 'viewed with equanimity', and 'even welcomed', the prospect of open rebellion.

55 See in particular Marianne Elliott, *Partners in Revolution: The United Irishmen and France* (New Haven, CT, 1982); Jim Smyth, *The Men of No Property: Irish Radicals and Popular Politics in the Late Eighteenth Century* (London, 1992); David Dickson and Hugh Gough (eds), *The French Revolution and Ireland* (Dublin, 1990), especially the contributions of Cullen, Dunne, Smyth and Whelan.

56 For the post-union period see S.J. Connolly, 'Aftermath and Adjustment', in W.E. Vaughan (ed.), *A New History of Ireland*, Vol. V: *Ireland Under the Union, I 1801–70* (Oxford, 1989), pp. 5–6, 17–20. For the long-term survival of proprietorial power see Hoppen, *Elections, Politics and Society*.

3

THE UNION OF IRELAND AND BRITAIN, 1801–1921

Liam Kennedy and David S. Johnson

'the Act of Union forms the matrix of modern Irish history.'[1]

INTRODUCTION

It is nearly 200 years since the passing of the Act of Union. Even after this length of time it is still difficult to divorce attitudes towards it from contemporary political stances on the 'Irish Question'. It is hard to imagine, for instance, many of today's republicans allowing that the Act conferred considerable economic blessings or loyalists arguing that its effects were largely damaging. And this has always been so. As we shall see, much of the historiography of the Union has been conducted within the framework of attitudes to the issues of the day, from repeal to home rule, to the arguments surrounding independence, and beyond.

Protagonists of the Union have usually, though not always, felt obliged to defend the status quo, the totality of the Union as it actually operated. This is not a logical necessity. To uphold the general framework of the Union does not imply support for every administrative detail or legal aspect of its operation. Nor does a disagreement with its basic principles necessarily involve an attack on everything that the British government did, or left undone, in Ireland since 1801, though opponents of the Union often acted as if it did. Many of the adverse judgments on the Union are in reality more in the nature of criticisms made by an opposing (and reforming) party to policies pursued by those in office. In areas like the tithe, the disestablishment of the Church of Ireland, poor relief or the land question, major reforms proved compatible with the Union, although it might be argued that a 'national' Irish government would have secured these ameliorative measures earlier. By the same token, it could also be argued that some of the problems might have taken an independent government longer to solve.

The first problem, then, in discussing the economic effects of the Union is to judge which elements were intrinsic to the Union, and which were not. We would suggest three essential implications of the Union. The first was the abolition of customs duties between Britain and Ireland and the creation of a single market. This was the clear intention of the sixth article of the Union, although it did not become fully operational until 1824. Internal free trade within the United Kingdom has to be seen in the context of the movement towards external free trade, which was largely completed by the mid-nineteenth century. The second central element was the harmonization of taxation within the United Kingdom. Ireland had its own exchequer and was taxed separately until 1817, however, and it was not until the 1850s that all the major imposts in the two countries were equalized. The logic of fiscal uniformity is encapsulated in Gladstone's famous remark when equalizing the whiskey duties in 1853: 'he could not see that it was part of the rights of man that the Irishman should be able to make himself drunk more cheaply than the inhabitant of Great Britain.'[2] Once it was allowed that, in theory anyway, all citizens of the United Kingdom of Great Britain and Ireland were equal under the same laws it followed that as individuals they should be subject to the same taxes, whether levied on income or on purchase.[3] The third central aspect of the Union involved a shift in the arena of economic decision-making from Dublin to London. The importance of this was two-fold. To an extent it may have led to increased absenteeism as politicians followed the transfer of power to Westminster. This would have led to increased remittances abroad and the reduction of purchasing power in Ireland. Less tangibly but perhaps more importantly, it may have led to a neglect of Irish economic interests which, on occasions, differed from those in more dominant parts of the United Kingdom.

If it can be agreed that the areas outlined above are those central to the Union, there remains another problem. What alternative framework to that of the Union is being envisaged? Those who praised or condemned the Union presumably had some alternative political arrangement in mind, however vague. Was it Grattan's reformed parliament, as Daniel O'Connell sometimes implied in the 1830s? This alternative came to look increasingly ridiculous as time went by and the British parliament reformed itself. Was it an Ireland as independent of Britain as France or Germany were, with plenary economic powers? This was the preferred option of those adhering to the revolutionary tradition in Ireland and was the one that eventually prevailed over most of the island after 1921. But this was not the alternative to the Union favoured by mainstream constitutional nationalism throughout the nineteenth century when various forms of Home Rule envisaged substantially less than full economic independence for Ireland.

Broadly speaking, the historiography of the Union can be divided into four phases, three of which coincided with periods of heightened political excitement. The first comes with the Repeal campaign of the 1830s and 1840s; the second upsurge of interest is associated with the Home Rule agitation of the later nineteenth century; the third centres on the movement for independence in the early twentieth century; and the fourth and qualitatively different phase relates to the stream of academic and professional historical writing, mostly in this century but especially since 1965.

THE EMERGING CRITIQUE OF THE UNION

The Union was under sporadic criticism from its inception. Petitions in favour of the repeal of the Act were made as early as 1810.[4] But it was not until the 1830s, after emancipation and the Reform Bill which increased 'popular' representation in parliament, that the Union came under more or less continuous attack from certain quarters. By that time the Irish economy was experiencing economic problems which had not been so apparent earlier. The period of the revolutionary and Napoleonic wars had generally been prosperous for the Irish economy. Although there had been problems in the years immediately after 1815 – a postwar recession on which were superimposed the subsistence crises of 1816–17 and 1819 – it was not until the second half of the 1820s that the more deep-seated nature of Irish economic problems became apparent. The continued population growth, coupled with agricultural prices that were lower in the 1820s and 1830s than in the previous twenty-five years, led to increased poverty among sections of the agricultural community. Ireland was also suffering from industrial problems. The woollen industry was acknowledged to be in decay although, in truth, its fortunes had probably been on the wane for many years. The cotton industry, too, was experiencing economic difficulties, partly a result of hand spinners and weavers losing employment through the spread of factories, partly because of Lancashire competition and partly through the rival attractions of linen production.[5] A range of other industries, admittedly not very significant ones like silk, glass, hatmaking, tinplating and brickmaking, were also in decay. In addition it was clear by the 1830s that Ireland had not benefited nearly as much as Britain from the reduction in taxation that had taken place after 1815. Thus the 1830s and 1840s led to an historical appraisal of the Union's economic effects. Of course, this appraisal was not, nor was it meant to be, impartial. In evaluating the Union, evidence was marshalled for and against repeal. Thus Daniel O'Connell, before making his important speech on the subject in 1834, which reviewed the history of the Union (and much more Irish history besides) requested information that would back up his anti-Union case: on 'the wrongs of the Irish distilleries' or how 'the bounty on imported linen yarn operated to shift the trade from Ireland to Scotland' for example.[6] Nor was the historical review by proponents of the Union any more even handed. R. Montgomery Martin, one of the most notable protagonists was patronized by government circles and dedicated his *Ireland Before and After the Union* to Sir Robert Peel.[7]

In assessing the economic effects of the Union both sides in the argument had by the 1830s and 1840s a considerable amount of statistical material at their disposal: figures for internal and external trade; for consumption of excisable commodities; for taxation; together with a miscellaneous selection of factual information, variable in quality, derived from governmental reports and the speeches and writings of private individuals. There were problems in using all of them.[8] But this was frequently compounded by two features in the disputants' mode of argument. First, facts were often used selectively, to make a case rather than to try to get at the truth of the matter. Thus figures for trade were cited for different points on the trade cycle – carefully chosen in a way that gave no indication of the underlying trend. Second, the connection between the statistics which were quoted and the Act of Union was not made explicit. The arguments were of the *post hoc ergo propter hoc* kind. This applied to both Unionists and Repealers, unless it suited them to do otherwise.

The war of ideas ranged over wide areas of Irish economic life. A principal battleground related to the very general question of whether living standards had improved or disimproved as a result of the Union. Direct indicators (as distinct from indirect ones, like export statistics) were difficult to come by. Selective quotations from parliamentary committees of enquiry could be used to support either conclusion.

A superior approach, at least from the viewpoint of methodology, exploited consumption figures for various dutiable commodities such as tea, tobacco or sugar. The data here generally supported the Repealers' argument. The rate of increase of consumption was more rapid under Grattan's parliament than after the Union.[9] Unionists in arguing the contrary either presented their data in an unconvincing form, or else used unrepresentative indicators such as the duty on wrought gold plate, 'an article of luxury . . . only used by persons of a superior class' which showed 'something of the condition of the higher orders' but little else.[10] The interpretation of the consumption data used by the Repealers could have been challenged, but generally it was not. This would have involved reasoning that the declining consumption of dutiable commodities was not necessarily an indication of declining living standards, as increased taxation had raised their prices relative to other goods. This would have led to a decline in the amounts consumed (for any given level of income), as people substituted other goods for those carrying heavier duties. Moreover, higher duties would also have served to promote an illicit trade in these goods which would not be reflected in official consumption figures.

Higher taxation under the Union was not something Unionists wished to concede, however. Unionists did sometimes shift the argument away from consumption patterns towards other kinds of indicators of living standards. Increasing prosperity could be inferred from the rising values of properties probated, the increased deposits in savings banks and the heavier tonnage carried on the canals.[11] Here they were on safer ground. While these measures say nothing directly about living standards for the majority of the population, they do suggest that some people, not always necessarily the very rich, were getting better off, and that the economy possessed a certain dynamism.

The performance of specific sectors of the Irish economy was also invoked in the debate. The external trade sector, it was agreed by both sets of antagonists, was an important window on the changing state of the economy, a view which would also command modern assent. 'There is abundant evidence of a high correlation between the rate of growth of exports and the rate of growth of GNP.'[12] By this test the Irish trade figures, for all their faults, tended to support the Unionist case. From the peak of the 1790s (Unionists were inclined to use the lower figures from the late 1790s, or even 1800–1 to reinforce their case) there was a rise, by the mid 1820s, of about two thirds in the official returns. The Railway Commissioners' Report, quite rightly attacked by Repealers as defective, even unbelievable, showed a doubling of exports between 1825 and 1835. The figures for tonnage cleared at Irish ports, though reflecting a change in the composition of trade towards bulkier agricultural produce, indicated a virtual trebling between the early 1800s and 1840.[13] Over the same period, population, itself regarded by some as 'a convincing test of the advancing state of the nation', had grown rapidly.[14] Although contemporaries were not as inclined as modern historians to see things in per capita terms, the clear implication from figures available at the time was that exports had grown more rapidly than population over the forty years since the Union.

This strong export performance created some embarrassment for Repealers seeking to assert the endlessly harmful effects of the Union, not least because the increase in external trade under Grattan's parliament had been interpreted as a sign of economic progress. They were driven, therefore, to argue that an active foreign trade sector – Ricardian notions of the benefits of economic specialisation and trade notwithstanding – could in some circumstances signify economic weakness. Barry, for example, claimed that it was fallacious to accept that an increase in the quantity of exports and imports over time was any 'test of prosperity'.[15] This seems an unusual position to adopt, not only on theoretical grounds but because of the historical evidence for an association between foreign trade and economic growth.[16] The pro-Union spokesman, Spring-Rice, remarked in mock-exasperation: 'Truly mine is a most unfortunate country. Whether the amount of imports or exports increase or whether they diminish, the one alternative or the other is a proof of her misery in the eyes of the advocates of Repeal. They are determined that in all circumstances, Ireland shall and must be poor. In argument they make poverty their divinity and they worship her with zealous devotion.'[17]

One can certainly make fun of the details and the logic of the economic reasoning employed by the Repealers. Nonetheless, they did have a point. The primary focus of the attack was the *composition* of Irish exports and imports, and how this changed over time. 'Indeed I am disposed to think, paradoxical as the position will appear to some', says Barry, 'that an export of food to any great extent, from a long-peopled country, which is *not* a large exporter of manufacturers, is, in itself, *prima facie* evidence of the poverty of that country'. While the argument is put in general terms, the example in mind is clearly Ireland after the Union:

> A country exporting agricultural produce largely, without any cor-responding export of manufactured articles, must, if it be fully peopled, be a poor country; because this exclusive export of food, shows that manufacturers have no existence in it – or that if they have existence, they must . . . be rapidly tending to extinction. The country must therefore be in, or be quickly advancing towards, a purely agricultural condition.[18]

There is no doubt that the composition of Irish exports changed signifi-cantly between 1780 and the 1830s. Although in absolute terms the value of industrial exports rose by about fifty per cent between the Union and 1826, their proportion of the total fell from forty-five per cent in the mid-1790s to thirty-two per cent by the mid-1820s, and to twenty-four per cent, according to the Railway Commissioner's Report, by 1835. Over the same period agricultural exports rose from forty-seven per cent of the total in the 1790s, to sixty-two per cent in the mid 1820s and to seventy-three per cent in 1835.[19]

But was the changing composition of Irish exports, and the structural change in the Irish economy which this implied, necessarily a bad thing? It would be hard to argue that trade liberalisation did not confer benefits on both economies in the short term – and there was confusion in the ranks of Repealers regarding the desirability of free trade – but this is not the same thing as saying that a country should be indifferent as to the patterns of specialisation emerging in the wake of economic integration. If comparative advantage, which hinges on differences in resource en-dowments, is conceived, not in static terms, but as being open to change (and perhaps manipulation) over time, then it is quite possible to argue that a switch of resources away from industry and towards agriculture was not in the best long-term interests of a country like Ireland.[20] Intuitively, the more perspicacious Repealers felt this to be the case.

This might seem to suggest that Repealers would be ardent supporters of economic protectionism. For those familiar with nationalist writings early this century, the surprise is how little protectionism featured in the policy ideas of these early critics of the Union. Certainly Repealers in- sisted that the alleged decline of Irish industry had been due to the Union (the removal of protective duties under the Union had 'unquestionably been attended with the ruin of a great number of our prosperous establishments'), but the fact remains that economic protectionism did not bulk large in their repertoire of arguments for the restoration of an Irish parliament.[21] This lightness of emphasis, even ambivalence on the subject, may have been due to the intellectual grip of free-trade ideology by the 1840s. Whatever the reason, few Repealers could bring themselves to advocate a reintroduction of protection as a remedy for Ireland's woes.

The Young Irelanders had fewer reservations and, it must be said, a more limited grasp of economic affairs by comparison with the main- stream Repeal campaigners. Thomas Davis, for example, assumed and asserted that Ireland could benefit from tariffs in much the same way as Germany apparently had done. Although temperamentally opposed to the new factory system, preferring instead an idealised version of do- mestic manufacture, he accepted that factory production was a necessary evil to combat Britain's industrial dominance. To promote a revival of industry, he advocated protective tariffs which would be sure to create 'vast manufactures' in Ireland. As in Germany, the price might be 'paying a little more for clothes, or furniture or utensils'. Though the great bulk of the population, which depended on the land for a livelihood, might have been less than enthusiastic about being penalised in this way, Davis felt that a break with free trade was necessary in the interests of Irish industry. Irish natural resources would also play a large part in this rather vague industrialisation story. Like Griffith later, Davis was inclined to exaggerate Ireland's natural resource endowments.[22]

Such arguments as existed for protection were of course strongly con- tested by other contemporary voices within Ireland. One of the most forceful statements was by C.G. Otway, as part of his report into the depressed conditions of the hand-loom weavers. This work, which was commissioned by the government, contained historical reviews of the most important Irish industries. According to Otway, protectionism under the old Irish parliament had been a disaster. 'Bounties, duties and premiums had created a situation in which manufacturers looked to the premiums and the Parliament instead of their own industry and the market, and expected that customers could be created by statute.'[23] The woollen industry, to take a prime example, deteriorated even under protection, because of shoddy Irish workmanship based on captive mar- kets for the cloth for the militia and the army. This led to 'shameful jobbing' and 'the worst description of cloth being produced'.[24] Conse- quently, customers preferred to buy English cloth even though it was dearer. The final collapse of the industry – which had already suffered a severe shock in 1810 – was brought about, not by the ending of protection but by the crisis of 1826, which led to dumping on the Irish market. Protection of the silk industry had led to inefficiency, as there was no inherent reason why Ireland could not have competed with the British.[25] All that protection did was to allow excessive wages and the growth of combinations. These could no longer be maintained after the Union duties were abolished. Nor could it be argued, Otway believed, that protectionism benefited the cotton industry. Duties were lower after 1800 than they had been before and were progressively reduced, yet down to 1825 the cotton industry had thrived. The industry suffered not from the removal of the protective duties but from the constant stream of improvements made to the industry in England. These had been difficult to replicate in Ireland because of England's 'direct access to raw materials' and because of 'all the advantages that capital and skill could accomplish to cheapen production and enlarge a market'.[26] The basic weaknesses in Ireland's competitive position had been revealed by severe crises in 1825 and 1837. It was these, according to Otway, rather than the absence of protectionism *per se*, that had led to the diminution in the importance of the Irish cotton industry.

Possibly in recognition of the difficulties associated with protectionist arguments, Repeal campaigners tended to concentrate their fire on two other issues: absenteeism among Irish landed proprietors and the allegedly excessive taxation of Ireland. These were unambiguously bad for Ireland, being held responsible for the drain of capital which caused both poverty and a lack of industrialization in Ireland.[27] 'Repeal', it was contended, 'would bring an end to this drain and so provide an abundant supply of capital, sufficient in itself, perhaps, to give new life to Irish industry'. Absenteeism was to be controlled by a tax on landlords who did not live in Ireland. (Nothing was said about these landlords, about two-thirds of all 'absentees', who were resident in other parts of Ireland.) An absentee tax required Repeal because, it was alleged, a Union parliament would never impose such legislation. It would never do so, in part because of self-interest: England gained at Ireland's expense. But the Union, by its very nature, also prevented discrimination against landlords absent from Ireland, in exactly the same way that it could not allow taxes on a 'Yorkshireman who should spend his fortune in Lancashire or Middlesex instead of in his own country'.[28] However, as Unionists pointed out, attempts to impose legislation against absentee landlords in the old Irish parliament had always failed even when, as in 1773, it had the support of the British government. In 1797 and 1799 motions to raise £240,000 by a tax on absentees were not supported in the Irish parliament.[29]

It was obvious to all, including Repealers, that the Union had not caused absenteeism. The argument was that it had increased it greatly.

The usual contention was that the money drained from Ireland as a result of it had risen from £2 million or less, before 1800, to £4 million annually by the 1830s.[30] The first figure was taken from the Irish Currency Committee of 1804. Newenham writing at the same time thought it was around £3 million each year. The figure for the later period of £4 million, was based partly on the belief that total rents had increased, and partly on *a priori* reasoning. The centre of political power had shifted from Dublin to Westminster and the landlords had followed. Though plausible, there was little hard evidence for this. Dr Malcolmson has argued that there was no mass exodus of would-be politicians across the water. The attendance of Irish MPs at Westminster was poor as was that of the Irish representative peers – for whom 'the principle was immediately established that residence in Ireland was an almost essential qualification.' The truth was that 'the Union did not cause a sudden exodus of those landlords who were resident at the time of its passing'.[31]

Not until the Emancipation and Reform Acts were passed, causing a gradual waning of landlords' political influence, was there a marked increase in absenteeism. Independent evidence would suggest a figure of £4 million for remittances to absentee landlords, but this is clearly an upper bound estimate. It implies that over 30 per cent of the gross rental of the country, or nearly 10 per cent of agricultural output was being remitted from Ireland to Britain.[32] In 1870, the first year for which there are anything like accurate figures, the transfer was of the order of fifteen to twenty per cent of the rental, or about four per cent of total output.[33] Even allowing for a possible shift towards greater residence as a result of the Encumbered Estates Act, the clear implication is that in the 1840s the annual figure was nearer to £3 million than £4 million, and possibly not much greater than the £2 million estimated by the Irish Currency Committee.[34]

Unionists would not have been satisfied with even this reformulation of the sums involved. Beginning with an estimate of around £2 million for the extent of absentee rents in the 1830s, they then contrasted this with a figure given by Newenham of £1.6 million for the year 1775. As the value of money had fallen since 1785, this comparison implied that absenteeism was actually lower in 1830 than before the Union![35] Unionists did not explain, though, how the Union could have produced this counter-intuitive outcome. Some in fact would have dismissed the whole argument about the drain of rents from Ireland, insisting that absentee landlords frequently made the best landlords, and adding the mischievous charge that Repealers were in any case almost equally uncomplimentary about resident as of absentee landlords.[36]

As the century progressed, the question of absenteeism was increasingly absorbed in the wider issue of the role of the landlords and land reform. In any case one of the cherished platforms of the Repealers, that only an independent Irish parliament could diminish absenteeism through a tax on non-resident landlords, had been shown to be false. At the same time that Repealers were arguing that an absentee tax was impossible under the arrangements of the Union, Peel was, effectively, imposing one. In 1842 he re-imposed the income tax on Britain, but not on Ireland. Rents to absentee Irish landlords resident in England were assessed under Schedule D as income from abroad and taxed at the rate of 7d in the pound. This was less than the rates proposed by the eighteenth-century Irish parliament or by the Repealers. But it was enacted. This situation lasted until 1853 when income tax was imposed on Ireland, creating equality of treatment in both countries.[37]

What of overtaxation, the question which bulked so large in any critical assessment of Ireland under the Union?[38] Indeed it still featured as a grievance in the twentieth century. A demand for the repayment ('without interest') of £400 million in overtaxation was made by Michael Collins in the Treaty negotiations of 1921 and by de Valera in the initial conference on the financial dispute between Great Britain and Ireland held in 1932 over the land annuities and other matters.[39]

During the first half of the nineteenth century discussion of this subject was hampered by a lack of accurate financial information. True, it was obvious fairly quickly after 1800 that the financial arrangements established by the Act of Union were working to Ireland's disadvantage. For although the Act created political union, fiscal separateness remained. Ireland and Britain, through separate exchequers, were to service their own debts incurred before 1801, and pay for their own local expenditure. Most important, Ireland was to contribute 2/17 of the money necessary to finance Imperial expenditure. According to Daniel O'Connell 'this fraction was purposely introduced in order that Ireland might be robbed with greater facility.'[40]

This was almost certainly untrue. Castlereagh had arrived at the figure of 2/17 on the basis of available information on consumption, exports, population and so on. This proportion might even have been reduced if a reasoned case had been made for a lower one; but the opposition concentrated on the principle of a contribution rather than the detail. As Boyce notes, unlike the closely-contested negotiations surrounding the union of England and Scotland a century earlier, British ministers had to attend to both sides of the bargain in 1799–1800.[41] In the circumstances, the agreement reached was generous. Still, as it turned out, the proportion *was* too high. With no income tax in Ireland, which would have been difficult to impose without a poor law valuation, the burden of increasing revenue fell on indirect taxes. By 1809–10 this source was subject to diminishing returns. As rates increased, revenue ceased to rise, except on whiskey. Despite more than doubling taxes, the Irish exchequer had increasingly to resort to loans to cover half of its expenditure. By the end of the war it was effectively bankrupt. Ireland's debt had risen from 1/15 to 2/13 of the British level. In 1817 the two exchequers and the two debts were amalgamated. Gradually many of the taxes in Ireland and Britain – except that on whiskey – were equalized, by abolishing some and reducing others in both countries. But as England had been a more highly taxed country to start with, complained the Repealers, these postwar developments brought a disproportionate benefit to England.[42] Of more significance, in terms of contemporary and also later debates, the Repealers identified an apparent revenue drain from Ireland (the poorer country) to England (the richer country). Ireland was overtaxed. The Unionist response was that tax rates in England had for many decades been higher than in Ireland, so in reality it was England which had been overtaxed.[43]

THE DEMAND FOR HOME RULE

As the century wore on the question of taxation became more widely discussed. This was probably caused by the large increase in taxation in the 1850s when Gladstone imposed income tax on Ireland for the first time and also raised the Irish whiskey duties to British levels. Despite a ten per cent fall in population, Irish tax yields rose by nearly sixty per cent in the course of the 1850s. The estimated annual 'drain' (gross of military and national debt expenditure in Ireland) in the form of the balance for Imperial Services, rose from £2.6 million in the 1840s to £5.4 million in the 1850s, falling to £4.5 million in the 1860s. Dissatisfaction with this state of affairs led to the establishment of a Parliamentary Select Committee which reported in 1865. The Committee recognised that there had been a considerable increase in taxation since 1853. Several witnesses blamed this for the distress that was apparent in Ireland in the 1860s. The Committee concluded, however, that the 'remarkably inclement' weather, which had persisted for several seasons, should be held responsible. Lowering tax rates in Ireland below those in Britain was seen as undesirable and unfair to the poor in Britain. The Committee instead recommended advances to agriculture, 'for drainage and labourers' cottages.'[44]

The problem of overtaxation was re-activated by the Home Rule League in the 1870s, but it was pushed from centre stage by the 'Land Question'. In 1894, however, Irish finances were thoroughly investigated by a Royal Commission. It could not agree on unanimous recommendations and, instead of producing one report, it produced a whole litter.[45] Still, eleven of the thirteen surviving members (two died in the course of its deliberations) reached several important conclusions. First, that Great Britain and Ireland would 'for the purpose of this inquiry, be considered as separate entities'.[46] As the inquiry stemmed from the Home Rule question, this was reasonable. But it was not logically necessary. If

Irishmen and Englishmen were seen simply as individuals in a unitary state then the problem of the 'overtaxation' of Ireland largely disappeared. Income tax was levied at a uniform rate throughout the realm. (What minor differences there were probably operated in Ireland's favour.) Customs and excise rates were also the same in all parts of the United Kingdom. Any injustice done to Ireland arose simply because indirect taxes bore most heavily on the poor and Ireland contained more poor people. Hence Nassau Senior's famous dictum: 'Ireland is overtaxed because she is poor rather than poor because she is overtaxed.'[47] The problem was at root, therefore, one of 'class rather than countries'.[48] If there was unfairness in the system as between individuals, the logical conclusion had to be that the whole United Kingdom tax structure should be overhauled, rather than that Ireland should be given special treatment.

Although this approach was a perfectly coherent one, it was increasingly recognised even in the nineteenth century that poorer regions might need special financial treatment. This usually took the form of regional subsidies. The grants to the 'congested districts' of the West of Ireland and the crofter communities of the Scottish Highlands are examples of this. In the twentieth century regional tax concessions to business have become common. But nineteenth-century Ireland also had an additional historic, legal reason for separate treatment. True enough, Article VII of the Act of Union envisaged a unified financial system between Britain and Ireland, although, as we have noted, it did not establish one immediately. With fiscal unification it was expected that all expenditure should be 'defrayed indiscriminately by equal taxes imposed on the same articles in each country'. But there was the important proviso that there should be 'particular exemptions or abatements in Ireland, and in that part of Great Britain called Scotland, as circumstances may appear from time to time to demand'.[49] This principle had effectively been recognised for more than thirty years after 1817. It had been applied in 1842 when the income tax was re-imposed on England, but not on Ireland. Although Peel increased the duty on spirits in Ireland to compensate for this, he repealed it a year later. Thus, under Article VII, a claim for separate treatment for Ireland could be admitted, something which was congenial to unionists as well as nationalists.[50]

The second important conclusion of the Committee was implicit in the first. By accepting the premise that Ireland could be treated as a separate part of the United Kingdom, it could be easily shown that Ireland had been overtaxed. 'Whilst the actual tax revenue of Ireland is about one-eleventh of that of Great Britain, the relative taxable capacity of Ireland is much smaller and is not estimated by any of us as exceeding one-twentieth.'[51] The concept of 'taxable capacity' was rather nebulous. Sir Robert Giffen had produced some speculative figures suggesting that Ireland's 'consumable stock', roughly national income, was one-eighteenth that of Britain. (This implies, incidentally, that incomes per head in Ireland were about half the United Kingdom average, certainly not ridiculously wide of the mark.) This figure corresponded more or less, with the ratios of death-duty yields and the gross assessments to income tax. The Committee argued that taxable capacity could not be assessed simply by comparing incomes. The richer a country was, the more comfortably it could afford to pay a higher proportion of its income in tax. So, accepting Ireland's taxable capacity to be around one-twentieth of Britain's[52] and given that Ireland contributed as much as one-eleventh of tax revenue, the conclusion to be drawn was that Ireland was paying nearly twice as much tax as it should have done, and this had been going on for at least forty years.

Another criticism of the financial system under the Union surfaced in several of the separate reports produced by members of the Committee. This related to the annual 'drain' on the taxation account from Ireland to England because of the surplus of revenue over expenditure. Put simply, Ireland paid more in taxation than was spent by the government in the country. Taking this back to 1817 produced a total by the 1890s in excess of £300 million. At least that is what the figures produced by the Committee suggested. The problem was in defining 'local expenditure'. It did not mean simply expenditure by the government in Ireland. This was because some items of Imperial Expenditure – particularly interest payments on the national debt held in Ireland, and spending in the country on the army and navy – were not taken into account. The former was running at £1.2 million annually in the 1860s, although it had fallen to £0.6 million by the late 1890s.[53] Expenditure on the army in Ireland is more difficult to quantify. Giffen estimated it cost between £3 million and £4 million annually in the 1880s.[54] Not all of this was spent in Ireland. Part was spent on ordnance in Britain. Part was remitted to Britain by British soldiers serving in Ireland. On the other hand this was offset by remittances back to Ireland from Irish soldiers serving out of the country. An intelligent guess might indicate net expenditure in Ireland at between £1 million and £2 million.[55] Thus by the 1880s the likelihood is that less than £1 million of Irish taxes failed to find their way back to the country in the form of expenditure. During the period from 1817 to the 1860s the true 'drain' was higher, possibly as much as £2–3 million a year on average. But by 1900 when the nominal surplus of revenue over expenditure was only £1.7 million, it was probably negative.

This element of Anglo-Irish financial relationships – the excess of revenue over expenditure – in time became important to Irish nationalists.[56] But this was not the element stressed in Home Rulers' submissions to the Financial Relations Committee. Their prime aim was to stress Ireland's overtaxation and they were disinclined to allow that any government expenditure could be allocated between local and imperial purposes. All expenditure was deemed to be imperial. This showed perspicacity, of a self-interested kind. First, if Ireland was to contribute according to its 'taxable capacity', it would pay not much more than half the amount it was currently paying. In this case there would quite clearly be a deficit of revenue over local expenditure, even as conventionally defined. Second, the trend of British policy was to increase expenditure in Ireland. Public expenditure had already risen from £2.9 million to £5.6 million annually between 1870 and 1895. By 1907–8, even before old age pensions swelled the total, it had risen to £7.8 million, thus reversing the drain. The pensions, introduced in 1909, created a large net inflow on taxation account. These net transfers to Ireland, courtesy of the British exchequer, would have been even larger had the principles embodied in the Home Rulers' case with respect to revenue been applied.

Nothing was done, however, to lighten Ireland's tax burden as a result of the Committee's work. The Committee itself was short on practical proposals. One suggestion made was to lower the tax rate on the alcohol content of spirits to that of beer. This would have saved Ireland £780,000 as there was some preference for whiskey over beer there. (It would, incidentally, have saved Scotland, where the preference was even more marked, a good deal more.) But this demand was half-hearted. There were good reasons, on social grounds, for maintaining the spirit duty.

The Unionist response to this was varied. It was generally acknowledged that Ireland had been hard done by in the past, largely as a result of Gladstone's budgets. But some thought it would not 'be fair to put on the great grandson of an English labourer at the time of the Union, an additional burden now to relieve the great grandson of an Irish peasant who paid too much in the earlier part of the century'.[57] Sir David Barbour in his minority report argued that, if there had been overtaxation in Ireland, there had also been overspending. If public expenditure in Ireland, in 1895 say, had been in the same proportion to her estimated taxable capacity (one twentieth), Ireland would have received in local services only £1.8 million compared to the actual figure of £5.6 million. Thus there had been overspending of £3.8 million. Set against the alleged overtaxation of £2.7 million, this meant that Ireland was a gainer to the tune of £1.1 million.[58] But this ingenious argument received little support, even amongst Unionists. Other Unionists were inclined to accept this part of the report and seek, like the Belfast Chamber of Commerce, additional spending in Ireland to compensate for the overtaxation. However, as unionists, they still disagreed with the Committee that Ireland and Britain should be treated as 'separate fiscal entries', resting their case rather on the 'exemption or abatements clause' of the Act of Union. In the ornate language of the Belfast Chamber of Commerce, Ireland was entitled to 'special treatment in the matter of wise and liberal expenditure in directions in which it can be arranged to be really reproductive'.[59]

We have dealt at length with the question of taxation because it was given so much prominence for so long.[60] But it is difficult to give it the weight attributed to it by contemporaries. Perhaps an independent Ireland could have governed itself more cheaply than Ireland was governed under the Union. This was most definitely believed by nationalists. There was a large and costly police force, for example. It is hard to understand, for example, why Ireland, with much the same population as Scotland, needed three times as many policemen in the 1890s. (Tim Healy's jibe that the RIC was 'the army of no occupation' contained some truth.) The 1893 Government of Ireland Act envisaged the phasing out of the Dublin Metropolitan Police and the RIC and their replacement by local police forces.[61] It is worth pointing out that this solution was perfectly compatible with the Union. Very much so, as under this legislation the police would have been organised in the same way as the rest of the United Kingdom, where they were largely paid for out of local taxes. There could also have been savings on Ireland's contribution to imperial expenditure if it had been self-governing. If the arrangements, for example, had been similar to those under either of the Home Rule Bills of 1893 (the original or the amended versions) then there would have been considerable savings in the earlier part of the century.[62] From the 1890s onwards, however, Ireland would have lost out.

But even if Ireland had saved £2 million annually in taxation in the nineteenth century, and there had been no imperial contribution, it is difficult to believe that this would have made an enormous economic difference to Ireland. If all the monies had all been productively invested, perhaps so. The growth rate of Irish national income in the nineteenth century has been estimated, perhaps overestimated, at 0.7 per cent per annum. If we assume a capital–output ratio of 3–4, this implies a net investment rate of 2–3 per cent of national income. National income in Ireland in the 1870s and 1880s must have been around £100 million, plus or minus 10 per cent.[63] So net investment in money terms must have been about £2–3 million. Thus, if all the savings on taxation had been invested, and if the incremental capital-output ratio had remained constant, Irish growth rates could have roughly doubled. Add to these tax savings the funds of absentee landlords and suppose these (or a proportion of them) were invested, then the exercise suggests that the growth rate could have been higher still. However, the likelihood of any of this happening in practice was exceedingly low. Lower taxes or a reduction in absentee remittances were much more likely to result in increased consumption. Indeed, in relation to absentee landlords, if there were opportunities for profitable investment on Irish estates, then there is no economic reason why an absentee as compared to a resident landlord should be any less likely to respond to such opportunities. Those revenues not consumed are likely to have been channelled into saving institutions, with little prospect of these savings being subsequently diverted into investment activity in Ireland.

Having discussed financial drains at some length, it is time to turn, or return to the question of economic protectionism. We saw earlier that support for protectionism was lukewarm during the repeal agitation of the 1830s and the 1840s. Subsequently, interest in this panacea for Ireland's problems declined further. Free trade ideas were in the ascendant, and went largely unchallenged within the United Kingdom and most of Europe at mid-nineteenth century. By the 1860s the 'dream of universal free trade appeared to be approaching reality'.[64] However, there was a revival of interest in the protectionist argument in Ireland, as indeed elsewhere in Europe, in the later nineteenth century. A measure of support for a highly selective set of tariffs, which in truth would have had only the mildest impact, can be found in the writings of Isaac Butt, the founder in 1870 of the Home Government Association.[65] It also featured in the speeches of the great nationalist leader of the later nineteenth century, Charles Stewart Parnell. But significantly, the case was heavily qualified. The industries that could benefit from protection were, he thought, 'not many in number' and should only be protected 'for two or three years'. Furthermore he admitted that 'Ireland could never be a manufacturing nation of such importance as to compete to any extent with England'.[66] Parnell's thought closely parallelled the findings of the 1884 Select Committee on Irish industry. Although this committee presented no report, an analysis of its findings suggests that almost half (twenty-eight) of the fifty-nine firms giving evidence blamed foreign competition either wholly or partially for their economic difficulties. Only fourteen saw protectionism as the remedy for their problems; the majority preferring instead government subsidies or patronage, more spending on education, or alterations in railway rates. All these types of change were, of course, perfectly compatible with the Union.[67]

TOWARDS AN INDEPENDENT IRELAND

The years before, during and immediately after the Great War witnessed renewed political controversy surrounding Home Rule and the question of Ulster. The script for a new Ireland was being written in blood. In the charged atmosphere of the times it is hardly remarkable that discourses bearing on the Union were highly polemical in tone. Discussions of the economic effects of the Union were often secondary to religious and political issues. Nonetheless, they played a part in the intellectual armouries of the antagonists. On the Nationalist side, the damage allegedly caused to Irish industry by the Act of Union received a prominence it had not enjoyed since the days of Repeal. More, in fact. As many of the twentieth-century exponents of this view were protectionists, they could be unequivocal in their condemnation of the removal of tariffs a century earlier. Thus the debate on the economic merits, or rather the demerits, of the Union was widened, extending far beyond a concern with over-taxation which had tended to dominate late-nineteenth-century interest.

Arthur Griffith, for example, traced the lack of industrialization in Ireland to the free trade introduced by the Act of Union. 'Under the operation of that infamous Act, one by one all her great industries, except linen, were again destroyed or reduced to skeletons of their former greatness.'[68] The absence of protectionism had not only devastated Irish industry, but had prevented the exploitation of Ireland's natural resources, which were assumed to be vast. Griffith purported to borrow his ideas from the German economist, Friedrich List, ignoring the fact that List had urged protectionism as a policy only for large countries, like Germany. For small countries, he had advocated a merger with larger units; Holland and Belgium with Germany, for example, and he had specifically commended Ireland's union with Britain as 'a great and irrefragable example of the efficiency of free trade between united nations'.[69] Obviously, the potential effects of protectionism on a large country with abundant natural resources are likely to be more beneficial than on a small country, heavily dependent on international trade, with meagre endowments. Griffith stresses the benefits of protectionism, despite the small size of the Irish market, and is equally uncritical in his exaggerated assessment of the extent of Irish natural resources. By comparison with the earlier Repeal arguments, this is fairly crude stuff.

The ideas of another of the separatist propagandists, Darrell Figgis, were even less convincing. The absence of protectionism as a cause of Ireland's industrial decline plays second fiddle to a series of *ad hoc* explanations, some bordering on the eccentric. He argued, for example, that the Irish railways were built to link military barracks rather than commercial centres, thereby damaging Irish industry. Belfast's economic progress is attributed to its being a 'military depot' at the time the rail network was established.[70] Additionally, he suggests that there had been constant attempts by the Castle administration to stifle promising areas of economic development: among the examples cited were Dunlop's pneumatic tyre and Galway's potential as a transatlantic port.[71]

The only really novel arguments to emerge from the fringes of militant Nationalism came from the labour activist and revolutionary republican, James Connolly. Although an opponent of the Union, his criticisms of it certainly did not run along traditional lines. (He had nothing but scorn for the 'parliamentary historians', an umbrella term embracing constitutional nationalists from Repealers to Home Rulers.) Thus the 'prosperity' – Connolly always used the inverted commas – of Grattan's parliament was 'as little due to that Parliament as the dust caused by the revolutions of the coach-wheel was due to the presence of the fly who, sitting on the coach, viewed the dust, and fancied him the author thereof'.[72] In reality, the advance of trade in the 1780s and 1790s was caused by the introduction of machinery, particularly in textiles, from England. However, Ireland could compete with Britain only as long as the machinery was controlled by hand. With the

> application of steam to the service of industry, which began on a small scale in 1785 and the introduction of the power loom, which first came into general use about 1813, the immense natural advantage of an indigenous coal supply finally settled the contest in favour of English manufacturers.

> A native Parliament might have hindered the subsequent decay, as an alien Parliament may have hastened it; but in either case, under capitalistic conditions, the process itself was as inevitable as the economic evolution of which it was one of the most significant signs.[73]

Although expressed differently, the analysis thus far is not dissimilar to that of the classical economists.

Connolly continues his analysis by pouring scorn on the views of the 'Parliamentary historians' with respect to the supposed effects of increased absenteeism after the Union. The decline of the woollen and leather industries, for example, had far deeper causes. 'Were the members of the Irish parliament and the Irish landlords the only wearers of shoes in Ireland?' Why did British manufacturers continue to supply the Irish market, whereas the Irish manufacturers did not? Did the latter really have to 'shut up shop and go to the poor house because My Lord Rackrent, and his immediate personal following had moved to London?'[74] Connolly proceeds to argue the paradox that the weakness of Irish manufacturers was a cause, not a consequence, of the Union on the Marxist grounds that a strong capitalist class would have reformed the parliamentary system and extended the franchise. This would have produced an electorate and parliament that would never have agreed to the Act of Union; an interesting counterfactual hypothesis, though one begging a large number of questions.

It is true that it is possible to extract protectionist sentiments from Connolly's writings, but the general thrust is against them. He specifically rejected Sinn Féin's economic ideology, to which protectionism was central. 'With its economic teaching, as expounded by my friend Mr Arthur Griffith in his adoption of the doctrines of Friedrich List, socialists have no sympathy.'[75] In so far as Connolly had any explanation, other than inexorable economic forces, for Ireland's industrial decline in the nineteenth century, it was that Irish capitalists did not treat their workers properly. 'Lots of important industries have disappeared from Ireland because Irish employers were encouraged' – by whom, he does not say – 'to refuse to treat their workers in a humane and reasonable fashion and so lost their trade to British competitors.' British employers, it appears, were always willing to compromise in industrial disputes and get back to making profits. Irish employers simply wanted to crush their workers, which, much to the delight of the British, led in turn to bankruptcy. British capital, he concludes, was 'grown up and had assumed the responsibility of the adult, but Irish capital is still immature and has all the defects of the "hobble-de-hoy", not big enough to be a man and too big to be a boy'.[76] This explanation of Ireland's industrial decline is not one that has received much support.

The Unionist response to the upsurge in nationalist writings went in two directions. First, it stressed the benefits of the Union but focused on the more recent period: the Union as it had operated between 1890 and 1913. Even if it might be granted that the arrangement had some damaging effects on Ireland in the early nineteenth century, and some Unionists were prepared to admit such a possibility, this did not mean that it continued to harm the country a hundred years on. The Union was not simply a one-off event but rather an evolving relationship which could accommodate a variety of economic and social changes and initiatives. During the late nineteenth and early twentieth century major changes *had* taken place. The land system had been altered to create a peasant pro-prietorship. Education had improved, culminating in a university system. Democratic, national and local government had been established. Subsidies had been given to the post office, housing and agriculture. The Congested Districts Board had been set up. Old age pensions had been introduced. Economic indicators showed a marked upturn – exports, bank deposits, railway receipts, for example. Unionist writers, like Pembroke Wicks, could even cite unguarded statements by nationalists to support the view that the history of the Union since 1890 was one of progress. Thus, for example, John Redmond in a speech in Detroit in 1910 had stressed 'what the last ten years had accomplished for Ireland'. T.P. Gill in 1911 referred to Ireland as being 'amongst the most rapidly and soundly progressive nations in the world'.[77]

The second point made by Unionists related to the long term effect of the Union on Ulster. By 1913 partition was firmly on the agenda. The possibility of Ulster (or part of it), rather than the whole of Ireland, remaining within the Union became a distinct possibility. The *Ulster* Unionist argument, therefore, stressed the benefits that the Union had brought, not necessarily to the whole island, but to the province and more particularly, the Belfast region. Under the Union Belfast had prospered almost continuously. Its population rose almost twenty-fold. It could 'show the largest shipyard, the largest tobacco factory, distillery, rope-works and linen factory in the world'.[78] It had the lowest rate of pauperism in the United Kingdom. It was the fourth largest port. This prosperity was based on the Union. Belfast and the north east alone had taken advantage of the opportunities offered by the Union to the whole of Ireland. The end of the Union would undermine this prosperity. Home Rule and, even more so, independence, would end 'good government', would cause a serious shock to business credit, and would lead to an increased burden of taxation upon the province.[79]

One way of summing up the state of these debates on the eve of partition is to observe that the historiography of the Union hardly conforms to the Whig view of history. On the contrary, the economic interpretation of the Union became less rather than more sophisticated in the hands of militant Home Rulers and the ideologues of Sinn Féin. The early Repealers had to fight for an audience, and they did so with some intellectual distinction. Later Nationalists inhabited a world in which the certainty of belief, and the imminence of the realisation of the nationalist dream (be it Home Rule or full independence), made close analysis less of a necessity. In the parallel universe, inhabited by Unionists, the case for maintaining the union was given an increasingly narrow and intransigent focus on 'Ulster'. The effect of these tendencies was intellectually impoverishing for both the Nationalist and the Unionist traditions.

MODERN ACADEMIC WRITINGS

With the publication early in the new century of Alice Murray's *History of the Commercial and Financial Relations between England and Ireland* we enter the modern period of the economic historiography of the Union.[80] Murray argued in fairly moderate terms, and with attention to evidence, for the harmful effects of a union between two economies at different stages of industrial development. A more subtle treatment of the Union and its aftereffects appeared the following year. D.A. Chart's *Ireland from the Union to Catholic Emancipation* was sharply critical of the handling of the Union negotiations and the political aftermath. On economic matters, however, Chart judged that while industry had been damaged, the Union had succeeded in benefiting agriculture. He found himself, therefore, unable to strike an overall balance between gains and losses[81] – a most unusual position given the weight of Unionist and Nationalist orthodoxies by this date.

But the best known, and by far the most influential work of scholarship from this period was by George O'Brien. Soon to become Professor of National Economy at University College, Dublin, O'Brien may be said to be the father figure of modern Irish economic history. (This image is not without irony: George never married and seems to have had a mysogynistic streak in his make-up.) O'Brien's *The Economic History of Ireland from the Union to the Famine*, which appeared in 1921, was the third volume in a trilogy of works on the Irish economy from the seventeenth to the mid-nineteenth century.[82] Undoubtedly coloured by the political passions of the time, these works represent the highest statement of the traditional nationalist interpretation of Irish economic history. In his treatment of the Union, O'Brien may be said to bridge the world of nineteenth-century polemical writings and the emerging world of academic historical scholarship. The historiographical significance of the trilogy lies in the fact that much of the writing in Irish economic history during the new era of the 1960s can be seen as a reaction to O'Brien. And, as enacted symbolically in Synge's *Playboy of the Western World*, there may even be an element of father-slaying in the historiographical revolution which later engulfed O'Brien's work.

In some respects O'Brien's case against the Union differs little from that of Repealers or Home Rulers. But it is generally much better argued and is buttressed by a greater array of factual information. For example, his discussion of the effect of the Union on the important cotton industry is greatly improved by the use of parliamentary returns, some of which were unavailable in the 1840s. Furthermore, in his historical writings – though not in his prescriptions for policy in the Ireland of the 1920s – O'Brien had few doubts about the benefits that resulted from protectionism under Grattan's parliament or the damage that occurred with its abolition. Thus the predominant reason given for the decline of the woollen industry was the ending of the duties in 1824, although O'Brien does allow that the depression of 1825–6 may also have contributed to its demise. The cotton industry, too, was affected by the depression. But the removal of protective duties and the consequent competition from Britain meant that Irish manufacturers 'through lack of capital' were prevented from modernising in the same way as in Britain. Other industries were also adversely affected by the Union: silk and glass by the ending of protection, paper by the extension of the copyright act to Ireland. In other areas, 'the importance of the adverse affects of absenteeism and taxation', for example, O'Brien essentially repackages earlier Nationalist views.[83]

There is no significant Irish unionist contribution on the subject of the Union to be set against O'Brien's achievement. Perhaps, with the disintegration of Irish Unionism, such an intellectual project would have seemed either anachronistic or premature. Nor were the decades after 1921 conducive to a reassessment from within the Nationalist tradition, even had there been a less limited infrastructure for academic and advanced studies in the new Ireland. National passions had been roused, and were not easily stilled. Critical historical scholarship was unlikely to flourish, or find acceptance, in a society which had just experienced the trauma of a national struggle of secession. The grandiosely titled 'economic war' between the Irish Free State and the United Kingdom during the 1930s kept existing animosities in good fettle.[84] Inevitably, creative energies were absorbed in the more immediate tasks of state-building and nation-moulding. The institutions of the new state had to be established and consolidated; the nation had to be shaped and reshaped, coercively if necessary, by policies aimed at restoring the Gaelic language and inscribing Catholic social thought in the public sphere. In a sense, the actuality of self-government was both a realisation of and a vindication of traditional orthodoxies.

The interwar period, therefore, witnessed no fresh scholarship on the Union, though there were the usual restatements of a polemical kind. Even after independence, that 'infamous act' was still the protean source of Irish problems, though increasingly its malign effects were combined with the 'evils of partition'.[85] Even within Northern Ireland, where different orthodoxies prevailed, the shock of secession by Nationalist Ireland gave no reason to question established verities, and the headlong flight into protectionism during the 1930s by the Irish Free State must have served to reinforce existing stereotypes regarding the financial dangers of life outside of the Union. Among academic studies, Curtis' valuable general history, first issued in 1936 and reprinted innumerable times, paid only limited attention to the Union. To the extent that it adopted a viewpoint on the economic consequences of union, it accepted that these had been negative.[86]

The first major re-statement of the case against the Union did not come for three decades after O'Brien, and then it came from an unlikely source, that of a Marxist pen. Strauss devoted a full, if less than original, chapter to the issue in his study of Anglo-Irish relations, arguing that it was the 'unfettered competition by English manufacturers, superimposed on the continuing drain of absentee rents, which completely crushed Irish industry outside Ulster'.[87] But the mid-century also saw the publication of two other pioneering studies, E.R.R. Green's *Lagan Valley* and T.W. Freeman's historical geography of Ireland (*Ireland: Its Physical, Historical Social and Economic Geography*).[88] There were virtually no references to the Union, and none of a positive or negative kind. By failing to acknowledge the Union, its centrality in Irish history had been brought into question, if only implicitly.

The crisis decade of the 1950s was of pivotal significance in terms of the evolution of new economic ideas within Irish society, and these were to exercise an influence on economic historiography. The shift in thinking, which was initially apparent at the level of policy makers, arose from a growing disillusionment with the practical outcomes of independence, in particular the policies of inward-oriented development and economic protectionism.[89] Reality had caught up with rhetoric. Despite the imaginings of Davis and Griffith, economic resources had proved less than ample and protectionism a mixed blessing. Emigration had not stopped in response to fiery speeches or Dáil decrees. By the mid-1950s economic stagnation seemed to have seized the recently declared Republic. With growing national self-doubt, and the adoption of policies which opened 'Fortress Hibernia' to the outside world, new intellectual possibilities, even a paradigm shift, became more likely.

In the succeeding decade old orthodoxies in the field of history, and particularly economic history, came under sustained attack. In relation to the Union, and its economic effects, the fundamental challenge came from an independently minded economist and historian, Raymond Crotty.[90] In *Irish Agricultural Production* Crotty launched a trenchant critique of the significance of the year 1800 for subsequent Irish economic and social change. According to Crotty the seminal date was 1815 and the changed market conditions which prevailed after the Napoleonic Wars. These included a lengthy deflationary period (1815–45), a shift in the relative price structure of foodstuffs on the British market in favour of livestock products and against tillage, and the effects of the British industrial revolution on Ireland. At the end of the 1960s L.M. Cullen edited a set of essays – in effect a manifesto of the new revisionism sweeping Irish economic history writing – the justly celebrated *Formation of the Irish Economy*, with contributions by Green, Lee, Goldstrom and Cullen himself.[91] The wider objective, it would seem, was to claim, or reclaim, great areas of history from the political and constitutional historians: 'Irish economic development is more independent of non-economic factors than has been generally believed', Cullen proclaimed.[92] Thus, the image of Grattan's parliament might burn brightly in the imagination of generations of Nationalists, and of earlier historians of Ireland, but its economic achievements were meagre. Or the Union might have been a major legislative measure but its economic impact was minor by comparison with the other economic processes of the early nineteenth century. The key fact was the onset of modern industrialization in some favoured regions of the British Isles. This resulted in massive price reductions through the application of new technologies and new forms of business organisation. The decline of handicraft production in the face of this competition was inevitable: this happened in rural England, and rural Europe more generally, not just in Ireland. The protectionism of Grattan's parliament would have been powerless to avert this fate. Cullen went further, however, arguing that in any case there had been relatively little industrial decline in Ireland, outside of textiles, during the first half of the nineteenth century, which is a thesis still being explored by historians.[93]

Ó Tuathaigh, in one of the most judicious modern assessments of the Union, sees the shift of economic decision-making powers from College Green to Westminster, where Irish affairs were the subject of lesser attention, as possibly the most serious consequence of the Union. He is not simply echoing earlier Repeal sentiment, however, and is quick to acknowledge the deep problems of Irish society, particularly the rural economy, in the decades before the Famine. He concludes by wondering if indeed any administration could have materially influenced the course of economic events. In line with the early revisionist school of economic history, he attaches key significance to the Industrial Revolution, and is doubtful of the possible benefits of a protectionist policy for Ireland.[94]

The economist O'Malley's contribution of the early 1980s might seem to hark back to an earlier age of nationalist scholarship but the primary intellectual influence is that of dependency theory, as developed by Latin American writers. Stressing the problems facing late-comers in the industrial race, O'Malley sees the absence of powers to impose tariffs as fundamental.[95] However, the arguments are based on speculative economic reasoning rather than a close historical analysis and the anomaly (within this framework of analysis) of the striking success of the North-East of Ireland is not readily reconciled with an emphasis on protectionist measures.

Why Ireland Starved is a dazzling contribution to the study of pre-Famine Ireland and the Great Famine itself. So much so that Mokyr's observations on the Union have tended to be obscured and hence somewhat neglected. His assessment is provocative: the arguments for protection are weak in the context of a small, open economy, such as that of Ireland in the nineteenth century; the Union conferred substantial benefits in terms of education, policing and law enforcement. Indeed in Mokyr's view the Union didn't go far enough: a more complete integration might have shielded Ireland from the worst effects of the subsistence crisis at mid-century, with the starving Irish being treated in a manner more akin to how a British government would have dealt with starving English people, or so he presumes.[96] Thus, in terms of the revisionist shift of the 1960s and 1970s, Mokyr edges the discussion a stage further: not only was the Union not negative, as was argued by most revisionist writers and is the position adopted by Ó Gráda in his monumental *Ireland: A New Economic History*,[97] but it actually gave rise to some very positive developments. It may be added that there is some tension between these integrationist conclusions and Mokyr's emphasis elsewhere in *Why Ireland Starved* on the malign impact of British intervention in Ireland up to the 1780s, in particular the pursuit of various mercantilist measures and, more fundamentally, the imposition of an alien landlord class which failed, and continued to fail in terms of the supply of investment capital and entrepreneurship.

The evolution of the historiography of the Union is summarised in Table 1. Obviously this categorisation involves a degree of simplification. For instance, the contributions by Black and Ó Tuathaigh have an agnostic flavour which brings them close to the neutral point on the continuum; O'Malley, by contrast, is in no doubt that the lack of economic autonomy made a major difference historically. Incidentally, the neutral

Table 1 The economic impact of the Union of Britain and Ireland: a summary of the views of academic writers

Ruinous	Negative	Neutral	Positive
	Murray (1903)		
		Chart (1910)	
O'Brien (1920)	O'Riordan (1920)		
	Curtis (1936)		
		Green (1949)	
Strauss (1951)			
	Black (1960)		
	Beckett (1966)	Crotty (1966)	
		Cullen (1969)	
		Green (1969)	
		Lee (1969)	
		Goldstrom (1969)	
	Ó Tuathaigh (1972)		
	Hechter (1973)		
	O'Malley (1981)	Daly (1981)	
			Mokyr (1983)
			J&K (1991)
		Ó Gháda (1994)	

Sources: as noted in the main text, with the additions of E.J. Riordan, *Modern Irish Trade and Industry* (London, 1920), pp. 264, 289–91, and Michael Hechter, *Internal Colonialism: The Celtic Fringe in British National Development, 1536–1966* (London, 1975)

category should be thought of as embracing such positions as 'non-negative' and 'unimportant' as well as net outcomes which were marginally positive or negative.[98] In all categories the assessment is conceived as a *net* outcome, that is, the author's conclusion having considered the possible, sometimes offsetting costs and benefits of the Union.

The dramatic change in the economic historiography of the Union in this century, which is illustrated in Table 1, deserves some explanation. Why the shift in interpretation, and its rapid acceptance within the academic community, all within the space of little more than a decade (1960–72)? The reasons would seem to be both material and intellectual. We have spoken already of the changing climate of ideas and circumstances around mid-century. There had emerged a new generation of scholars, some of them specialists in economic history, who felt free to examine old orthodoxies with fresh vigour. This freedom owed something to the fact that they were well-distanced in time from the passions of the

Nationalist–Unionist confrontation, the Anglo-Irish conflict and the nationalist civil war. An intellectual assurance, as well as expanded resources for academic scholarship, must have owed something also to the remarkable expansion of the two economies in Ireland and, more generally, to the air of optimism and critical inquiry present in Irish society in the period. Moreover, due to its history of subordination to political history, economic history had accumulated a wealth of untested assertions and dubious propositions. Thus, some of the hoarier fruits of earlier scholarship and polemic were ripe for plucking, and clearly there were intellectual rewards and professional reputations to be made in shaking the tree of knowledge planted by earlier generations.

Like all good short stories, there has to be a twist in the narrative. While it is true that the Union has provoked a surge of reflection and reasoning on the Union and its implications, it is also the case that little new research has focused exclusively on the subject. The Famine, the Land War, the role of landlords in Irish society, the 'Economic War' of the 1930s, population and marriage patterns – all of these subjects have been the focus of intensive re-examination using primary sources. This is not really true of the Union. Despite the undoubted merits of the discussions by Cullen, Daly, Ó Tuathaigh and Mokyr, the Union has not attracted the attentions of a comprehensive new study in its own right. Until the essay by Johnson and Kennedy, which looked *inter alia* at the public finances of the period in a preliminary way, and the more recent paper by Geary on the composition of trade flows between the economies of Britain and Ireland before and after 1800, there were no sustained efforts to go back to the primary source materials. This would seem to be a prerequisite for firmly grounded, new interpretations.[99] The reasons for the relative neglect of the Union in the monograph literature are not altogether clear. Perhaps the revisionist potential seemed unpromising, once some of the more obvious points had been made. The possibilities of quantitatively testing hypotheses in relation to the Union were obviously limited. This is further complicated by some major cross-currents, of which war with France and the underlying changes being effected by the Industrial Revolution, are the most important. Perhaps the temporal location of the Union, at the end of the eighteenth century and the beginning of the nineteenth, leaves it in a no-man's land between the interests of the early modern and the modern historians. Less speculatively, it is surely the case that there is a stochastic element in the choice of research agendas and perhaps the subject of the Union will in time engage a new set of scholars. Whatever the reason, the surprise remains, in a quarter century when the winds of revisionism blew most strongly, the Union has not been exposed to the full force of these gales of creative destruction.[100]

ALTERNATIVE HISTORICAL PATHWAYS

A fault line running through most of the debates of the last two centuries on the economic impact of the Union is the failure to show how the Union produced the effects, benign or malign depending on viewpoint, which Unionists and Nationalists claimed were caused by the Union. The fallacy of *post hoc, ergo propter hoc* ruled the roost on both sides of the debate.

In fairness, it is no easy task to assess the economic impact of the Union. Strictly speaking, one needs to fabricate an alternative historical world, that is, an Irish history without the Union, against which to measure the experience (as reconstructed by historians) of nineteenth-century Ireland. The major hypothetical alternatives would appear to be some variation on Grattan's parliament, a federal United Kingdom and an independent Ireland. A further possibility, giving formal recognition to the economic and political divergences of interest on the island, would have envisaged two separate parliaments of North and South, thereby foreshadowing the Government of Ireland Act of 1920.[101]

Such was the flexibility of the Union in practice, it is difficult to see how the first of the two counterfactual scenarios could have produced economic outcomes radically different from those actually observed. However, the more extreme alternative of an independent Ireland could have made a difference, and not necessarily a benign one. To take a single but catastrophic event, the potato blight of the 1840s: would an independent Irish parliament have dealt more effectively with this ecological bolt from the heavens, this force of devastation which was independent of all political and constitutional frameworks? There is more than a little room for doubt. The rural poor would have been underrepresented in any Dublin parliament. It is unlikely that the politically powerful Catholic and Protestant bourgeoisies would have countenanced a ban on food exports, at their own expense. The debacle of the rates-in-aid controversy of 1849, which sought unsuccessfully to spread the burden of poor-law expenditure more evenly across Ireland, suggests that altruism among Irish property holders was in limited supply. Empathy with the malnourished masses was circumscribed by forces of kinship, religion, locality, and social class. A succession of harvest failures would have seriously weakened the public finances of an independent Irish state, both on the revenue and the expenditure sides. There is a real likelihood, therefore, that an Irish parliament would have been less rather than more capable of mounting relief operations on the scale attempted by the United Kingdom government. Indeed, these lines of speculation might be taken a stage further. While hardly anyone, outside the ranks of a few polemicists, would suggest there was a direct causal relationship between the Act of Union and the Great Famine, there are some grounds at least for saying that a *closer* union between the peoples of the two islands might have resulted in larger transfers of resources, and hence fewer Famine deaths. From the perspective of the welfare of the most vulnerable people in Irish society, several million cottiers and labourers, the process of union may not have gone far enough.

What of the more routine features of the functioning of the Irish economy? Firstly, independence raises the issue of *market access*: under what conditions might an independent Ireland have been allowed to export its goods to the markets of Britain and the Empire? Under the Union, Ireland had unrestricted access to British and Empire markets. Moreover, the United Kingdom operated protectionist policies which benefited the two major sectors of the Irish economy, agriculture and linen production, and disadvantaged foreign competitors.[102] Outside the Union there could be no guarantee of such favourable terms.

Yet the potential problems may not have been as severe as might appear at first sight. Unless an independent Ireland operated belligerent trading policies, in the manner of De Valera and Fianna Fáil during the 'economic war' of the 1930s, the presumption must be that the general movement towards free trade in industrial goods, which is apparent from Huskisson's duty reductions of the 1820s, would have applied to Ireland also. In the specific case of linen manufacture it is worth noting that the main centres in Britain, those of Dundee and Leeds, were not major producers. Consequently, no powerful interest groups clustered round linen manufacture. Furthermore, much of the British produce was of low quality and hence did not experience direct competition from the more expensive textiles of the Ulster linen industry.

One might be somewhat less confident about trade in agricultural produce before the 1840s. Here protectionist sentiment was only gradually eroded by free-trade notions, as is evidenced by the re-introduction of the Corn Laws after Waterloo and limits on the import of cattle into the United Kingdom. As against this, the landed interest in Ireland had business as well as kinship links to the landed ascendancy in Britain. Whether this would have been sufficient to guarantee fully privileged access for the produce of Ireland's most important economic sector, it is impossible to say, but for strategic, security and kinship reasons it seems unlikely that Britain would have discriminated heavily against Irish food exports in the decades after Waterloo. The issue of tariff barriers does not arise after 1846 as in that year, with the repeal of the Corn Laws, Britain committed itself to comprehensive trade liberalisation.

These assessments err deliberately on the side of optimism and may well downplay the possible difficulties of market access which might have occurred. In other words, they are best-case scenarios under conditions of independence. Any uncertainty associated with independence, and some would have been inevitable, was likely to have deterred investment to some degree. However, the most serious problems with an independent Ireland may well have been located outside the sphere of trading relationships between the two islands. Fundamental to economic development is a structure of social order, security and contract enforcement, on which the functioning of economic institutions and market mechanisms are predicated. In view of the deep ethnic, religious and social cleavages on the island, it is highly improbable that an independent Ireland could have provided such a framework. A separate legislature, had it been launched any time between 1815 and 1845, would have encountered a sea of difficulties. The long phase of deflation which affected the British and Irish economies during the decades after Waterloo exacerbated social tensions in Irish society. Politico-sectarian struggles such as the Protestant evangelical movement, the Catholic campaign for religious 'emancipation', the tithe wars, and the activities of the Rockites, Ribbonmen and Orangemen all served to heighten sectarian and ethnic feeling. An independent Ireland, almost irrespective of the composition of its legislature, was likely to have brought the contradictory forces in Irish society into more direct confrontation than was the case under the Union. The Union, it is worth recalling, was a response, not only to the threat posed by the French but the crisis within the Irish social order itself. Less effective public order and a separatist image would have had the effect of deterring investment, innovation, and inflows of technology and entrepreneurship. When one reflects that much of Ireland's industrial progress in the eighteenth and nineteenth centuries was due to immigrant businessmen, and the technologies embodied in them – Quakers and Huguenots during the formative phase of fine linen production, Nicholas Grimshaw, James Wallace and Robert Gemmill in the case of cotton spinning, Harland, Wolff, and Clark in shipbuilding, Mackie in engineering, Henderson and Tillie in the shirtmaking industry, Jacob's in biscuitmaking – maintaining the social networks and political identifications which connected industrial Ireland to the north of England and the west of Scotland was vital to safeguarding supplies of entrepreneurship and technology to the developing Irish economy. It is difficult to see how parliamentary legislation in Dublin could have substituted effectively for these growth factors.[103] It is even less clear how it might have induced the dynamic or high-productivity sectors which defined early industrialisation. Independence carried very high risks, not only politically but economically as well.

Viewed in this perspective, that of ensuring some of the basic conditions for economic progress, the Union conferred very substantial benefits on the peoples of Ireland. Of the hypothetical alternatives, an independent Ireland seems to have had little to commend it on economic grounds during the first half of the century. The economic arguments for independence are more attractive for the second half: the taxation burden could have been reduced, there was the possibility of economic protectionism without the fear of British retaliation, and the relationship between people and land resources was more favourable. By then, however, the separate economic development of the North-East of the island was more pronounced and more visible, and the human and intellectual resources for opposition to any form of secession correspondingly strengthened. Civil conflict, extensive economic disruption and partition would seem to have been the inevitable concomitants of a drive towards independence.

CONCLUSION

So much discussion of Irish economy, politics and literature comes back eventually to a consideration of the Union of Britain and Ireland, and the consequences which issued from this constitutionally momentous event. The paradox, nonetheless, is that the Union, either in its political or its economic forms, has not been subjected to close analytical study using the techniques of modern scholarship. In relation to the economic dimensions of the Union, there is clearly a case for further primary research, and the application of economic theory and quantitative methods in exploring its short and long-term ramifications. Moreover, much of the revisionist literature of the 1960s, while opening up new spaces for enquiry, was both defensive and reactive in its revisionism, arguing essentially that the Union had not produced the damaging effects usually ascribed to it by its critics. The emergence of a post-revisionist phase in the writing of Irish economic history – in turn reacting against some of the overstatements of the early revisionist claims in relation to the Great Famine and the role of Irish landlords, for example – might seem to suggest the desirability of a shift backwards towards earlier, negative views of the implications of the Act of Union.

The reactive mode of writing is not necessarily conducive to enduring scholarship. The current state of knowledge on the Union and our reflections on it, which are of course subject to future change in the light of new evidence and fresh insights, suggest to us that the process of revising the Union debate has not gone far enough. Relative to the alternative courses of action, the Union and the net economic effects seem to have been clearly favourable. In arriving at this conclusion, we have found it necessary to bring into the reckoning socio–political features of Irish society during the nineteenth century. It is virtually impossible to pass judgement on the post-Union economy in isolation from political and social considerations.

There is, in any case, an argument for broadening the debate to attempt a more ambitious assessment of the Union in its entirety. That it was 'the most important single factor in shaping Ireland as a nation' and that the experience of the Union was 'truly traumatic' are a set of assumptions that pervade Irish history writing.[104] Such sacred ground is still virtually

beyond the pale of critical enquiry. Having argued against the 'failure' of
the Union economically, we would also wonder if the presumed failure of
the Union politically is just as implausible, not least as the two sets of
issues are partly intertwined. A simple but fundamental fact is that the
Union lasted for one hundred and twenty years, outliving many constitutional and political arrangements elsewhere in nineteenth-century
Europe. It remains to be seen if the current European Union can look
forward to an existence of comparable length. The Union was not maintained by force of arms (with the exception of a few years immediately
preceding its demise), it facilitated constitutional opposition and an
apprenticeship in democratic politics, and it ensured a degree of internal
and external security that was conducive to social and economic development. While the constitutional framework in being between 1800
and 1920 proved resistant to change, the political processes it contained
were highly variable. The latter could accommodate extensions to the
electoral franchise, a reform of the tithes and disestablishment of the
Church of Ireland, institutional provision for the poor, a legislative onslaught on Irish landlordism, state intervention in regional economic
development through the medium of the Congested Districts' Board,
local self-government in urban and county affairs, and the beginnings of
major social reform such as the state provision of housing for labourers'
families, old-age pensions and insurance against unemployment. As the
redistributive role of the state strengthened, so poorer regions like Ireland
benefited from net transfers of income from the British treasury,[105] and
not always to the delight of critics of the Union.

In fact there is a case to be made that an independent Ireland – ab-
stracting for a moment from the problems posed by the Ulster question –
would have found it more, rather than less difficult to go down the road
of social reform. The example of France, where a similarly large rural
electorate blocked attempts at welfare reform because these costly ex-
penditures would have favoured disproportionately urban workers and
their families, offers little reassurance to the Irish reformer.[106] The
widening scope of social reform at a United Kingdom level from the turn
of the century onwards, while hardly endangering the Home Rule project
(though some conservative Nationalists feared this), did raise the economic cost of independence. The embryonic welfare state inherited from
the United Kingdom by the Irish peoples, and the ending of subsidies
once the Irish Free State had come into being, put heavy pressure on the
budgets of the new state. A moment of truth was reached in 1924 when an
independent Irish parliament, sitting in Dublin, cut old age pensions to a
point well below British and Northern Irish levels.[107] Looking forward in
time, it is intriguing to reflect on the dilemmas that would have been
posed had Irish independence come a decade or several decades later, in
view of the reforming thrust of British social policy and the benefits

which would have accrued to lower-income regions such as Ireland. All one can say with certainty is that the cost of sacrificing economics on the altar of Nationalism was rising through time.

There are two major conclusions to this survey of debates surrounding the Act of Union and its ramifications. First, we have argued the Union was profoundly important in fashioning a framework for the development of the economy of Ireland. This was true both at an island-wide level and in relation to its two constituent regions – the industrial North and a largely agrarian South. Nationalists and Unionists of the nineteenth century, though agreeing on little else, would have shared this presumption of the historical significance of the Union. This reinstatement of a traditional view, it must be added, is not one which would find acceptance among a fair number of modern academic historians (see Table 1). The second, more controversial conclusion is that, on balance, the Union was a benign rather than a malign framework for the evolution of the Irish economy, and perhaps of Irish society more generally.

All this may tell us little, of course, about how people actually experienced or perceived the Union. What of the noise, the tumult, the party colours that attached to the divisive questions of loyalty to the Crown or to Home Rule, to Hibernia or to Britannia? Indeed, modern Irish history is frequently presented as a series of struggles centring on the making and the unmaking of the Union.[108] Such a narrow perspective has the effect, however, of robbing people in earlier generations of much of the complexity and diversity in their lives. It may be particularly misleading in relation to the exploration of *mentalités*. It is doubtful if the typical peasant awoke many mornings during the course of the nineteenth century to contemplate the necessity of undoing the Union. Sickness, funerals, pregnancy, the price of tea, and the state of one's soul were probably of deeper concern.

NOTES

1 Oliver MacDonagh, *Ireland: The Union and Its Aftermath* (London, 1977), p. 9.
2 Quoted in Thomas Lough, *England's Wealth and Ireland's Poverty* (London, 1896), p. 50.
3 This logic was never entirely followed through. Differences in taxation remained, although they were relatively minor.
4 Maurice O'Connell (ed.), *The Correspondence of Daniel O'Connell*, vol. I (Dublin, 1972), p. 343.
5 F. Geary, 'The Rise and Fall of the Belfast Cotton Industry: Some Problems', *Irish Economic and Social History*, viii (1981), pp. 30–49.
6 *Correspondence of Daniel O'Connell*, vol. V, pp. 119–20.
7 F. King, *Robert Montgomery Martin, 1801–1868: A Draft Bibliography and Biographical Sketch* (Hong Kong, 1972), pp. 108–110. R. Montgomery Martin, *Ireland Before and After the Union with Great Britain* (London, 1843), pp. xiii–xviii.

8 The problems simply put were as follows.

   1 For trade: trade was generally valued using official valuations of commodities rather than market values. See L.M. Cullen, *Anglo-Irish Trade 1660–1800* (New York, 1968), pp. 216–20 for a discussion of the problems. Furthermore, trade figures end in 1825. After that date no figures were produced until 1904, with the exception of the year 1835 when not very satisfactory estimates were made by the Railway Commissioners.

   2 For exciseable commodities: the problems are twofold. First, some exciseable goods paid duty in England before being sent to Ireland (and vice-versa). Thus the commodity was consumed in a different part of the United Kingdom from the one in which it paid duty. The second problem was a variable, but significant, degree of smuggling.

   3 For taxation: there was a difference between the revenue collected in Ireland and the revenue which Ireland truly paid. This arose because there was sometimes a difference between where exciseable goods paid duty and where they were actually consumed.

   4 For reports, and enquiries: here the problem is the usual one of differing opinions on the part of witnesses, often amounting to special pleading.

9 See, for example, Speech of Daniel O'Connell, 22 April 1834, *Hansard, Parliamentary Debates*, Third Series, 22, cols 1150–1.

10 Speech of Thomas Spring Rice, 23 April 1834, *Hansard, Parliamentary Debates*, Third Series, 22, col. 1277.

11 *Ibid.*, cols 1276–8.

12 Jan Hogendorn, *Economic Development* (New York, 1992), p. 492.

13 Martin, *Ireland Before and After the Union*, pp. 54, 65. For a critique of the Railway Commissioners' figures, see P. Solar, 'The Agricultural Trade Statistics in the Irish Railway Commissioners' Report', *Irish Economic and Social History*, VI (1979), pp. 24–40.

14 Martin, *Ireland Before and After the Union*, p. 165.

15 M.J. Barry, *First Repeal Prize Essay: Ireland As She Was, As She Is, and As She Shall Be* (Dublin, 1845).

16 An early statement, with qualifications, is J.R.T. Hughes, 'Foreign Trade and Balanced Growth: The Historical Framework', *American Economic Review*, xlix, May, 1959, pp. 330–7.

17 Spring-Rice, *op. cit.*, col. 1240.

18 Barry, *op. cit.* pp. 55–7.

19 Taken from Ralph Davis, *The Industrial Revolution and British Overseas Trade* (Leicester, 1979) Statistical Appendix and *Report of the Commissioners Appointed to Consider and Recommend a General System of Railways in Ireland*, B.P.P., 1837–8, xxxv.

20 P. Krugman (ed.), *Strategic Trade Policy and the New International Economics* (Cambridge, 1987).

21 R.D.C. Black, *Economic Thought and the Irish Question 1817–70* (Cambridge 1960), pp. 141–2.

22 Arthur Griffith (ed.), *Thomas Davis: The Thinker and Teacher* (Dublin, 1916), pp. 162–3, 198.

23 *Report from Assistant Hand-loom Weavers' Commissioners*, B.P.P., 1840, xxiii. Report from C.G. Otway, p. 592.

24 *Ibid.*, p. 560

25 *Ibid.*, pp. 601–11.

26 *Ibid.*, pp. 599–600.

27 R.D.C. Black, *Economic Thought and the Irish Question*, p. 140.

28 Michael Barry, *First Repeal Prize Essay*, pp. 67–8.
29 Martin, *Ireland Before and After the Union*, p. 279.
30 Alderman Staunton, *Second Repeal Prize Essay: Reasons for a Repeal of the Legislative Union between Great Britain and Ireland* (Dublin, 1845), p. 633.
31 A.P.W. Malcomson, 'Absenteeism in Eighteenth-Century Ireland', *Irish Economic and Social History*, I (1974), pp. 15–35.
32 C. Ó Gráda, *Ireland Before and After the Famine: Explorations in Economic History, 1800–1925* (Manchester, 1993), p. 62.
33 *Return for the Year 1870 of the Number of Landed Proprietors in Each Country . . . ,* B.P.P., 1872, xlvii, 775.
34 *Report from the Committee on the Circulating Paper, the Specie and the Current Coin of Ireland*, reprinted in F.W. Fetter, *The Irish Pound 1797–1826* (London, 1955), p. 67.
35 Martin, *Ireland Before and After the Union*, pp. 280–1.
36 Apologists for the Union were not, though, inclined to use the highly theoretical arguments of J.R. McCulloch to the effect that absenteeism, whatever its level, inflicted no economic damage on Ireland whatsoever. This is probably because, however firmly based this argument is in Ricardian logic, it did not appear grounded in common sense. See R.D.C. Black, *Economic Thought*, ch. III, for an exposition of this argument.
37 Josiah Stamp, *British Incomes and Property* (London, 1916), pp. 210–11.
38 See, for example, Thomas Lough, *England's Wealth, passim*.
39 Deirdre MacMahon, *Republicans and Imperialists: Anglo-Irish Relations in the 1930s* (New Haven and London, 1984), p. 88.
40 Speech by O'Connell, 22 April 1834, col. 1136.
41 D.G. Boyce, *Nineteenth-century Ireland: The Search for Stability* (Dublin, 1990), p. 20; T.R. McCavery, 'Finance and Politics in Ireland 1801–17' unpublished Ph.D. thesis, Queen's University, Belfast (1983), pp. 28–33.
42 Alderman Staunton, *Second Repeal Essay*, pp. 67–9.
43 Martin, *Ireland Before and After the Union*, pp. 229–41.
44 *Report from the Select Committee on the Taxation of Ireland*, B.P.P., 1865, xii, pp. xiii–xiv.
45 Speech of Lord Landsdowne, 5 March 1897, *Hansard, Parliamentary Debates*, Fourth Series, 47, col. 21.
46 *Report of the Royal Commission Appointed to Inquire into the Financial Relations of Great Britain and Ireland*, 1896, xxxiii, 2.
47 Quoted in speech of Horace Plunkett, 30 March 1897, *Hansard, Parliamentary Debates*, Fourth Series, 48, col. 158.
48 C.F. Bastable, 'Ireland's Place in the Financial System of the United Kingdom', *Economic Journal*, VI (1896), pp. 185–203.
49 Quoted in Martin, *Ireland Before and After the Union*, p. 402.
50 See, for example, speech of Col. Saunderson, 30 March 1897, *Hansard, Parliamentary Debates*, Fourth Series, 48, col. 174. Saunderson thought taxation should remain the same in Ireland as in Britain, but Ireland should get more by way of expenditure.
51 *Financial Relations*, B.P.P., 1896, p. 2.
52 One of the minority reports, by arbitrarily imposing a subsistence element for both countries, arrived at an even lower proportion of one-thirty-sixth. See the report by Mr Sexton and others, *BPP*, 1896, pp. 61–106.
53 Figures taken from *Financial Accounts of the United Kingdom of Great Britain and Ireland, B.P.P* (various years).
54 Evidence of Sir Robert Giffen, Q.7906 in *Second Volume of Minutes of Evidence to the First Report from the Royal Commission on Financial Relations*, 1896, xxxiii.

55 Dr Vaughan in a valuable survey of the problem of Irish finances c.1870 suggests £1.5 million. W.E. Vaughan, 'Ireland c.1870' in W.E. Vaughan (ed.), *Ireland Under the Union, I, 1801–70. A New History of Ireland* (Oxford, 1989), vol. V, p. 789.

56 See, for example, Darrell Figgis, *The Economic Case for Irish Independence* (London, 1920), p. 14.

57 Speech of Viscount Goschen, 30 March 1897, *Hansard, Parliamentary Papers*, Fourth Series, 48, col. 229.

58 *Financial Relations, B.P.P.*, 1896, Report by Sir David Barbour, pp. 109–26.

59 Quoted in speech of Arnold Foster, 30 March 1897, *Hansard, Parliamentary Debates, Fourth Series, 48, col. 178.*

60 See Thomas Kennedy, *A History of the Irish Protest Against Overtaxation from 1853 to 1897* (Dublin, 1897) for a detailed historical account.

61 The 1896 bill implied that Ireland would have two separate police forces, but this may have been due to sloppy drafting.

62 The most sensible of the financial arrangements were probably those contained in the first draft of the Home Rule Bill of 1893. This earmarked the yield from customs as the imperial contribution.

63 This figure is based on data in K.A. Kennedy, T. Giblin and D. McHugh, *The Economic Development of Ireland in the Twentieth Century* (London, 1988).

64 A.G. Kenwood and A. Lougheed, *The Growth of the International Economy* (London, 1971), p. 76.

65 Isaac Butt, *Protection to Home Industry: Some Cases of Its Advantage Considered* (Dublin, 1846).

66 Quoted in Liam Kennedy, 'The Economic Thought of the Nation's Lost Leader' in D.G. Boyce and A. O'Day (eds), *Parnell in Perspective* (London, 1991), pp. 171–200.

67 *Report from the Select Committee on Industries (Ireland) with the proceedings, evidence and index, B.P.P.*, 1884–5, ix, 1, appendix no. 26.

68 Arthur Griffith, 'The Economic Oppression of Ireland', Appendix III, *The Resurrection of Hungary* (Dublin, 1918).

69 Richard Davis, *Arthur Griffith and Non-violent Sinn Fein* (Dublin, 1974), p. 130.

70 Darrell Figgis, *The Economic Case for Irish Independence* (Dublin, 1920), p. 37.

71 *Ibid.*, pp. 40–3.

72 James Connolly, 'Labour in Irish history' in *Collected Works* (Dublin, 1987), vol. I, p. 58.

73 *Ibid.*, p. 61.

74 *Ibid.*, p. 62.

75 James Connolly, 'Sinn Féin, Socialism and the Nation' in *Collected Works*, vol. I, p. 369.

76 James Connolly, 'Dublin Trade and Dublin Strikes' in *Collected Works*, vol. II, pp. 364–5.

77 Pembroke Wicks, *The Truth about Home Rule* (London, 1913), ch. II, quotations from pp. 11–12.

78 *Ibid.*, p. 54.

79 *Ibid.*, pp. 73–82.

80 Alice Murray, *A History of the Commercial and Financial Relations Between England and Ireland from the Period of the Restoration* (London, 1903), pp. 337–5.

81 D.A. Chart, *Ireland from the Union to Catholic Emancipation* (London, 1910), pp. 35, 305.

82 George O'Brien, *The Economic History of Ireland from the Union to the Famine* (London, 1921).

83 O'Brien, pp. 521–5, 574. For an assessment of O'Brien's ideas see D.S. Johnson and Liam Kennedy, 'Nationalist Historiography and the Decline of

the Irish Economy', in Sean Hutton and Paul Stewart, *Ireland's Histories: Aspects of State, Society and Ideology* (London, 1991), pp. 11–35.

84 This also provoked some critical thinking. See, for example, J. Johnston, *Irish Agriculture in Transition* (Dublin, 1951).

85 The flavour (as well as the poverty) of this literature is well conveyed in such works as Frank Gallagher, *The Indivisible Island* (London, 1957).

86 Edmund Curtis, *A History of Ireland* (London, 1936), pp. 353, 358 (page references are to the 1968 reprint).

87 E. Strauss, *Irish Nationalism and British Democracy* (London, 1951), p. 76.

88 E.R.R. Green, *The Lagan Valley 1800–50* (London, 1949) and T.W. Freeman, *Ireland: its Physical, Historical, Social and Economic Geography* (London, 1950). Curiously, Green uses 1800 as the starting date in his title, in deference to conventional thought perhaps, but it has no interpretative significance in his scheme of things.

89 T.K. Whitaker, *Economic Development* (Dublin, 1958).

90 Raymond Crotty, *Irish Agricultural Production: Its Volume and Structure* (Cork, 1966).

91 L.M. Cullen (ed.), *Formation of the Irish Economy* (Cork, 1969).

92 L.M. Cullen, *Irish Economic History: Fact and Myth* in Cullen, *loc. cit.*, p. 113.

93 L.M. Cullen, *An Economic History of Ireland since 1660* (London, 1972), pp. 108–9.

94 Gearoid Ó Tuathaigh, *Ireland Before the Famine, 1798–1848* (Dublin, 1972), pp. 35–40, 119–21.

95 Eoin O'Malley, 'The Decline of Irish Industry in the Nineteenth Century', *Economic and Social Review*, xiii, 1981, pp. 21–42.

96 Joel Mokyr, *Why Ireland Starved* (London, 1983), pp. 287–92.

97 Cormac Ó Gráda, *Ireland: A New Economic History 1780–1939* (Oxford, 1994), pp. 45–6, 306–7.

98 Mary Daly, for example, is clear that the usual litany of negative effects flowing from the Union is exaggerated or untenable, and that there were some benefits also. See Daly, *Social and Economic History of Ireland since 1800* (Dublin, 1981), pp. 63–88.

99 Johnson and Kennedy, 'Nationalist Historiography', *loc. cit.*, pp. 11–35; Frank Geary, 'The Act of Union, British-Irish Trade and Pre-Famine Deindustrialization', *Economic History Review* (forthcoming).

100 The image is borrowed from J.A. Schumpeter, 'The Instability of Capitalism', *Economic Journal*, xxxi, 1928, p. 361.

101 The possibility of separate parliaments in Dublin and Belfast was raised as early as 1833 in the House of Commons by Thomas Macaulay. See Fergus O'Ferrall, *Catholic Emancipation: Daniel O'Connell and the Birth of Irish Democracy, 1820–30* (Dublin, 1985), p. 280.

102 Johnson and Kennedy, 'Nationalist Historiography', pp. 19–23.

103 This is not to deny that some forms of state intervention might have been helpful, ranging from subsidising new technologies to selective forms of protection, but convincing contemporary proposals on how to use political independence to advance the Irish economy were conspicuously lacking. This dearth of ideas does not augur well for the adoption of effective, alternative policies.

104 McDonagh, *Ireland*, p. 9.

105 Johnson and Kennedy, 'Nationalist Historiography', p. 19.

106 See, for example, Norman Stone, *Europe Transformed 1878–1919* (London, 1983), pp. 293–6.

107 F.S.L. Lyons, *Ireland Since the Famine* (London, 1973), p. 668.
108 But see K.T. Hoppen, *Elections, Politics and Society in Ireland 1832–1885* (Oxford, 1984), which is an especially fine study of nineteenth-century politics, observed from the vantage point of local rather than national concerns.

4

REVISIONISM AND IRISH HISTORY

The Great Famine

Mary Daly

The Great Famine is arguably the only event in modern Irish history to have achieved widespread international recognition. The steady sales of Cecil Woodham-Smith's *The Great Hunger*, which has been in print for more than thirty years, testify to a continuing wish to be informed about this crisis. The more recent runaway success of the spurious *Famine Diary*[1] – allegedly the diary of school teacher Gerald Keegan who emigrated with his wife to Canada on a 'coffin ship' where both died of fever – and its continuing sales despite being revealed as a piece of late nineteenth-century Canadian–Irish fiction – suggest a strong desire to wallow in its emotional horrors, perhaps at the cost of a wider understanding. For some US and Canadian citizens of Irish descent the Famine is in danger of becoming their answer to the Jewish Holocaust: evidence that the Irish too are a nation of victims, a causal explanation for mass Irish emigration and a symbol of national unity. With the sesquicentennial of the Famine in 1995 and the promises of Famine walks, Famine museums and the commemoration of Famine-era graveyards the Famine seems set to become part of the Irish heritage industry.

Despite such popular interest, scholarly research in the Famine has been limited,[2] and contemporary perceptions of the subject, both in Ireland and abroad, have been virtually untouched by revisionist scholarship. The controversy surrounding the event and its subsequent exploitation by Nationalist polemicists have meant that the narrative of events and the related debate have been dictated not by scholars but by politicians: men such as John Mitchel, Charles Gavan Duffy or Isaac Butt.[3] A further ingredient consists of eye-witness accounts by journalists such as T.C. Foster, or aid workers attached to the Society of Friends[4] to which can be added the drawings featured in the *Illustrated London News*. The Irish Famine was arguably the first media famine of the modern era. Later versions drew heavily on these accounts. Although Canon John O'Rourke, author of the first scholarly history of the Famine sent query sheets to eye-witnesses, the thrust of his work is largely derived from the

71

coverage in the Nationalist press.[5] W.P. O'Brien, author of the other nineteenth-century account, had served as a Poor Law Inspector in 'Kerry, Clare, Galway, Roscommon, Leitrim etc.' during the Famine years, however he offers little sense of that fact, relying instead on 'the elaborate and careful compilation of the facts then made by Sir Charles Trevelyan, who had in the preparation of it official access to all the best and most authentic sources of information existing on the subject'.[6] Sir Charles Trevelyan, Chief Secretary to the Treasury, published his justification of the British government's stance anonymously in 1848.[7] More recently, the dominant version of the Famine has come from Cecil Woodham-Smith, a professional writer, though one with considerable historical skills;[8] her chief contribution has been to focus the question of English guilt around the person of Sir Charles Trevelyan. In the widely read historiography of the Famine professional historians have been on the sideline.

The most evocative recurring image comes from the pen of John Mitchel; each relief ship sailing into an Irish port with a cargo of grain was 'sure to meet six ships sailing out with a similar cargo'. According to Mitchel, 'during all the famine years Ireland was actually producing sufficient food, wool and flax, to feed and clothe not nine but eighteen millions of people'.[9] Thus the Famine was an artificial event, caused not by a shortage of food, but by the failure on the part of the British government to close the ports and by the need to export food to pay rents to profligate, absentee landlords. This viewpoint, which was common during the Famine years dominates the first scholarly history written by Canon John O'Rourke, which was first published in 1874. P.S. O'Hegarty signals its central place in his Famine chapter by beginning with a quotation from George Bernard Shaw's *Man and Superman*:

> *Malone* . . . Me father died of starvation in Ireland in the black '47. Maybe yourself heard of it?
> *Violet* The Famine!
> *Malone (with smouldering passion)* No, the Starvation. When a country is full of food, and exporting it, there can be no famine. Me father was starved dead; and I was starved out to America in me mother's arms. English rule drove me and mine out of Ireland.[10]

The charge most consistently levelled against the British government in many older accounts is not one concerning the adequacy of the relief measures adopted, which tends to dominate much of the more recent debate,[11] but the failure to prevent the export of food from Ireland. The extreme variant of the Nationalist viewpoint assumes that closing the Irish ports together with a scheme of public works *financed from Irish resources* would have been fully capable of meeting the Famine crisis. O'Hegarty cited Daniel O'Connell's speech to the Mansion House Committee in December 1845: 'let it not be pretended that we seek alms at the

hands of England. We are doing no such thing', which outlined a programme of taxes on absentee landlords and proposals to raise a loan to
fund relief works secured by the income of Irish Woods and Forests,
sources which O'Connell deemed to be 'exclusively Irish funds'.[12] Land
League leader Michael Davitt and Sinn Féin activist and historian P.S.
O'Hegarty were among the writers who denounced Irish politicians for
failing to prevent food exports by organising popular resistance.[13] The
division in ranks between O'Connell and the Young Irelanders over the
theoretical possibility of resort to physical force was seen as contributing
to national misery. O'Rourke, in a chapter entitled 'Irish ranks split'
summarises the position as follows:

> Thus at a most critical moment, standing between two years of
> fearful, withering famine, did the leaders of the Irish people by their
> miserable dissensions, lay that people in hopeless prostration at the
> mercy of the British Cabinet, from which, had they remained united,
> they might have obtained means of saving the lives of thousands of
> their countrymen.[14]

These however were subsidiary matters: responsibility for both the
immediate and long-term causes of the Famine were laid at Britain's door.
According to George O'Brien pre-Famine Ireland presented the 'anomaly
of a fertile country being disfigured by wretched agriculture and a starving people'; both the 'condition of the Irish agricultural labourers and the
state of Irish agriculture . . . were miserable in the extreme'. Despite the
wealth of unexploited Irish resources, as demonstrated by Robert Kane's
The Industrial Resources of Ireland (published in 1844), Ireland remained in
a state of chronic poverty, exemplified by the recurrence of minor famines
for several decades prior to the Great Famine.[15] Responsibility for this
condition, however, rested in the political rather than the economic sphere.
Although O'Rourke focused attention on Irish overreliance on the
'prolific but uncertain' potato, he attributed its widespread adoption to
the dispossession of the native lands which forced the 'poor Celtic natives
. . . to take themselves to the despised wastes and barren mountains' and
to the 'poverty of the English colony itself' which resulted from unjust
fiscal treatment by England.[16] George O'Brien accounted for pre-Famine
poverty by referring to 'the unjust distribution of the produce of the land
actually cultivated, and the failure to bring waste land of the country into
cultivation' for which he held the government directly responsible. 'Was
it not the government's duty to see that the Irish gentry should do their's?'[17]
Such a viewpoint transforms the Famine into another episode in the
long-running saga of British mistreatment of Ireland: a nineteenth-
century equivalent of the Cromwellian Plantation or the Penal Laws.

The most striking point about the views explored above is the degree
to which they focus on the political sphere. Analysis of causal factors or

responsibility for the Famine focused on Whitehall, Westminster or Dublin Castle rather than on Mayo or Skibbereen. This tendency to view economic matters as politically determined is not unique to the Famine, nor did it begin in the 1840s. Until relatively recently, as Louis Cullen has shown, most commentators writing about the eighteenth-century Irish economy assumed that

> economic development was subsidiary to political issues; not only subsidiary but its achievement or negation a product of policy. Contemporaries in Ireland argued in effect from two postulates, firstly that Ireland was on the evidence before them an economically depressed country, and secondly, that this depression was a consequence of certain aspects of British policy . . . Economic ill-effects were as a matter of course polemically attributed to constitutionally objectionable legislative measures.[18]

Most writers have attributed major responsibility for both Irish poverty and the Famine disaster to the free trade, market-driven approach which had by the 1840s come to dominate the British economy. British Prime Minister Sir Robert Peel was commonly accused of exploiting the Famine to achieve political support for repeal of the corn laws – the final step in the triumph of free trade. Such accusations were frequently made at the time both by English protectionists and disgruntled Irish landlords.[19] O'Rourke, writing in the 1870s, when the impact of repeal was evident in the form of stagnant or falling grain prices and soaring imports, was particularly bitter on this point.[20] George O'Brien, some fifty years later, was equally critical condemning repeal (of corn laws) as 'one of the legislative aids to depopulation'.[21] If Peel can justifiably be accused of using the Famine to achieve a longer-term political ambition – repeal of the corn laws – the historians quoted above are equally guilty of viewing the issues of repeal and food exports from the perspective of the adverse affects of free-trade on the post-Union Irish economy and the imagined joys of protection. In the *Last Conquest of Ireland*, John Mitchel claimed that during the Famine Ireland had died 'of political economy'. As an alternative to economic liberalism most Irish writers favoured a more mercantilist approach: a protected market (closing the ports), together with a government-financed programme for economic development. The vision of an Irish economy declining in the nineteenth century because of the removal of protection and the ending of the mercantilist measures enjoyed under the late eighteenth-century Grattan's Parliament strongly informs the critique of British government policy in the Famine and immediate pre-Famine years. The long-term solution to Irish economic problems is seen as resting on the implementation of the report of the *Poor Inquiry* of the 1830s, which recommended an ambitious programme of infrastructural development;[22] government-funded Famine relief works are criticised for failing to spend money on 'productive' works while the abortive proposal of renegade Tory Lord George Bentinck for government-financed railway development as a form of Famine relief, is much applauded.[23] In fact, Bentinck's scheme would have brought little relief to starving Irish labourers: irrespective of the time-lag between planning and implementation, only one-third of the money spent would have actually accrued to labour, most of the remainder would have gone on materials.[24]

The partisan counter-case to the above, epitomised by Trevelyan's *The Irish Crisis* shared some common features. This too regarded pre-Famine Ireland as poor, backward and underdeveloped with famine as virtually inevitable; once more the land system and specifically Irish landlords were seen as the culprits. In this scenario, however, the solution was seen as lying in full exposure to the liberal market economy which would weed out incompetent landlords and indolent peasants alike, replacing them with a modern capitalist agriculture. The clash of views on the Famine should not simply be seen as one between Ireland and Britain, but a more complex one centred on widely differing views on economics and specifically the merits or evils of the market economy: a clash which echoes aspects of the British 'standard of living debate'.

Revision of the above analysis was slow to come and what remains striking is the degree to which so-called revisionists retained key features of the earlier analysis. The key revisionist contribution, *The Great Famine*, edited by R.D. Edwards and T.D. Williams, has been described by Cormac Ó Gráda as a work 'which reads more like an *administrative* history of the period'.[25] Originally intended to mark the centenary of the Great Famine, and to have been edited by the founding fathers of *Irish Historical Studies*, Edwards, Moody and Quinn, (Quinn and Moody subsequently dropped out),[26] the book epitomised that journal's commitment to writing 'value-free' history while also reflecting the primarily political focus of that school. The volume's revisionism centres on the chapters dealing with the political background and the administration of relief by K.B. Nowlan and T.P. O'Neill respectively; essays on emigration by Oliver McDonagh and on the medical history of the Famine by William MacArthur reinforce the overall tendency to replace a previous picture of 'great and deliberately imposed evil in high positions of responsibility' with one characterised by 'human limitation and timidity'. This is achieved by a detailed examination of political and administrative sources, which chronicle a picture of men overwhelmed by the task in hand. In contrast Roger McHugh's essay on the Famine as viewed in Irish folklore reiterates the strength of traditional views and, as the introduction states, 'makes it clear that there was no disharmony between the folk memory and the writings of the political commentators' – a comment whose implications were unfortunately not explored. Although the introduction seeks to shift responsibility for the

Famine from individuals or nations to the prevailing social system, promoting the analysis of James Connolly – '"No man who accepts capitalist society and the laws thereof can logically find fault with the statesmen of England for their acts in that awful period"'[27] – in place of John Mitchel in an effort to gain historical legitimacy, the examination of socio–economic questions is insufficient to sustain this line of approach. The sole essay dealing with economic matters by E.R.R. Green, which occupies less than ten per cent of the volume, consists of a primarily descriptive account of pre-Famine agriculture; other socio–economic issues are briefly noted in R.B. McDowell's general account of pre-Famine Ireland. Despite the existence in print by this stage of the pioneering work of K.H. Connell,[28] there is no section dealing specifically with population growth with the exception of two cursory pages in McDowell's survey. The book also suffers from the rather smug assumption that both the responsibility of the state for economic management and the effectiveness of state involvement in such matters are self-evident:

> The timidity and remoteness of the administrators in the eighteen-forties may irritate the modern observer who unhesitatingly accepts the moral responsibility of the state to intervene in economic affairs in a time of crisis. But it needs patience to realise that what is obvious and uncontroversial today was dark and confused a century ago to many persons of good will.

Peel, Russell and their colleagues therefore deserve our sympathy for failing to see the light. This assertion may have seemed obvious in the 1950s; its validity appears less so in the post-Thatcher and post-Reagan 1990s.

If *The Great Famine* had devoted more attention to economic conditions it appears probable that the effect would have been to blunt its revisionist cast. As Cullen has pointed out, although works such as K.H. Connell *The Population of Ireland* and Lynch and Vaizey *Guinness's Brewery in the Irish Economy*[29] broke new ground in adopting an economic as opposed to a political focus, they continued to propagate the well-established picture of an economy mired in poverty and distress which was not explicable in terms of economic cycles.[30] According to Lynch and Vaizey all Ireland with the exception of a small coastal 'maritime economy' subsisted in a primitive pre-monetary state. Despite his pioneering efforts in quantifying population growth, Connell's analysis of pre-Famine Ireland is seriously flawed. All except a tiny upper class were consigned to the generalised category of peasant (a word so all-pervasive that it does not feature in the index), who married early because life and particularly an exploitative land system offered little else, subdivided their holdings and subsisted on potatoes.[31] In this scenario the Famine becomes a Malthusian disaster, caused by the relentless tendency to young, improvident marriages and the inexorable drive of population on to marginal wasteland, a process facilitated by the potato which permitted settlement on wasteland and prevented population growth being arrested by higher mortality. For Connell the Famine constituted a watershed: leading to the abandonment of sub-division and early marriages in favour of late marriages, dowries and match-making. This picture is not radically different from that painted by George O'Brien though the causes are now sought in economics rather than politics. A broadly similar analysis was presented by the historical geographer T.W. Freeman:

> Ireland in the pre-Famine years was heading for the human disaster which came with greater force and horror than its people could possibly anticipate. Poverty was stark, housing wretched, trade inadequate, agriculture backward, industry faltering,

though the picture of stagnation was qualified somewhat by his emphasis on major improvements in transport and communications.[32]

Fundamental revision of this economic analysis with the more rigorous use of economic methodology and statistical analysis did not begin until the 1960s. The key writers were Raymond Crotty, an economist whose primary interest lay in contemporary economic issues, and economic historian Louis Cullen. Crotty's book *Irish Agricultural Production: Its Volume and Structure* adopted an explicitly Marxist interpretation of the type hinted at, but not developed in the introduction to Edwards and Williams. Where Connell saw the growth in Irish population as a reaction to the misery of peasant life, Crotty argued that it was economically determined: a response to the rising demand for labour which was triggered in turn by an increase in Irish grain exports to feed the expanding English labour force of the Industrial Revolution. The reversal of these demand stimuli in the 'years of crisis' after 1815, when continental Europe began to compete for the British market, brought a shift from tillage to pasture farming, reduced demand for labour and a struggle to reduce population growth. The rate of increase slackened and emigration rose. Crotty's analysis de-throned the Famine from its position as the pivotal economic event in nineteenth-century Ireland in favour of the Battle of Waterloo. According to Crotty trends which were generally associated with post-Famine Ireland such as the shift to pasture farming and the end of sub-division were all established after 1815.[33]

While Crotty devoted little time to the Famine *per se*, he presented it as an almost inevitable outcome for a society unable to respond to rapidly changing market circumstances. Cullen's controversial argument that the potato was a consequence rather than a cause of population growth also focused heavily on market trends.[34] He linked the spread of the potato to the increasing commercialisation of Irish agriculture in the eighteenth and early nineteenth centuries as growing markets for butter, bacon and grain led to their disappearance from many rural diets.[35] Cullen also played down the significance of the Famine, reiterating Crotty's views that many of the subsequent trends which were commonly attributed to the Famine were already inevitable. For Cullen the disaster was a regional rather than a national phenomenon; only in the impoverished West was the whole community threatened.[36] This phase of economically focused revision served to marginalise the Famine as a major factor in Irish history and led to a greater focus on pre-Famine economy and society.

The quantity and quality of intellectual input focused on Ireland both during and after the Famine in the past twenty years far exceeds all previous research. Economic analysis has continued to dominate with increased use of statistical data and econometric techniques, allied with a comparative dimension. Ireland is no longer seen as *sui generis*. Solar has compared pre-Famine Irish agricultural productivity not unfavourably with Scottish levels;[37] writing on Irish demography has been strongly influenced by emerging evidence emerging concerning British and European trends.[38] Ireland's relatively light escape during the European Famine of 1816–17[39] has forced some rethinking about its alleged chronic vulnerability to famine as has Joel Mokyr's analysis of the Potato Famine of 1845–6 in the Low Countries.[40] Amtya Sen's work on Indian and other Third World famine has also proved influential, particularly his argument that famines are often caused by lack of entitlement to food – i.e., an inability to buy or otherwise obtain food in the market – as opposed to mere food scarcity[41] has raised new questions concerning government relief measures and the precise causality of famine deaths.

The pre-Famine Ireland which has emerged from this revision is a much more complex society. The gulf in interpretations is best captured by reading contrasting chapters in the *New History of Ireland*: the late T.W. Freeman presents a largely traditional picture of a country reeking of poverty with a sense of imminent crisis whereas Ó Gháda presents a more positive and a more nuanced account.[42] Although images of poverty survive, the picture is not totally bleak. Irish pre-Famine peasantry have little hope of winning the prize for the most exploited race in Europe. Clothing was ragged and housing conditions primitive, but those with access to turf had adequate heating. Labourers and small farmers in all areas except Ulster were almost totally dependent on the potato, but the potato is the only staple crop which does not carry the risk of a deficiency disease and statistics showing that Irish military recruits were taller than their English counterparts confirm that the diet was a healthy one.[43] On the other hand they may have been vulnerable to famine: unlike grain, potatoes cannot be stored from year to year, and they are too bulky to transport in large quantities; they may also be more vulnerable to failure than other crops. Cottiers faced specific problems, being forced to plant their crops late in the season when paid farm work was unavailable, depending increasingly on the prolific but vulnerable lumper.[44]

Although contemporary travellers described the Irish countryside as primitive and untidy, pre-Famine Irish agriculture is no longer regarded as backward or remarkably inefficient. Improvements were taking place in animal breeding stock; land was being cleared and improved – often by landlords.[45] The picture of an idle peasantry lazing around without any work to do for most of the year, which was central to Trevelyan's analysis, 'a fortnight planting, a week or ten days digging and fourteen days turf cutting suffice for his subsistence. During the rest of the year he is at leisure to follow his own inclinations',[46] has been replaced by one of intensive peasant cultivation. Productivity yields compared favourably with those in continental countries; pre-Famine Ireland was capable of feeding over nine million people both in Ireland and overseas.[47] New roads brought virtually all areas within reach of the market economy (this had been emphasised for many years by Freeman);[48] new export routes emerged for produce such as eggs and grain from places such as Westport.[49]

Although the population continued to rise, Connell's picture of an undifferentiated peasantry rushing lemming-like into matrimony no longer survives. The rate of population increase appears to have been falling slowly from 1791.[50] Irish age at marriage and numbers marrying immediately prior to the Famine were similar to those in other parts of Northern Europe.[51] Emigration was rising rapidly, particularly in areas which had lost the income from domestic textiles, although the latter fact had been known for many decades.[52] Marriages *may* have been taking place at a later age;[53] dowries were common. Although the decades prior to the Famine were marked by crop failures, there is no evidence to suggest that they resulted in significant excess mortality, perhaps, because as Timothy O'Neill suggests, government relief measures proved adequate,[54] despite the absence of a poor law system. Pre-Famine poverty is no longer seen as the poverty of a nation, but the product of highly unequal distribution of income and resources. Many people were prospering in pre-Famine Ireland; the majority of them not landlords. Prior to the mid-1840s, this poverty did not appear to have resulted in mass mortality.

Fewer minds have concentrated on the Famine than on pre-Famine Ireland; the revision is less clear-cut and many unanswered questions remain. Recent research has however re-established both the magnitude of the Famine and its longer-term economic significance. Solar's figures showing that Irish food production in the years 1846–50 averaged only sixty per cent of the 1840–5 output – the drop for 1846 was substantially greater[55] – should conclusively refute any argument of a non-existent or artificially created Famine. The Irish Famine constituted the most severe episode of food shortage in nineteenth-century Europe. Food imports for the years 1846–50 exceeded exports by a ratio of three to one. Analysis of the Irish grain trade by Austin Bourke – one of the unsung heroes of Famine studies – confirms that a ban on Irish food exports would not have compensated for losses in the potato crop: grain exports in 1846 had a food equivalent of less than ten per cent of the lost potato crop. However Bourke throws a crumb to supporters of the traditional line, conceding that the

> nationalist argument, stripped of gross exaggeration still retains a small hard kernel of truth. The grain crop of 1846, if entirely retained in Ireland, could have made an appreciable gap between the destruction of the potato crop in August and the arrival of the first maize cargoes in the following winter.[56]

The short-term impact of the Famine on the overall Irish economy remains a murky area. The Famine coincided with an international commercial crisis which brought about rising distress in Britain, added to Ireland's difficulties and blunted the edge on English generosity; the relationship between the two events remains to be explored. Lynch and Vaizey suggested that the maritime – e.g., the commercial monetised Irish economy – was virtually untouched by the Famine: figures showing a significant decline in bank note circulation suggest that this was not so,[57] while a virtual tripling of maize prices during the autumn/winter of 1846[58] and the sharp fluctuations in potato prices[59] suggest that Ireland in the 1840s offered a more responsive market economy than Bengal did a century later.[60]

What of Famine deaths? Two independently derived estimates both suggest a figure of one million excess deaths.[61] Deaths doubled over the whole age spectrum: the majority of victims were children or elderly. The birthrate fell as a result of fewer marriages and of Famine-related infertility. Most regional variations are explicable in terms of an area's economic structure; the heaviest deaths were in the West, but both Limerick and Donegal appear to have had lower than expected death rates.[62] The major advance in our knowledge of Famine-era disease comes from Margaret Crawford's examination of diseases caused by dietary deficiency: blindness especially among children caused by xerophthalmia emerges as a hitherto little-recognised consequence of the famine.[63]

The explosion of historiography dealing with emigration merits a separate study.[64] Famine emigration is now largely seen as a continuum from the immediate pre-Famine pattern of the early 1840s: areas with exceptionally high Famine emigration, south Ulster, north Connacht and parts of the midlands had all experienced heavy depletion in previous decades. This makes Famine emigration seem less the panic-stricken flight into the unknown of earlier accounts, more a departure of those with some prior knowledge of the process. Emigration and deaths proved largely complementary: the young and the old died; those in active age groups emigrated. Areas with high excess mortality had low emigration and vice versa. Although most emigrants were labourers or sons of farmers, the most impoverished were often incapable of leaving because of lack of resources; many emigrants in the early 1850s would have left during the Famine years if they could have afforded to do so.[65] The saga of the notorious coffin ships has undoubtedly been overstated. Death from fever on the passage was heavily concentrated on ships going to Canada where a fare one-third of the cost of going to New York brought three times the risk of death.[66] Although Famine-era emigration is traditionally seen as the prime cause of growing anti-Irish sentiment in the US, it seems to have predated the Famine influx.[67]

Sen's entitlements analysis has proved most useful as a mechanism for exploring the process of distress. Most Famine victims were poor, victims both of potato failure and of their inability to buy alternative food. Cottiers and small farmers sold animals and any other possessions to buy the cheapest food; cattle numbers fell between 1847 and 1850 on farms under fifteen acres. In contrast larger farmers benefited both from high grain or potato prices and from small farmers' distress: cattle numbers rose by twenty-five per cent on farms over thirty acres.[68] Relief works, which were designed to provide the poor with the money (entitlements) to buy food proved ineffective in the winter of 1846–7 because prices rocketed and the wages paid were inadequate. Higher wages would only have dragged more workers away from productive employment and further distorted the economy. Paradoxically, by the spring of 1847 when they were ending, relief works *might* have proved effective because food prices were falling rapidly. Many questions relating to Famine relief are only beginning to be explored. While a somewhat sterile debate has taken place on the inadequacy of Britain's relief contribution of £7 million when contrasted with its expenditure of almost ten times that amount on the Crimean War[69] – a point which can be made with equal, if not greater validity about the disproportionate resources currently devoted to military expenditure versus Famine relief, little attention has been devoted to Irish society's capacity to absorb relief funds, or the extent to which these were targeted at those most in need. Devine's work on the Scottish Highlands had highlighted the role of landlords in organising relief and subsidising emigration. The most effective were not traditional landlords but new men with substantial financial resources.[70] This pinpoints the need to examine the location, composition, and actions of relief committees. Little light can be shed to date on these issues though figures suggest that some acutely distressed areas derived relatively little benefit from the public works of 1846–7.[71] Equally telling is the fact that Scotland applied for £803,804 in grants for relief works under the Drainage Act by January 1847 against a mere £39,171 from Ireland.[72]

Although not designed to cope with major famine, the Irish poor law

played a major role in Famine relief. Kinealy's work does much to reha-
bilitate its overall reputation given the strictures of Woodham-Smith and
others. In the winter of 1846–7 individual unions broke the rules and
pioneered the establishment of soup kitchens; by 1848–9 the Commissioners in Dublin had become increasingly critical of government policy.
She sees the 1847 Poor Law Extension Act which made the poor law the
sole agency responsible for Famine relief as a consolidation rather than a
reversal of government relief policy.[73] However many unanswered
questions remain about the actual working of the system. A recent study
of the Enniskillen Board of Guardians in 1847 indicates the potential of
such local studies.[74]

Most accounts of the Famine until recently virtually ended in the
summer of 1847.[75] Having ploughed through two Famine seasons, 1845–7,
scholars appear to have succumbed to research fatigue, an academic
version of the compassion fatigue which caused the Society of Friends
and the British government to wind up their relief efforts at that time. In
doing this, historians have missed some significant aspects of the story:
many Famine deaths occurred after 1847; it was then that the notorious
Gregory Clause began to bite and the burden on the poor law intensified.
Workhouse numbers peaked in 1849, evictions in 1850. The regressive
burden of poor relief, with the poorest areas carrying the heaviest poor
rates undoubtedly delayed economic recovery particularly in the West.
The tax burden crippled larger farmers in these areas, causing some to
emigrate, with possible long-term damage to the social fabric. The argument
that the British government was ungenerous to Ireland during the famine
seems much stronger for the years after mid-1847 than for any other period.

Current consensus sees a greater measure of continuity between pre-
and post-Famine Ireland in demographic matters such as marriages,
births and emigration than was the case in the past. Post-Famine emigration is attributed to 'pull' factors: the attraction of better conditions
elsewhere, rather than the 'push' of misery.[76] The exception is Joel
Mokyr's speculation that 'had there been no Famine, Ireland's population
would have continued to grow like any other European country in the
second half of the nineteenth-century'.[77] In economic terms however the
Famine's status as a watershed has been firmly restored. If the pre-
Famine economy is no longer seen as utterly backward, the post-Famine
scenario appears less rosy. The Famine administered a serious, long-term
shock to Irish agriculture.[78] By 1854 Irish agriculture had only three-
quarters of its pre-Famine labour force and output had fallen by sixteen
per cent.[79] Crop yields also suffered, mainly because of falling potato
yields – the result both of recurrent potato blight and a shift to less
labour-intensive cultivation because lower potato yields and higher
potato prices meant a sharp rise in labour costs.[80] Irish agriculture shifted
from tillage to pasture. Whether this shift was the result of the repeal of

the corn laws which opened the British and Irish markets to cheap American grain or of the Famine has been a matter of some controversy. While the impact of the corn laws should not be ignored, O'Rourke argues that the sharp increase in labour and therefore tillage costs which resulted from the Famine was the critical factor.

As the above pages suggest, most of the momentum in Famine studies has come from economists and economic historians. To date however economics has failed to provide a definitive explanation for the Famine, though in the process it has destroyed some hardy perennials in the Famine's history and mythology. For those who subscribed to the older picture of relentless population growth in an impoverished society, the Famine was a virtually inevitable Malthusian disaster, though Malthus never actually envisaged such an outcome.[81] The revised picture of pre-Famine society requires a major reassessment of causation. The most direct attempt to do this in economic terms is Joel Mokyr's book, *Why Ireland Starved* – which could perhaps be described as the ultimate quest for the value-free history beloved of *Irish Historical Studies*. Despite accepting and originating much of the revisionist analysis of the pre-Famine Irish economy outlined previously, Mokyr argues that pre-Famine Ireland was undoubtedly poor: in support of this term he employs 'a new definition of poverty', one which 'views poverty in terms of famines and their demographic impact.'[82] Mokyr advances the hypothesis that differences in Famine mortality between various counties should be explicable in terms of factors such as comparative levels of over-population, dependency on the potato, the system of land-tenure, quality of land or access to non-agricultural employment. Despite heroic and highly complex econometric calculations, none of the above provide statistically significant explanations. However these indecisive (or statistically insignificant) results may reflect the inaccuracy or inadequacy of nineteenth-century statistics, or the fact that analysis on a county basis was simply too crude to reveal the underlying statistical relationships. It may therefore be premature to reject over-population, or the other hypotheses out of hand. Having failed in his search for economic explanations, Mokyr turned to politics, specifically the Act of Union and the growing integration of the British and Irish economies. According to Mokyr, Ireland's problems resulted, not from the integration of the two economies and politics but from the fact that it 'did not go far enough'; Britain considered Ireland 'an alien and even hostile country'. As a result 'English and Scottish capital shied away from Ireland'. As evidence of this foreignness Britain viewed Irish poverty 'as being caused by laziness, indifference, and ineptitude', unlike British poverty which was the result of economic fluctuations and structural change. 'Most seriously of all, when the chips were down in the frightful summer of 1847, the British simply abandoned the Irish and let them perish.'[83]

With Mokyr's book the wheel has come full circle; a work setting out to conduct a quantitative economic analysis of the causes of the famine concludes with highly charged political rhetoric. Others have opted to explain the Famine as a case of bad luck or divine Providence. Solar has focused on the sudden and sharp shortfall in food supplies; the coincidence of the Irish Famine with the sharp rise in grain prices in the 1840s and the international commercial depression of 1847 and concluded that Ireland was 'profoundly unlucky'.[84] This renewed interest in random events, or 'the Visitation of God'[85] marks a return to older interpretations. The famine as divine punishment is a theme which recurs in folklore.[86] Canon O'Rourke's account contains several descriptions of unnatural weather conditions which heralded the coming of the blight.[87] However the strongest belief in the Famine as an act of Providence originated, not in superstitious peasant Ireland, but among significant numbers of the English political and administrative elite: a group which included figures close to both Peel and Russell of whom Trevelyan numbered only one.[88]

Boyd Hilton's work on the moral predestination analysis which underlay much of early nineteenth-century political economy, the belief that the invisible hand of the market economy reflected the working of divine Providence and that measures which thwarted its functioning were inherently evil, is one of the most important recent contributions to Famine historiography.[89] This has now been supplemented by Peter Gray's recent Ph.D. thesis which examines the Providentialist analysis with specific reference to the Irish Famine.[90] Gray's work showing the wide currency in British politics of views similar to those held by Trevelyan, the Chief Secretary to the Treasury, brings into question the tendency, common to both Woodham-Smith and K.B. Nowlan to differentiate between the pragmatic Peel and the dogmatic Russell. Both shared broadly similar ideological values; Peel was lucky to confront the relatively milder Famine of 1845–6.

According to Providentialist theory, Irish rural society, as exemplified by cottiers, other small landholders and slipshod easy-living landlords had to give way to a modern commercial farming system ruled by profit and worked by wage-earning labourers. To those who subscribed to Providentialism, such as Trevelyan, the Famine was 'the judgement of God on an indolent and unself-reliant people'; as God had 'sent the calamity to teach the Irish a lesson, that calamity must not be too much mitigated'.[91] Providentialism would appear to afford the most important boost to anti-revisionist Famine historiography, revealing as it does a British establishment which saw the Famine as inevitable punishment for Ireland, and were less likely to make heroic efforts to ease its impact. Yet while superficially lending weight to interpretations of the Famine as genocide carried out by the British establishment, such images are belied by the picture of a British people, led by Queen Victoria, engaged in a national day of Atonement, (24 March 1847), fasting and doing penance for Irish famine.[92] As Ó Gráda points out, the wish to change rural Ireland was strongest not among wicked men, but among those motivated by a 'vision of a better world';[93] furthermore the Famine did much to discredit Providence theory in Britain, leading to a re-evaluation of social policy.[94]

CONCLUSION

It is no doubt premature to proclaim the end of the revisionist/anti-revisionist conflict on the Famine, though it remains doubtful whether it can serve any useful future purpose. Many key facts are clear: the Irish Famine was real, not artificial, food was extremely scarce; it could not have been solved by closing the ports; charges of genocide cannot be sustained. However it is undoubtedly the case that the British response was inadequate and was unduly influenced both by domestic political concerns such as repeal of the corn laws and by Providentialism. On the other hand, it is equally clear that the Irish political response was also dictated by matters such as Repeal of the Union and the power struggle between O'Connell and Young Ireland. Mitchel's subsequent savage indictment of British government Famine policy conceals the fact that he and his colleagues offered no workable alternative at the time. All, including the radical land theorist James Fintan Lalor looked to the Irish landlord class to solve the Famine crisis;[95] at least the British government was less naive. The renewed attention to politics and ideology should hopefully begin to reveal the precise Irish reaction to the Famine. Donnelly ends his contribution on the Famine and Irish politics by asking, 'Who today should be surprised that many of "Erin's boys" wanted "revenge for Skibbereen"?' – a reincarnation of the traditional view that the Famine gave a new impetus to Irish nationalism. Elsewhere in the same volume Comerford is less certain: emphasising that the 'Famine experience induced doubt about the country's capacity for self-government'.[96] The curious reticence about the Famine, the failure to use the word, in Fenian novelist Charles Kickham's best-selling novel, *Knocknagow* suggests a more ambivalent response to the tragedy on the part of nationalist Ireland than is generally painted.

The primary need at this stage is further research, concentrating at local and regional level: who died, when and where; relief committees which functioned or failed to function; where landlords were involved in Famine relief or acted in an uncaring manner; where larger farmers turned a blind eye to the plight of cottiers or held out a helping hand; where Catholic and Protestant clergy worked in co-operation or in opposition. The outcome may reveal new targets for vilification closer to home than Westminster or Whitehall, generating in the process a new wave of revisionist or anti-revisionist arguments.

The danger remains that much current and future scholarship on the Famine will make its mark in academic circles but not in the wider world where images of genocide will persist. One entry in Dudley Edwards' diary during the years when *The Great Famine* was in gestation noted *the danger of dehydrated history.*[97] Somewhat similar accusations have been levelled at my work in this area.[98] Ultimately only a blend of analysis and emotion, an account of the Famine which takes stock of its legacy in economics, politics, folklore, and poetry will meet the needs of scholarship and popular memory alike. Whether historians can deliver this, it is impossible to say.

NOTES

1 Gerald Keegan, *Famine Diary. Journey to a New World* (Dublin, 1991). For the background to what was in fact a work of fiction, see Jim Jackson, 'Famine Diary. The Making of a Best-Seller', *The Irish Review*, 11 (winter 1991–2), pp. 1–8.

2 The first hundred issues of *Irish Historical Studies* contained a mere five articles on the Famine; *Irish Economic and Social History* did not publish a single article on the Famine over the years 1974–87. Cormac Ó Gráda, *Ireland Before and After the Famine. Explorations in Economic History, 1800–1925* (Manchester, 1988), p. 78.

3 Charles Gavan Duffy, *My Life in Two Hemispheres* vol. i (London, 1898); John Mitchel, *The Last Conquest of Ireland (Perhaps)* (London, 1876); Isaac Butt, *The Famine in the Land* (Dublin, 1847).

4 T.C. Foster, *Letters on the Condition of the People of Ireland* (London, 1847); *Transactions of the Central Relief Committee of the Society of Friends During the Famine in Ireland in 1846 and 1847* (Dublin, 1852).

5 Canon John O'Rourke, *The History of the Great Irish Famine of 1847, with Notices of Earlier Famines* (Dublin, 1875).

6 W.P. O'Brien, *The Great Famine in Ireland and a Retrospect of the Fifty Years, 1845–95* (London, 1896), pp. 83–4.

7 C.E. Trevelyan, *The Irish Crisis* (London, 1848).

8 Cecil Woodham-Smith, *The Great Hunger* (London, 1962).

9 Mitchel, *op. cit.*, p. 208.

10 George Bernard Shaw, *Man and Superman* (1903), p. 150 as cited in P.S. O'Hegarty, *A History of Ireland Under the Union* (London, 1952), p. 291.

11 James S. Donnelly, Jr. 'The Administration of Relief, 1847–51', in W.E. Vaughan (ed.), *New History of Ireland, V. Ireland Under the Union, Part 1. 1801–70* (Oxford, 1989), pp. 328–9.

12 O'Hegarty, *op. cit.*, p. 259, citing *The Nation*, 6 December 1845.

13 Michael Davitt, *The Fall of Feudalism in Ireland*, (London, 1904), pp. 52–3. O'Hegarty, *op. cit.*, pp. 311, 324.

14 O'Rourke, *op. cit.*, p. 89.

15 George O'Brien, *The Economic History of Ireland from the Union to the Famine* (London, 1921) pp. 222–31. This and other similar accounts derive from Wilde's appendix to the 1851 census.

16 O'Rourke, *op. cit.*, pp. 16, 6, 20.

17 O'Brien, *op. cit.*, pp. 4–5, 271.

18 L.M. Cullen, 'Problems in the Interpretation and Revision of Eighteenth

Century Irish Economic History', *Transactions of the Royal Historical Society*, 5th series, vol. 17 (1967), p. 1.

19 Kevin B. Nowlan, 'The Political Background' in R. Dudley Edwards and T. Desmond Williams (eds), *The Great Famine* (Dublin, 1956), p. 135.

20 O'Rourke, *op. cit.*, p. 56.

21 O'Brien, *op. cit.*, pp. 262–8.

22 *Poor Inquiry (Ireland)*. 1836 (35), xxx; 1836 (369) xxxii.

23 O'Rourke, *op. cit.*, pp. 172–6.

24 Mary E. Daly, *The Famine in Ireland*, (Dublin, 1986), p. 77.

25 Ó Gráda, 'Making History', p. 95. This article provides a fascinating account of the background to this book.

26 Ó Gráda 'Making History', pp. 87–91.

27 Edwards and Williams (eds), *op. cit.*, pp. ii, viii–ix.

28 K.H. Connell, *The Population of Ireland, 1750–1845*, (Oxford, 1950).

29 P. Lynch and J. Vaizey, *Guinness's Brewery in the Irish Economy, 1759–1856*, (Cambridge, 1960), chapter 1.

30 Cullen, 'Interpretation and Revision' pp. 7–11.

31 Connell, *op. cit.*, chapter III.

32 T.W. Freeman, *Pre-Famine Ireland. A Study in Historical Geography* (Manchester, 1957), pp. 3, 107–27.

33 Raymond Crotty, *Irish Agricultural Production. Its Volume and Structure* (Cork, 1966), p. 50.

34 L.M. Cullen, 'Irish History Without the Potato', *Past and Present*, 40 (July 1968).

35 L.M. Cullen, *The Emergence of Modern Ireland, 1600–1900* (London, 1981), pp. 140–71.

36 L.M. Cullen, *An Economic History of Ireland Since 1660* (London, 1972), pp. 131–2.

37 Peter Solar, 'Agricultural Productivity and Economic Development in Ireland and Scotland in the Early Nineteenth Century', in T.M. Devine and David Dickson (eds), *Ireland and Scotland, 1600–1850* (Edinburgh, 1983).

38 In particular Wrigley and Schofield's focus on the birth-rate as the key variable in English population growth. E.A. Wrigley and R.S. Schofield, *The Population History of England: A Reconstruction* (London, 1982).

39 John D. Post, *The Last Great Subsistence Crisis in the Western World* (Baltimore and London, 1977).

40 Joel Mokyr, 'Industrialization and Poverty in Ireland and the Netherlands: Some Notes Towards a Comparative Case-study', *Journal of Interdisciplinary History*, vol. X, 3 (winter 1980), pp. 429–59.

41 Amartya Sen, *Poverty and Famines, an Essay on Entitlements and Deprivation* (Oxford, 1981).

42 T.W. Freeman, 'Land and People, c. 1841', pp. 242–71; Cormac Ó Gráda, 'Poverty, Population and Agriculture'; 'Industry and Communications, 1801–45', pp. 108–57; in Vaughan (ed.), *op. cit.*

43 E.M. Crawford, 'Indian Meal and Pellagra in Nineteenth Century Ireland' in J.M. Goldstrom and L.A. Clarkson (eds), *Irish Population, Economy and Society: Essays in Honour of K.H. Connell* (Oxford, 1981), p. 126.

44 Joel Mokyr, 'Uncertainty and Pre-Famine Irish Agriculture', in Devine and Dickson, *op. cit.*; Austin Bourke, 'Towards the Precipice'; 'The Use of the Potato Crop in Pre-Famine Ireland'; 'The Visitation of God' in Jacqueline Hill and Cormac Ó Gráda (eds), *The Visitation of God* (Dublin, 1993).

45 James S. Donnelly, *The Land and the People of Nineteenth Century Cork* (London, 1975), pp. 52–72.

46 Trevelyan, *op. cit.*, p. 4.
47 Solar 'Agricultural Productivity and Economic Development in Ireland and Scotland in the Early Nineteenth Century', in Devine and Dickson, *op. cit.*, p. 81.
48 Freeman, *Pre-Famine Ireland*, p. 112.
49 Peter M. Solar, 'The Agricultural Trade Statistics in the Irish Railway Commissioners' Report' *Irish Economic and Social History* vi, (Dublin, 1979), p. 35.
50 Stuart Daultrey, David Dickson and Cormac Ó Gráda, 'Eighteenth-century Irish Population: New Perspectives from Old Sources' *Journal of Economic History*, xli, 3 (September 1981), pp. 601–28.
51 Joel Mokyr and Cormac Ó Gráda, 'New Directions in Irish Population History, 1700–1850', in *Economic History Review*, xxxvii, 4 (November 1984).
52 W.F. Adams, *Ireland and Irish Emigration to the New World from 1815 to the Famine* (New Haven, 1932).
53 Cormac Ó Gráda, 'Dublin's Demography in the Early Nineteenth Century: Evidence from the Rotunda', *Population Studies*, 45 (1991), p. 52 shows that the average age of first-parity mothers rose from 22.4 in 1811–12 to 23.3 in 1824 and 23.7 in 1840.
54 Timothy P. O'Neill, 'The State, Poverty and Distress in Ireland, 1815–45', Ph.D. thesis N.U.I. (U.C.D), 1971. Timothy P. O'Neill, 'Poverty in Ireland, 1815–45', *Folklife*, xi (1974) pp. 22–33.
55 Peter Solar, '"The Great Famine Was No Ordinary Subsistence Crisis"', in E.M. Crawford (ed.), *Famine: The Irish Experience, 900–1900* (Edinburgh, 1989), p. 123.
56 Austin Bourke, 'The Irish Grain Trade, 1839–48', *Irish Historical Studies*, xiii (1962), pp. 26–32.
57 Cormac Ó Gráda, *The Great Irish Famine* (Dublin, 1989), pp. 46–8.
58 Daly, *op. cit.* pp. 58–9.
59 Ó Gráda, *Ireland Before and After the Famine*, pp. 90–106.
60 See, *op. cit.*
61 For age and sex mortality, P.P. Boyle and C. Ó Gráda, 'Fertility Trends, Excess Mortality and the Great Irish Famine', *Demography* 23 (1986) pp. 542–62; J. Mokyr, 'The Deadly Fungus: An Econometric Investigation into the Short-Term Demographic Impact of the Irish Famine, 1846–51', *Research in Population Economics*, 2 (1980).
62 James S. Donnelly, Jr. 'Excess mortality and emigration', in Vaughan, *op. cit.*, p. 351.
63 E.M. Crawford, 'Subsistence Crises and Famines in Ireland: A Nutritionist's Views', in Crawford, *op. cit.*, pp. 198–200.
64 Kerby A. Miller, *Emigrants and Exiles: Ireland and Irish Exodus to North America* (New York, 1985); see ch. 10, below.
65 James S. Donnelly, *Cork*, pp. 227–8.
66 David Fitzpatrick, 'Emigration, 1801–70', in Vaughan, *op. cit.*, pp. 581–2.
67 Dale Knobel, *Paddy and the Republic. Ethnicity and Nationality in Antebellum America* (Middletown, CT, 1986).
68 Daly, *op. cit.*, p. 65.
69 Donnelly, 'The Administration of Relief, 1847–51' in Vaughan, *op. cit.*, p. 329.
70 Tom Devine, *The Great Highland Famine. Hunger, Emigration and the Scottish Highlands in the Nineteenth Century* (Edinburgh, 1988).
71 Daly, *op. cit.*, pp. 82–4.
72 Devine, *op. cit.*, p. 111.
73 Christine Kinealy, 'The Poor Law During the Great Famine: An Administration in Crisis' in Crawford, *op. cit.*, pp. 157–75.

74 Joan Vincent, 'A Political Orchestration of the Irish Famine: County Fermanagh 1847', in Marilyn Silverman and P.H. Gulliver (eds), *Approaching the Past: Historical Anthropology Through Irish Case Studies* (New York, 1992), pp. 75–98.

75 James Donnelly's chapters in the *New History of Ireland* provide one of the best accounts of the later Famine Years.

76 Kevin O'Rourke, 'Rural Depopulation in a Small Open Economy: Ireland 1856–76', *Explorations in Economic History*, xxvii, pp. 409–32.

77 Joel Mokyr, *Why Ireland Starved: A Quantitative and Analytical History of the Irish Economy, 1800–1850* (London, 1983), p. 64.

78 Kevin O'Rourke, 'Did the Great Irish Famine Matter?' *Journal of Economic History*, LI (1), pp. 1–22.

79 Cormac Ó Gráda, 'Irish Agricultural Output Before and After the Famine', *Journal of European Economic History* (Spring 1984), pp. 151–4.

80 Austin Bourke, 'The Average Yields of Food Crops in Ireland on the Eve of the Great Famine', in Hill and Ó Gráda, *op. cit.* pp. 114–24.

81 Cormac Ó Gráda, 'Malthus and the Pre-Famine Economy' in A. Murphy (ed.), *Economists and the Irish Economy, 1800–1850* (Dublin, 1984) pp. 77–80.

82 Joel Mokyr, *op. cit.*, p. 15.

83 Mokyr, *Why Ireland Starved*, ch. 10, pp. 278–94; quotations from p. 291.

84 Solar, in Crawford, *op. cit.*, pp. 127–9.

85 Bourke, '"The Visitation of God": The Role of the Potato in Ireland on the Eve of the Famine', p. 52.

86 McHugh, in Edwards and Williams, *op. cit.*, p. 395.

87 O'Rourke, *op. cit.*, pp. 29–30, 95.

88 Peter Gray, 'Potatoes and Providence', Paper read to Irish Famine Network, Dublin, November 1992.

89 Boyd Hilton, *The Age of Atonement. The Influence of Evangelicalism on Social and Economic Thought, 1785–1865*, (Oxford, 1988).

90 Peter Gray, 'Potatoes and Providence: The British Government's Response to Irish Famine' Ph.D. thesis, Cambridge (1992).

91 Jennifer Hart, 'Sir Charles Trevelyan at the Treasury', *English Historical Review* 75, (1960).

92 Hilton, *op. cit.*, p. 113.

93 Ó Gráda, *Ireland Before and After the Famine*, p. 113.

94 Hilton, *op. cit.*, p. 250.

95 Mary E. Daly, 'James Fintan Lalor', in Ciaran Brady (ed.), *Worsted in the Game: Losers in Irish History* (Dublin, 1989), pp. 110–20.

96 James S. Donnelly, Jr., 'A Famine in Irish Politics' and R.V. Comerford, 'Ireland 1850–70: Post Famine and Mid-Victorian' in Vaughan, *op. cit.*, pp. 371–385.

97 Cited in Ó Gráda, 'Making History', p. 101.

98 Cormac Ó Gráda review of Daly, *The Famine in Ireland in Irish Historical Studies* (99) May 1987, p. 333.

5

THE NATIONAL QUESTION, LAND, AND 'REVISIONISM'

Some reflections

Paul Bew

In an eloquent article, 'Nationalism and historical scholarship in modern Ireland', published in *Irish Historical Studies* in 1989, Dr Brendan Bradshaw launched an interesting and engaging assault on what has come to be known as 'revisionism' in Irish historiography.[1] For Bradshaw, the revisionists had rejected 'value-based interpretation in the name of value free history and had overlooked the intellectual processes by which the historical past is reconstructed and represented'.[2] Culpably, they lacked the imagination and sensitivity needed to appreciate the catastrophic nature of England's colonisation of Ireland. Even more culpably, they had 'normalised' the violence of colonial subjugation, treating 'the abnormality . . . in terms of a more normal historical process' and ignoring a 'central dimension of the Irish historical experience',[3] namely, the prolonged suffering of the Irish people. Like Professor Roy Foster before him, Bradshaw was concerned by what he saw as a 'credibility gap' opened up between academic history and the Irish reading public;[4] but unlike Foster, he drew a conclusion sharply unflattering to the community of Irish professional historians – obsessed with the pursuit of professional objectivity and insensitive to the burdens of Irish history, they had spurned 'the historian's role of mediation'. The revisionists had failed to see how 'the bitter reality recalled in song and story, continues to haunt the popular memory'.[5] The bulk of Bradshaw's specific references were based – and indeed, his own considerable expertise as a scholar – on the period before the nineteenth century; Bradshaw did, however, criticise recent revisionist work on the Famine of 1846 for its 'inhibited' and 'austerely clinical tone'.[6] It was guilty of 'cerebralising and desensitising the trauma'[7] of the Famine tragedy. Dr Bradshaw has also explicitly made a link between his critique of revisionism and his own admiration for the 'militant' Nationalist tradition[8] of Patrick Pearse and the Rising of 1916. But there is a problem here: laying aside the merits or demerits of particular works, does the fully empathetic account – which historians are understandably urged to produce – validate any particular political project, Unionist or Nationalist?

Let us open with two texts, both equally honest and equally lucid and both touching on the interpretation in the Irish Famine. They both concern the place of the Famine in the argument about Ireland's place within the United Kingdom: a subject which continues to exercise both the general public and specialist historians with some – to borrow the recent terminology of Professor L.P. Curtis – taking a rather condemnatory 'green'[9] and others taking a more 'white' view of the British government's responsibility for the crisis.

The first text is entitled 'Old Fenian Passes Away' and appears in the *Weekly Freeman* for 24 February 1912, at the beginning of the third Home Rule crisis. It records the death in Haslingden at the age of seventy-five of one Patrick Macintyre, an intimate and life-long friend of Michael Davitt, who like Davitt, was associated with all the Irish 'patriotic' organisations from the Fenian movement to the United Irish League. Patrick Macintyre did not die in poverty. Though he began his working life as an operative in a Lancashire cotton mill, Macintyre subsequently started a business as a furniture broker eventually building up a 'splendid business' in Haslingden. Yet *embourgeoisement* did not lead to any slackening in commitment to Nationalist and Catholic causes. Why? We are left in no doubt as to the core historical experience of this successful emigrant:

> He had a wonderful memory and could recall many remarkable incidents of the Irish famine, and the fact that he and his father walked all the way from Ballina to Dublin, over 160 miles, before setting sail for England, and that after reaching Liverpool they walked all the way to Haslingden, his father having only 6s.6d in his pocket when he reached that town. They spent the first night in a cellar along with 28 other emigrants.[10]

Inevitably, then it appears, Patrick Macintyre became one of those Lancashire Fenians – with broad northern English accents – who so impressed Irish American revolutionary leader, John Devoy, when it came to the organisation of the New Departure and Land League movement in 1878–9.[11] One of Patrick Macintyre's last public actions was to place a tablet in St Mary's Catholic Church in Haslingden – a church whose existence owed much to his efforts – to the memory of Michael Davitt: Davitt who, as David Krause has recently pointed out, was the first to use the term 'holocaust'[12] (with its clear implication of British governmental intent at some level) about the Famine. From all this, it is a simple matter to read off the subsequent history. As Ann Kane has recently reminded us, the invocation of the memory of the Famine played a major role in Land League rhetoric in Mayo at the start of the Land War of 1879.[13]

The second text has a rather different provenance. It appears in an article 'Modern Ireland' which appears in the first issue (vol. 1, no. 1) of a serious liberal journal *Ulster Magazine* published in Belfast in 1860. The *ethos* of the *Ulster Magazine* is clear enough: it aimed to appeal to 'liberal-minded men of all parties' in Ireland but did not expect support from 'extreme Tories' or the 'ultras of the opposite side of the question'.[14] It revels in the social progress made in Ireland in the late 1850s which had helped all classes, religions, and regions. 'Thus while England has one pauper for every twenty-five of her population, and Scotland one for every twenty-four of her people, Ireland, so often in recent days stigmatised as the hot-bed of poverty has only one pauper for every one hundred and forty of her population.'[15] As a result, in a graphic phrase, the journal concludes, 'Tipperary emulates Down in its peaceable habits and determined industry'.[16] Such beneficial signs contrasted profoundly with the firm recollection of the Famine: by the end of October 1846, 'so rapidly did the vegetable plague spread itself [that] four-fifths of the entire produce had been totally destroyed. Nothing could exceed the destruction and dismay of Ireland's poor when the dark cloud of that sad calamity fell around their miserable abodes'.[17] There is no lack of sympathy here; no lack of admiration for the achievements of the famine exiles in America:

in the most secluded of the inland states the language of the ancient Celt is at this day to be heard in all the glory of the rich brogue which never fails to ring like the tones of the harp on the ear of the Connaughtman. America is now the richest quarter of the globe in its annual yield of industrial products; and how much of these fruits of toil is produced by the labour of the millions of American immigrants, who are either the direct or remote descendants of the Isle of the West? The poor half-clad and half-famished who fled from the scenes of desolation in 1847, soon made some way in the new scenes of toil; and when they had succeeded in realising a little money, the first act of their prosperity was to send home means to bring out to them the dear relations they had left behind. During that first five years which succeeded that of the Famine, upwards of five millions was remitted from different parts of the world – chiefly America – by the poor Irish, in aid of their poorer friends at home; and since that date, the sum of money forwarded would reach nine millions! What a world of kindly feeling and benevolence is to be found in this remarkable trait of the character of our self-exiled countrymen.[18]

While many would question the phrase 'self-exiled', the warmth of these comments is undeniable – they are quite free from any narrow taint of 'little Ulsterism' but are based on a broad Irish sympathy. The same writer celebrated what was presented (not uncontroversially) as a non-sectarian response to the crisis: 'in the desire to mitigate the effects of the calamity, creeds and crochets were soon forgotten'. Lord Lurgan and the Rector of Schull were called as among the many 'hundreds of Samaritans'[19] who gave their own lives alongside Catholic priests to the Famine pestilence. The conclusions remained sombre:

> The events of the spring of 1847 have yet to be written, and it is questionable whether any historian will ever be able to give in their dread realities, the actual results of fever and famine during that period. About the end of March, there were three quarters of a million of labourers engaged at the different operations under the Board of Works – making with their wives, children and other dependants on their labours, a total of about two and a half million individuals dependent on state alms. Then came the pestilence – and for several months, tens of thousands were swept into eternity under circumstances so appalling as to leave far in the shade the more heart-rending histories of suffering in the Crimea. During the period intervening between the summer of 1846 and that of 1850, upwards of two million of the Irish people had either died of famine and disease, or emigrated to other lands.[20]

But all this heart-felt sympathy provokes one obvious question: what were the political implications of the Famine? Here the *Ulster Magazine* is in no doubt: 'The British government did all that was possible under the circumstances'.[21] The problem was apparently one of information; or rather the lack of it:

> At the seat of Government, all was confusion; Somerset House officials gazed at each other in mute despair of even comprehending a tithe of the tales told of Irish famine; and, in the celebrated halls of Downing Street, routine sat with hands folded, unable to get beyond the barricades of red tape and sealing wax. With every disposition to aid to the uttermost of dearth-stricken millions of the wretched isle, John Bull found himself quite unequal to the task – not because of want of means or lack of will, but in reality in consequence of the total ignorance of his people on all subjects connected with Ireland . . . the English officials from Sir C. Trevelyan, down to the lowest clerk, were as fairly bewildered in the wilds of Connaught as if they had fallen among the aborigines of Timbucktoo. Totally ignorant of the habits of the people and quite incapable of forming a correct estimate of their wants, they were left completely at the mercy of a class of greedy landlords and others, who cared little for future interest, and were only anxious for present benefit . . . but still a noble few of the landlords held faith by the social faith of their fathers, and, in the greatness of true nobility, fought side by side with their overburdened tenants.[22]

This is a version of events which is not complimentary to a British government – 'routine sat with hands folded' – apparently unaware of important realities about 'a part of its own state'. Nor is it complimentary to Irish landlords – only a 'noble few' are presented as doing their duty in the crisis. Yet the *Ulster Magazine* drew no Nationalist message from its own analysis; rather it prepared to say from the vantage point of 1860: 'after centuries of strife and struggling peace and, at least, comparative prosperity dawn on the face of Ireland'.[23] Commenting savagely on the Young Ireland movement of 1848, it added:

> Would that some of the more boisterous of that school of patriot who so eloquently denounced the Saxon and so shamefully forgot the Celt, had lived to see the wonders which have been performed in every district of Ireland. Not one of that band of self-elected leaders . . . ever made the least effort to raise their countrymen's thoughts from imaginary causes of discontent to the necessity of industrial exertion, frothy declamation and vapid political economy formed the staple for their rhetoric, and, beyond those boundaries, no Young Irelander ever attempted to pass.[24]

The lesson then of the *Ulster Magazine* text is rather different from that of the *Weekly Freeman*; there is no automatic move from an analysis of the Famine, which is most certainly not an exercise in 'cerebralising and desensitising' the 'trauma' of the event to a nationalist politics. However understandable and unproblematical Patrick Macintyre's transition from Famine emigrant to Lancashire Fenian might appear to be, and indeed actually was, there exists, as the *Ulster Magazine* text shows, another possible political interpretation of the lessons of the mid-nineteenth century – an interpretation which owes nothing to heartlessness or indifference in the face of a national calamity.

In the last two decades, the historiography of the Irish land war has changed markedly. The landlords are now the subject of a treatment which is considerably less unsympathetic.[25] The role of Fenian or neo-Fenian calculation in the strategy of the Land League has received a renewed emphasis.[26] Finally, the notion of the essential unity of the challenging collectivity of the peasantry has been contested by the majority of writers.[27] As Dr Cormac O Grada has aptly summarised: 'Few historians now believe that Irish landlords were typically the predatory and vindictive ogres of nineteenth-century farmer propaganda (though some were) or that the Land War of the 1880s was the inevitable outcome of landlords' injustice'.[28] But mid-Victorian Irish landlords were not frequent evictors or rank rankers; they were often dangerously close to being pure rentiers. In this respect Frederick Engels was correct when he placed Irish landlords in the 'superfluous' category in his much criticised 1881 pamphlet 'Social Classes – Necessary and Superfluous'. The economic peripherality of Irish landlordism justifies the point. The effect of such research – while in no sense denying the existence of a genuine realm of tenant grievance – has been to place a renewed emphasis on the political conditions of the Land War. As Professor Don Jordan has recently demonstrated with great clarity, the Fenians were key figures in the early genesis of the land struggle in Mayo in 1879.[29]

Over five decades later, the nature of Fenian involvement in the Land League was recalled by an activist in 'Land League Days' published in *An Phoblacht* on 5 April 1930.[30] Commenting on the last Land League meeting at Irishtown in April 1879, this article noted: 'Of the men who took the platform that day 90% were sworn Republicans – among them a member of the Supreme Council of the IRB'. The same writer outlined the basis of the Fenian Land League compact – at a secret Claremorris conference in March 1879 the Fenians agreed to support the Land League as individuals but not as an organisation. In exchange, they received the naming of official organisers for the county and province. 'The pact was faithfully kept on both sides.' As a result, the IRB, under 'cover of Land League meetings', recruited the 'full strength of the farmers' sons and labourers in general'. It is also the case that these meetings were characterised by much rhetoric hostile to the claims not only of the British government and landlords but also of Irish strong farmers or graziers.[31]

In the summer of 1880, in an effort to make the land agitation truly national in scope, the Land League's central executive – not without certain misgivings – sought to draw the large eastern and southern graziers into the Land League. In particular, the new League policy of 'rent at the point of the bayonet' whereby the Land League subsidised a policy of delay in payment (rather than outright refusal) reflected the interests of the rural bourgeoisie. Land League neo-Fenian radicals like Matthew Harris fretted over the accession of the large farmers but ultimately accepted it – only to renege on it later when the consequences became apparent.[32] Others like Anna Parnell saw the form of struggle embodied in 'rent at the point of bayonet' as a 'great sham'.[33] In a typical comment, P.J. Lynam wrote from Queen's County at the 'request of many prominent members of the land league':

> they are of (the opinion) that there is a useless expenditure in paying all the costs at sheriff's sales, as it is a pity to have the money subscribed by the friends in America getting into the clutches of bailiffs and sheriffs, and going towards the support of all the paraphernalia of landlord rascality, and, moreover, there are some I know well who are imposing themselves on the country as cheap martyrs.[34]

It is clear that many tenants in 1880–81 faced a choice between the 3 Fs as these were to be enshrined in the Land Act of 1881, and some form of land purchase – voluntary or compulsory – whereby the state would help tenants buy their holdings from landlords.[35] Effectively, the 3 Fs emerged in the short term, as the outcome of the land agitation – in part, because it was the Liberal government's response but also, in part at least, because peasant proprietorship was sponsored by revolutionary men. Fenians were anxious not simply for national independence but also to re-settle the poorest tenants of Mayo and adjacent counties on new farms carved out of rich pasturage. The play of these conflicting forces helps to explain the peculiar nature of Parnell's political dominance in the 1880s.

In his neglected memoirs *Old Ireland: Reminiscences of an Irish KC*, Sergeant A.M. Sullivan gives us a powerful insight into Parnell's place within the configuration of Irish political forces at this moment. Sullivan stresses Parnell's displays of disdain for even his most prominent colleagues: at a very important central Land League meeting, for example, 'while Tim Harrington was speaking, Parnell left the chair and amused himself tossing scraps of biscuits to Grouse',[36] his beautiful red setter. Yet the fact remained that 'the threat to his power levelled by the continuation of Fenianism and the Land League, compelled him to assume the role of land agitator and compelled him to associate with him of a social and intellectual order that he must have disliked'.[37] This compulsion at the key point in early May 1882 may have even operated to make Parnell take the IRB oath provided that this action remained a secret.[38] Yet despite these pressures, in the final analysis Parnell survived the turbulence of the land war and helped to ensure a reformist rather than revolutionary outcome of the crisis and this, in Sullivan's inelegant but revealing phrase, 'by a dispensation hard to understand Parnell became the hero of the bourgeoisie'.[39]

The difficulties posed by the land question – the source of both vitality and division within popular Nationalism – did not diminish for Parnell's successor, John Redmond. At least in 1881 the Land League had a unifying object of hostility: the 'alien' landlords. In the period of the United Irish League (1898–1918) divisions within the tenantry became much more visible: after the massive land purchase reform embodied in the Wyndham Act of 1903, the likelihood of a *united* movement of the Irish farmers receded even further. The continuation of agrarian militancy after 1903 generated considerable disunity within the Nationalist bloc; Catholic Nationalist was set against Catholic Nationalist – it was not simply or even, in many places, mainly the now increasingly marginalised landlord stratum who felt the heat. Yet officially, at least – and despite Redmond's certain reluctance – the Irish party remained committed to a left of centre agrarian radicalism.

Yet as more and more of its cadre became themselves the dominant social forces in the countryside, the party was thus condemned to live by an increasingly visible 'double standard' on agrarian matters. Let us take the vexed question of cattle 'ranching', condemned in Nationalist social theory because it increased dependence on the English market and aided the process of rural depopulation. Yet the embarrassing fact remains that a remarkably high proportion of the principal Irish party leaders of the 'ranch war' of 1906–10 were or became graziers or were intimately related to graziers – John Hayden MP, John Fitzgibbon MP and Patrick McKenna all belong in this category. Others were guilty of attempting to call off the struggle against the graziers when it affected the interests of friends, associates or even potential supporters in internal Nationalist political disputes – W.J. Duffy MP, 'Farmer' Hogan MP and David Sheehy MP fell into this category.[40] By 1917 the Irish party found that the land issue – so long a source of votes and excitement – no longer worked for it in any simple way; a development which in no small way assisted the rise of Sinn Féin.

In his powerful anti-revisionist article, Dr Bradshaw invites professional scholars to display more empathy for the trauma suffered both by the Nationalist and Unionist people of Ireland. Yet the history of the process which sets the contours of modern Ireland – the country's massive agrarian revolution – invites a different subversive reflection. It seems rather to validate a research project infused by a probing (even sceptical) attitude; demands for greater empathy with either the Nationalist (or Unionist) past are often demands to ignore not only experiences shaped by class, sexual or regional experience but even considerations of objective reality or political choice.

The popular Nationalist reading of the Famine – and Ireland's post-Famine transition – was a powerful one based on the reality of a sharp fall in population. It argued that Britain had an interest in Irish population decline; mass emigration helped to turn the country into a ranch designed to feed cheaply British industrial cities – from the IRB, founded in 1858, until the Whitaker Report 1958 shattered Fianna Fáil's orthodoxy, the answer was believed to be Irish self-government, radical land redistribution supplemented by a policy of protection. This was Irish Nationalist political economy, the final flowering of which in the mid-1950s was to see vastly higher rates of emigration than those which characterised the last quarter century of British rule. The depth of the tragedy of the Famine contained within it no guarantee that a Nationalist political economy could restore Irish population levels – a fact which Michael Davitt began to grapple with (at the expense of some personal discomfort and confusion) towards the end of his life.[41] Indeed, the rural bourgeoisie of Nationalists – and indeed, large sections of the middling farmers – became the natural beneficiaries of a post-Famine transition to pasture which, in theory, official Nationalism resisted.

The attempt to restore the veil of Nationalist propriety to this period – in the name of a common trauma suffered by all equally, when clearly all did not suffer it equally – is to remove the possibility of a serious dis-cussion of the mainstream social programme of Irish Nationalism despite the huge implications that programme has had for the majority of Irish people. The Whitaker Report's demolition of this programme in 1958 reflected its profound failure – a government led by one of the 1916 Easter insurgents, Eamon de Valera, presided over its complete and visible failure; a 'vapid' political economy indeed. The phenomenon of 'revision-ism' is integrally related to the collapse of 'Sinn Féin' orthodoxy in this period; perhaps those who forget this are too condemned to 'eloquently denounce' the Saxon while 'shamefully forgetting' the Celt.

The disillusionment of the 1960s has a material base: the comprehen-sive failure of the 'Sinn Féin' approach to the problem of Irish development. Thus in 1966 after forty years of independence, the population of the Republic at 2.88 million was less than it had been in 1926 (2.97 million) whilst that of the part of Ireland 'still unfree' was larger (1.25 million in 1926; 1.48 million in 1966). The fortunes of the Republic have vastly improved since then but, to a considerable degree, this is a product of the Lemass revolution in Irish economic and social policy; a revolution which explicitly effected a veritable *bouleversement* of the principal elements of the social programme of the national revolution. It is not at all clear how a 'public' national version of Ireland's history can illuminate this phenomenon. It is rather an invitation to be silent about some of the most important and revealing aspects of the Irish past.

NOTES

1 *Irish Historical Studies*, vol. XXVI (1 and 4) November 1989, pp. 329–51.
2 *ibid*.
3 *ibid*.
4 But see Roy Foster's recent comments on this in his interview, 'Our Man in Oxford', *History Ireland*, vol. I (3) autumn 1993, pp. 11–12. For Professor Foster's refined view on this point, see *Paddy and Mr Punch* (London, 1993).
5 Bradshaw, *op. cit.*, p. 340.
6 Bradshaw, *op. cit.*, p. 338.
7 Bradshaw, *op. cit.*, p. 341.
8 See Dr Bradshaw's *History Ireland* interview, 'A Man with a Mission', vol. 1 (1) p. 52.
9 'The Greening of Irish History', *Eire-Ireland*, vol. XXIX (2) summer 1994, pp. 7–28.
10 *Weekly Freeman*, 24 February 1912.
11 John Devoy, 'Michael Davitt's Career', *Gaelic American*, 22 September 1906.
12 David Krause, 'The Conscience of Ireland, Lalor, Davitt and Sheehy-Skeffington', *Eire-Ireland*, vol. XXVIII (1) spring 1993, p. 13.
13 In chapter 4 of her UCLA Ph.D. 'Culture and Social Change: The Formulation of Ideology in the Irish Land War', pp. 879–81, Ann Kane quotes James Daly, 'Were they to wait as they did in '46 and '47 until they allowed themselves to be evicted from their homesteads and left no alternative but to take the

ocean-hearse, or seek the shelter of those places of despair, the workhouses (cries of no, no). The forefathers of these lords of the soil took it by force, but we want to treat them better now than they treated our forefathers; we are willing to compensate them.

A Voice: Three cheers for tenant-right.

We want more than tenant right. As long as you have landlords you will have rack-rents. We want to have no owners between the Lord of the soil and the State, *Connaught Telegraph*, 10 April 1879.

14 *Ulster Magazine and Monthly Review of Science and Literature*, 1860, p. 1.
15 'Modern Ireland', *Ulster Magazine*, vol. 1 (1) 1860, p. 43.
16 *ibid.*
17 *ibid.*, p. 43.
18 *ibid.*
19 *ibid.*, p. 41.
20 *ibid.*, p. 42.
21 *ibid.*, p. 39.
22 *ibid.*
23 *ibid.*
24 *ibid.*, p. 44.
25 Most recently, see the impressive work of W.E. Vaughan, *Landlords and Tenants in Mid-Victorian Ireland* (Oxford 1994).
26 Paul Bew, 'The Nature of Irish Political Biography', in James Noonan (ed.), *Biography and Autobiography: Essays on Irish and Canadian History and Literature*, Ottawa 1993, ch. 2, pp. 19–26.
27 Professor A.C. Hepburn makes this point in *Irish Economic and Social History*. A review of C.H. Philpin (ed.), *Nationalism and Popular Protest in Ireland*, vol. XVII, 1990, pp. 122–5.
28 C. Ó Gháda, 'Too Slow to Evict', *Times Literary Supplement*, 22 July 1994.
29 Donald Jordan, *Land and Popular Politics in Ireland: Co Mayo from the Plantation to the Land War*, Cambridge 1984, pp. 227.
30 The author was almost certainly T.J. Quinn. For Quinn on this see Patrick Maume's forthcoming article in *Irish Historical Studies*, May 1995.
31 Jordan, *op. cit.*, p. 7.
32 Bew, *Land and the National Question in Ireland 1858–82*, Dublin 1978, pp. 134–6.
33 Anna Parnell, *The Tale of a Great Sham*, ed. by Dana Hearne (Dublin, 1986).
34 J.W.H. Carter, *The Land War and Its Leaders in Queen's County 1879–1882* (Portlaoise, 1994), p. 179.
35 Bew, *Land and the National Question*, pp. 145–213.
36 *Old Ireland* (London, 1927), p. 47.
37 *ibid.*
38 See Quinn's other article, 'Memories of Kilmainham', *An Phoblacht*, 8 March 1930. This is the subject of Maume's important *Irish Historical Studies* essay.
39 *Old Ireland*, p. 47. Jordan, *Land and Popular Politics*, p. 228, writes that Parnell believed in land reform as a route to Irish social unity as a precondition of self-government – 'in contrast the Fenian plan would pit class against class and could result in an Irish state that was unacceptable to many in Ireland'.
40 Paul Bew *Conflict and Conciliation in Ireland, 1890–1910* (Oxford, 1987), p. 287.
41 *ibid.*, pp. 126–8.

6

IRISH NATIONALISM

John Hutchinson

I

Explaining nationalism has not been easy for scholars, and indeed, the distinguished historian E.J. Hobsbawm has argued that very little of value has been written on the subject until recently.[1] The central problem is that the discipline of history has formed since the emergence of nationalism and the modern nation state and is redolent with their assumptions. In many countries the founders of the historical profession have been leaders of the national revival, concerned to forge on authoritative foundations the claims of their community to an independent and distinctive culture and politics against the sometimes wounding quips of foreign detractors. The histories they constructed have provided the mythic legitimations of the drive for a nation state and (after independence) of the domestic and international policies of these polities.

In Ireland the 'father' of modern Irish historiography, Eoin MacNeill, Professor of History at UCD and founder of the Irish Manuscripts Commission in 1929, had been the Vice President of the Gaelic League, President of the Irish Volunteers and the first Minister of Education in the newly independent Irish state. His sophisticated and pioneering work on Ireland's medieval Gaelic past, when vulgarised by non-academic historians such as Alice Green and conveyed in school textbooks, reinforced the mythologies of popular tradition that presented Ireland as an independent national and democratic civilisation that had fought for independence for over six hundred years against the English invaders.[2] Teachers in the new state were instructed to stress the continuity of the separatist idea from Tone to Pearse and to imbue their pupils with the national idealism of Thomas Davis and Patrick Pearse.[3] Such nationalist teleologies were invoked powerfully to define the character of the Irish state under Eamon de Valera as Gaelic and Catholic, based on the land, and with unfinished irredendist claims over the North. Most subsequent Irish politicians have found it sensible to re-invoke these mythologies.[4]

This chapter will examine the gradual transformations within Irish historiography since the late 1960s in the interpretation of Irish nationalism. These represent a shift from perspectives that, although shaped by the canons of 'scientific history', regarded the Irish nation and nationalism as given and therefore available to 'objective' description, to those influenced by developments in social history which problematised the nation as the master concept of Irish history and emphasised its multiple meanings and derivations. As in other countries a radical questioning of the nationalist paradigm was precipitated by political factors. Whereas in contemporary Germany the issue of the German state's responsibility for both the First and Second World Wars addressed by the historian Fritz Fischer was the catalyst of a revolution in national historiography;[5] in the Irish Republic it was the revival of the inter-communal violence in Northern Ireland shortly after the fiftieth commemoration of the Easter Rebellion and a growing disillusion with the performance of the existing state that has inspired alternative approaches.

I shall argue that despite advances in research revisionists largely fail to explain Irish nationalism, and this is due in part to their political agenda. For revisionism itself, despite an apparently anti-nationalist agenda, is vitiated by the fact that it operates within national assumptions about the organisation of knowledge and research. Whether they are aware of it or not, most Irish historians are methodological nationalists since they tend to take for granted the nation as the proper unit of analysis. Revisionism as a tendency can be seen in various ways as an attempt to broaden the definition of the nation, to qualify its pervasive appeal by reference to other factors or to liberalise the practices of the nation-state. But nationalism is a global phenomenon and cannot be explained in any one country by local peculiarities. It follows that Irish nationalism can only be properly understood within an international perspective. The chapter points to the necessity to employ social scientific models and comparative historical frameworks in order to contextualise and explain the rise of nationalism in Ireland and examines some approaches that do so.

II

When the modern historical profession in Ireland might be said to have formed in the late 1930s it was in conscious reaction against the excesses of nationalist history, then politically embodied in de Valera's constitution that declared Ireland as Gaelic, Catholic and indivisible. Irish history was to become a scientific profession imbued with the norms of international scholarship. The three men responsible, R.D. Edwards, T.W. Moody and D.B. Quinn, were individuals of different religious backgrounds who after a common experience of training in England at the Institute of Historical Research returned to take up positions at Irish

101

colleges (University College Dublin, Trinity College Dublin and Queen's respectively), where they rapidly dominated teaching and research, established the journal *Irish Historical Studies* and academic forums such as the Ulster Society for Irish Historical Studies and the Irish Historical Society.[6] There was an explicit policy to avoid the contemporary period as too enmeshed with partisan political interests and passions.

Through this nexus, as R.F. Foster has observed, a school of Irish history at the research level evolved, transcending the political, religious and cultural divides of the two Irelands, which has attempted to recuperate the past from the fantasy of folk mythologies. The preferred mode of writing was the historical monograph based on thorough archival research, careful contextualisation, critical questionings, and rigorous documentation of sources which replaced a hagiographical focus on national heroes and repudiated the teleologies of national development.[7]

The earliest studies of nationalism were in the field of politics, examining in biographical studies both the role of individuals and the analysis of political organisations. The work of scholars such as F.S.L. Lyons, C.C. O'Brien and D.A. Thornley disrupted the republican conception of an apostolic succession of revolutionary leaders from Tone to Pearse by establishing the historic importance of the Irish Parliamentary Party as the vehicle of national aspirations in the late nineteenth century and the essentially constitutional character of the politics of Parnell whom Republicans had sought to appropriate.[8] Nevertheless, given the tendency of biographers to find coherence and virtue in the lives of their subjects, writing history through the genre of biography even in the hands of such skilled practitioners as Lyons could reinforce the nationalist interpretation of the Irish past as a story of an emerging national consciousness embodied and made coherent by the heroic will of its great men.

On the whole, academic studies such as those by T.W. Moody on Davitt and by Oliver MacDonagh on O'Connell have avoided this by identifying the different aspects of their personalities and by a careful contextualisation that discusses the impact of the subject in relation to political organisation, but they could be criticised as implying an individualistic concept of political change.[9] Other works from a younger generation implicitly or explicitly undermine this model by revealing the contingent and sometimes fleeting 'successes' of their subjects, and the ambivalence of their motives. Notable in this category is Ruth Dudley Edwards' life of Pearse (subtitled 'The Triumph of Failure'), whom she depicts as channelled into the pursuit of martyrdom by personal and professional inadequacy and Tom Dunne's study of Wolfe Tone who is presented as a frustrated social climber.[10]

This increasingly critical stance to the nationalist 'heroes' is part of a broader critique emerging since the 1960s of the nation as a concept for understanding the development of Irish history. This trend can be seen as part of a more general international rejection of political history as legitimating the hegemony of official elites in favour of a history of society presented as a plurality of competing groups. Although Marxists such as E.P. Thompson were major influences, this history from below was aimed at disrupting the winner's histories and giving minorities a voice.[11] In the hands of E.J. Hobsbawm writing in the late early 1980s the nation was presented as an invented tradition created from above by official elites in the nineteenth century who projected back the assumptions of primordialness, unity and continuity.[12]

This international movement in Anglo-American historical scholarship resonated with a disillusionment with the legacy of nationalism emerging in the late 1960s as a result of the resurgence of sectarian violence in Northern Ireland and the sense of failure of the Irish Republic as a state, marked by economic decline and puritanical restrictions on civil liberties, to realise the dreams of independence. It would be too much to dub their project 'Irish History Without the Nation', but in reaction against the nightmare of popular history, Irish historians have come to call into question almost all the verities of the nationalist perspective: the idea of a pre-conquest Irish nation, the conception of Ireland as a victim eternally set against a ruthless and manipulative British oppressor, and in the modern period the idea that the nationalist tradition is continuous, nonsectarian, popular, necessarily primary, and all-Ireland.

One of the targets of the revisionist historians is what they regard as the anachronistic retrojection of modern nationalism into the Gaelic past. Steven Ellis has taken to task historians who by their framework and terminology assume the medieval Gaelic Ireland to be an autonomous actor and to interpret the Gaelic-English interaction in terms of the modern period.[13] Hence Ellis and others stress that the Gaelic society in Ireland was interconnected with the Scottish Highlands and had no concept of a unitary state until the English invasion. He argues that to describe occasional acculturation of the English in Ireland as Gaelicisation and to designate the English of Ireland as Anglo-Irish and Irish parliamentary assertiveness in the fifteenth century as a home rule movement are seriously misleading. In these accounts Gaelic Ireland looks separate because it has been treated as a separate island by historians without reference to links and developments in Britain when it would be more proper to treat it as a borderland similar in its experience and treatment to its other territories like Wales and North England.

At same time the demonological model of Irish–British relations in the modern period which differentiated the virtuous Irish from the malign British has been rejected in favour of an interactive approach that allows for the possession of dual identities and for the fact that nationalism found its leadership among the upwardly aspiring, not the immiserated. Examples include Alan O'Day's study which, examining the members of the Irish parliamentary party, demonstrates how many had arrived at Irish political nationalism through participation in British radical causes.[14] This internalisation of the social norms of Victorian respectability was not confined to constitutional nationalists as R.V. Comerford's work on the Fenians makes clear.[15] Charles Townshend has commented that Irish nationalism was very much a product of the British-led state intervention which contributed to the modernisation of Irish society in the nineteenth century.[16]

A third feature of revisionism is a repudiation of any simple apostolic tradition of nationalism. This comes in several varieties. Boyce has highlighted the discontinuities between periods of nationalism by disentangling the very different concepts of Irish nation employed by such leaders as Grattan, Tone and O'Connell.[17] Garvin has analysed the ambiguous relations, sometimes complementary, sometimes oppositional between the physical force and constitutional advocates during the nineteenth century.[18] In discussing the gradual elaboration of an Irish cultural identity, Lyons has resisted a 'winners' history by presenting it as developing in the course of a tragic conflict that, squeezing out a cosmopolitan Anglo-Irish conception, resulted in the polarisation between increasingly narrow Gaelic Catholic and Ulster Protestant loyalties.[19]

Although reproducing Eoin MacNeill's dichotomisation of Ireland as a religious community confronted by a secular political English culture, Patrick O'Farrell's powerful and original *Ireland's English Question* subverts the secular republican interpretation by emphasising the role of religion in defining the modern Irish identity (and by implication the depth of the divisions between Ulster Protestants and rest of Ireland).[20] Irish nationalism is presented as a modern expression of profound religious mentalities that shaped Catholic Irish apprehension of the world and gave Irish nationalism a utopian quality that demanded violent retribution for its martyrdoms. O'Farrell brilliantly brings out the different tenets of secular nationalism and the Catholic religion and the essential tensions between them. Although he shows how the two could be harnessed by charismatic leaders such as O'Connell or Parnell, who could tap the messianic dreams of the peasantry, he demonstrates how the split between Church and the Home Rule Party was an inherent possibility. On its own, he argues, a secular political nationalism lacked roots in Irish society, and he was the first to identify the rise of strong neo-traditionalist religious sentiments that channelled nationalism and shaped the definition of modern independent Ireland.

Since the 1970s a considerable body of scholarship has problematised the relationship between nationalism and class identities, destroying in the process the idea of modern nationalism as the expression of a pre-existing people 'awakened' to consciousness by patriotic leaders to recover the national estate from an alien conqueror. Instead the nation is seen as constructed out of diverse and often contradictory interests and attention has been paid to the questions of which groups were crucial at the organisational level in both the centre and localities, and the extent to which nationalism was adopted to promote class interests and functioned to contain class conflicts. Recent work by Garvin has centred on the way in which an emerging Catholic (lower) middle class of professionals and white collar workers in the early twentieth century used the Gaelic revival to legitimate their drive to power, forming the new governing classes in independent Ireland.[21]

Much of the focus, however, has been on the relationship between the land question and national movements. Historians such as Joseph Lee and Tom Garvin disagree over the extent to which early nineteenth-century agrarian secret societies such as Ribbonism should be regarded as motivated by local peasant grievances or by a populist nationalism against an alien socio–political order.[22] Similar arguments continue about the characterisation of the land war, regarded as decisive for the collective mobilisation of Irish farmers, and whether, as Samuel Clark suggests urban strata such as shopkeepers and publicans, or as David Fitzpatrick argues, farmers formed the local leadership.[23] But the effects of these debates are to open up the topic of when the mass nation formed rather than to presume its existence and to reveal the nation as one (and not necessarily the most potent) among many potential sites of individual and collective loyalty.

This process of deconstructing the nation has been carried further in the work of Hoppen, which focuses on the period 1850–70.[24] These years, usually dismissed as an interlude in organised nationalist movements, he argues, in fact, reveal the underlying forces in Irish society: the politics of locality and kinship on which the national politics of O'Connell and Parnell were only an unusual superimposition. This scepticism about the directive power of nationalist ideology accords well with that of Fitzpatrick's notable examination of County Clare, revealing that although there was a dramatic shift of power at the centre in this period, there was remarkable continuity at the provincial level with local factions struggling for control and Sinn Féin largely stepping into the shoes of the older nationalist organisations.[25] The geographical basis of nationalism is an important one given, as Erhard Rumpf, A.C. Hepburn and Fitzpatrick have shown, there were marked regional variations in the distribution of nationalist violence and voting between 1916 and 1921, with the commercialised Munster the centre of violence and the impoverished Connaught most electorally committed to Republican nationalism.[26] In stressing the importance of looking for local reasons to explain why individuals joined nationalist organisations, Fitzpatrick proposes (amongst others) what would be perhaps the most insulting explanation to the romantic nationalist: the role of such institutions in keeping the monotony of country life at bay! Vincent Comerford drew similar conclusions from his research on the Fenian movement.[27]

Finally, historians have come to demolish the 'achievements' of the post-independence state. Clare O'Halloran has argued that one of the major declared objectives of this state – Irish unification – was little more than hollow rhetoric. Lee has fired another such fusillade, pointing to the state's failures in economic policy (producing, he claims, the weakest growth in western Europe), its repression of civil liberties, its inability to stem emigration, its reinforcement of Unionist fears and hence of partition.[28]

III

It should be clear from this brief and far from exhaustive survey of recent approaches that they have brought a new sophistication to the analysis of Irish nationalism, not only in the range and variety of records consulted but in the application of research methods: from the use of statistics by Fitzpatrick, Garvin, and Rumpf to the iconographic analysis of cultural artefacts by Peter Alter and Jeanne Sheehy and the application of social scientific models adapted from Charles Tilly and others.[29]

But revisionist historians have been the subject in recent years of a broad ranging critique by Brendan Bradshaw in *Irish Historical Studies*, 'house journal' of the Irish historical profession, for fundamentally distorting the understanding of the Irish past and failing in their duty as historians to sustain the capacity of the Irish people to build a better future.[30] This critique and the ripostes it excited disclose important limitations in the conceptualisation and interpretation of nationalism within Irish historiography, as well as the attitudes within the historical profession about the responsibilities of academic historians to the nation state.

Bradshaw's polemic was initially inspired by an article in the same journal from Steven Ellis who rejected as Whiggish the tendencies of some medieval historians (including Bradshaw himself) to treat Gaelic Ireland as an emergent nation.[31] But his target is much broader than this: the capture of the modern historical profession since the 1930s by the paradigm of scientific history which imbues its practitioners with an ethos of value neutrality to the past, a commitment to empirical enquiry and a critical stance to all received tradition. The effects of this, he argues, are to distance the academic historian from the general public and to fail to recognise the necessary role of historical tradition (in this case national myths) as a way of making sense of the present and giving hope for the future.

The authors of this lamentable situation are R.D. Edwards, T.W. Moody, D.B. Quinn and Desmond Williams who dominated Irish history through their chairs at Trinity College Dublin, University College Dublin and Queen's. Although of different religious backgrounds, they shared a common commitment to the liberating power of a rational history to dissolve the popular myths that encouraged misunderstanding between the different communities of Ireland. Bradshaw pays tribute to the scholarly achievements of these men and their pupils but complains that their very commitment to a scientific method and a value-free ethos has produced dullness, a loss of a sense of the catastrophic dimension of the Irish experience (suffered during the Conquest and the Famine), and a destructive scepticism with respect to the national tradition, which is still a living force in popular culture.

Since the 1960s, he argues, the stance on nationalism has become more hostile, with a refusal to empathise now turning into a delight in an iconoclastic debunking. This takes three forms. The first is a corrosive cynicism directed at national heroes who are prosecuted as a motley bunch of war lords, defenders of narrow class interests, or, when national sentiment is acknowledged as an animating force, as politically inept and intellectually confused ideologues. The second is an 'inverted anachronism' in which historians, influenced by fashionable social scientific interpretations of nationalism as a product of modernisation, have eliminated all conceptions of national consciousness from the Gaelic past evident in the early middle ages in the exilic laments of Christian poems and Gaelic origin legends, later in the development of the legend of *insula sacra*, and, during the sixteenth century, in the political commentaries found in Gaelic literature. The third is the rejection of the idea of a continuous national tradition in favour of interpretations that present the Irish past as a foreign country characterised by complexities and discontinuities between generations. Although this rejection is correct at an academic level, professional historians have failed to understand the vital functions of this 'purposeful unhistoricity'. Just as Butterfield, after his initial assault on the Whig interpretation of the English past as ideological, came to appreciate its value in enabling English society to assimilate innovation to tradition and hence avoid the revolutionary upheavals of its neighbours, so in Ireland the notion of a continuous nation has performed important integrative roles in allowing the absorption of new waves of settlers from the tenth century to the generations of Hyde, Pearse, and Griffith. As an alternative to the revisionist enterprise which would deprive the Irish community of heroic figures and sense of rootedness, he does not advocate a return at the academic level to an uncritical nationalism but to the empathetic history practised by MacNeill and Edward Curtis.

Bradshaw's polemic has received some well-directed blows from Ellis and others.[32] The utility of the term 'revisionist' and its equation with value freed history has been questioned since the days of Eoin MacNeill, whose work overturned an 'Anglo-Saxon' dismissal of the Gaelic past, falls into this category. Does not 'revisionism' simply mean a willingness to revise received historical interpretations in the light of new questions and evidence? And who could quarrel with that? To the uncommitted observer, his rejection of Ellis's borderland model as a device for understanding Gaelic developments *vis à vis* Britain in the medieval and early modern periods in favour of treating Ireland as the unit of analysis and of a focus on Anglo-Irish political separatism does seem to have a strong whiff of anachronism. Finally, his plea to historians to respect national myth-making has raised well justified alarms among those who see this (despite Bradshaw's protestations to the contrary) as sustaining the divisions in the island of Ireland.

Nonetheless, Bradshaw has highlighted what one might call a modish debunking attitude to the subject of nationalism prevalent in recent Irish historiography and has rightly pointed to its failure to understand the salience of national identities in the modern world. But these limitations, I would argue, cannot be blamed on a commitment to value neutrality. What lies behind this is an understandable if, at times, undisciplined revulsion on the part of significant sections of a new generation of historians against the consequences of the Gaelic republican triumph so evident in the utopian terrorism of the IRA and the repressive character and economic failures of the Irish Republic.

Of course, the process of professionalising history has been a contributing factor. As historians have been formed into guilds by virtue of their extensive scientific training in universities, they have tended to define themselves as custodians of the past and developed at times a sense of mission, articulated by J.H. Plumb as the liberation of humanity from myth, which he argues has been often used to legitimate tyranny and privilege.[33] In Ireland, a country unusually obsessed by dangerous fictions, historians have come to see themselves as having a special responsibility to disenchant in the interests of a tolerant democratic politics. Mark Finnane has made these points in what is the most penetrating discussion of the topic to date.[34] He points to the closing paragraph of *Ireland Since the Famine* in which Lyons writes in 1973 of the quiet historiographical revolution and his hopes for it in the education of an intellectual elite:

And since it is this elite which is making its way into politics and into the public service, the fact that its attitude towards the past should have become less romantic, less distorted by prejudice and by patriotic over-simplification, than that of its predecessors may yet prove one of the formative influences upon the future. . . . To understand the past fully is to cease to live in it, and to cease to live in it is to take the earliest steps towards shaping what is to come from the materials of the present.[35]

Since then the de-mythologising goals have taken on a new intensity with the emergence of a new secularly minded and better-educated middle class, impatient of the contrast between the complacent nationalism of their elders and Ireland's lamentable economic and social record compared to its European neighbours. Two recent books by Tom Garvin and by Joseph Lee exemplify the depth of the current revulsion against the present Irish nation state and the hope (among the historical profession) that history might lend support to liberalise it. Garvin begins his acute (although unbalanced) study of the ideological make-up of the Gaelic–Catholic activists, whom he flays as petty-bourgeois anti-modernists with affinities to fascism, by celebrating the approaching death of their revolution as Ireland integrates hesitantly into the liberal democratic states of Europe.[36] Lee, in a savage indictment of the performance of the Irish state since independence for its cultural dependence, demographic decline and economic stagnation relative to comparable European countries, attributes some of the blame to a history of grievance which has substituted for systematic self-appraisal, and advocates that policy-makers take advice from historians.[37]

It cannot be gainsaid that the critical stance to conventional pieties has resulted in a more sophisticated analysis that examines nationalism as one among many possible factors in a given situation, and that has been productive in encouraging research into those (for example, Protestants, women, peasants) given little status in their own right (i.e., independent of their allegiance to the nation) by nationalists. But this focus on changing received opinions at the elite and popular level about the formation of the nation state has been at the expense of accounting for nationalism. Most Irish historians have assumed the nation as a given and they have treated nationalism as a datum to be critiqued, relativised, demoted or even exorcised but not to be explained. Andrew Orridge's observation made in 1977 remains valid today:

> The difference between most of the inhabitants of Ireland and the rest of the population of the British Isles and the expression of this in the form of nationalism has been such a massive fact of modern Irish history that its very existence has hardly seemed a cogent question for most Irish specialists.[38]

But nationalism as we understood it today – a belief that humanity is divided into culturally distinctive communities which should be politically autonomous – is a post-eighteenth-century phenomenon which is now embraced globally. Historians of Ireland need to stand back and ask why in Ireland as in much of the rest of the world did having this political nationality become so essential as an attribute of full human worth? What was the relationship of this ideology to pre-existing religious sentiments? Was it quite novel or shaped by earlier ethnic sentiments? To the extent that it was novel, when did the modern nation form, and to what extent was the Irish route to nation-building distinctive or comparable to the experience of other countries? All these questions are germane to Ireland but require for cogent answers to be possible that the Irish case be placed in broad comparative framework rather than examined as if nationalism was an emanation from Irish particularities. For it is elementary logic that one cannot explain what is a general phenomenon in terms of the peculiarities of each case of the phenomenon. To do so is to adopt the assumptions of nationalism itself: that each (national) population is unique and can only be discussed in its own terms.

IV

In Irish as in many other national historiographies, the question raised by scholars from many disciplines, 'Why Nationalism?', has rarely been addressed let alone answered, although there is some recognition of the importance of 'modernisation' perspectives for understanding of Irish nationalism.[39] Outsiders have made occasional forays into the field. Michael Hechter has explained the rise of nationalism in Ireland (as in other parts of the Celtic fringe) by the structuring by an English metropolitan core of industrialisation along ethnic lines, creating patterns of dependent development in the peripheries and a cultural division of labour.[40] But this internal colonialist approach has had little take-up in Ireland, and its rather mechanical analysis of cultural revivals as arising out of a sense of economic discrimination has been criticised in the wider scholarship.

It might be argued that many of these perspectives (modernisation and otherwise) are too abstract for easy application, for example, Ernest Gellner's interpretation of nationalism as a product of the transition from agro-literate to industrial societies.[41] But attention deserves to be given to Benedict Anderson's conceptualisation of the nation as an imagined community made possible by the rise of print capitalism and new genres such as the newspaper and the novel.[42] Although it would be unwise to place too great weight on the reading of William Carleton, the roles played by institutions of journalism and the circulation of the British and Irish metropolitan and provincial press in the development of a modern national consciousness have been grossly underresearched.

One variant of the modernisation perspective – the work of Anthony D. Smith – does seem to have particular relevance to Ireland, and John Hutchinson has employed it in a recent study of Irish cultural Nationalism.[43] Nationalism, according to Smith, is the outcome of a prolonged legitimation crisis generated by the expanding impact of a modernising bureaucratic state on societies regulated by religious conception of the social order. This conflict tends to produce three competing yet also complementary cultural responses in populations – a secular modernism,

110

a religious reformism, and a neo-traditionalism – each of which may evolve into a variety of nationalism. At this level, nationalism is a concern of the intellectuals. But one effect of a modernising state is to create a professional middle class (or intelligentsia) through its expand- ing educational system and its bureaucratic apparatus. Nationalism becomes a serious political project when the career expectations of significant sections of this aspiring intelligentsia are 'blocked' so that, disillusioned with the existing state, they become the cadres of nationalist organis- ations, seeking an autonomous nation in which their leadership talents will achieve appropriate recognition.[44]

This model has general application to the mass political movements for legislative autonomy in nineteenth-century Ireland. Hutchinson has used it to analyse the origins and consequences of the three cultural nationalist 'revivals' that formed since the late eighteenth century. Although there was in practice often an overlap between the two types of movement, he argues that for analytical purposes Irish cultural nationalism, with its focus on the moral regeneration of an (allegedly) distinctive historic community, should be differentiated from political nationalism, whose goal was the establishment of a autonomous modern state (or quasi-state) based on citizenship equality. Although the former were generally small in scale, they performed important integrative functions, emerging at times of crisis and conflict, often generated by the mass political nationalist movements whose unstable coalitions of secular liberals and religious tradi- tionalists would periodically break down. Indeed, one can see something of an alternating pattern in modern Irish history, where a young and ambitious intelligentsia periodically turn to the communitarian vision and strategies of cultural nationalist intellectuals at times when the statist politics of political nationalists seem to be breaking down. What then ensues is a conflict of generations within Irish nationalism.[45]

Hutchinson's analysis concentrates on the late nineteenth–century Gaelic revival which, recoiling against the growing assimilation of Irish society (including the Irish parliamentary party) to secular liberal British norms, proposed to restructure Irish social, economic, and political institutions around indigenous values. He examines its roots in and complex relations with first liberal reform, and then (more potent) neo-traditionalist campaigns of the Catholic lower clergy. But through an examination of census and other employment data, he concludes that its political dynamics derived from an excess of socially aspiring educated lower-middle-class Catholics to positions available in a society where Protestants still wielded disproportionate socio-economic power. Under these circumstances, the Gaelic revival served to channel and legitimate the drive of these new social strata who felt excluded from power and status both by the British state and the ageing oligarchies of the Irish parliamentary party.

This analysis is in many respects complemented and empirically deepened by Tom Garvin's perceptive study which sets the modern Irish case in a broad European context and provides an extensive analysis of the social background and ideological mind set of Gaelic and revolutionary activists in the period 1858–1928.[46] A particular strength of this book is its attention to regional factors. Influenced by the Czech historian Miroslav Hroch,[47] who identifies the petty bourgeoisie of 'intermediate' economic zones as the strategic group in stateless nationalities, Garvin has established the central importance of province of Munster in the framing the character of the revival and hence of modern Ireland. Although both Garvin and Hutchinson stress the increasing anti-modernism of the Gaelic revival, they differ in some notable respects. Garvin interprets the Gaelic revival as comparable to proto-fascist movements in Germany in expressing the pathological fears of modernity of a threatened petty *bourgeoisie*, and as destined to disappear with Ireland's integration into liberal democratic capitalism. Hutchinson, by contrast, explains its early appeal in more positive terms: it infused young educated Catholics with pride in being descended from a unique civilisation of European importance. He also stresses its early modernising thrust and the interest of its leaders in the lessons of other small nationalities in Europe. Although a puritanical and traditionalist Catholicism became dominant, it is worth noting that by comparison with other post-colonial states, Ireland has been relatively stable, democratic, and liberal.

Garvin's model can be criticised as economistic (he explains radical nationalism as a disease of development) and over-influenced by once-fashionable (but now discredited) notions about the regressive and transient character of the petty *bourgeoisie*.[48] A long-term perspective on the revival of interest in things Gaelic since the eighteenth century will show that the ideal has come in several different varieties which in turn have had the support of different classes and ethnic groups, suggesting it cannot be explained by economic or social reductionism.[49] Nor do the patterns of recurrence in Irish history suggest its life has come to an end.

A second topic that has as yet lacked systematic exploration is the relationship of modern nationalism to pre-modern collective identities. As in European scholarship there is a tendency among contemporary Irish historians to dismiss as anachronistic attempts to locate national identities in the medieval period, but it is arguable that the issue is over-simplified by adopting a narrow political definition of the nation. In fact, both Ellis and Bradshaw overstress a statist conception in their recent debate about the interpretation of the late medieval period. Although Bradshaw maintains that in this period Gaelic Ireland was an ethno-cultural unity integrated by myths of common origins, he is concerned to prove it was also a political entity and characterises as nationalist and separatist the fifteenth-century campaign of the English settlers for greater powers for the Irish parliament.[50] In disputing this, Ellis points out that unlike Spain, Italy and Germany, Gaelic Ireland had never been a unitary sovereign state, it shared its Gaelic culture with Scotland, and the appropriate model for Irish medieval history was that of a borderland within a British archipelago. A national model was being invalidly employed to describe Irish revolts against the centre which in fact were directly comparable with regional struggles in the similar borderlands of Northern England and Wales.[51]

The issue, however, is much more complex than this, and John Armstrong and Anthony Smith have published substantial studies that have thrown doubt on the equation of nations with statehood and citizenship.[52] Armstrong has argued the modern nation needs to be examined in *la longue durée* in terms of a long-term cycle of ethnic resurgence and decay in history, and that nations are ethnic groups integrated by means of common descent, myths and symbols which persist even if the values, culture and demography change over time. Smith goes further and locates two types of ethnic (or ethnic community) – lateral–aristocratic and vertical–demotic – in the pre-modern world. The first is based on an aristocratic stratum which identifies with state institutions and, although ethnic consciousness is territorially extensive, it is socially thin. In the second case ethnic consciousness penetrates well down the social scale, is usually identified with religious institutions and a smaller, more compact territory. In Smith's schema Ireland is an example of a demotic tribal confederation knit by Gaelic themes and origin myths highly coloured by the institutions of a monastic Christianity. Religious institutions, however, were secondary to local aristocratic dynasties which were unable to generate a sufficient solidarity to withstand the Anglo-Normans. But as a result of the English Protestant conquest of the sixteenth and seventeenth centuries which overthrew the native aristocracy, an Irish ethnic millenarian consciousness formed amongst the peasantry, focused on the restoration of the Catholic Church and of the traditional landed order.[53]

This subject might be of limited interest to modern Irish historians but for the fact Smith argues that modern nations are heavily shaped by their premodern ethnic structures (or lack thereof). Whereas the modern great powers are usually based on lateral ethnics, nations based on demotic ethnics are often small in scale but claim a religiously based moral mission. The routes to nation formation differ in each case. In the case of lateral ethnics, the bureaucratic state – perceived, as in France, to be the embodiment of the nation – plays a major role in the national incorporation of the mass of the population through public education systems, military conscription, and economic integration of the country. In the case of the vertical ethnics (usually stateless) the transformation of a traditional community into a modern political nation is more a bottom-up process, performed by a rising intelligentsia. This secular intelligentsia has not only to struggle against the existing (alien) state but also, in seeking to reconstruct and politicise ethnic sentiments, to compete with native religious institutions jealous of their custody of collective traditions. In many cases there is a prolonged internal struggle between the secular nationalists and religious leaders over the definition of the nation which at the grass roots is heavily inflected by religious values.[54]

Smith's model illuminates the Irish pathways to national formation which were and are still marked by recurring patterns of accommodation and conflict between secular nationalists and the Catholic Church. Like all such ideal-typical models it needs to be adapted to particular cases. As Boyce points out, nationalists could look to a secular heritage – the existence of a separate Irish parliament from the Anglo-Norman era to the modern age and a history of resistance to defend its rights – in order to assert Ireland's claims to be an autonomous nationality.[55] Liberal middle-class nineteenth-century constitutional nationalists appealed to this heritage in their struggle for power with the Catholic Church, and this sense of shared political traditions with Britain lent, as O'Day has demon- strated, a strong assimilative cast to sections of the Irish Catholic elites.[56] Nonetheless, O'Farrell is essentially correct in arguing that the power of secular nationalists was heavily circumscribed by the underlying ethno-religious conceptions rooted in popular culture, dating from the seventeenth century, of the Irish as a martyred nation.[57] Although by the late nineteenth century, deference to ecclesiastical opinion in the political arena was being challenged among sections of a growing urban secular middle class, there was at the same time a strong communitarian nationalist rejection of British *secular* modernisation which allied with a resurgent neo-traditionalism. Further intensified by the war of independence these ethno-religious conceptions served to define the independent Irish state.

Although such issues remain underexplored, one Irish scholar, Tom Garvin, drawing on the comparative frameworks of Stein Rokkan and Miroslav Hroch,[58] has blazed the way in exploring the manner in which premodern ethnic and other identities and institutions have shaped the modern Irish nation state. In his first book, he takes as his starting point the unusual characteristics of the post-independence Irish state in a Western European context – the authoritarian populist nature of Irish political parties and degree to which kinship and localistic networks override abstract civic conceptions and class loyalties, and he points to the distinctive patterns of political mobilisation in Ireland.[59] Whereas in other countries modernising elites inducted the masses into national politics, in Ireland mass national mobilisation and organisation under O'Connell came early, long predating industrialisation. The result was that 'modern' political forms were colonised by the conspiratorial practices and the xenophobic Catholic sentiments of a subjugated peasantry that in many areas still organised in secret societies against the hated Protestant landed and religious settlement. Although the urban middle-class leadership of the national parliamentary parties might espouse a respectable constitutional nationalism, their fervent support among the rural population was based on their apparent violation of British political norms and their abilities to tap underground local traditions and millenarian sentiments.[60]

Garvin's focus in this book is on political organisation and on the timing of social mobilisation. In his later study,[61] where he examines the formative period of the Gaelic revival, there is a greater stress on ideology, although as I have indicated above his approach is overly reductive. As Fitzpatrick observed, Garvin oscillates between decrying the baneful effects of the Gaelic revival and interpreting Gaelicism as just the vehicle of a reactionary and threatened petty *bourgeoisie* in search of power.[62] In his comments Fitzpatrick is also critical of elite-centred analysis (a somewhat unfair point given Garvin's pioneering work on secret societies). It might be said that a concentration on the study of popular mentalities by themselves leads to a directionless social history, but Fitzpatrick is correct to argue that the two levels of analysis must be brought together.

This discussion of the relationship between nationalism and the social mobilisation of populations raises the further question of when one can say the nation has become a reality. This has been opened up in the general scholarship on nationalism by the American political scientist Walker Connor,[63] who has argued that if the nation is defined as a mass phenomenon (because of its basis in doctrines of popular sovereignty), then it is very doubtful that one can date the emergence of nations before the twentieth century. Referring amongst other works to Eugene Weber's classic study,[64] he argues that even in late nineteenth-century France, one of the most advanced states in Europe, the horizons of the bulk of the population were regional, religious or class-based. It is only with the development of integrated territory-wide systems of communications, production and exchange, of universal education and military conscription, and later universal suffrage that one might speak of the formation of nations.

Although the question of when the modern nation comes into being has not been *explicitly* addressed, it is a strength of the recent revisionists to recognise the multiple levels of identity in existence in any population and to refuse to assume that even in nationalist campaigns individuals or groups are necessarily inspired by the goals attributed to them by their leaders. Can one then trace the formation of an Irish national community in linear terms, evolving from local pre-political secret societies into an integrated territory-wide community through the agency of modern party organisations, improved communications, and newspapers?[65] Some would propose the land war as the formative experience in drawing the peasantry, formerly confined to local politics, into a national political consciousness. But even here, others such as Foster are prepared to argue that even as late as the Land League agitations, much of the rural population was inspired by religious or class antagonisms.[66] Later still, with respect to the war of independence Fitzpatrick indicates the partial regional and class participation in national movements and the many non-patriotic reasons individuals might have for membership.[67] And after independence local loyalties remain powerful.

In fact, Connor argues that national-formation is a process, not a final state, and it is a reversible one: even in contemporary societies national identity oscillates in political and social salience as it competes with class and other loyalties. At first, these reflections might seem to support positions that modern nationalism is a much weaker force in history than has been assumed, and that the nation can be easily deconstructed by Irish historians, with the corollary that it can be reconstructed and given a more pluralistic definition. But it would be simplistic to suppose this, for it can be argued that Connor's definition of the nation as a mass community is too stipulative: what is important for judging whether the nation is hegemonic is not how many at any one time identify themselves primarily in national terms, but the extent to which the acknowledged leaders of the community appeal successfully to nationalism as a mobilising device and are themselves motivated by nationalist goals.[68] It is also the case that while nationalism is only one of several motivations of individual and collective actions, historians must also recognise and seek to account for the fact that nationalism is a potent recurring force embedded in the modern Irish experience which among the indigenous Catholic population expresses itself in certain repetitive thematic patterns. In the Irish case, it is often artificial, in practice, to make sharp distinctions between religious, agrarian and national goals since Irish ethnicity has been closely aligned with a sense of religious mission and religio-economic grievance, and since (as argued above) nationalism can emerge from both religious and secular imperatives. This suggests that any academic attempts to remould popular traditions and to re-invent the nation are likely to have limited success.

CONCLUSION

Behind much of this discussion lie the questions of whom Irish historians are addressing and why, when they study and publish on Irish nationalism. The answers will be various, but it is clear that as Finnane has argued as in many other countries a profession armed with the mystique of 'science' is seeking to claim control of the past from popular traditions, justified by an ethical, even political, mission to liberate their society from (national) myth.[69] I have argued that this project insofar as it is directed to undermining nationalism *per se* is doomed because national identities are not contingent elite constructs but are rooted in modern social conditions and draw strength from an older ethnocultural heritage. It is also impossible to understand Irish nationalism and its place in the modern world without reference to the near universal emergence of nationalism among human communities since the late eighteenth century. Indeed, a 'national history' approach reinforces nationalism by the false assumption that the Irish are *sui generis*.

The way forward for the further study of Irish nationalism does not lie primarily in the filling of empirical gaps or the cultivation of an ironic detachment from popular mythologies, but rather in a willingness to embrace comparative perspectives and to conceptualise the history of modern Ireland as part of the human story.[70] An 'internationalisation' of historical practice may achieve considerably more than a corrosive scepticism by lessening the claustrophobic intensity with which the Irish are wont to examine themselves. Fortunately, there are signs that some historians are weary of performing as tribal historians and desire to address a wider audience.[71]

NOTES

1 Eric J. Hobsbawm, *Nations and Nationalism Since 1780* (London, 1990).
2 On MacNeill, see the essays in *The Scholar Revolutionary: Eoin MacNeill, 1867– 1945*, F.X. Martin and F.J. Byrne (eds) (Shannon, 1973).
3 Roy Foster, 'History and the Irish Question', *Transactions of the Royal Historical Society*, xxxiii, 1983, pp. 185–7.
4 Roy Foster, 'The Problem of Writing Irish History', *History Today*, 34, 1988, pp. 27–30.
5 See J.J. Sheehan, 'What is German History? Reflections on the Role of the "Nation" in German History and Historiography', *Journal of Modern History*, 53 (1), March 1981, pp. 1–23.
6 Roy Foster, 'History and the Irish Question', pp. 188–9. Moody spent a brief period at Queen's, but spent the rest of his career in TCD.
7 *Ibid., loc. cit.*
8 See F.S.L. Lyons, *The Irish Parliamentary Party (1890–1910)* (London, 1951); *Idem., Charles Stewart Parnell* (London, 1977).
9 T.W. Moody, *Davitt and the Irish Revolution (1846–82)* (London, 1981); Oliver MacDonagh, *The Hereditary Bondsman* (New York, 1988) and *The Emancipist* (New York, 1989). Unlike MacDonagh's magisterial study, Moody's book could be accused of an almost fetishistic accumulation of detail on his subject.
10 Ruth Dudley Edwards, *Patrick Pearse: The Triumph of Failure* (London, 1977); Tom Dunne, *Theobold Wolfe Tone: Colonial Outsider* (Cork, 1982).
11 E.P. Thompson, *The Making of the English Working Class* (Harmondsworth, 1963).
12 Eric J. Hobsbawm and Terence Ranger (eds), *The Invention of Tradition* (Cambridge, 1983); Eric J. Hobsbawm, *op. cit.*
13 Steven G. Ellis, 'Nationalist Historiography and the English and Gaelic Worlds in the Late Middle Ages', *Irish Historical Studies*, xxv (57), May 1986, pp. 1–18.

14 Alan O'Day, *The English Face of Irish Nationalism* (Dublin, 1977).
15 R.V. Comerford, *The Fenians in Context* (Dublin, 1985).
16 See Charles Townshend, 'Modernisation and Nationalism: Perspectives in Recent Irish History', *History*, 66 (217), 1981, pp. 233–43.
17 D. George Boyce, *Nationalism in Ireland* (London, 1982).
18 Tom Garvin, *The Evolution of Irish Nationalist Politics* (Dublin, 1981).
19 F.S.L. Lyons, *Culture and Anarchy in Ireland (1980–1939)* (Oxford, 1979); see also J. Beckett, *The Anglo-Irish Tradition* (London, 1976) and Oliver MacDonagh's elegant *States of Mind* (London, 1983), which addresses the place of Ulster in modern Irish history.
20 Patrick O'Farrell, *Ireland's English Question* (London, 1971).
21 Tom Garvin, *Nationalist Revolutionaries in Ireland (1858–1928)* (Oxford, 1987).
22 See J.J. Lee, 'The Ribbonmen' in *Secret Societies in Ireland*, T.D. Williams (ed.), (Dublin, 1973) pp. 26–35 and Tom Garvin, 'Defenders, Ribbonmen and Others: Underground Political Networks in Pre-Famine Ireland', *Past and Present*, 96, 1982, pp. 133–55.
23 See Samuel Clarke, *Social Origins of the Irish Land War* (Princeton, 1980); David Fitzpatrick, 'The Geography of Irish Nationalism, 1910–21', *Past and Present*, 78, 1978, pp. 113–43.
24 K. Theodore Hoppen, *Elections, Politics, and Society in Ireland 1832–55* (Oxford, 1984).
25 David Fitzpatrick, *Politics and Irish Life 1913–21: Provincial Experience of War and Revolution* (Dublin, 1977).
26 A.C. Hepburn and E. Rumpf, *Nationalism and Socialism in Ireland* (Liverpool, 1977); David Fitzpatrick, 'The Geography of Irish Nationalism'.
27 *Ibid.*, p. 131. R.V. Comerford, *The Fenians in Context: Irish Politics and Society 1848–82* (Dublin, 1985).
28 Clare O'Halloran, *Partition and the Limits of Irish Nationalism* (Dublin, 1987); J.J. Lee, *Ireland 1912–1985: Politics and Society* (Cambridge, 1989).
29 See Peter Alter, 'Symbols of Irish Nationalism', *Studia Hibernica*, 14, 1974, pp. 104–23; Jeanne Sheehy, *The Rediscovery of Ireland's Past: The Celtic Revival (1830–1930)* (London, 1980). Charles Townshend's *Political Violence in Ireland* (Oxford, 1948) is one of the most sophisticated studies informed by a knowledge of such models.
30 Brendan Bradshaw, 'Nationalism and Historical Scholarship in Modern Ireland' *Irish Historical Studies*, xxvi (104), November 1989, pp. 329–51.
31 Steven G. Ellis, *op. cit.*
32 *Idem.*, 'Historiographical Debate: Representation of the Past in Ireland: Whose Past and Whose Present?, *Irish Historical Studies*, xxvii (108) November 1991, pp. 289–308; see also Hugh Kearney, 'The Irish and Their History', *History Workshop*, 31, 1991, pp. 149–55.
33 J.H. Plumb, *The Death of the Past* (Harmondsworth, 1973).
34 Mark Finnane, *Irish Nationalism* (Griffith University, 1984).
35 Cited in *ibid.*, p. 21.
36 Tom Garvin, *Nationalist Revolutionaries*.
37 J.J. Lee, *Ireland 1912–85*.
38 A.W. Orridge, 'Explanations in Irish History', *Journal of the Conflict Resolution Society*, 1, 1977, p. 32.
39 See note 16.
40 M. Hechter, *Internal Colonialism: The Celtic Fringe in British National Development 1536–1966* (London, 1975).
41 Ernest Gellner, *Nations and Nationalism* (Oxford, 1983).
42 Benedict Anderson, *Imagined Communities* (London, 1983).

43 Anthony D. Smith, *Theories of Nationalism* (London, 1971), ch. 10; John Hutchinson, *The Dynamics of Cultural Nationalism: The Gaelic Revival and the Making of the Irish Nation State* (London, 1987). See also Jacqueline Hill's use of Smith's model in 'The Intelligentsia and Irish Nationalism in the 1840s', *Studia Hibernica*, 20, 1980, pp. 73–110.

44 For his discussion of the blocked mobility thesis, see Anthony D. Smith, *The Ethnic Revival* (Cambridge, 1981), ch. 6.

45 John Hutchinson, *op. cit.*, chs 2 and 8.

46 Tom Garvin, *Nationalist Revolutionaries*.

47 Miroslav Hroch, *Social Preconditions of National Revivals in Europe* (Cambridge, 1985).

48 L. Weiss, *Creating Capitalism* (Oxford, 1988), ch. 3.

49 J. Hutchinson, *op. cit.*, ch. 8.

50 Brendan Bradshaw, *op. cit.*, pp. 332–3.

51 Steven G. Ellis, 'Historiographical Debate', pp. 296–306.

52 J. Armstrong, *Nations Before Nationalism* (Chapel Hill, 1982); Anthony D. Smith, *The Ethnic Origins of Nations* (Oxford, 1986).

53 *Ibid.*, pp. 95, 110–11.

54 See Anthony D. Smith, 'The Origins of Nations', *Ethnic and Racial Studies*, 12 (3), 1989, pp. 95, 340–67.

55 D. George Boyce, *op. cit.*

56 Alan O'Day, *op. cit.*

57 Patrick O'Farrell, *op. cit.*

58 See Stein Rokkan, *Citizens, Elections, Parties* (Oslo, 1970).

59 Tom Garvin, *The Evolution of Irish Nationalist Politics*.

60 For a summary, see *ibid.*, pp. 180–3.

61 Tom Garvin, *Nationalist Revolutionaries*.

62 David Fitzpatrick, 'Still in the Grip of Myth', *Times Literary Supplement*, 22–8 July 1988, pp. 813–14.

63 Walker Connor, 'When is a Nation?', *Ethnic and Racial Studies*, 13 (1), 1990, pp. 92–103.

64 Eugen Weber, *Peasants into Frenchmen: The Modernisation of Rural France* (Stanford, 1976).

65 For a linear view, see Roy Foster 'Introduction' in C.H.E. Philpin (ed.), *Nationalism and Popular Protest in Ireland* (Cambridge, 1987). For a rejection of such perspectives, see the introduction in Samuel Clarke and James Donnelly (eds), *Irish Peasants, Violence and Political Change 1789–1914* (Manchester, 1983).

66 This question is raised in a critical review of Sean Cronin's *Irish Nationalism* by Roy Foster, 'Splits and Reactions', *Times Literary Supplement*, 31 July 1981, p. 870.

67 David Fitzpatrick, 'The Geography of Irish Nationalism'.

68 For a critique of Connor, see John Hutchinson, *Modern Nationalism* (London, 1994), ch. 1.

69 See note 34.

70 One of the areas still seriously neglected at a conceptual and empirical level is that of gender and nationalism.

71 Among the hopeful signs are the involvement of Irish historians in the European Science Foundation project 'Comparative Studies on Governments and Non-Dominant Ethnic Groups in Europe, 1850–1940' published in 8 volumes between 1990 and 1993.

7

IRISH UNIONISM

Alvin Jackson

The Irish, North and South, are as bound by their history as they are divided by it. Their abuse of the past has for long been shared. Their historical inheritance, though different in content, shares the same form: Derry beseiged or Limerick beseiged, 1641 or Drogheda, 1916 on the banks of the Liffey or on the banks of the Somme. History for all the Irish is a mantra of sacred dates, an invocation of secular saints: though the enshrouding flags differ, the martyr's coffin is a shared icon. National identity for both sides is a cocktail distilled by external assault and internal confidence. Most nations, colonial or indigenous, have produced clearly defined notions of their community's strengths and weaknesses, of the experiences of injustice and of the superior qualities which permit survival or triumph: the 'varieties of Irishness' are not exceptional in this respect.[1]

The Protestant sense of the past in contemporary Northern Ireland is as fragmentary and limited as most popular historical awareness – it is a sense of the past which, as we shall see, has been tailored by the public history provided by the Unionist movement and, before 1972, by the Northern Irish government. This is not to suggest, however, that the demands of political unity have wholly spirited away those aspects of a complex inheritance which do not suit contemporary needs. The Protestant past is an uncomfortable and ugly garment, and a gaudy Orange sash never fully conceals the stains of denominational conflict, or the patches of class division. Rural Protestant communities in eastern Ulster retain tortured memories of 1798, of the struggle for tenant right, and of the sectarian rivalries between Presbyterian and Episcopalian. They resent Dublin, surely, but then they resent Belfast as a font of degeneracy; and their irritation at Dublin's interference predates Irish independence. As Terence Brown has argued, Protestant history *is* more complex than contemporary rhetoric would suggest.[2] But then, a fundamental aspect of the Irish tragedy is that the past is continually and ritually sacrificed to a caricature of the present. Threads are plucked from

120

both past and present, and woven into a smothering ideological blanket of a uniform green, or orange.[3] A monochrome history deceives only a minority, but it is the few, purblind zealots who have sculpted so much of our environment.

Unionism neither supplies nor demands a complex vision of its own past. This is very far from saying that the Unionist historiographical tradition is as sporadic and monodimensional as the needs and perceptions of its beneficiaries would appear to imply. On the contrary, late nineteenth-century Unionist visions of the past were as varied and shifting as the demands of political debate. The fissiparous nature of Irish Unionism, no less than of Irish Nationalism, meant that there was always a tendency towards producing a simplified and unifying historical creed for the consumption of the pious. But the emphases of this creed certainly changed according to political necessity, and a more complex historiographical dogma has always been available to a material and intellectual elite.

Unionism remains fissiparous, and retains a need for its catechisms of historical faith. The broadening of political debate since 1972 has made ideological and strategic demands for which the Unionist movement, schooled disastrously at Stormont, has had no response. As the demands of Anglo-Irish politics have become more intricate, so the political and historical perceptions of Unionism have become more simplified. The historical and historiographical legacy is rich and complex, but the legatees squander their inheritance by their very frugality.

The definition of Unionist history is as intangible as the definition of Unionism itself, but in the interests of clarity the arguments here are structured around two alternative propositions. Unionist history may be at once a matter of Unionists engaged in the writing of history and, at the same time, the study of the Unionist tradition in Ireland by those not necessarily committed in one political direction or another: the distinction between 'Unionist historian' and 'historian of Unionism'. Defining the definition – defining the 'Unionist historian' – is by no means easy, partly because of the diversity of Unionist political commitment, and partly because it is self-evidently unreasonable to ascribe political sentiments to those contemporary historians who have not made some unambiguous expression of political faith. No, the intention here is not to speculate about personal conviction from uncertain evidence, or to offer a definition of Unionism so flaccid as to be meaningless, but rather to identify a type of historian who has either been politically active in the interests of Unionism, or who (like A.T.Q. Stewart) has unequivocally published his or her political convictions.[4] Against this grouping I want to juxtapose a tradition of scholarship concerned with the evolution of Unionist politics and society in Ireland. Clearly the two categories – 'Unionist historian' and 'historian of Unionism' – are not mutually exclusive but the overlap is, in practice, much slighter than one might expect. And it will become clear that the categories are also discrete when judged within the context of the historical profession's evolution in Ireland.

The period between the emergence of Home Rule within the mainstream of Irish politics and the emergence of two states in Ireland saw a dramatic upsurge both in political pamphleteering and in the manipulation of history, or exploitation of historical evidence, for partisan intent. The historical profession, defined as those pursuing the discipline of history within a university, emerged in Ireland at the same time as the national revival, and it should come as no disappointment (especially given continental precedents) that the two events were so closely interwoven. The dialogue between the Irish cultural revival and political nationalism is an obvious historical phenomenon, as are the political commitments of historians like Eoin MacNeill and Alice Stopford Green – R.B. McDowell's 'passionate historian' – or the historical commitments of politicians like Arthur Griffith expressed through *The Resurrection of Hungary* (1904) or Eamon de Valera through works such as *Ireland's Case against Conscription* (1918).[5] Of course parliamentary Nationalists such as William O'Brien and T.M. Healy were no less eager to seek legitimisation through historical evidence, whether in polemical works such as Healy's *Stolen Waters* (1913) or his *The Great Fraud of Ulster* (1913) (titles which themselves signal that these are no mealy-mouthed works of consensus), or tendentious autobiographical reminiscence. But the phenomenon of the scholar–politician was as much a Unionist as a Nationalist creation, and the frequently historical nature of the Home Rule debate ensured that the writing of history was high among the priorities of the Unionist intelligentsia. If, as Lloyd George and other British pragmatists so often complained, Irish politics *were* a matter of perceived historical grievance, then the all-too-familiar centuries of Saxon occupation were as actively scrutinised by Unionists as by Nationalists.

Unionist historical scholarship had several institutional focuses in Ireland, but chief amongst these was Trinity College Dublin. Trinity College was land-owning and Anglican, and (as its parliamentary representation repeatedly indicated) predominantly Unionist. Its law school supplied technically adroit advocates to the Irish Unionist leadership, and its lawyers and historians supplied Unionism with ideological substance and with a shifting vision of the Irish past.[6] Among the Protestant intellectual elite of Victorian Dublin was a recognisable cultural Irishness and constitutional anti-separatism, married within the Royal Irish Academy, among the pages of the *Dublin University Magazine*, or the writings of a Samuel Ferguson. Of course mainstream, popular politics in the Ireland beyond College Green were pressing towards a more ambitious Nationalism and a more rigorously exclusivist definition of Irishness (judged whether in terms of religion, perceptions of ethnicity, or xenophobia). The radicalisation of Irish politics after 1870 outstripped the expectations and desires of most Trinity intellectuals, however liberal or Irish in terms of self-perception. Certainly an historian such as Lecky, as Donal McCartney has demonstrated, was being shunted from an early and generous liberalism in the 1860s towards an increasingly circumspect conservatism by the 1890s, an evolution to be traced in the successive revisions to his *Leaders of Public Opinion in Ireland*. In the preface to the edition of *Leaders* which appeared in 1903, at the end of his life, Lecky repudiated 'the worst excesses of boyish rhetoric' evident when the volume first appeared in 1861, as well as the contemporary political analysis which prefaced the version of 1871.[7] And Lecky was only the most prominent of a group of Trinity and other scholars who, by the end of the nineteenth century, had emerged as active proponents of Unionism and active investigators of the origins of the Unionist tradition in Ireland.

Unionist historiography was thus, as with its Nationalist counterpart, partly a response to the prevailing political climate in Ireland. Caesar Litton Falkiner, an important, yet neglected Unionist historian, admitted candidly in the preface to his *Studies in Irish History and Biography* (1902) that it was impossible to approach his subject with 'absolute colourlessness'; and he found himself in agreement with Lord Rosebery's dictum that 'the Irish question has never passed into history because it has never passed out of politics'.[8] Predictably, given these statements, Falkiner was active in the defence of his Unionist convictions. Falkiner together with his close friend and contemporary, Frederick Elrington Ball, the historian of County Dublin and of the Irish judiciary, fought comfortable crusades for the Union in the suburbs of south Dublin at the end of the nineteenth century: Ball stood in south County Dublin as a rogue Unionist candidate at the election of 1900.[9] Falkiner ventured north once, in 1892, as Unionist parliamentary candidate for South Armagh, but he did not choose to repeat the experiment at later elections.[10] Lecky, mentor to both Falkiner and Ball, sat as the parliamentary representative for Trinity College Dublin between 1895 and 1903, having migrated from liberalism (indeed from an insipid form of Nationalism) to Liberal Unionism at the time of the first Home Rule Bill. Other scholars were associated with Lecky and his Trinity acolytes: Richard Bagwell from Clonmel, the historian of Tudor and Stuart Ireland, and Irish Unionist Alliance activist; Samuel Henry Butcher, the Kerry-born classicist and President of the British Academy; and Edward Dowden, dismissed by Yeats as the archtypal Victorian drudge, but rated rather more highly within the hierarchy of the I.U.A.[11]

But, conspicuous though scholar-apparatchiks like Butcher and Dowden were, it was the historians who were of the greater ideological importance to the development of Unionism. Falkiner, Ball and Lecky supplied Irish

Protestants with histories of the Anglo-Irish political tradition, and with celebrations of its values and achievements. Lecky offered an account of the Anglo-Irish gentry in the form of a five-volume *History of Ireland* (1892), one of the most obviously Anglo-centric general histories of Ireland (if only because it was directly a by-product of a survey of English history).[12] Falkiner pleaded eloquently and fruitlessly for more local and more social history in Ireland in his *Illustrations of Irish History and Topography* (1904); but he devoted another book of essays largely to the late eighteenth-century gentry, providing sympathetic portraits of Viscount Castlereagh and John Fitzgibbon, Earl of Clare, the architects of Union.[13]

The strength of the bond between Unionist politics and Unionist historical scholarship is indicated both by the political concerns of the historians themselves, as well as by the evolving nature of their scholarly enthusiasms. The historical nature of Gladstone's Home Rule apologetic, and the encouragement which he gave to others similarly disposed to argue from historical principles (like the Parnellite J.G. Swift MacNeill) created a need for a Unionist response. Thomas Dunbar Ingram, a Belfast-born lawyer and brother to John Kells Ingram (the Trinity classicist and author – ironically – of 'Who fears to speak of '98?') rose to the occasion: T.D. Ingram composed *The Passing of the Act of Union* (1887) in order to demonstrate to the British public the strength of contemporary support for the measure, and the purity of the circumstances of its passage into law.[14] Successive Unionist writers returned to consider and to vindicate the Act – Falkiner through his biographical essays, Lord Ashbourne, the egregious Lord Chancellor of Ireland, through his biography of William Pitt the Younger, and J.R. Fisher, the editor of the *Northern Whig*, through his monograph, *The End of the Irish Parliament*, published, significantly, in 1911, on the eve of the crisis arising from the third Home Rule Bill.[15] Only Lecky among the Unionists felt that faith in the Act of Union was compatible with a sceptical vision of its genesis; and in 1892 he referred bitterly to 'those discussions about the advantages and disadvantages of Home Rule in Ireland' which drew on 'the perceived merits and demerits of the Irish parliament of the eighteenth century, with a complete forgetfulness of the fact that this parliament consisted exclusively of the Protestant gentry'.[16]

In this context it is worth emphasising that there was a clear division among these late Victorian Unionists between a Whig school which looked back, reverentially, to Edmund Burke, and a more robust and polemical tradition which owed much to J.A. Froude, and to his philosophy of history.[17] Lecky (like Gladstone) deeply admired Burke, lavishing praise on his literary style, his political insight, and, above all, on the purity of his personality: Burke's letters on Irish affairs, his speeches and correspondence 'contain some of the best lessons of political wisdom in the language' while Burke himself was 'not only a very great man but emphatically a good one'.[18] For Lecky political and intellectual well-being was rooted in personal morality, and Burke's combination of a high-minded patriotism and social compassion reflected the strength of his moral principles. Having abandoned Whiggery in the national interest, Burke was an obvious totem for late nineteenth-century liberal Unionists.[19] Both Lecky and his young disciple, Falkiner, quoted Burke as a scriptural authority; indeed Falkiner's first venture into print, 'The New Voyage to Utopia' (1886) was described by Dowden as ' a kind of appeal from the New Whigs to the Old'.[20]

T.D. Ingram, by way of contrast, embraced Froude as a more appropriate model of style and judgement than Burke. Froude's bracing polemical style, his hostility to the Gaelic Irish tradition, and his anti-Catholicism all found a ready imitator with Ingram. The fullest expression of this intellectual debt comes with Ingram's *A Critical Examination of Irish History* (2 vols, 1900), a work which lamented the 'pathetically' sensitive British conscience regarding Ireland, and which intermittently snarled its contempt for Burke. But *A Critical Examination* was much less concerned with the master, Burke, than with the most eloquent of his acolytes, Lecky – 'the most respectable among the teachers of the doctrine that no good can come out of the British Nazareth'.[21] And the work is largely cast as a refutation of Lecky's historical methodology and interpretations.

More widely ranging Nationalist indictments of British rule in Ireland, which proliferated in 1886 and after, were countered by Unionist historical propaganda, scouring the centuries for a sharper illumination of the present. Lord Midleton's *Ireland: Dupe or Heroine?* (1932), hailed by the *Evening Standard* as 'this authentic record by the greatest living authority on Ireland', was merely a late addition to a peculiar form of Irish historical apologetic, which sought to annex the lessons of history in the service of present political need. The point of Midleton's polemic was a defence of W.T. Cosgrave and his Cumann na nGaedheal administration (his last chapter, entitled 'St Patrick or de Valera?', came down decisively on the side of St Patrick); but earlier Unionist historians and controversialists (Peter Kerr-Smiley, A.W. Samuels) had shaped their narratives along similarly expansive lines in order to indict Parnell or Redmond.[22]

The responses of Irish Unionist historians and historical polemicists were not exclusively tied either to Home Rulers, real or imagined, or to the Home Rule debate. Celebrating the loyalist tradition in Ireland also, inevitably, meant celebrating the contribution of Irish soldiers to the British war effort in the years 1914–18. War simultaneously united and divided the Irish people: 1916 came to represent a different form of magic number to different types of Irishman and woman, even though Protestants and Catholics were fighting and dying together on the Western Front. The Great War, and the Battle of the Somme in particular, dominated Unionist history-writing in the 1920s, when the Irish Free

State was being supplied with a revolutionary mythology and hagiography by its scholarly and polemical defenders. Celebratory accounts of the struggle against the British and of its protagonists filtered into print in the 1920s and 1930s, reaching a literary apex with Ernie O'Malley's *On Another Man's Wound* (1936); they were paralleled within Unionist historiography by celebratory accounts of the Irish struggle against the Kaiser. Piaras Beaslai's portrayal of Michael Collins (1926) appeared only months before the commemoration of another Irish commander who was assassinated in 1922 – Field Marshal Sir Henry Wilson, Unionist MP for North Down and military adviser to the Northern Irish cabinet, whose *Life and Letters* was devoutly compiled by a fellow Irish Unionist and war veteran, General Charles Callwell. Other Irish Unionist writers supplied regimental and divisional histories: Bryan Cooper, Unionist MP for South County Dublin in 1910, and subsequently a convert to Cumann na nGaedheal, commemorated the Irish dead of Gallipoli through his account of the *Tenth (Irish) Division* (1917). Cyril Falls, son of a prominent Fermanagh Unionist, began a distinguished scholarly career with the publication of his immensely popular *History of the 36th (Ulster) Division* (1922), and his *History of the Royal Irish Rifles* (1925). Lord Ernest Hamilton, a rather less-skilled but no less-committed historian, paid his homage to the war dead through *The First Seven Division* (1916). In the midst of these war requiems only W. Allison Phillips, holder – significantly – of the Lecky chair of Modern History at Trinity, offered a substantial, contemporary and Unionist analysis of the Anglo-Irish struggle.[23]

The blood sacrifice called for by Pearse had been offered, but by different loyalties and on different altars. War had fully exposed the tensions within Irish politics, and historians, divided both politically and now by their choice of subject matter, compounded these tensions. Commemorating their respective dead, historians supplied two distinctive devotional literatures to the two Irish states, and helped to fashion two distinctive iconographical traditions.

Although commentators as diverse as Peter Gibbon and Tom Paulin have recognised the partitionist sympathies of individual Irish historians, the extent and importance of the work celebrating 'Ulster' and the origins of Northern Ireland have too rarely been recognised.[24] In aggregate, northern historians and writers, working from the end of the First World War through to the 1940s, supplied a comprehensive legitimising and apologist literature. War histories were only one, indirect contribution to the historical vindication of loyalism and of the unionist state: indeed, historians themselves only offered one form of contribution to a more complex literature which explored the Ulster Protestant 'condition'. Edwardian novelists (George Birmingham, St John Ervine, F. Frankfort

Moore), taking their cue from the political arena, were drawn to northern loyalism, and perpetuated a stereotype of the Belfast character.[25] If fiction echoed politics, then history echoed fiction. Popular Unionist historians like Ernest Hamilton followed in the path of the Orange writer and politician, William Johnston, in celebrating the planter tradition, delineating its qualities and publicising its tribulations. The onslaught of 1641 was a recurrent theme, taken up by Johnston in his novel *Under Which King* (1873) (a strangely lachrymose work from an otherwise ferocious Orange commander), and expounded in detail by Hamilton in *The Irish Rebellion* (1920). Of course the Anglo-Irish war provided an essential stimulus, and the apparent resonance linking 1641 and 1921 further motivated writers: Hamilton himself offered semi-fictional accounts of 1641 in his *Tales of the Troubles* (1925). Both Hamilton in Elizabethan Ulster (1923) and Cyril Falls in his *The Birth of Ulster* (1936) – a highly suggestive title – explored the early development of the Ulster plantations, Falls referring to his own planter origins and to his admiration for that tradition.[26]

The partition era was characterised both by these historicist explorations of the 'birth of Ulster' and by a more general literature commemorating the Ulster unionist achievement and celebrating the qualities of the 'Ulsterman'. The omnipresent Ernest Hamilton provided a selective and schematic history of his native province in *The Soul of Ulster* (1917), a work damned by the *Freeman's Journal* as an exemplar of the Junker mentality: tellingly, J.J. Lee has annexed and developed this analogy.[27] Hamilton's polemical target was Sinn Féin. Ramsey Colles supplied a less tendentious and more comprehensive *History of Ulster* (4 vols, 1919), an enterprise justified by 'the Province's magnificent record, and the greatness of her achievements in so many spheres of activity'. Colles's *History* was dedicated to Lecky, and included an appendix which documented and celebrated Ulster's contribution to the British war effort: the work appears to have had a popularity in the North as marked as E.A. d'Alton's *History of Ireland* (6 vols, 1910), which also bore the imprint of the hustling Edwardian publishing house, Gresham. The inevitability of partition was further adduced through the writing of contemporary historians and political commentators in the 1920s such as H.D. Morrison and J.W. Logan.[28] And the events leading to the found- ation of Northern Ireland were chronicled with a piety worth of a P.S. O'Hegarty or a Beaslai by the Ulster Unionist MP Ronald McNeill in his influential *Ulster's Stand for Union* (1922).[29]

All these works, whatever their scholarly merits or demerits, were essentially period pieces, because, consciously or unconsciously, they represented an Ulster Unionist response to the partition question. The writers were often politically active, and where, like Cyril Falls, they were professional scholars, they expressed their particular communal loyalty.[30] This was Unionist history, not necessarily because it was uniformly and absolutely committed, but because it was written by Unionists on historical themes of particular relevance to the Unionist community, and occasionally with a contemporary political purpose. James Craig's Northern Ireland had therefore a more formidable literary vindication than is generally assumed. If Northern Ireland was an instant and arbitrary political formulation, then Unionist writers saw, with Whiggish confidence, only a more ancient pedigree and an inevitable constitutional denouement.

Ronald McNeill's work was important, and not only because he was the most able exponent of Unionist historiography in the 1920s. His *Ulster's Stand for Union* represented a key historiographical transition as the first substantial, documented and public account of organised Unionism. McNeill looked forward to the evolution of scholarly interest in the structures of the Unionist movement, and his narrative, important as much for its personal insights as for its political balance, is still required reading. A Unionist historian of organised Unionism, McNeill pioneered a shift away from other forms of partitionist historiography, and was the precursor of a tradition which has been sustained through the work of scholars such as A.T.Q. Stewart.

McNeill was therefore a father to the literature which celebrated the Unionist founders of Northern Ireland, and the events surrounding its foundation: he was father to the public history of the Northern Irish state. In the 1930s, and after, celebratory biographies of Carson and Craig appeared, written by historians and propagandists, like McNeill, from within the Unionist tradition, and frequently drawing upon McNeill's own narrative. Edward Marjoribanks and Ian Colvin wrote the first major assessment of Carson, published in three volumes between 1932 and 1936: this was followed in 1953 by Montgomery Hyde's *Carson* and in 1981 by a brilliant synthesis of these pioneering works written by A.T.Q. Stewart. The early assessments were essentially positive, as indeed the nature of their authorship might suggest. The ill-starred Marjoribanks – he killed himself in 1932 – was a Conservative MP, while Colvin was a leader-writer for the ultra-Tory *Morning Post*: both men saw a great deal of Carson while they were writing.[31] Montgomery Hyde, though he later repudiated his convictions, was an Ulster Unionist MP at Westminster in the 1950s. James Craig was nearly as fortunate in his biographers, Hugh Shearman writing sympathetically, though professedly from a non-partisan standpoint in *Not an Inch* (1942). St John Ervine's massive semi-official biography, *Craigavon: Ulsterman* (1949) was composed partly 'to expound and interpret . . . the beliefs and political faith of Ulster Unionists' of whom he declared himself to be one.[32] Through works such as these, the cult of the Unionist commanders, so vital a political phenomenon during their lifetime, was sustained after death. Celebratory biographies helped to reaffirm the integrity of the state's purpose and leadership in Northern

Ireland no less than popular portrayals of revolutionary leaders in the Irish Free State. These were the lives of the Founding Fathers, and as such they fulfilled an essential ideological function for successive Stormont governments. One need not look further than the career of Ian Paisley to observe the influence and burden of Carson's mystique; and panegyrical biographies were crucial in the bequest of such political reputations and mythologies.[33]

It should not be assumed, however, that such panegyrics automatically found favour with either the families of the these titans, or with the Northern Ireland government. Ervine's *Craigavon* distressed Lady Craigavon on account of 'the large amount of scurrilous material directed against southern Irish personalities'; and Ervine's invective caused equal alarm among the members of Sir Basil Brooke's cabinet, who refused any association with what had originally been cast as an official biography.[34] Ervine's gift for polemic, combined with his hard-headed commercial sense probably cost him the commission for the official history of Northern Ireland in the Second World War. This celebration of the Northern contribution to the Allied war effort was eventually composed by John Blake, a lecturer in the Queen's University, Belfast, who came cheaper than the veteran man of letters.[35]

Celebrating the origins and founders of Northern Ireland also occasionally, involved a reconsideration of some of the more dramatic and controversial aspects of Ulster Unionist politics. The gun-running of 1914 was of crucial political and psychological significance, bringing credibility to Unionist threats, and representing a successful defiance by an embattled and minority community of an unsympathetic government: as such it was the focal point for Ulster Unionist self-congratulation and pride. A leading gun-runner, like F.H. Crawford, though an idiosyncratic, even apocalyptic figure, enjoyed patronage from the Northern Ireland government: indeed leaders of that government (Craig, for example) had themselves been directly involved with Crawford's activities. McNeill celebrated the gun-running in his *Ulster's Stand for Union*. Crawford offered his own, often inaccurate memories of the episode in *Guns for Ulster* (1947); and more minor figures like R.J. Adgey were equally anxious to recall their participation in the events of April 1914. A.T.Q. Stewart provided a vivid and intricately produced portrayal of the gun-running through his *The Ulster Crisis* (1967). The date of publication is significant. Stewart's was a highly acclaimed work of professional scholarship, and therefore to be distinguished from earlier accounts. But it was written by a friendly observer in the context of a still stable Stormont administration. *The Ulster Crisis* is among the last works of Unionist Whiggery, works which cast the founders of Northern Ireland and their actions in an heroic mould. In this sense the Stewart of 1967 stood as virtually the last representative of a tradition which had its roots in the origins of Northern Ireland itself.[36]

Since 1969 the historical analogy which has dominated the minds of the Unionist leadership has been that supplied by the events of 1912–14. Earlier generations of Unionist leader validated their actions by evoking comparisons with 1641 or with 1690; but, while the Boyne is never far from the historical consciousness of the Unionist movement, the precedents suggested by loyalist activity in 1912 have recently exercised a more thorough fascination and restraint. This may be partly related to divisions within Unionism, and in particular to the search by the Democratic Unionist Party for domination of the Unionist past, no less than of the Unionist present. Ian Paisley has repeatedly identified himself as the successor to Edward Carson – from his association with Carson's son in 1966 through to his Carson Campaign Trail of 1981. In doing so, he has implicitly challenged the validity of rival claimants, as Terence O'Neill and his successors within mainstream Unionism have speedily recognised.[37] But both Democratic and Official Unionists have agreed in seeing their resistance to the Anglo-Irish Agreement as a reconstruction of their forefathers' opposition to the third Home Rule bill, even if they differ over the inheritance of different roles. The immutability of their dilemma has impressed all types of Unionist. As with Frank McGuinness's, Kenneth Pyper ancestral hands exercise a guidance and a restraint from beyond the grave.[38] A particular sense of history and a particular cast of mind permit the present to be fulfilled by the events of a long-dead struggle.

If Unionist commentators, from Dr Paisley to the newly formed Ulster Society, have been engaged by the events of 1912–14, then recent scholarship has opened up broader perspectives on the historical development of the Unionist movement. The resurgence of violence in Northern Ireland after 1969 has radically altered the character of the study of Unionism. Broader interest in the politics of the North has promoted a more comprehensive and politically complex examination of Unionist history, even if – as I shall argue – there remain striking imbalances within this literature. In addition, the expansion and professionalisation of Irish history-writing since the 1930s, and especially since the 1960s, has brought to Unionism more rigorous scholarly standards and a greater scholarly scrutiny (not to say a greater scepticism).

Setting aside ephemeral anti-partitionist polemic (such as James Winder Good's *Irish Unionism* (1920)), those writing on Unionism before 1969 tended themselves to be Unionist: indeed, as has been indicated, some of the most important commentators were active in contemporary Unionist politics (Ernest Hamilton, Ronald McNeill). Well-publicised violence since 1969 has attracted a more diverse range of analysis, for – as John Whyte has pointed out – 'Northern Ireland is a small stage on which great issues can with relative ease be tested'.[39] External comment, combined with the exponential growth of historical research in Ireland has created new historiographical traditions within the study of Unionism as well as a more weighty literature. 'Unionist history' is no longer the preserve of Unionist principle.

Much has been written about the nature of contemporary Protestant politics, but this lies largely beyond the parameters of the present essay. The concerns here are with the historical development of organised Unionism, and not with any broader treatment of contemporary Ulster Protestantism. It may be briefly observed, however, that there *is* a bias within much of the recent literature towards the consideration of radical loyalism. In part this reflects a general weighting within Irish and British historiography which, as Brian Harrison has pointed out, tends to neglect centrist themes, and to favour the radical periphery of politics.[40] So Ian Paisley and his movement have been anatomised in three important works (Steve Bruce's, *God Save Ulster* (1986), Moloney and Pollak's *Paisley* (1986), Clifford Smyth's *Paisley: Voice of Protestant Ulster*? (1987)), whereas James Molyneaux has been almost thoroughly neglected: there is one conversational essay in biography, and no extended analysis of his leadership.[41] Equally, since 1972 there have been several substantial examinations of loyalist paramilitary politics – David Boulton's *The U.V.F.* (1973), Sarah Nelson's *Ulster's Uncertain Defenders* (1984), Martin Dillon's *The Shankill Butchers* (1989) and his *Stone Cold* (1992), and Steve Bruce's *The Red Hand* (1992) – while there has been no published study of Official (Ulster) Unionism, which since its evolution in 1973–4 has been the single largest Unionist party, and indeed, to purloin W.D. Flackes's label, 'the single biggest political entity in the Province'.[42] There have been no detailed assessments of Molyneaux's predecessors, Harry West, Brian Faulkner and James Chichester-Clark; Terence O'Neill's epochal rule, setting aside the general histories, has been examined only once – in David Gordon's stimulating and polemical *The O'Neill Years* (1989). After twenty-five years of violence the plain of Unionism, suburban and constitutional, remains apparently more accessible than the ganglands stalked by Lennie Murphy.

The historical development of organised Unionism has stimulated even less scholarly enthusiasm, yet the work produced in the twenty-five years since 1969 is still far more extensive than that produced in the fifty preceding years. The intellectual origins and implications of this scholarship are exceedingly diverse, but a starting point may be located with the broad organisational dichotomy employed by Whyte in his reviews of the literature on Northern Ireland: that separating Marxist from non-Marxist.[43]

Of course the divisions within the Marxist literature are as striking as the differences between Marxist and non-Marxist work. Divisions over the national question and partition have coloured Irish socialism from the Edwardian disputes between William Walker and James Connolly: such disputes were bequeathed to the Labour Party in Northern Ireland, and are reflected in Marxist and socialist analysis of Ulster Unionism.[44] The now disbanded British and Irish Communist Organisation produced an important and partitionist analysis, *The Birth of Ulster Unionism*, which links that movement to the uneven development of Irish capitalism, and to the existence of two nations, an Irish and a British, on the island. Anti-partitionist Marxists such as Desmond Greaves and Michael Farrell have what Whyte would call a more 'traditional' conception of a single Irish nation, with the island of Ireland as its natural territory: partition, for Greaves, was a cynical British imposition favouring an economically privileged and dissident minority of the Irish people.[45] Farrell's conception of Ulster Unionist nationality is more ambiguous, for while he accepts that Protestants may perceive themselves as part of a British nation, he has also inherited Connolly's bemused impatience with the unionism of the Protestant working classes: populist unionism, rather than being a corollary of Britishness, is instead an unhealthy admixture of bigotry and bourgeois manipulation.

Starting from intellectual premises so thoroughly opposed, the analyses of Unionism profferred by BICO and by Greaves and Farrell embody very different emphases: indeed BICO and Farrell have come into direct confrontation, the BICO pamphlet *The Two Irish Nations* being cast, in its edition of 1975, as a rejoinder and a rebuke to Farrell. Farrell, particularly in his *Northern Ireland: The Orange State* (1976), dwells on the injustices experienced by the Northern minority at the hands of Unionist government and documents the 'carnival of reaction' prophesied by Connolly. Unionism, as embodied in its governmental structures, reflects superannuated economic relationships, and inevitably – though ineffectually – tends towards repression. For BICO commentators, by contrast, it is Unionism, rather than its Nationalist critics, which reflects the historically more advanced economic conditions; and it is Nationalism, through its relationship with Catholicism, which is socially regressive and oppressive. BICO commentators frequently stress the radical political and social potential of Ulster Protestantism, expressed whether in the United Irishmen, or in farmer agitation, or in the populist opposition to Belfast Toryism.[46] But the BICO ideologues and Farrell have at least this in common – that they have approached Unionist historiography from the perspective of contemporary commitments: Farrell has represented his *Orange State* as 'not an impartial work', but rather a socialist clarion call; while the BICO activists were, by definition, political crusaders first and historians second, working from a comprehensive critique of contemporary Ireland back to historical first principles.[47]

Paul Bew, Peter Gibbon and Henry Patterson constitute a third school of Marxist comment on Irish Unionism: in John Whyte's terms they represent the 'apex' of the Marxian dialectic on Northern Ireland. Influenced by the French revisionist critique supplied by Althusser and others, Bew, Gibbon and Patterson have sought to break away from the more banal aspects of the partition controversy, and have concentrated more on examining the internal dynamics of Unionism. As with BICO and Farrell, Bew and Patterson are each anxious to offer a critique of British government in Northern Ireland, although the partnership tends to emphasise the opportunities for positive British intervention (in contradistinction, say, to the convictions of Farrell). Bew and Patterson's contemporary and historical analyses are more sharply distinguished than those of BICO and Farrell for their contemporary analysis is now segregated in discrete volumes and the contemporary implications of their historical research have now become rather allusive: their writing is more subtle and expansive in terms of its ideology, more radical in its methodology, and less rebarbative in its tone. They do not subscribe to the rigid economism of other Marxian writers; they substantiate their theoretical positions with a more thorough historical research than earlier Marxian commentators. 'The central critique which the three writers offer of the prevailing Marxist analysis of Ireland', Bob Purdie has observed, 'is of the inheritance from James Connolly and Second International Marxism of a simplistic view of Unionism which sees it as an artificial entity held together by manipulation and deceit'.[48] Their fundamental achievement, certainly so far as the themes of this essay are concerned, has been to probe the depth of economic and political tension within, especially urban Unionism, whether at the level of the Stormont cabinet (*The State in Northern Ireland* (1978)), or among the Protestant working classes of Edwardian Belfast (Patterson's *Class Conflict and Sectarianism* (1980)). Peter Gibbon has explored the interrelationship of urban and rural Unionism, and the political supersession of the landlord caste by a dynamic, export-oriented unionist manufacturing and mercantile elite (*The Origins of Ulster Unionism* (1975)). Through these works Bew, Gibbon and Patterson have shifted from re-mapping the interface between Unionism and Nationalism towards a new dimension in the analysis of Unionist development. The nature of the partition question is much less important than the nature of the partitionists themselves: qualitative distinctions between unionism and nationalism are much less important than qualitative distinctions *within* Unionism and Nationalism.

The fullest and most thoughtful reaction to the work of Bew, Gibbon and Patterson has been provided by Paul Stewart in his essay, 'The Jerry-Builders'.[49] Stewart rejects what he sees as the trio's attempt to 'normalise' unionist government in Northern Ireland by treating Stormont as an 'ordinary' bourgeois regime and Northern Ireland as an 'ordinary' class society. He argues that they exaggerate the progressivism of the Protestant class alliance in the North East of Ireland, and are guilty of at best, an 'undue optimism' concerning the class awareness and radical potential of Protestant workers. As a corollary, Stewart returns to Connolly, salvaging what he can from *Labour in Irish History* (1910) and

The Re-Conquest of Ireland (1915), and underlining the radical and progressive elements within the Nationalist tradition. In effectively favouring the 'normality' of northern Protestant politics (however squalid in certain respects), in treating Unionist and Nationalist within separate spheres, Bew, Gibbon and Patterson are seen by Stewart to be as partitionist as the two nations advocates of BICO.

Recent non-Marxist historiography represents rather less of a break with earlier analyses of Unionism than the work of Bew, Gibbon and Patterson. Works such as John Biggs-Davidson and George Chowdharay-Best's *The Cross of St Patrick* (1984), an exploration of the Catholic Unionist tradition, certainly share similarities with an older, laudatory historiography both in terms of the overt political sympathies of their authors, and in terms of source material. More recent celebrations by Unionist politicians and writers living in Ireland tend to appear rather lightweight when judged alongside their late Victorian precursors – yet they also stand as clearly within a tradition of loyalist self-assessment as *The Cross of St Patrick*. The fiftieth anniversary of Carson's death stimulated James Allister, a Democratic Unionist Assemblyman, and Peter Robinson, Democratic Unionist MP for East Belfast, to compose a reverential essay on their perceived political forebears.[50] This, and a number of works on the 1912–14 period produced by the Ulster Society, a body created in 1985 'to promote an awareness and appreciation of our distinctive Ulster-British culture' recall in both their tone and purpose the historical reflections of Victorian Unionist activists.[51] Neatly packaged, well-illustrated, and cheaply priced, these recent publications are evidently designed for a mass market – designed to promote a more active consideration of the loyalist tradition. Standing within a Unionist historiographical lineage, it is ironic that the evangelical tone of these works should recall the zeal of Gaelic revivalist literature no less than the apologetic of Victorian loyalism.

But the work of the majority of non-Marxist commentators is less overtly politically committed, and therefore less uniformly centred on Ulster Unionism than either loyalist or Marxist reflection. Southern Unionism was virtually rediscovered by Patrick Buckland after a scholarly neglect of almost fifty years.[52] In so far as Brendan Bradshaw's 'Irish Historical Studies school' is a meaningful label, then Buckland may be located within this school: a doctoral student working with Beckett, he stands in an intellectual tradition and discipline which may be traced back to T.W. Moody and to the progenitors of *Irish Historical Studies* in the 1930s.[53] His trail-blazing articles and monograph (*Irish Unionism I: The Anglo-Irish and the New Ireland* (1972)) opened the way in the 1970s to a succession of studies of southern loyalism or ex-loyalism (those of Ian d'Alton, Jack White and Kurt Bowen).[54] Indeed, although Buckland completed two studies devoted to pre-partition Unionism – one on the North and one on the South – the latter is a more substantial volume than the former. J.C. Beckett has contributed to this debate and this emphasis through his *The Anglo-Irish Tradition* (1976), the peroration of which embodies a quotation from William Drennan: 'the Catholics may save themselves, but it is the Protestants must save the nation'. 'The words are as true today as when they were written', comments Beckett drily and intriguingly, 'and as little likely to be heeded'.[55]

D.C. Savage and F.S.L. Lyons have provided studies of Ulster Unionism during two key phases of its evolution, in 1885–6 and 1904–5; John Harbinson has written a pioneering general account of organised Unionism from its foundation through to 1973.[56] David Miller, through his influential *Queen's Rebels* (1978) and Andrew Gailey in *Ireland and the Death of Kindness* (1987) have explored aspects of the loyalist relationship with British government. But, even allowing for these works, it is arguable that as much is known about the institutional evolution of Southern Unionism as of Northern Unionism for the period before 1972 – a curious imbalance given the numerical inferiority and ultimate demise of the Southern movement. And, although the literature on Protestantism in Northern Ireland is relatively large, little has been written on any aspect of Ulster Unionist history and even on organised Ulster Unionism. Only in 1987 was the first critique of Nationalist attitudes towards Ulster Unionism offered (Clare O'Halloran's *Partition and the Limits of Nationalism*); only in 1988 were the first studies of the Unionist press and of Viscount Brookeborough offered by, respectively, Dennis Kennedy and Brian Barton.[57]

The impact of contemporary political debate on these non-Marxist scholars is certainly subtle, yet it is surely as profound as for the more deterministic. To some extent political controversy has dictated both the subject matter and the evidence of those scholars researching Unionism. Just as the struggle surrounding the first Home Rule bill has a historical dimension, so critics of partition have looked to the historical record of unionism in order to substantiate their allegations. The Government of Ireland Act plays much the same role in late twentieth-century polemic as the Act of Union did in the Home Rule controversies of the late nineteenth century: the record of British Chief Secretaries for Ireland was analysed minutely in 1886, 1893, and 1910–14 (through, for example, R. Barry O'Brien's *Dublin Castle and the Irish People* (1912)), in much the same way as the record of Stormont ministers has been tested since the late 1960s. The issues of polemical concern have become the issues attracting scholarly research; polemical literature has become the substance of scholarly research; to a limited extent the polemicists have *become* the scholarly researchers, just as historiographical and party political activities were not deemed to be incompatible in the nineteenth century, before the popularisation of a 'scientific' methodology.

The critics of Unionist government have indirectly encouraged a greater consideration of their subject. Michael Farrell, through *The Orange State* and the more measured *Arming the Protestants* (1983), has provided more thoroughly researched versions of his work as an ideologue and leader within People's Democracy. Volumes such as these reflect both an increasing research interest in Stormont, itself the offspring of polemical debate, and in turn excite further scholarly rejoinder. John Whyte, for example, has tested a central feature of the critique of the Unionist record (the allegation of sustained and comprehensive discrimination), weighing the available historical evidence against verdicts of commentators such as Farrell and the Unionist A.J. Walmsley.[58] Tom Wilson, a distinguished economist and adviser to Terence O'Neill, has taken up this theme, and engaged other aspects of the debate over Stormont government, in a measured defence of the Unionist record (*Ulster: Conflict and Conciliation* (1989)).

More generally, there has been a proliferation of commentary on the politics and history of Northern Ireland, as scholars respond to the demands of heightened political awareness and of political discussion. Works such as Patrick Buckland's *Factory of Grievances* (1979), or his *History of Northern Ireland* (1981) offer considered assessments of the Unionist record, and help to satisfy the popular appetite for reliable and accessible historical comment on Northern Ireland, especially and increasingly within the schools. David Harkness's *Northern Ireland Since 1920* (1983) and Sabine Wichert's *Northern Ireland Since 1945* (1991) fulfil a similar function. Naturally, these works address issues of contemporary political concern (economic performance, employment practice, security policy), and thereby become themselves part of the political agenda, informing and provoking debate. Writing history becomes making history: historiography becomes once again, as in 1886 or 1912, part of the historical process.

Contemporary debate also, inevitably, intrudes into the historian's sources. There is both an institutional and a personal dimension to this intrusion. Government and civil service in London, Dublin and Belfast have proved to be extremely reticent when processing historical materials bearing on Northern Ireland. The restrictions governing such material tend to be much more oppressive than for other, less controversial, areas of administration; and the processes of selection are performed apparently with much greater vigour. In the Public Record Office at Kew there remains Irish documentary material from the 1890s which is withheld from scholarly scrutiny. Of course all historians working in official archives are informally bound to an agenda devised by government – but this is emphatically true of those working on modern Ireland. Nor is there much consolation to be gained elsewhere. Leading Unionist politicians have been reluctant, understandably, to place their archives on public access, and their descendants, often fearful of the consequences of publicity, are generally no less coy. Autobiographical reminiscence – Lord

Brookeborough's autobiographical articles in *The Belfast Telegraph*, Terence O'Neill's *Autobiography* (1972), Brian Faulkner's posthumously published *Memoirs of a Statesman* (1978) – is, almost by definition, less concerned with factual reconstruction than with the protection of political reputation. The opponents of Unionism are generally as unforthcoming as their targets. Violence in Northern Ireland, allied to the peculiarly acrimonious nature of political exchange, has meant that the penalties of unconsidered frankness, of sweeping disclosure, are very considerable. Given these constraints of evidence, even the most disinterested historian is bound to the sectarian arena.

A thoroughly diverse and vibrant historiography has therefore emerged since 1969 – but an historiography characterised by both old and new varieties of imbalance. The achievements of 'revisionist' scholarship – particularly the recent radical revisionism which Brendan Bradshaw has identified – have, until comparatively lately, made little impact on the historiography of Unionism.[59] The historiography of unionism remains a historiography of crisis, detailed examinations of politics in 1885–6, or 1912–14, proliferating at the expense of the investigation of institutional evolution or of Unionist society. Southern Unionism before 1922 has evoked a comparatively great scholarly regard, while many features of popular Unionism in the North remain obscure. Perhaps scholars have found Belfast, Louis MacNeice's 'country of cowled and haunted faces' a less congenial territory than the 'islands' of Anglo-Irish civilisation inhabited by Somerville and Ross, or by Elizabeth Bowen.[60] Or perhaps the general predominance of elite history within European political historiography has an Irish reflection in a literature which says more about Ascendancy landowners than about Orange labourers.

Unionist historiography retains an inevitable connection with contemporary political perspectives, but this connection has been both tempered by the development of professional scholarship and mitigated by new varieties of interpretation. Moreover, the evolution of Unionist historiography reflects the evolution of Unionism itself, from early political triumphs and an uncertain command of parliamentary power at Stormont through to division and defeat. The confident tones of Trinity Unionists, defending the constitutional *status quo* of the 1890s, or of the Unionist polemicists of the 1920s, defending their particular Brave New – Northern – World, have scarcely survived 1969 and 1972: the evangelical tone of recent popular historiography seems more firmly rooted in despair than in hope. A schismatic and fissile Unionism is reflected in a scholarship which, itself divided by political and methodological sympathy, focuses on analyses of Unionist division. In this sense, therefore, the political revolution in Northern Ireland has evoked a revolution among its chroniclers.[61]

NOTES

1 Oliver MacDonagh, *States of Mind: A Study of Anglo-Irish Conflict, 1780–1980* (London, 1983), p. 14: 'In the last analysis they [Ulster Protestants] share the historical cyclicalism of nationalist Ireland, or at least the two mental habits tend to converge.' R.F. Foster, 'Varieties of Irishness' in Maurna Crozier (ed.), *Cultural Traditions in Northern Ireland: Proceedings of the Cultural Traditions Group Conference* (Belfast, 1989).

2 Terence Brown, *Ireland's Literature: Select Essays* (Mullingar, 1988), pp. 226, 238.

3 A.T.Q. Stewart, *The Narrow Ground: Roots of Conflict in Ulster*, 2nd edn (London, 1989), p. 15.

4 A.T.Q. Stewart, 'The Siege of Ulster', *Spectator*, 11 January 1986, pp. 15–16. Though see Hiram Morgan, 'A Scholar and a Gentleman: Interview with A.T.Q. Stewart', *History-Ireland*, 1 (2), summer 1993, p. 58.

5 J.J. Lee, 'Some Aspects of Modern Irish Historiography' in E. Schulin (ed.), *Gedenkschrift Martin Goehring* (1968), pp. 432–43. R.B. McDowell, *Alice Stopford Green: A Passionate Historian* (Dublin, 1967).

6 Alvin Jackson, *The Ulster Party: Irish Unionists in the House of Commons, 1884–1911* (Oxford, 1989), pp. 57–9.

7 Elizabeth Lecky, *A Memoir of W.E.H. Lecky* (London, 1909), pp. 76–7, 337, 350, 359–60.

8 C.L. Falkiner, *Studies in Irish History and Biography* (London, 1902). For Falkiner's career see the memoir by Edward Dowden prefacing C.L. Falkiner, *Essays Relating to Ireland: Biographical, Historical and Topographical* (London, 1909), pp. v–xvi. Lecky, *Memoir*, p. 351: 'He [W.E.H. Lecky] had followed for some time past with much interest and sympathy the historical studies of a friend of his, Mr. C. Litton Falkiner.'

9 Alvin Jackson, 'The Failure of Unionism in Dublin, 1900', *Irish Historical Studies*, xxvi (104), November 1989, pp. 377–95. F.E. Ball, *The Judges in Ireland*, 2 vols (London, 1921).

10 Falkiner, *Essays*, pp. vi–vii. Public Record Office of Northern Ireland (hereafter PRONI), Irish Unionist Alliance Papers, D.989: C.L. Falkiner to Mr Cox, 5 September, 11 September, 12 September, 1890.

11 Brown, *Ireland's Literature*, pp. 29–31. See Richard Bagwell's contribution to S. Rosebaum (ed.), *The Case for the Union: Against Home Rule* (London, 1912), pp. 182–8. There is a case for including the historian of medieval Ireland, G.H. Orpen, in this category: see the obituary notice in *Jn.R.S.A.I.*, lxiii, 1933, pp. 145–7. I am grateful to my colleague, Marie-Therese Flanagan, for this reference and for this suggestion.

12 Donal McCartney, 'Lecky's *Leaders of Public Opinion in Ireland*', *Irish Historical Studies*, xiv (54), September 1964, pp. 119–41. Lecky, *Memoir*, p. 227.

13 C. Litton Falkiner, *Illustrations of Irish History and Topography, Mainly of the Seventeenth Century* (London, 1904), p. xiii. C. Litton Falkiner, *Studies in Irish History and Biography, Mainly of the Eighteenth Century* (London, 1902).

14 James Loughlin, *Gladstone, Home Rule and the Ulster Question* (Dublin, 1986), pp. 193ff.

15 Lord Ashbourne, *Pitt: Some Aspects of his Life and Times* (London, 1898).

16 W.E.H. Lecky, *The Political Value of History* (London, 1892), p. 16. McCartney, 'Lecky's *Leaders*', pp. 134–5.

17 See Loughlin, *Gladstone*, pp. 194–5, for the fight over Burke's legacy.

18 Lecky, *Memoir*, pp. 310–11.

19 Lecky, *Political Value of History*, pp. 53–7.

20 Falkiner, *Essays* p. vi.
21 T.D. Ingram, *A Critical Examination of Irish History, Being a Replacement of the False by the True*, 2 vols (London, 1900), i: pp. 1, 14, 184, 196; ii: 10, 166, 171.
22 See for example: Peter Kerr-Smiley, *The Peril of Home Rule* (1911); A.W. Samuels, *What is Home Rule?* (1911) and *Home Rule Finance* (1912); 'Irish Imperialist', *The Old Conspiracy, 1848–1911* (1911); anon., *Ireland & the Union* (1914).
23 W. Alison Phillips, *The Revolution in Ireland, 1906–23* (London, 1923). There are also more narrowly focused catalogues of the IRA campaign written by a Unionist official of Dublin Castle: C.J.C. Street, I.O., *Ireland in 1920* (London, 1921); C.J.C. Street, *Ireland in 1921* (London, 1922).
24 Peter Gibbon, *The Origins of Ulster Unionism: The Formation of Popular Protestant Politics and Ideology in Nineteenth Century Ireland* (Manchester, 1975), pp. 4–5, 20n. Tom Paulin, *Ireland and the English Crisis* (Newcastle, 1987), pp. 25, 118–19, 142, 155–6.
25 George Birmingham, *The Red Hand of Ulster* (London, 1912); W. Douglas Newton, *The North Afire* (London, 1912); St John Ervine, *Mrs Martin's Man* (London, 1914); F. Frankfort Moore, *The Ulsterman* (1914). See Norman Vance, *Irish Literature: A Social History* (London, 1990), pp. 176–92.
26 Cyril Falls, *The Birth of Ulster* (London, 1936), p. xii: 'I may as well admit it now . . . that I was brought up to admire the Ulster colonists.' For William Johnston as novelist see Aiken McClelland, *William Johnston of Ballykilbeg* (Lurgan, 1990), p. 15.
27 *The Freeman's Journal*, 14 April 1917; J.J. Lee, *Ireland 1912–85: Politics and Society* (London, 1989), pp. 4–6.
28 H.D. Morrison, *Modern Ulster*, (London, n.d.); J.W. Logan, *Ulster in the X-Rays* (London, n.d.).
29 For the significance of McNeill see Jackson, *The Ulster Party*, pp. 284–5.
30 Falls, *The Birth of Ulster*, p. xii. For Falls's father, who was an important functionary within the Ulster Unionist Council, see Jackson, *The Ulster Party*, pp. 200, 204, 311.
31 PRONI, Edward Carson Papers, D.1507E: Correspondence between Carson and his biographers, 1930–35.
32 St John Ervine, *Craigavon: Ulsterman* (London, 1949), p. vii. For Carson's biographers see Alvin Jackson, *Sir Edward Carson* (Dublin, 1993), p. 74.
33 Steve Bruce, *God Save Ulster! The Religion and Politics of Paisleyism* (Oxford, 1986), pp. 212–13.
34 PRONI, Northern Ireland Cabinet Papers: CAB.9F/123/37. I am grateful to Sean MacDougall, University of Birmingham, for this reference. See also CAB.3A-3E for further material on Blake's *History of Northern Ireland in World War II*.
35 *Ibid.*
36 Morgan, 'A Scholar and a Gentleman', p. 56: 'I was not writing an academic book for Faber – it was going to be a kind of political thriller. But I could not shake off the academic training.'
37 Alvin Jackson, 'Unionist Myths: 1912–85', *Past & Present*, 136, August 1992, pp. 168–9, 175.
38 Frank McGuinness, *Observe the Sons of Ulster Marching Towards the Somme* (London, 1986), p. 56: 'I couldn't look at my life's work for when I saw my hands working they were not mine but the hands of my ancestors interfering, and I could not be rid of their interference. I could not create. I could only preserve.'
39 John Whyte, *Is Research on the Northern Ireland Problem Worthwhile?* (Belfast, 1983), p. 16.

40 Brian Harrison, 'The Centrist Theme in Modern British Politics' in *Peaceable Kingdom: Stability and Change in Modern Britain* (Oxford, 1982), esp. pp. 353–77.

41 Anne Purdy, *Molyneaux: The Long View* (Antrim, 1989).

42 W.D. Flackes, *Northern Ireland: A Political Directory, 1968–79* (Dublin, 1980), p. 143.

43 Whyte, *Research on the Northern Ireland Problem*, pp. 11–16.

44 Paul Stewart, 'The Jerry-Builders: Bew, Gibbon and Patterson – the Protestant Working Class and the Northern Ireland State' in Sean Hutton and Paul Stewart, *Ireland's Histories: Aspects of State, Society and Ideology* (London, 1991), p. 180.

45 John Whyte, *Interpreting Northern Ireland*, paperback edition (Oxford, 1991), pp. 180–1.

46 See for example: *The Two Irish Nations* (1975), *The Birth of Ulster Unionism*, revised edition (1984), *The Belfast Labour Movement* (1974).

47 Michael Farrell, *Northern Ireland: The Orange State* (London, 1976), p. 12.

48 Bob Purdie, 'The Demolition Squad: Bew, Gibbon and Patterson on the Northern Ireland State' in Hutton and Stewart, *Ireland's Histories*, p. 167.

49 See note 44.

50 Jim Allister and Peter Robinson, *Carson: Man of Action* (Belfast, 1985).

51 Jackson, 'Unionist Myths', pp. 175–6.

52 See Patrick Buckland, *Irish Unionism I: The Anglo-Irish and the New Ireland, 1885–1922* (Dublin, 1972).

53 Brendan Bradshaw, 'Nationalism and Historical Scholarship in Modern Ireland', *Irish Historical Studies*, xxvi (104), November 1989, pp. 329–51.

54 Ian d'Alton, 'Southern Irish Unionism: A Study of Cork Unionists, 1884–1914', *Transactions of the Royal Historical Society*, xxiii (3), January 1973, pp. 71–88; d'Alton, 'Cork Unionism: Its Role in Parliamentary and Local Elections', *Studia Hibernica*, xv, 1975, pp. 143–61; Kurt Bowen, *Protestants in a Catholic State: Ireland's Privileged Minority* (Kingston and Montreal, 1983); Jack White, *Minority Report: The Protestant Community in the Irish Republic* (Dublin, 1975).

55 J.C. Beckett, *The Anglo-Irish Tradition* (London, 1976), p. 153.

56 D.C. Savage, 'The Origins of the Ulster Unionist Party, 1885–6', *Irish Historical Studies*, xii (47), March 1961, pp. 185–208; D.C. Savage, 'The Irish Unionists, 1967–1886', *Eire-Ireland*, ii (3), 1967, pp. 86–101; F.S.L. Lyons, 'The Irish Unionist Party and the Devolution Crisis of 1904–5', *Irish Historical Studies*, vi (21), March 1948, pp. 1–22; John Harbinson, *The Ulster Unionist Party, 1882–1973: Its Development and Organisation* (Belfast, 1973).

57 Dennis Kennedy, *The Widening Gulf: Northern Attitudes Towards the Independent Irish State, 1919–49* (Belfast, 1988); Brian Barton, *Brookeborough: The Making of a Prime Minister* (Belfast, 1988).

58 John Whyte, 'How Much Discrimination was there Under the Unionist Regime, 1921–68' in Tom Gallagher and James O'Connell (eds), *Contemporary Irish Studies* (Manchester, 1983), pp. 1–35.

59 Bradshaw, 'Nationalism and historical scholarship', p. 342.

60 Louis MacNeice, 'Belfast' in *Poems* (London, 1935).

61 An earlier version of this essay appeared in the *The Irish Review* (winter, 1989, and summer 1990).

8

HOME RULE AND THE HISTORIANS*

Alan O'Day

INTRODUCTION

'Our knowledge of the past is seriously affected if we learn how that knowledge came into existence', observes Herbert Butterfield in *Man on his Past*.[1] He was not addressing the work of Irish historians then, despite the book's origins as the Wiles Lectures at the Queen's University of Belfast in 1954, but deploring the baleful effect of an earlier German historiography which, Butterfield believes, had contributed to the tragedy of modern Germany. He goes on to suggest that

> the historian in fact played an important part in the German national story . . . for in effect it was he who said to the country: 'See, this is your tradition, this is the line which the past has set for you to follow'. And now it is dawning on the Germans that their historians may have made the wrong diagnosis.

To begin with Butterfield and Germany may seem curious at first sight though less so if they are placed in the context of historians' presumed pre-eminence in the construction of national traditions, especially of emergent states. His words are a clarion call for re-examination of nationalistic history, a plea for a 'revisionism' which detaches historical writing from xenophobia. Older Irish historical writing has stood in the dock accused by 'revisionists' of having much the same deleterious effect as Butterfield attributes to German historiography. Writings in the nationalist tradition have been charged with contributing to the post-1968 'troubles' in Northern Ireland by legitimising an interpretation of Ireland's history glorifying violence. Butterfield is an appropriate starting point, also, because Brendan Bradshaw has singled out his influence in undermining traditions of patriotic Irish historical writing.[2] The inter-action of contemporary politics and history is not a new phenomenon, a recently discovered danger to national values. Between the 1880s and the Great War intellectuals in the British Isles readily lent their prestige to one

141

or another panacea for the Irish problem.[3] No issue was subject to greater attention, none raised more emotion than home rule.

Irish Home Rule, like many aspects of Ireland's past, has been re-written under the impact of new evidence, changing techniques and different perspectives. It has been a battle ground of 'revisionism', but 'revisionism' with a difference. Interest in the subject has been higher among foreign scholars than among the Irish themselves in the last thirty years. In his critique of 'revisionism', Fr Bradshaw particularly is incensed by the intrusion of anti-patriotic agendas in much modern work. However, as will be seen, the traditional writings on Home Rule were notable for their political bias fully as much as any of the recent studies. Discussions of Home Rule have had a polemical side to be sure but more often this has been linked to contemporary British politics or intellectual fashions rather than to Ireland, north or south. Interpretations of Home Rule seem far removed from the intense debates in Irish circles over the Famine, land war and Irish revolution. 'Revisionism', on Home Rule has been cooler and discussed mainly among academics rather than intrud-ing into the public arena. It is surprising, however, that Irish institutions, specific plans for self-government, have not been placed under a micro-scope more often in recent studies emanating from Irish universities for these have certainly played a substantive part in both the character of the contemporary Republic of Ireland and in the 'troubles' of post-1968 Northern Ireland. Various attempts since the early 1970s, and especially the Framework Document issued in February 1995, exemplify the present-day significance of the devolution or Home Rule disputes of an earlier era. Alan Ward's recent book demonstrates that very point.[4] Contemp-orary republican rhetoric and assumptions of what constitutes a legitimate majority owe much to the Home Rule debates between 1886 and 1914.

ORIGINS AND DEFINITION OF HOME RULE

What do I mean by Home Rule? I mean by Home Rule the restoration to Ireland of representative government, and I define representative government to mean government in accordance with the constitu-tionally expressed will of a majority of the people, and carried out by a ministry constitutionally responsible to those whom they govern. In other words, I mean that the internal affairs of Ireland shall be regulated by an Irish Parliament – that all Imperial affairs, and all that relates to the colonies, foreign states, and common interests of the Empire, shall continue to be regulated by the Imperial Parliament as at present constituted. The idea at the bottom of this proposal is the desirability of finding some middle course between separation on the one hand and over-centralisation of government on the other.

(John Redmond in Australia, 1883)[5]

142

It must also be considered that an examination into the different forms of Home Rule, while it shows that no scheme of legislative indepedence for Ireland offers any promise of finality, also suggests that the form of Home Rule least injurious to England is the form which gives Ireland most independence. The inference from these facts cannot be missed. Home Rule is the half-way house to Separation. Grant it, and in a short time Irish independence will become the wish of England. If any thorough-paced Home Ruler admit this conclusion and suggest that Home Rule is a desirable transition towards Separation, the answer is that Home Rule is such a transition, but assuredly that such a transition is not be desired.

(A.V. Dicey, 1886)[6]

Irish self-government has a distant lineage. It was given flesh in the late eighteenth century under Henry Grattan when Ireland enjoyed substantial though not complete autonomy. The crown remained head of state in Ireland and the Irish Parliament did not engage in independent relations with foreign potentates. In fact, the London regime retained considerable authority in Ireland and could decline to accept legislation passed by the Dublin Parliament. Neither the Viceroy nor Chief Secretary were responsible to the Irish Parliament. This was a Protestant Parliament that excluded Catholics, though those who met the property qualification were admitted to the franchise in the early 1790s. Ireland possessed representative but not responsible institutions. As an alternative to limited autonomy republicans such as Wolfe Tone sought complete separation from Great Britain. His aim was 'to break the connection with England, the never-failing source of all our political evils'.[7] He was followed by Robert Emmet, another disaffected Protestant, who tried 'to effect a total separation between Great Britain and Ireland – to make Ireland totally independent of Great Britain'.[8] After the success of Catholic Emancipation, Daniel O'Connell wanted to revive Repeal of the Union as a means of squeezing concessions out of the British Parliament. In 1831 he announced, 'we only want a Parliament to do our private business, leaving the national business to a national assembly.'[9] In 1843 the Repeal movement proposed

the restoration of a separate and local parliament for Ireland – the restoration of the independence of Ireland. The first would necessarily include the making of all laws that should be of force within the entire precincts of Ireland – by the Sovereign, the Lords, and the Commons of Ireland, and the total exclusion of any other legislature from any interposition in affairs strictly Irish. The second would necessarily include the final decision of all questions in litigation by Irish tribunals seated in Ireland, to the total exclusion of any species of appeal to British tribunals.[10]

143

O'Connell's more mundane goal was 'a parliament inferior to the English Parliament but vested with powers of "independent legislation"'. But, he was prepared to accept 'a subordinate Parliament'.[11] 'The Liberator' conceived of an Irish Parliament in which popular influences, at least in the lower chamber, would be substantial. For a brief time in 1844 O'Connell took up Sharman Crawford's ideas on 'federalism' though these never achieved popularity among repealers.[12] Young Ireland broke with O'Connell, in part, because of his vacillations and modest ambitions. James Fintan Lalor would 'never contribute one shilling, or give my name, heart, or hand, for such an object as the simple Repeal by the British Parliament of the Act of Union'.[13] He would be satisfied with nothing short of 'independence'.

Fenianism, like its republican forbears, tended to be stronger on sentiment and rhetoric than in working out finely calculated structures. The Proclamation in 1867 decreed

> all men are born with equal rights, and in associating to protect one another and share public burdens, justice demands that such associations should rest upon a basis which maintains equality instead of destroying it.
>
> We therefore declare that, unable longer to endure the curse of Monarchical Government, we aim at founding a Republic based on universal suffrage, which shall secure to all the intrinsic value of their labour.
>
> The soil of Ireland in the possession of an oligarchy, belongs to us, the Irish people, and to us it must be restored.
>
> We declare, also, in favour of absolute liberty of conscience, and complete separation of Church and State.[14]

A republic was the announced intention though individual Fenians were less committed to a precise formula and were open to variations on the self-government principle.

In 1870 the Home Government Association tried to formulate its aims which under Isaac Butt's guidance were defined as 'federal home rule'. His rationale was that 'England, Scotland and Ireland, united as they are under one sovereign should have a common executive and a common national council for all purposes necessary to constitute them, to other nations, as one state, while each of them should have its own domestic administration and its own domestic Parliament for its own internal affairs'.[15] He wanted an autonomous responsible Parliament of two Houses with exclusive jurisdiction in Ireland. There was to be a House of Commons of 250 to 300 MPs and an upper chamber composed of resident peers. The powers of the Irish body were to be those of the old Irish Parliament under Grattan but it would surrender the right of taxation for imperial needs. The Westminster Parliament would have authority over imperial expenditure, the national debt, the civil list, the cost of the military, nomination and maintenance of ambassadors and the colonial establishment. Ireland would retain the present number of MPs in the Westminster House of Commons. Like its predecessors this new movement did not succeed in drawing up proposals that answered key questions such as the proportion of taxation payable by Ireland or the powers of intervention a British regime might exercise. At the Home Rule Conference in November 1873 'federalism' was accepted as the official platform but many delegates expressed preferences for other plans. Clearly, the movement's commitment to details was sufficiently vague that in 1875 Parnell might say that he 'could never see the difference between Home Rule and Repeal. It was a fact that to obtain Home Rule they must first repeal the Union'.[16] The ambiguity surrounding the term Home Rule allowed an Irish Chief Secretary in the 1870s to observe, 'it seems to me that every class in Ireland has interpreted the cry . . . to mean the fulfilment of its own particular desires'.[17]

Parnell was unwilling to define what he meant by Home Rule though he later denied being a separatist and promised that the 'Queen would be our Queen'.[18] John Redmond's concept cited at the beginning of the section, was a clear statement of the broad principle but not enlightening about details. Parnell's testament at Cork in January 1885 contained a generous measure of ambiguity. He stated that

> I do not know how this great question [national self-government] will be eventually settled. . . . It is given to none of us to forecast the future, and just as it is impossible for us to forecast the future, and just as it is impossible for us to say in what way or by what means the national question may be settled, in what way full justice may be done to Ireland, so it is impossible for us to say to what extent that justice shall be done. We cannot ask for less than the restitution of Grattan's Parliament with its important privileges and wide and far-reaching constitution. We cannot, under the British Constitution, ask for more than the restitution of Grattan's Parliament. But no man has the right to fix the boundary to the march of a nation; no man has a right to say to his country: 'Thus far shalt thou go and no further', and we have never attempted to fix the *ne plus ultra* to the progress of Ireland's nationhood, and we never shall.[19]

Typically, his declaration was more remarkable for sentiment than detail; it was about the closest Parnell came to defining Home Rule in public prior to 1886. However, this and other similar references gave substance to the belief that Home Rule was supported by nationalists as the maximum Britain was likely to concede, not the end patriots would prefer.

Home Rule was given reasonably definite form not by the Irish but in Gladstone's Government of Ireland bill in 1886. Gladstone held 'that there is such a thing as local patriotism, which in itself is not bad, but good'.[20] In order to enable that local sentiment to flourish he proposed to 'establish a Legislative Body sitting in Dublin for the conduct of both legislation and administration in Irish as distinct from Imperial affairs'. In his proposed structure many powers were permanently or for a specified time retained by the Westminster Parliament. It was acknowledged, even by Nationalist representatives, that the Dublin Parliament could be suspended or revoked as befell the Northern Ireland Parliament in 1972. Parnell in his final speech before the second reading of the bill accepted it as a 'final' solution but he was soon repudiated by some of his own supporters. Subsequently, the meaning of Home Rule was well understood though the details of plans changed over time. Thomas Sexton, speaking for the nationalist parliamentary majority in 1893, stated that the 1886 proposal had 'narrowed . . . the area of the controversy . . .'.[21] When Irish Home Rule was placed before Parliament again in 1912 it was as the first instalment of a devolution of powers to local assemblies in the United Kingdom, a far from reassuring prospect for those who might otherwise be induced to shed Ireland in the interest of preserving the Constitution. But the actual scheme did not greatly deviate from the principle laid down by Gladstone in 1886.[22] Critics of Irish plans were often more precise about structures and concepts than advocates of home rule, none more so than A.V. Dicey.

Both advocates and opponents of Home Rule used terminology like 'self-government', 'responsible self-government', 'local self-government', 'federalism', 'devolution', and 'independence' without careful distinctions as to the differing meanings.[23] Some greater clarity emerged after 1886 though that was not invariably the case. John Redmond in 1910 could say that the concession of Home Rule was valuable as a means to 'strengthen the arm of the Irish people to push on to the great goal of national independence' and shortly thereafter that 'by Home Rule we mean something like you have here [in the USA], where Federal affairs are governed by the Federal Government and state affairs by the state government'.[24] A recent commentator outlines the differences in a useful fashion. He notes that Irish Home Rule was an example of devolution, a system of government in which a central legislature creates subordinate regional assemblies to which it devolves responsibility for regional affairs.[25] This he distinguishes from 'Home Rule all round' which describes a comprehensive plan for devolution to regional legislatures in England, Scotland and Wales, something never proposed except as a future possibility in the various Home Rule bills. Finally, federalism is a constitutional system in which a central legislature and regional legislatures exercise co-ordinate powers, the two levels of authority being defined in a constitution that can only be revoked or amended by extraordinary means, not by ordinary legislation. Home Rule proposals after the 1870s, he observes, were devolutionary, no matter that some were called 'federal'. Despite the fact that many nationalists were lawyers, it remained the case that they tended to be blasé about institutional structures, no doubt because the language and uses of Home Rule had a deeper utility than concrete schemes. Irish Home Rule was a middle course between integration into Britain and separation and when the men of 1916 acted out their 'blood sacrifice', it was not for the sake of domestic autonomy but in pursuit of an 'Irish Republic as a sovereign independent state', one claiming, indeed, insisting upon 'the allegiance of every Irishman and Irishwoman'.[26] At the conclusion of the Irish revolution Home Rule became obsolete for nationalists. For them it was a movement and concept chiefly pertinent to the decades between 1870 and the Great War.

INTERPRETATIONS OF HOME RULE

It is doubtful whether Hercules could shoulder the weight of writings on Home Rule. These can be categorised by perspective, chronology, origin of the authors or some combination of approaches. There has never been a shortage of raw material for a study of Home Rule. Newspapers, periodicals, public records, the parliamentary debates, numerous recollections and biographies have been available in abundance since the Home Rule era itself. To this vast array of materials later academic studies, published diaries, and private papers have widened and deepened the possibilities for exploring the motives and expectations of participants in the controversy. The literature can be placed in four broad schools – unionist, liberal, nationalist and modern revisionist. These designations mirror to some extent the classifications employed by the late J.H. Whyte's treatment of the literature on the present-day 'troubles' in Northern Ireland.[27] His categories were traditional unionist, traditional nationalist, Marxist and internal conflict schools of writing. This period and the home rule era are linked and Whyte's classification scheme is pertinent to the earlier episode as well.

Between 1886 and 1914 unionist literature, mainly polemical writings, was rich in numbers, argument and emotion. Already, Anthony Froude and W.E.H. Lecky had found previous periods of Irish history fruitful as illustrations of Ireland's unsuitability for self-government.[28] Lecky threw on the scales the weight of his acknowledged expertise of eighteenth-century Ireland to counter the claims of Nationalists. No writer of the era was more influential than A.V. Dicey but others, including Arthur Balfour, made significant contributions as well.[29] An important collection compiled by Simon Rosenbaum in 1912, *Against Home Rule: The Case for the Union*, further highlights the tone and quality of much Unionist writing.[30] Though prepared for a partisan purpose the Rosenbaum volume makes telling points. Similarly, the political cartoons of Tom Merry and his contemporaries added to the rich harvest of anti-Home Rule propaganda.

Dicey's many articles and two further books, *A Leap in the Dark* (1893) and *A Fool's Paradise* (1912) along with his first volume in 1886 stated the intellectual case against the Home Rule plans. In 1886 he forcefully maintained

Home Rule does not mean National Independence. This proposition needs no elaboration. Any plan of Home Rule whatever implies that there are spheres of national life in which Ireland is not to act with the freedom of an independent State. . . . A *bona fide* Home Ruler cannot be a *bona fide* Nationalist.[31]

In that same book he considered the alternatives of Grattan's Parliament, federalism and separation and found them wanting. Balfour, likewise, criticised the concept of Home Rule for he believed that the peoples of the British Isles were too entwined to form separate states. He challenged, 'ask an Irish Nationalist what institution he desires to see restored to his native county. If he replies at all, the institution he names will almost certainly prove to be of English origin and to have been abolished because it failed'.[32] There also was a strong economic argument. In 1893 the Belfast Chamber of Commerce petitioned against the second Home Rule bill on a combination of socio-economic, political and religious grounds essentially employing the two nations theory for intellectual underpinning. It held

we believe that the Economic and Social condition of Ireland renders it singularly unfitted for Home Rule. The population is not homogeneous – it is radically divided on the lines of race and of religion, and the two parties are filled with distrust and with historical jealousy of each other. . . . The resources of Ireland are unequal to supporting a national government.[33]

Excepting Dicey's writings, little of this vast body of material retains currency. The settlements of 1920–21 largely undermined interest in the unionist case as it applied to the whole of Ireland. Able biographies of certain of the chief participants, notably of Lord Salisbury, Arthur Balfour and Sir Michael Hicks Beach, offer a defence of their anti-Home Rule stances but most post-1920 work, even that generally sympathetic to Conservatives, has been bashful about unionist opposition to Ireland's demand for autonomy. Two active members of the present-day Tory party display this reticence. Lord Blake's sympathetic accounts of Disraeli and Bonar Law are reserved on the Irish vision of the two Conservative party leaders. Of Law's stance on Ulster between 1912 and 1914 Blake remarks, 'undoubtedly in making a declaration of this sort Bonar Law was going far to break the conventions upon which Parliamentary democracy is based'.[34] In his later general survey of the Conservative party he states that 'whatever the errors of the Liberals, the fact remains that the Conservatives were launched on a very perilous course'.[35] John Ramsden's official history of the Conservative party in the age of Balfour and Baldwin advances the view that Law as 'leader of the opposition in Parliament approved and supported the destruction of both the practice and authority of Parliament'.[36] Whyte's treatment of Unionist writings on the current 'troubles' parallels the pattern.[37] Revival of traditional Unionist interpretation has been unfashionable for more than seventy-five years though a few studies such as those of A.T.Q. Stewart constitute exceptions.[38] Nevertheless, it is important not to ignore the quantity, quality and influence that traditional Unionist interpretations exerted or to overlook that they surely won the propaganda war before 1900 and more than held their own down to 1914.

The Conservative interpretation was never allowed unchallenged hegemony and the chief rivals, Liberal and Nationalist perspectives, have dominated the field since the early 1920s. John Morley's classic biography of Gladstone, initially published in 1903, was a powerful salvo for Home Rule. Morley, of course, was a political colleague of Gladstone, a politician–journalist staking out a position, not a dispassionate scholar intent upon weighing up and balancing evidence before pronouncing judgement. During the penning of the three volume *Life* Morley declined to take a large role in Liberal party affairs. For him the biography's purpose was to bring Liberals back to their true mission. Gladstone's adoption of Home Rule in 1886 was not just an Irish crusade but a stand for the liberal humanitarian commitment to justice. He strove to show that Gladstone's conversion to Home Rule was not a response to freak parliamentary arithmetic or the whim of an 'old man in a hurry'. Morley's admiration of Gladstone's high motives spring to life in the observation, 'among his five spurious types of courage, Aristotle names for one the man who seems to be brave, only because he does not see his danger. This, at least, was not Mr Gladstone's case. No one knew better than the leader in the enterprise, how formidable were the difficulties that lay in his path'.[39] According to Morley 'few are the heroic moments in our parliamentary politics, but this was one'. No-one would describe this as detached history.

Morley's influence reached widely. In the 1930s studies by George Dangerfield, R.C.K. Ensor, J.L. Hammond and Nicholas Mansergh re-affirmed and extended his perspective advocating the view that Home Rule was the best solution we never had. Unionists were for them and others the 'guilty men' of the Irish imbroglio. No-one slapped down unionists more thoroughly than Dangerfield. His *The Strange Death of Liberal England* (1935), sees them as among the chief villains in the destruction of the liberal values of later Victorian and Edwardian Britain. They had been obstructionists over Ireland and bore responsibility as wreckers of Liberal Britain. In a real sense, they were forerunners of the inter-war menace of fascism and intolerance. Dangerfield's subsequent foray into Irish affairs, *The Damnable Question* (1977), published in his later years, repeats his early opinions and argues forcefully against any Liberal concession to Ulster separatism.

R.C.K. Ensor's *England, 1870–1914* (1936) written for the Oxford Modern History syllabus, influenced a future political elite. Hammond, like Ensor, belonged to the progressive left in British politics. He had spent time in Ireland reporting for *The Manchester Guardian* on the Anglo-Irish war. His newspaper was then the leading voice of Liberalism and a critic of British actions in Ireland. Hammond was appalled by the atrocities committed, especially at the hands of the crown forces, and saw in Gladstone's Home Rule proposals the best means to have averted the tragedy he witnessed. Emotion bubbled to the surface in Hammond's declaration in his *magnum opus, Gladstone and the Irish Nation* (1938) that, 'on the day of Judgement the British people may be glad to remember that in 1886 nearly half the nation and in 1893 more than half the nation was ready to follow this old man's summons to a splendid adventure'.[40] Due to the timing of the book's publication, it had only a modest impact until after 1945 when it became indispensable to the rising generation of history students.

Mansergh shared Ensor's and Hammond's outlook. As a southern Irish Protestant he felt the bloody last chapter of the Home Rule episode with special poignancy. In *Ireland in the Age of Reform and Revolution* (1940) he maintains that

> in the long unhappy history of Anglo-Irish relations only one event is more truly tragic than the rejection of Home Rule in 1886. The opportunity of settlement had come, perhaps the greatest of English statesmen was ready to grasp it and yet the unique chance was destroyed by a failure in perception whose consequences not even time can wholly repair.[41]

Mansergh's account, like Dangerfield's and Hammond's, retains its place up to the present day on higher education and popular reading lists for the Irish Question. Slightly revised editions, under the new title, *The Irish Question, 1840–1921*, have been re-issued several times since the mid-1960s. He returned to Irish matters at the close of his life when he examined the Ulster dimension in *The Unsolved Question: The Anglo-Irish Settlement and its Undoing 1912–72* (1991). Mansergh's initial account was among the earliest by a respected academic rather than the labour of a journalist or politician though his passionate eloquence was not dulled thereby. Common threads running through liberal interpretations include Gladstone's grand vision, the possibility of Home Rule ending 'centuries' of Anglo-Irish antagonism, and a disinclination to place the successive schemes under close scrutiny.

Nationalist writings (note Whyte's category, Traditional Nationalist) offered a variant on the liberal perspective. These flowered particularly in the post-1922 Irish Republic but were earlier adumbrated in the skilful works of R. Barry O'Brien, an indefatigable journalist-historian. O'Brien, too, was a participant as well as an observer having been Parnell's Boswell during the last campaign of 1890–91. The most impressive of his many books, the magnificent two-volume study of Parnell published in 1898, like Morley's *Life*, is a monument to the craft of late Victorian biography. During the period when he was preparing the biography O'Brien was cavorting with Lady Gregory's set and trying to persuade the Unionist, Sir Horace Plunkett, to take up Parnell's mantle.[42] The biography was a conscious comparison of the greatness of Parnell's era with the sad fate of Irish politics in the 1890s. O'Brien's emotions burst through when he declaimed that Parnell had 'brought Ireland within sight of the Promised Land. The triumph of the national cause awaits other times, and another man.'[43] O'Brien did not repudiate the importance or greatness of Gladstone but put emphasis on Parnell's power, strategic insight and magnetism. His centre of gravity was Irish. Subsequent works of the Nationalist vein have stressed the Irish aspect of the story, though it remained usual to laud Gladstone's attempt to satisfy Ireland. Denis Gwynn and P.S. O'Hegarty, though in differing ways, exemplify this style of historical writing. On the whole, however, home rule, as compared with revolutionary politics, has not facinated the post-1922 generation of historians in Ireland writing in the Nationalist tradition. For most of them Home Rule seemed what it had been to Redmond and Dicey, a middle course that diverted some Nationalists between the Famine and Irish Revolution but never could meet Ireland's legitimate expections. T.A. Jackson's, *Ireland Her Own*, first published in 1947 but reprinted several times, states this widely held view. Of the home rulers, only Parnell entered the new age with a reputation largely unsullied. The others were seen as Irish 'uncle Toms'. Whereas earlier Nationalist writing sought to legitimise the revolutionary tradition, to salute its accomplishments, later scholars were drawn to the same subject matter in order to quash the prevailing republican orthodoxy. For reasons not wholly explicable, Home Rule has not often been a preferred battleground between the old and new history, 'anti-revisionists' and 'revisionists'.

The new or research-driven history that mushroomed after the Second World War has been mainly university based. The majority of earlier writings were by contemporaries, politicians and journalists. Mainstays of the academic approach can be summarised as careful sifting of evidence, fidelity to information, balance and a professed refusal to employ history as a handmaiden to politics. F.S.L. Lyons captured the essence of academic professionalism when he explained, 'I have a historian's loyalty to my sources and, once having seen this material would find it impossible to behave as if it didn't exist. . . . A public man belongs in the last analysis to history and the ordinary rules of privacy don't apply – or at least not in the way that they do to private people'.[44] This approach did not originate in Ireland but was transported there by scholars who in the 1930s had been research students in Britain, principally at the Institute of Historical Research in the University of London. Nor was it even a British Isles innovation for the real beginning point of academic inquiry had been in nineteenth-century German universities from whence it jumped over the sea to America before being transported from there into Britain.

The two centres of academic interest in Home Rule in Ireland were Trinity College where T.W. Moody and his disciples dissected the Irish parliamentary party and at The Queen's University of Belfast where students re-examined unionist resistance to Home Rule. Students and scholars at University College Dublin were frequently drawn to other controversies though under the guidance of Desmond Williams and R. Dudley Edwards they employed the same academic methodology. University College, though, never developed into an important centre for the training of doctoral students, preferring to send its own abler graduates on to British universities. This literature introduced many caveats to received icons and greatly refined understanding of the Home Rule controversy. Although the Trinity group turned a cool eye on traditional republican interpretations, their work has not greatly departed from the liberal-nationalist perspective. Lyons, *Ireland since the Famine* (1971) reflects the continued potency of those traditions. He begins

the tired old witticism that every time the English came within sight of solving the Irish question the Irish changed the question, contains, like most jokes about Ireland, a small grain of truth submerged in a vast sea of misconception. The Irish did not change the question between the Famine and the war of independence any more than they had changed it between the Union and the Famine. The 'national demand', as it used to be called remained in essence, what Wolfe Tone had declared it to be as long ago as 1791, 'to break the connection with England, the never-failing source of all our political evils'. It is true, of course, that men differed in the nineteenth century, as they have continued to differ, in the twentieth, about how complete the break should be, or more precisely, perhaps, about how far the full separatist idea was practicable. But whether they took their stand on the rock of the republic, or were prepared to settle for repeal of the Union and some form of Home Rule based upon a reanimated Irish Parliament, they were emphatic that the first step towards real independence was to recover for Irishmen the right to control their own affairs.[45]

Lyons' last major study, *Culture and Anarchy in Ireland, 1890–1939* (1979), based on his Ford lectures at the University of Oxford, is written within the Nationalist perspective while identifying reasons for its failure. This volume was composed under the impact of the violence in Northern Ireland and undoubtedly is sombre in tone. Though often seen as a signal piece of 'revisionism' by 'anti-revisionists', mainly because Lyons identifies four antagonist cultures in Ireland which divide rather than unite the country's peoples, in one sense supporting the two nations theory so much hated by traditional Nationalists, there is little directly in the account that can be called demonstrably anti-national. Despite his credentials as an authority on the Home Rule movement, Lyons does not fully flesh out an implicit part of his theme that in the halcyon days of Parnell, Nationalism had not been Celtic, Catholic and sectarian, the roots of partition being found in the post-1890 changes in the nature of the movement. Roy Foster essentially takes over Lyons' outlook that in the aftermath of the divorce scandal Ireland lacked sufficient consensus on essential matters to live happily under a single liberal democratic regime based in Dublin. This analysis is within the Liberal–Nationalist tradition though perhaps one showing increasing signs of being frayed at the edges. Similarly, Conor Cruise O'Brien's *Parnell and his Party, 1880–90* (1957), places the Irish leader and his movement in the constitutional Nationalist tradition, then a 'revisionist' perspective which attracted its share of criticism from patriotic historians. The doyen of Trinity historians, T.W. Moody did not see his vast enterprise *Davitt and the Irish Revolution, 1846–1882* (1982), appear until shortly before his death. Although meticulous in his adherence to scholarly methodology, Moody's perspective is hardly distinguishable from R. Barry O'Brien's at the end of the nineteenth century.

Differing academic outlooks were largely a product of training and fashions in historiography elsewhere, mainly in British universities. Some of this work roughly approximates Whyte's internal conflict categorisation. Michael Hurst, an Oxford scholar, published a careful study, *Joseph Chamberlain and the Liberal Reunion: The Round Table Conference 1887* (1967), establishing a framework of analysis based on intensive use of private correspondence and adherence to strict chronology. Hurst argues that the issue was used by most of the participants as a means to solidify their respective standings with supporters and reunion was not what they actually wanted to achieve. Implicit in this argument is the assumption that issues and ideology must not be accepted at face value but may very well stand as codes or publicly acceptable objectives behind which a more complex agenda can be found. His insight was being replicated and extended in other studies of British politics, notably in Cambridge, at around the same time. Hurst's argument found a strong echo in D.A. Hamer's biography, *John Morley: Liberal Intellectual in Politics* (1968). Hamer, a New Zealander who did research at Oxford, asserts that the Liberal party leadership was internally divided between advocates of programme politics and those who favoured concentration on a single great unifying cause. Hamer subsequently elaborated this theme suggesting that Gladstone's motivation for the adoption of home rule was less idealistic than the liberal interpretation admitted. After exhaustive investigation of original and published sources Hamer concludes that while Gladstone no doubt believed in his panacea for resolving Irish disaffection, home rule was devised essentially for internal Liberal party needs. He maintains, 'the Home Rule preoccupation offered a temporary remedy for faddism, a temporary answer to the problem that had plagued the Liberal leaders for many years of fixing priorities among reform demands'.[46] This assertion turned Home Rule historiography on its head. Gladstone was neither an 'old man in a hurry' nor pandering to Irish susceptibilities but a cool calculating leader intent upon patching up dissension within the Liberal party by using Ireland as the common denominator, the all-embracing cause.

An influential increment in the interpretation was introduced in the many works of A.B. Cooke and J.R. Vincent, culminating in *The Governing Passion* (1974). They assert that only private materials were reliable for assessing motivation, thereby rejecting the usual reliance upon public as well as private pronouncements. For them

the 'Irish question' was the temporary and particular name given in the 1880s to a continuous and permanent existential problem which party managers inflict upon themselves. This is the task of finding party lines, divisions, and alignments, and then rationalising these for the benefit of that great majority of even their senior colleagues who hold themselves bound by habit, honour, loyalty, and decency to an existentialist view of party definitions of which they then loyally expect the moral entrepreneurs of the party to evolve for them from their own inner Nihilism.[47]

Behind their thesis lies the belief that the 'greasy pole' of politics was a contest for power between individuals; issues and principles have only a subsidiary role. This took Hurst's essential proposition and added a large twist of cynicism to it. They contend that Gladstone took up home rule as a tactic to out-manoeuvre Joseph Chamberlain and other rivals within the Liberal party. This approach, often referred to as 'high politics' was employed in Maurice Cowling's study of the Reform Act of 1867. It has been associated especially with Peterhouse, Cambridge and has been applied to other disputes by scholars from many backgrounds. The main features of 'high politics' are that it developed outside Ireland and was initially used for questions unrelated to Irish affairs, only latterly being applied to Home Rule. It does echo Arthur Balfour's trenchant comment

154

in 1914 that 'Home Rule is not a constitutional remedy, it is a parliamentary device'.[48] For practitioners of 'high politics' Westminster is the centre of the political matrix, the venue where all vital alignments and issues are worked out. Also, the technique is employed essentially to explain British leaders' motivations and ignores nationalists. 'High politics' is often alleged to be 'conservative' as a consequence of the political stance of some of its originators, also because it de-emphasises ideas and issues and correspondingly stresses personal ambition and the quest for power. Few would suggest, however, that this sort of 'conservatism' was akin to the Unionist writings of an earlier generation. What this whole school or approach potentially spells out for discussions of Home Rule is that the scheme devised in 1886 contains much more than a means of satisfying Irish wants, that home rule has had a variety of uses both within and outside Ireland, and that the term Home Rule contained symbols and meanings beyond being a formal description of a form of self-government.

'High politics' had some influence in the 1970s and 1980s although its appeal crested then; in the late 1980s and 1990s a Liberal counter-attack resurfaced. 'High politics' has been applied in numerous studies including Peter Marsh's *The Discipline of Popular Government* (1978), which sees the home rule issue in Lord Salisbury's hands being worked as a device to subdue rivals and discipline followers in his own coalition and found further support in Roy Foster's *Lord Randolph Churchill: A Political Life* (1981). Andrew Gailey's *Ireland and the Death of Kindness: The Experience of Constructive Unionism 1890–1905* (1987) offers a similarly inspired assessment of the Conservative alternative to Home Rule. The approach was only partially applied to Irish nationalism, although traces can be found in subsequent studies of the first Home Rule crisis. Sophisticated reprises of the liberal interpretation by T.A. Jenkins *Gladstone, Whiggery and the Liberal Party 1874–1886* (1988) and by the distinguished editor of the Gladstone diaries, stand as a reminder that the spirit of Morley, Hammond and Gladstone is alive and well in academic circles. Jenkins endorses Hammond's claim that Gladstone had been converted to Home Rule some months before the general election of 1885, although he accepts that his decision in the circumstances of late autumn and winter 1885–6 may well have been dictated by personal ambition, by a desire to be called upon one more time to solve a great national problem. Thus, while rejecting the conclusions of Cooke and Vincent, Jenkins is prepared to see Gladstone as an 'old man in a hurry'.[49] Colin Matthew's painstaking labours which assimilate modern scholarship to thorough research on Gladstone refutes an interpretation of his subject as driven only by political self-preservation. Yet, he gives close attention to the context that encouraged Gladstone to take up Home Rule. Curiously, while rejecting a 'high politics' analysis for Gladstone, Matthew endorses

Marsh's explanation for Salisbury's motivation, confirming not so much the truth of the hypothesis but its continued attraction when the technique fits historians' arguments. Matthew also confounds the 'Greek-like chorus' of pessimists who have shouted down the feasibility of Home Rule, especially the financial provisions of the 1886 bill, by demonstrating that it would have proved very much to Ireland's benefit. His intervention acknowledges that Gladstone's 'mission was still to pacify Ireland, not to liberate it' and Matthew's laconic conclusion that 'the gold of the moment of 1886 indeed turned to lead' is something distinct from a simple reversion to the good old days of Morley just as Jenkins' study confirming Hammond's contention about Gladstone's conversion does so with a post-'high politics' twist.[50] Little of the new research originated in Ireland, indeed, the bulk of post-1965 'revisionism' has been produced in, or influenced by, British universities and, though scholars in Ireland were undoubtedly familiar with 'high politics' ideas, they have made little use of it in their own work. Foster, of course, is a partial exception but by the time he fell under its sway he was settled at Birkbeck College, University of London, and probably should be treated as an English rather than an Irish academic.

On the whole, academic interest in approaches to the institutional and political facets of Irish politics have been superseded by an emphasis upon localism and internal class divisions (see Whyte's Marxist category for a parallel). David Fitzpatrick's study of County Clare during the revolutionary decade, *Politics and Irish Life, 1913–21* (1977), focuses attention on change and its absence on the ground in rural Ireland, while K.T. Hoppen's writings, particularly his huge tome, *Elections, Politics and Society in Ireland 1832–1885* (1984), establishes a framework for interpreting Irish national politics from the bottom up rather than the traditional way, top down. Tom Garvin's analysis of Revolutionary Nationalism uses an occupational and geographical basis for treating Nationalists of all varieties.[51] Traces of Paul Bew's provocative Marxist-inspired contributions emphasising internal class conflict are found in some recent writing on Home Rule that use class or interest models to explain divisions within nationalist ranks.[52] His subsequent endorsement of Unionist objections to Home Rule because of uneven economic development and that Home Rule was a British manufactured solution not unlike the Anglo-Irish Agreement of 1985, adds a note of vitality to the discussion of the objects of the Gladstonian self-government proposals which may bear fruit in the future. Indeed, it is rather surprising that the core–periphery scheme employed by Michael Hechter's *Internal Colonialism: The Celtic Fringe in British National Development, 1536–1966* (1975), has not been utilised more systematically to explain the motives for advocacy of, and resistance to, Home Rule. Quantitative analyses of Nationalism have added an ingredient to the discussion though, these have not been employed systematically to the home rulers over an extended period. Alan O'Day's attempt to quantify the parliamentary performance of the Parnellites between 1880 and 1885, interposing a Namierian concept of 'interest' – though only for a limited time – encountered some hostility from those who prefer a conventional model based a neat polarity dividing Nationalists from its opponents.[53] Garvin's studies also attempt to see revolutionaries from the standpoint of 'interest' but his subjects, of course, were opponents of simple constitutional Home Rule. William Lubenow's treatment of the Home Rule Parliament of 1886 also employs a Namierian framework and relies upon analysis of voting patterns, but the study has attracted only modest attention in Ireland.[54] His chief concern is British, rather than Nationalist, political alignment; to date the study has not inspired a parallel Irish investigation, though the implications of his work are considerable. If, as Lubenow and others note, the Irish party in the 1880s was an 'ideologically monolithic' grouping with a pronounced tendency to take radical or progressive stands on social issues, this has importance for the Home Rule debate. These and other investigations have amplified and shifted academic discussion but they have not sought to explain why Redmond's or Dicey's middle way was advocated with so much enthusiasm by bourgeois patriots. An orthodox Nationalist interpretation that sees the commitment to home rule as simply the art of the possible has never been altogether persuasive, but to date no alternative perspective or methodology has displaced it.

'Revisionism' as it is understood or vilified in Ireland – reinterpretation of the patriotic past with the intent of undermining the nationalist and revolutionary tradition, has not scarred the debate on home rule to any great degree. New perspectives on Home Rule have not had the same emotive force as, for instance, those on the Famine, land war, or Easter Rising. 'High Politics', for sure, sparked a controversy, but it mainly took place within British academic circles. Nothing in 'high politics' is inherently anti-national and its findings, in fact, can be used to sustain an orthodox Nationalist interpretation. The wider public has been immune to many of the changes in academic fashion, continuing to prefer familiar Liberal or Nationalist themes. Robert Kee's Liberal–Nationalist writings enjoy extensive readerships.[55] Also, North American academics, many from Irish ancestral origins, mostly have stood outside the fist-'a-cuffs of recent academic disputes often seeming to be unaware of the heady controversies, oblivious to the learned discourse in Ireland and Great Britain. Alan Ward, working from an American college, makes no reference even by implication to the swirling cross-currents of intellectual debate on Home Rule in an otherwise skilful synthesis, *The Irish Constitutional Tradition* (1994). Emmet Larkin's multi-volume investigation of the politics of the Catholic Church and Lawrence McCaffrey's survey books with a market in American higher education, scarcely budge from traditional Nationalism and show no evidence of having taken on board the historiographical disputes at the cutting edge of scholarship in the British Isles. William Lubenow, in contrast, labouring outside the ambit of Irish studies in America, devotes several pages to consideration of 'high politics' in his book, *Parliamentary Politics and the Home Rule Crisis: The British House of Commons in 1886.*

CONCLUSION

Approaches to Irish history have changed over time. Journalistic history has not wholly disappeared (note the success of Robert Kee) but it has fought an uphill battle against the onward march of academe. Partly as a consequence of the triumph of rigorous academic methodology reliance upon, and treatment of, evidence is far more systematic today from what it was in the time of O'Brien and Morley. Neither O'Brien nor Morley was disdainful of what might be called scholarly adherence to sources. They and fellow journalists made liberal use of public and private materials, often with every bit as much fidelity as university dons, but they did not, as Fr Bradshaw would say, do so to the exclusion of empathy with their subjects. Yet, as noted already, new methodology and insights have not had so huge an impact upon the traditional view of Home Rule as they have had on other issues in Irish history. 'Revisionism' of the sort deplored by Brendan Bradshaw has not played so prominent a role in the reevaluations. Hoppen and Fitzpatrick are not notably lacking in empathy even if their language is more restrained but these and similar works have been mined mainly for insights on questions other than Home Rule. The main line of a by no means negligible change in the historiography has come from British universities and mainly applied to the British side of the home rule story. Curiously, even Foster's treatment of Churchill makes no attempt to apply the method to the Irish dimension of home rule. No-one would say that the conclusions today are identical to the assessments of Morley, Dangerfield, Hammond and Mansergh. T.A. Jenkins and Colin Matthew writing in a similar tradition have none the less made a more measured defence of Gladstone. The struggle for Home Rule is seen as more complex, more variegated, less inspired by single-minded nobility of purpose than these earlier writers allowed. As already indicated, the discussion has generated considerable heat, but the principal forum has been within British historiography rather than its Irish counterpart. Also, it is a debate which has for the most part eluded the wider public. If politicians, civil servants and journalists have been contaminated with a 'revisionist' view of Home Rule, as allegedly is true in Ireland where anti-national historiography supposedly has had a enervating influence, the real problem outside this narrow world has been how to elicit any sustained interest in Irish history at all. 'Revisionism' in this instance has been confined to a rarefied section of the community. Foster's much misquoted aphorism, 'we are all revisionists now' certainly applies to Irish Home Rule and in the sense he undoubtedly meant the remark to be taken. Foster, in the finest Trinity tradition espoused by Lyons, was expressing approval of critical historical inquiry not promoting an overtly anti-patriotic agenda.

'Revisionism' on the Home Rule question may be taken as an exemplary illustration of the internationalisation of intellectual life, where the strains of historical writing from several traditions have induced reassessment of the Home Rule era. None perhaps has been more intriguing, but less applied, to the period than the Germanic approach to myths and symbols pioneered by Peter Alter.[56] Except for occasional flashes of interest, such as seen in Garvin's writings, studies of Irish nationalism generally and home rule in particular have taken little notice of the methodology pioneered by Miroslav Hroch and the Cologne school. Likewise, the important theoretical insights of Benedict Anderson, Ernest Gellner and Anthony Smith among others have received no more than faint responses from the fraternity of Irish historians, although John Hutchinson's *The Dynamics of Cultural Nationalism* (1987), holds out suggestive possibilities of how these conceptual ideas might be put to good use.[57] Likewise, the huge storehouse of pictorial materials has enticing prospects for a different approach to many aspects of Home Rule and more generally, Victorian Ireland. Attempts by L.P. Curtis Jr to exploit some of this imagery is done within a traditional Nationalist outlook and failed to advance either understanding or methodology; indeed, the discrediting of his work may have retarded serious interest in these important sources.[58] His assertion that racism was the key to rejection of the Home Rule Bill in 1886 has a grain of truth that ought not to be ignored, but the suggestion is hardly new and the motives behind the measure's defeat were much more complicated that this facile explanation allows. His studies seem to owe more to the America of the racially-torn 1960s than to Victorian Ireland, a 'revisionism' so removed from mainstream Irish concerns as to reduce its value to passing notice. While E.H. Carr's reminder that history is shaped by contemporary perspectives is certainly part of the story of 'revisionism' in all ages,[59] the strife of Afro-America and Vietnam then were too far removed from Ireland to elicit much interest except occasionally from one of the author's countrymen. Curtis, at least, could not be accused of being hide bound by a parochial Irish outlook.

In what senses was Home Rule a symbol, a code for other expectations, as much as a precise formula for governing institutions? This and other questions remain largely unasked, much less answered, for insularity and an insistence upon Ireland's uniqueness is the hallmark of 'revisionism' as surely as it is in the tradition 'revisionists' set out to challenge.

Significantly, it is not the provincialism of Irish historical writing that incurs the wrath of Fr Bradshaw. Indeed, the impetus for his assault on 'revisionism' is the comparative analysis employed by an early modernist, Stephen Ellis, and his argument that the Irish experience under English rule was the norm for regions on its geographical fringes.

Comparative disregard of Home Rule must, in the end, seem extremely curious. Post-1968 violence in Northern Ireland has been a stimulus to reassessments of many facets of Ireland's past. Institutions have played an important part in British policy objectives since 1969 and the reiteration of the need for new structures has been a theme of communiqués, agreements and joint declarations for over two and a half decades. The Framework Document of February 1995 is but a further instalment of the attempt to reconstruct a workable fabric of government. There is no more significant effort at a structural solution to the Irish problem than the Home Rule schemes between 1886 and 1921. If Ireland, north and south, is to forge some different and viable sets of constitutional relationships, it is certainly in order to assess with renewed vigour those institutional ambitions of the not so distant past. Once again the question of whether or not Gladstonian Home Rule was the best solution we never had rears its head, beautiful or ugly depending on the eye of the beholder. Finally, examination of the literature on Home Rule does not sustain the usual assumption that 'revisionism' is most pronounced in Irish political history. Economic studies of the Famine and land holding, for example, are much more advanced along the path of 'revisionism' than the political topic of home rule.

NOTES

* I am pleased to acknowledge the assistance in preparation of this article of George Boyce, Miles Bradbury, Michael Bromley, Dennis Dean, Barbara Gauntt, Sheridan Gilley, Michael Hurst, Jonathan Moore, my aunt Col. Helen O'Day and Genevieve Schauinger.
1 Herbert Butterfield, *Man on his Past* (New York, 1962 edn), p. 26.
2 Brendan Bradshaw, 'Nationalism and Historical Scholarship in Modern Ireland', *Irish Historical Studies*, XXVI, November 1989, pp. 329–51; reprinted in Ciaran Brady (ed.), *Interpreting Irish History: The Debate on Historical Revisionism* (Dublin, 1994), pp. 191–216.
3 Thomas Dunne, 'La Trahison des Clercs: British Intellectuals and the First Home Rule Crisis', *Irish Historical Studies*, XXIII, November 1982, pp. 134–73; Christopher Harvie, 'Ideology and Home Rule: James Bryce, A.V. Dicey and Ireland, 1880–1887', *English Historical Review*, XCI, April 1976, pp. 299–314.
4 Alan J. Ward, *The Irish Constitutional Tradition: Responsible Government and Modern Ireland, 1782–1922* (Washington DC, 1994).
5 Quoted in Denis Gwynn, *Life of John Redmond* (London, 1932), p. 52.
6 A.V. Dicey, *England's Case Against Home Rule* (Richmond, VA, 1973), pp. 286–7.
7 Quoted in F.S.L. Lyons, *Ireland since the Famine* (London, 1976), p. 15.

8 Quoted in Alan O'Day and John Stevenson (eds), *Irish Historical Documents since 1800* (Dublin, 1992), pp. 14–16.
9 Quoted in Ward, *op. cit.*, p. 42.
10 *Ibid.*, p. 44.
11 Quoted in O'Day and Stevenson (eds), *op. cit.*, p. 60.
12 Ward, *op. cit.*, p. 45.
13 Quoted in O'Day and Stevenson (eds), *op. cit.*, pp. 68–70.
14 *Ibid.*, pp. 76–7.
15 Isaac Butt, *Irish Federalism: Its Meaning, Its Objects and Its Hopes* (4th edn, Dublin, 1874).
16 *The Nation*, 23 October 1875.
17 *Parliamentary Debates [PD]*, 218 (1874), cc. 110–18.
18 *Ibid.*, 305 (1886), cc. 1168–84.
19 *United Ireland*, 24 January 1885.
20 *PD*, 304 (1886), cc. 1036–85.
21 *Ibid.*, 8 (1893), cc. 1313–27.
22 Patricia Jalland, *The Liberals and Ireland: The Ulster Question in British Politics to 1914* (Brighton, 1980), pp. 19–49.
23 John Kendle, *Ireland and the Federal Solution: The Debate over the United Kingdom Constitution, 1870–1921* (Kingston and Montreal, 1989), pp. 4–5.
24 Quoted in Ward, *op.cit.*, pp. 85–6.
25 *Ibid.*, p. 51.
26 Quoted in O'Day and Stevenson (eds), *op. cit.*, pp. 160–1.
27 John Whyte, *Interpreting Northern Ireland* (Oxford, 1990).
28 R.F. Foster, 'History and the Irish Question', *Transactions of the Royal Historical Society*, Fifth Series, 33, 1983, pp. 169–92; reprinted in revised form in Brady (ed.), *op. cit.*, pp. 122–45.
29 A.J. Balfour, *Nationality and Home Rule* (London, 1913).
30 Simon Rosenbaum (ed.), *Against Home Rule: The Case for the Union* (Washington, New York and London, 1970).
31 Dicey, *op. cit.*, p. 33.
32 Balfour, *op. cit.*, p. 12.
33 Quoted in O'Day and Stevenson (eds), *op. cit.*, pp. 122–9.
34 Robert Blake, *The Unknown Prime Minister: The Life and Times of Andrew Bonar Law 1858–1923* (London, 1955), p. 130.
35 Robert Blake, *The Conservative Party from Peel to Thatcher* (London, 1985), p. 195.
36 John Ramsden, *The Age of Balfour and Baldwin 1902–1940* (London, 1978), p. 85.
37 Whyte, *op. cit.*, pp. 147–74.
38 A.T.Q. Stewart, *The Ulster Crisis* (London, 1967); *The Narrow Ground: Aspects of Ulster, 1609–1969* (London, 1977).
39 John Morley, *The Life of William Ewart Gladstone* (London, 1903), III, p. 308.
40 J.L. Hammond, *Gladstone and the Irish Nation* (London, 1938), p. x.
41 Nicholas Mansergh, *Ireland in the Age of Reform and Revolution* (London, 1940), p. 150.
42 John Kelly, 'Parnell in Irish Literature', in D. George Boyce and Alan O'Day (eds), *Parnell in Perspective* (London, 1991), pp. 256–8.
43 R. Barry O'Brien, *The Life of Charles Stewart Parnell* (London, 1898), II, p. 367.
44 F.S.L. Lyons to Myles Dillon, 13 July 1967, Lyons Papers, Trinity College Dublin.
45 Lyons, *op. cit.*, p. 15.
46 D.A. Hamer, *Liberal Politics in the Age of Gladstone and Rosebery: A Study in Leadership and Policy* (Oxford, 1972), pp. 129–30.

47 A.B. Cooke and J.R. Vincent, *The Governing Passion: Cabinet Government and Party Politics in Britain 1885–86* (Brighton, 1974), p. 18.
48 Quoted in Ward, *op. cit.*, p. 53.
49 T.A. Jenkins, *Gladstone, Whiggery and the Liberal Party 1874–1886* (Oxford, 1988), pp. 248–9.
50 H.C.G. Matthew, *The Gladstone Diaries, July 1883–December 1886* (Oxford, 1990), XI, pp. ccxxvi–clxi.
51 Tom Garvin, *The Evolution of Irish Nationalist Politics* (Dublin, 1981); *Nationalist Revolutionaries in Ireland 1858–1928* (Oxford, 1987).
52 Paul Bew, *Land and the National Question in Ireland, 1858–1882* (Dublin, 1978).
53 Alan O'Day, *The English Face of Irish Nationalism* (Dublin, 1977; 2nd edn, Aldershot, 1994).
54 William C. Lubenow, *Parliamentary Politics and the Home Rule Crisis: The British House of Commons in 1886* (Oxford, 1988).
55 Robert Kee, *The Green Flag* (London, 1972); *The Laurel and the Ivy* (London, 1993).
56 Peter Alter, 'Symbols of Irish Nationalism', *Studia Hibernica*, 14, 1974, pp. 104–23; reprinted in Alan O'Day (ed.), *Reactions to Irish Nationalism 1865–1914* (London, 1987), pp. 1–20; see also, Gerhard Brunn, 'Historical Consciousness and Historical Myths', in Andreas Kappeler, Firket Adanir and Alan O'Day (eds), *Comparative Studies on Governments and Non-Dominant Ethnic Groups in Europe, 1850–1940: The Formation of National Elites* (Aldershot and New York, 1992), VI, pp. 327–38.
57 E.g. Ernest Gellner, *Nations and Nationalism* (Oxford, 1983); Anthony D. Smith, *National Identity* (London, 1991); Benedict Anderson, *Imagined Communities* (London, 1983). Also see Peter Alter, *Nationalism* (2nd edn, London, 1994).
58 L.P. Curtis Jr, *Anglo-Saxons and Celts: A Study of Anti-Irish Prejudice in Victorian England* (Bridgeport, CT, 1968); *Apes and Angels: The Irish in Victorian Caricature* (Washington, DC, 1971); see Ned Lebow, *White Britain and Black Ireland* (Philadelphia, 1970). For a thorough-going critique, S.W. Gilley, 'English Attitudes to the Irish in England, 1780–1900', in Colin Holmes (ed.), *Immigrants and Minorities in British Society* (London, 1978), pp. 81–110.
59 E.H. Carr, *What is History?* (New York, 1962), p. 5.

9

1916, INTERPRETING THE RISING

D. George Boyce

In 1966, at a conference held in a Belfast hotel to mark the fiftieth anniversary of the 1916 rising, one of the participants criticised Professor J.C. Beckett for having devoted only one page of his 496-pages-long book *The Making of Modern Ireland* to Patrick Pearse. Since the book surveyed Irish history from 1603 to 1923, this may seem unreasonable; and it is true to say that Patrick Pearce and the 1916 Rising have had many pages devoted to them in the last twenty-five years. But the incident, small in itself, epitomises the difficulty in placing the rising in its appropriate context in the history of modern Ireland. And this is because it has several resonances: the making of 1916, and the aims and intentions of its leaders; its immediate impact on events; its implications for Irish politics in the longer run; and the significance of the rising in Irish political ideology, as a 'recycled' inspiration to would-be revolutionaries, and indeed, to would be constitutionalists as well. This chapter will assess these four topics, which, of course, are not mutually exclusive. This assessment will be preceded by a short historiographical section.

I

It is very often the case that in the interpretation of an historical event those who get their explanation in first influence subsequent generations, if only because they set the agenda for future debate.

The Easter Rising of 1916 did not undergo this kind of treatment. That the rising was an important episode could not be doubted. But professional historians very largely ignored it, and it was left to those whose purpose was to eulogise the heroes of the rising to write interesting, if sketchy, lives of the leading participants. The rising bubbled to the surface of Irish politics, but it cannot be said to have attracted the attention of Irish historians, and nothing about it appeared even in the pages of the house journal, *Irish Historical Studies*, in the first thirty years of its life. Yet the first major advance was made through the medium of

Irish Historical Studies, now moving tentatively away from its caution over publishing material relating to recent Irish history. Moreover, the breakthrough came in a most unlikely section of that most unlikely publication: in that part of the journal devoted to an occasional series which printed original source material. An article entitled 'Eoin MacNeill on the 1916 Rising' was edited with an introduction by Professor F.X. Martin, using documents which he had unearthed in the National Library of Ireland while compiling a bibliography of MacNeill's writings (published in *Irish Historical Studies* in 1948). Martin published two memoranda by MacNeill (who was Chief of Staff of the Irish Volunteers), with extensive footnotes and commentary.[1]

These memoranda revealed important aspects of the rising: that it was planned by the Irish Republican Brotherhood, whose origins lay in the Fenian movement launched in the 1850s, but which has been marginalised since the failure of its insurrection in 1867; that it was finally decided upon by an inner circle, without the knowledge of MacNeill and Bulmer Hobson; that Pearse deceived MacNeill into thinking that he, MacNeill had succeeded in his aim of persuading James Connolly from leading his Citizen Army into rebellion on its own. MacNeill's memorandum had been seen, but not used, by L.N. Le Roux who published a biography of Pearse in 1932; and in any case Le Roux had confused it with a letter written by MacNeill to Pearse much earlier than the memorandum, which was composed only weeks before the rising took place. A second memorandum, compiled by MacNeill some time in 1917, gave his analysis of the personalities and events of 1916 from 'backstage'.

These documents were significant not only for revealing that MacNeill sought to prevent an armed uprising and took practical steps to do so but also for raising the question of the morality, and in a sense, legitimacy of the rising: was it a just uprising in a just cause? MacNeill weighed up the possibilities of a 'reasonably calculated or estimated prospect of success, in the military sense', believing that 'without that prospect, military action . . . would in the first place be morally wrong and that consideration to my mind is fatal and decisive'. He concluded that 'to kill any person in carrying out such a course of action is murder'. 'The success which is calculated or estimated must be success in the operation itself, not merely some future moral or political advantage which may be hoped for as the result of non-success.' This could be decided only by the application of rational judgement, not by instinct or feeling; and maxims such as 'Ireland has always struck too late' were no guide to action. MacNeill did not set aside the claim that 'lives must be sacrificed, in order to produce an ultimate effect on the national mind'; he simply denied that this was a 'military act in any sense', and thus 'does not come within the scope of our military counsels'.[2]

MacNeill, then, distinguished between military and non-military action;

and he based his objection to the rising on what he saw as military criteria. He made his case well. But he did not address the deeper issues raised by the concept of the impact of 'non-military' action on the 'national mind'. Yet this posed one of the central questions surrounding the rising: was it a 'coup d'état' or a 'bloody protest'? Was it a rebellion aimed at provoking or inspiring a general uprising against the British, in the fashion of nineteenth-century European risings? Or was it a deliberate bid to create martyrs in order to shock the nation out of its 'torpor' and into a more radical nationalist mood, the blood of the martyrs acting, as it were, as the seed of the church? And what was the Ireland that the rebels hoped to serve through risking their lives? MacNeill, for his part, warned that Ireland was not an abstraction, but a real place with real people who must be won over to the side of the Volunteers. He denied that there was any serious discontent in Ireland in 1916.[3] In his editorial contribution, F.X. Martin drew attention to the fact that in 1916 there were some 150,183 Irishmen serving with the British forces, of which 99,837 were recruits who joined up after mobilisation in August 1914; that there were 1,121 members of the Dublin Metropolitan Police and 9,501 members of the Royal Irish Constabulary, and, in addition, 105,000 Irish Volunteers loyal to John Redmond, the leader of the Irish Parliamentary Party which supported the British war effort: a total of 265,000 Irishmen serving with or in alliance with the British forces, against 16,000 Irish Volunteers who were not.[4]

These valuable documents not only attracted much public interest, causing an unusually high sale of *Irish Historical Studies*; they also drew attention to the many-sided nature of the rising, and the issues it raised, and in particular to the rising in the wider context of the Great War and Ireland's role in it. The celebrations in 1966 of the fiftieth anniversary of the rising encouraged a closer examination of these and related questions – a nice example of a political event that stimulated not polemic, but a genuine interest in recovering a past that was not necessarily the past that politicians and public were commemorating. It was entirely appropriate that this should be done through the medium of the Thomas Davis Lectures, a series of radio broadcasts which sought to bring the results of historical scholarship to the public, while in no way sacrificing the historian's craft. F.X. Martin's *Leaders and Men of the Easter Rising* cast the net widely, drawing in themes and topics hitherto hardly associated with the rising at all. For example, it related the rising to the Ulster Crisis of 1912–14, and to other political developments before 1916. Thus the Ulster Volunteer Force, Sir Edward Carson, Dublin Castle, Lloyd George and Asquith, were all woven into the texture of the rising, and the historiography of the event moved from the narrow (though of course important) focus on conspiracy and martyrdom to the more general question of the rising as an episode in the history of all Ireland and indeed of the British Isles.[5]

In one sense the question, 'Why was there a rising?' was easily answered, and P.S. O'Hegarty, the veteran Sinn Feiner, answered it: 'the Supreme council of the Irish Republican Brotherhood decided that it would come . . . it was the Supreme Council of the IRB which decided the Insurrection, planned it, organised it, led it, and financed it'.[6] But this hardly scratched the surface of the event. The rising was a complex affair, and the fact that the IRB was able to plan it was not merely a matter of their free choice, but that choice itself was influenced, perhaps shaped, by events quite outside their control, or even understanding. Thus Professor J.C. Beckett drew attention to the role of Sir Edward Carson, whose stand for Union helped to encourage 'the development of a more militant nationalism and hastened the establishment of an Irish Republic'.[7]

Martin's *Leaders and Men* did not entirely free itself from the more traditional interpretations of 1916. David Thornley quoted Le Roux's judgement (made in 1932) that Patrick Pearse 'possessed all the qualities which go to the making of a saint. . . . It would not be astonishing if Pearse were canonised some day', adding that it was 'not merely difficult but almost blasphemous to discern a human being of flesh and blood'. Yet Thornley did attempt to make a historical assessment if 'only an interim one'.[8] Edward MacLysaght sought to reaffirm, rather than analyse, Connolly and the Labour movement's role in the gaining of Irish freedom, ending his chapter by quoting with approval Connolly's last statement to the court martial which condemned him to death.[9] Roger McHugh saluted Roger Casement and his decision to 'reject the sectarian and colonial basis of armed Ulster Protestant action and to substitute the principle upon which the Irish Volunteers were founded, "to defend the rights and liberties common to the whole people – Protestant and Catholic"'.[10] Yet three volumes which appeared between 1966 and 1969 illustrated the advances which historical research was making at the expense of more traditional interpretations. T. Desmond Williams' *The Irish Struggle, 1916–1926* (1966) also examined the Ulster and British dimensions of the rising, adding analyses of the failure of socialism to make any appreciable impact on the freedom struggle, and the growing conservatism of Sinn Féin, a conservatism exacerbated by Sinn Féin's need to hold its mixed band of supporters together. In 1967 W.I. Thompson published a fine literary investigation into the rising, stressing the artistic vision of the rebels, and their failure to cope with reality: hence their desire to turn towards destructive, almost nihilistic revolution.[11] Owen Dudley Edwards and Fergus Pyle's *1916: The Easter Rising* (1968) mixed quotations and extracts from contemporary documents with essays which, again, asked searching questions about the motives as well as the actions of the rebels.[12] In 1969 a collection of essays commissioned by an official state body to mark the fiftieth anniversary of the rising appeared. But it proved to be no mere eulogy of the rebels. The contents ranged from an assessment of the influence of the Gaelic movement on the rebels to a sober chapter by F.S.L. Lyons on the home rulers, and, most useful of all, a detailed and careful examination of the strategic and tactical aims of the rebels, with a close description of the course of the fighting during Easter Week – a timely reminder that a rebellion does require military planning and execution, even if improvisation, central to the art of war, is found to be necessary.[13]

Yet all this research, valuable though it was, lacked an important dimension. The rising still needed a close study of the kind of politics that it stood for, that it represented. What kind of political system, if any, had the rebels in mind with which to supplant British rule? The Irish Parliamentary Party's model was based on the British Westminster tradition, and indeed on a Home Rule constitution granted by a Liberal government. Ireland's political culture would not necessarily be altered by this, though it was axiomatic that under Home Rule it would change for the better. But there was no change envisaged in the fundamentals of political life, except for John Redmond's assumption that, freedom won, the party would no longer have a raison d'être and might step down to open the way to new parties, new interests. But the political future of Ireland, the consequences for Ireland of an armed revolt, the result of protest in arms for Irish democratic processes – all were as yet unexplored, even though, as Maureen Wall noted in a perceptive essay on the Ulster Question, the revolt 'was as much a revolt against the Irish Parliamentary Party as against British rule in Ireland.[14]

It is important to make a distinction, though by no means a completely stark one, between the 1916 Rising as a subject attracting historical attention, with that attention enhanced by the general climate of opinion in Ireland (just as the Great War produced a series of historical reinterpretations as its various anniversaries fell due), and the rising as an influential factor in Irish political thought. Therefore a consideration of Father Francis Shaw's essay on 'The Canon of Irish History: A Challenge'[15] will be left to later on in this chapter. The next important breakthrough came not in essays, articles or monographs, but in the field of biographical study; and this was helped by the unearthing of new material, or the reinterpretation, by a younger generation, of works already available. Biographical studies enabled advances to be made where they were most needed: in unlocking the minds of the rebels and revealing the kind of political and social system they wished to establish in Ireland.

Ruth Dudley Edwards' life of Patrick Pearse started out by declaring that 'the Irish have always tended to impose on their patriots, posthumously if necessary, impossibly high standards'.[16] Dudley Edwards perhaps over-compensated for the hitherto high standards imposed on Pearse. The flawed man was stripped bare in his mysterious cloak of heroism. But she also laid bare his vision of what the rising would do for

– or perhaps to – Ireland. A Home Rule Ireland would not be the Ireland that he dreamed of: not Gaelic, not a model to the world of what his nation should be. Pearse's model was one that stressed economic self-sufficiency (Ireland would be capable of supporting twenty million people),[17] but also sought to change the very nature of the Irish people: they would become different, they would become loving, caring and they would be busily absorbed in helping each other, intensely communal, very self-conscious, and, above all, totally insular, that is, cut off from the horror of the modern world. Human nature would be different – or at least the Irish part of it would.[18]

Ruth Dudley Edwards' method was to test Pearse's ideology against his own life; to explain the personal and psychological reasons why, in the end, self-immolation was his only choice. Death compensated for failure in life: failure on personal, family and financial grounds. This was perhaps reductionist; Pearse was deeply influenced by the Romantic and cultural mood of his time, and it is possible to imagine even a successful Pearse deciding that the European World, the bourgeois civilisation that war was now putting to the test, was a weary and profoundly unspiritual place.

Pearse was deeply influenced by two, apparently contradictory, themes. The Roman Catholic religion; and the pagan tradition embedded in ancient Irish sagas and popularised in the historical works of Standish O'Grady. Pearse could think and act upon, two contradictory impulses because he welded them together in his desire for martyrdom. It was this that inspired his notion that immortality, not death, would be his reward, just as it was the reward of the pagan heroes of the pre-Christian world, and, at the same moment, the reward of the martyred Christ. Pearse was no born soldier, he did not translate his bloody words into murderous deeds. His words applied to himself; his blood would be the red wine of the battlefields.

Ruth Dudley Edwards was right in assessing the long-term influence of Pearse upon Irish nationalist thinking. He forged a link between the prophets of Irish nationality, Tone, Davis, Mitchel, Lalor and Parnell (whose ideas bore only the most superficial resemblance to each other) and created a kind of legal justification for what he planned to do: and 'those who survived him would have a standard work on nationalism by which they could check their own consciences'.[19] This was to get to the heart of the idea and purpose of the rising: that it would not stop at 1916, but that it would be an event that would work its magic on future generations, now and in time to come. Past rebels, even Tone and Mitchel, had been capable of adoption by pragmatic politicians, for even Redmond could praise the men of 1798 (while warning that they must not be emulated by the present generation of nationalists). But now 'The idealists sought to put [Pearse] beyond criticism . . . the pragmatists, despairing of making him their own, tried to ignore him.[20] Pearse's unworldiness was evident even – or especially – in his attitude to the Protestants of Ulster. He admired the Orangeman with a rifle more than the Nationalist without one; and his vision even extended to the improbable call to the Ulster Unionists to make their provisional government of Ulster 'a Provisional Government of Ireland and we will recognise and obey it'.[21]

What Pearse was to Nationalism, James Connolly, the other great pillar of the rising, was to Irish Socialism.[22] Here again biographical study threw down the gauntlet. In 1988 Austen Morgan published his *James Connolly: a Political Biography*,[23] which, in his own words, 'queried the claim that Connolly has successfully married socialism and nationalism'.[24] Morgan's sources were Connolly's own writings, but writings read carefully and in a non-selective way. The result was that, 'on the evidence of the last twenty months of Connolly's life, it is very difficult to associate Easter 1916 with international proletarian revolution'.[25] Morgan traced the process by which Connolly's desire to create an international working class culture gave way, ever more quickly, after 1914 to 'support for German victory; his invocation of a continent-wide anti-war movement was eclipsed by a parochial national concern'.[26] This was because the 'seed of nationalism was nurtured by a historical crisis until it dominated his politics. By 30 August 1914, socialism had ceased to be his guiding ideology'.[27] As he moved towards committing himself to a rising, Connolly became less concerned with the question of gaining the support of the people; and so he became part of a revolutionary junta planning something of a militarized state. He turned his back on the Irish Transport and General Workers Union, and joined 'a group of five, later six, petty-bourgeois cultural nationalists'.[28] Thus after August 1914 nationalism, which had hardly dominated his twenty-five years of political commitment, came to command 'his very being', and he went to his death with no discernible socialist project. His death in 1916 ensured that Irish Socialism would essentially be a 'one national perspective'.[29]

Morgan's conclusions attracted much criticism. But his findings have been borne out by other researchers in the field,[30] and have not been refuted historically, even if they have been denounced politically. But by the end of the 1980s the material, the perspectives and the insights of the previous twenty years, whatever their drawbacks or arguable points, had set the rising firmly in an historical context. It was possible to construct at least an historically sound picture of the event, the motives of its leaders, its immediate and longer term impact on Irish politics, and – on the seventy-fifth anniversary of the rising in 1991 – to assess its continuing resonances in Irish political thought.

II

In one sense the 1916 Rising was a product of the Great War; without it, Pearse's mysticism, Connolly's nationalism, arising from his disappointed socialism, and the Irish Republican Brotherhood's long awaited day of reckoning with Britain would have come to nothing. The outbreak of war in August 1914 postponed the Home Rule crisis of 1912–14, but in its place confronted the Irish Parliamentary Party with the prospect of a Home Rule parliament now enacted as an Act of Parliament, but postponed for the duration of the war, and with no clear resolution of the Ulster Question. Nevertheless, and despite some disillusionment as the war lengthened, and casualties amongst those Nationalists who enlisted in the British army rose, the home rulers remained firmly in command of the votes of Nationalist Ireland. Yet Nationalists – constitutional Nationalists – always claimed that rebellion was justified, and praised rebel heroism in the past, provided that their audiences understood that it was the past that was being praised, and listened carefully to the advice that no such rebellion should be attempted again, especially as the British would easily overwhelm the insurgents.[31]

The controversy over the revisionist analysis of 1916 has obscured rather than clarified the issues. Modern historians' determination to see the rising in its conspiratorial setting, to stress the importance of Irish Republican Brotherhood planning and preparation, to cast the event in terms of human choice and endeavour, may have failed to place the rising in its wider political/cultural context.[32] It is impossible to separate the culture of the rising from the growth of the Gaelic ideal in the late nineteenth and early twentieth centuries. Irish nationalists between Parnell and Redmond looked to the past to justify their beliefs and their programme. Parnell and Redmond took as their reference point the Constitution of 1782, Grattan's Parliament, and the whole Patriot movement of the last two decades of the eighteenth century. But the Gaelic revival of the 1890s and in its own, less popular way the literary revival inspired by W.B. Yeats (which was itself partly inspired by the writings of Standish O'Grady in the 1870s and 1880s), introduced a new strand into Irish Nationalist thinking: that of the warrior-prince, Cuchulainn, valiant, noble, and willing to sacrifice himself for his people – and for eternal fame and glory. Ireland must find her true roots, her true past; and this lay not in the eighteenth-century Irish parliament, but in the kind of social order that Gaelic Ireland was believed to have represented: a sovereign people, a people free and equal, holding everything in common (this, of course, was attractive to James Connolly), and a language revival that was not narrowly linguistic in inspiration, but sought to impose barriers between this free and equal Ireland, and English-speaking, metropolitan, capitalist, imperialist England. Thus labour leaders, including W.P. Ryan and even James Larkin, were persuaded that Gaelic Ireland could be recreated in the shape of socialist Ireland.[33]

This was a revolution of the mind that preceded, and necessarily proceeded, the 1916 Rising. It was not incidental, but central to the whole enterprise. It was not yet an ideal with mass appeal; but it was one that permeated the opinion-makers, and certainly influenced members of the Gaelic League and the Irish Volunteer Movement that sprang up in response to the Ulster Volunteers in 1913. The sense of a lost, destroyed Gaelic past; a world that could be re-enacted, providing sacrifice was willingly embraced; a search for everlasting fame; the heroic language of the 1916 proclamation (a document more mentioned in passing than read or understood by many historians today) – all these speak of a revolution of the mind. Ireland 'summons her children to her flag and strikes for her freedom'; 'The Irish Republic is entitled to, and here by claims, the allegiance of every Irishman and Irish woman'; 'we pray that no one who serves the cause will dishonour it by cowardice, inhumanity or rapine'; 'in this supreme hour the Irish Nation must, by its valour and discipline, and by the readiness of its children to sacrifice themselves for the common good, prove itself worthy of the august destiny to which it is called'.[34] Here indeed is the cult of the Mother Eire, of her heroic offspring, Cuchulainn; even the repetition of the word 'children' speaks of this cult-mother and child, Eire and her sons and daughters. W.B. Yeats was exaggerating when he mused on the possibility that his play, 'Cathleen ni Houlihan' had 'sent out/certain men the English shot'; but he was summarising the context in which the rising was made possible in the form and style that it assumed. It is important that modern, professional historians, scientifically trained to examine documents, do not therefore lose sight of a more elusive, but nonetheless deeply significant aspect of 1916, and of modern Irish Nationalism: the rediscovery of ancient, Gaelic, free and equal Ireland, inspired by the Revival movements of the turn of the century, and spread through a range of Nationalist publications, organisations and clubs. Even the Irish equivalent of the boy scout movement, the Fianna, was based on the Cuchulainn idea of youth enlisted in the service of the nation, and trained to die, if need be, for the nation.

The men of 1916 were what might be called professional students of Irish, and other, risings. When Pearse pondered on past misfortunes, he singled out the failure of the leaders: 'Stephens refused to 'give the word' in '65; he never came in '66 or '67. Connolly believed that the disasters of the past had happened because the leaders had refused to take that 'leap in the dark which all men must take who plunge into insurrection'.[35] The lessons of the past were that leaders must act resolutely and in time: the moment for the action must not be allowed to slip by. Moreover, a rising must be one that would attract the people; it must not degenerate into fiasco as it did in 1848 and 1867, nor suffer the fate of the uncoordinated risings of 1798. The central planners of 1916 – Pearse, Connolly, Ceannt, MacDiarmada, Clarke, MacDonagh and Plunkett, accepted Connolly's plan: to seize key buildings in Dublin, and stand on the defensive.[36] This would give the British forces a difficult task, for Connolly knew that street-fighting tested even the most experienced regular troops, and would protect the rebels from any accusation that they were wantonly aggressive or destructive. As students of rebellion, the leaders knew that secrecy was a vital ingredient of success (hence their deception of Eoin MacNeill) and that scrupulous honesty need play no part in conspiracy (hence their concoction of the Dublin Castle Document purporting to show that the authorities were about to arrest the leaders of the Irish volunteers and disarm their men). This was planted on MacNeill early in Holy Week to incite the Volunteers and precipitate action, and to create an acceptance of the inevitability of insurrection.[37] They also learned from past risings that it was vital for those who would want to supplant an existing political elite not to go out of their way to make enemies: therefore they

> scrupulously refrained from attacking what today would be called 'the establishment'. They did not deliberately antagonise any section of Irish life, whether Irish Parliamentary Party, Catholic Bishops and Clergy or any of the other customary targets of revolutionaries.[38]

Public opinion could then be moulded, and this could be done if the rising were one where the courage of the rebels might gain praise even from those sections of the political and religious elites, and the general public, which would not necessarily support either a rebellion or the separatist aims of the rebels. The last minute disasters, the orders given and then countermanded, might have indeed produced just such a fiasco; but the rebels were helped by the total lack of preparedness on the part of the authorities, and by the success of the defensive strategy. British officers, predictably enough, led their men to disaster in some areas, notably Mount Street Bridge.[39] The fighting lasted a week, which was long enough to attract the admiration of those who saw Irishmen putting up a good fight; and even though the rebels were initially unpopular, and were jeered at when they surrendered, they managed to maintain their dignity, to avoid any wholesale condemnation by the Catholic Church (with even the atheist Tom Clarke accepting the last rites of the church, and Connolly, possibly an atheist, doing the same)[40] and to place the Irish Parliamentary Party in the difficult position of having to condemn the rising while admitting and even admiring the courage of those who were misled into participating in it. The rising was not a 'crime'; and General Maxwell's executions, few in number, it is true, but sufficient to create martyrs, were remembered while the restraint of British and Irish regular soldiers under fire in what they regarded as an 'unfair fight' was soon forgotten. The worst atrocity – one of the very few breaches of this restraint – was the murder of Francis Sheeny Skeffington, which was perpetrated by a demented officer of Anglo-Irish extraction.

But the rising, far from resolving the problems of Irish nationalism, set it a more difficult problem. As David Fitzpatrick wrote

> The 1916 Rising left Irish politicians of all parties with a pretty problem. As a dramatic pageant it had been a spectacular success, quickly generating a popular cult of the dead which politicians would ignore at their peril. Yet as a military enterprise it had been a spectacular failure which even the most bloodthirsty Republicans were reluctant to see reenacted. Former opponents of violent Republicanism were faced with four choices, all hazardous. They might condemn both the rebels and the consequences of their acts; praise the rebels while denouncing the consequences; praise both the rebels and consequences without becoming Republican; or become Republican . . . Inconsistency and ambivalence proved increasingly frequent responses, as politicians sought to exploit the popular mood of veneration for the dead in order to promote policies which the dead would have deplored.[4]

The rising had an immediate impact on Irish public opinion, in that it launched a new, or rather revived, cult of martyrdom, with the men of 1916 replacing the Manchester martyrs, the Fenians executed in 1867 for their part in the murder of a policeman while attempting to rescue some Fenian prisoners. These martyrs' sacrifice had been celebrated in song and story, and processions were held every November to honour their memory. Now 'St Pearse' and his fellows were given pride of place. But the rising alone would not have swung the nationalist public and electorate round to a rejection of the Irish Parliamentary Party. As Austen Morgan put it

> Four points can be made: one, Irish Catholics remained loyal to Redmond after he accepted the principle of partition (in the negotiations for a settlement which Lloyd George undertook in the aftermath of the rising); two, Maxwell's executions undoubtedly shocked many, but only a minority turned to separation, and the rising destroyed Fenian insurrection for ever; three, the Irish Party collapsed in the anti-conscription campaign of 1918 . . . and this mass mobilisation which was legitimised by the Catholic Church, showed that the majority of nationalists had reached the limits of conditional loyalty to Britain; four, just under a third of the electorate voted in December for Sinn Fein . . . In the political sea change of Catholic Ireland in the First World War then, the 1916 rising came to

assume a symbolic importance over a shift in legitimacy produced by the 1918 anti-conscription campaigning.[42]

The focus, then, is not upon some miraculous instant change of mind on the part of Nationalist Ireland, nor even upon the evocation of a tradition, however important that might be to some Nationalists; but upon the way in which events after the rising continued to shape public opinion, and help create Sinn Féin's election victory of 1918. Here, the rising in the context of British history must be considered. It can be said that by 1914 Ireland was, to put it no more strongly, confused by the British handling of the third Home Rule crisis of 1912–14. In Ireland, there was the spectacle of a crumbling and increasingly ineffective Dublin Castle administration; yet in Britain there was the furious Unionist opposition to Home Rule, the Liberal government's indecisive response to the Ulster question, and the Liberal intention to exercise a guiding hand over Irish affairs, even if Home Rule were to be conceded. Redmond even admitted that, once Home Rule came, the Irish Parliamentary Party might well dissolve itself, its task now accomplished.[43]

By the outbreak of war in 1914 it was clear that, whatever the outcome of the crisis, a British government was in a position that no British government had ever faced before with regard to Irish affairs since the Union of 1800: that of losing its power to mediate and control events in Ireland. The initial Irish Nationalist and Unionist enthusiasm for the war disguised that serious position; but the 1916 Rising again threatened to remove the initiative from the British. The British response to the rising, once the newspaper press began to report events from Ireland, was one of condemnation, but also affirmation of the fact that it did not represent Ireland's loyalty to the war effort.[44] Lloyd George's mission to negotiate a settlement in the aftermath of the rising came to grief on the sturdy, and it must be said principled opposition of Southern Irish Unionists and of some British Unionists in the Cabinet, most notably Walter Long, Landsdowne and the Earl of Selborne.[45] But his negotiations cleared up one aspect of the problem: that any discussion of the future government of Ireland must begin with a consideration of the Ulster Question, and would almost certainly end with partition of some kind or another. The 1916 Rising could not blast that rock out of the path of the nation; nor, in all truth, was it meant to. Its effect was to make Ulster Unionists all the more determined to stand fast, and the rising, coming as it did shortly before the great Somme offensive, enabled Unionists to claim that they were loyal to the British war effort, whereas Nationalists had at last shown their true colours.

Even the failure of the Lloyd George negotiations, compromising as they were for John Redmond, did not immediately open the way to the inexorable rise of Sinn Féin. During the following year there were increasing signs of support for the rebels, yet still the Country Inspector for Clare reported that Sinn Féin was something of a mystery: not yet having shown 'any life', yet 'not dead'.[46] As Sinn Féin began to reorganise, and to challenge the home rulers in by-elections, it sought to find a balance between sympathy for the rebels, and the need to win over supporters from the Irish Parliamentary Party: for, after all, Sinn Féin voters could not be made anew; they must be converts from Home Rule, and, like all converts, they needed reassurance that Sinn Féin did not stand for any radical departure from the even tenor of Irish political ways, but could claim the support of the Roman Catholic Church, and could claim also to be the 'real' inheritors of Parnell's – not Pearse's – mantle.[47] Sinn Féin was assisted by the British government's preoccupation with the war effort, which made Lloyd George and his Cabinet essentially reactive when it came to Irish policy. The decision to take powers to impose conscription in Ireland was a wartime emergency decision, made in the wake of the German Army's breakthrough on the Western Front in March 1918; and the general election of December 1918, which could not have come at a worst time for the Irish Parliamentary Party, and which was conducted on the British 'first past the post' system, not only gave Sinn Féin its best chance of success, but even distorted the electoral results to give them seventy-four seats, an over-representation in terms of the percentage of votes cast for them.[48]

III

What light has recent historical scholarship thrown on the place of the rising in Irish history, viewed in the longer perspective?

This issue was first raised by Professor J.C. Beckett in a seminal article published in 1967 in the American occasional series Topic.[49] Beckett argued that the Union was neither the illegal imposition upon Ireland that Nationalists like to claim, nor did it conform to the Unionist version of a great experiment that went sadly wrong. Beckett drew attention to another dimension of the Union; that of the British capacity to suppress a revolution, a revolution that would have gone much further than a change of political elites, and would have attacked Protestant social and economic privilege as well. This suppression of a revolution in one sense did not in the end prevent the overthrow of the Union by a violent revolution in 1916–23. But the slow revolution carried out by Britain, with its programme of reform, beginning with Catholic Emancipation in 1829 and ending with the destruction of landlordism, ensured that the violent revolution that followed the 1916 Rising was one in which the Irish Free State could 'set out on its course without the burdens of ecclesiastical or social privilege'. There was, then, much truth in A.J. Balfour's jibe, 'What was the Ireland that the Free State took over? It was the Ireland that we made'.

175

Beckett explained the 'two revolutions' in these terms:

The revolution with which Ireland seemed to be threatened in 1800 was, first, postponed by the legislative union, and then under the shelter of that union, carried out by constitutional means. But the British government, though ready to carry out revolutionary changes in Ireland, though ready to sacrifice the church and the landlords, was not ready to sacrifice what it regarded as the national interests of England; and it was only at this point . . . that violent revolution took the place of constitutional revolution. In short, the union enabled Ireland to get through one revolution peacefully, but subjected her to another revolution which was violent.

Beckett argued that, although these two revolutions were different not only in method but in character, there might be a relationship between them:

It would be tempting to regard the latter simply as a completion of the former; but the facts do not warrant our assuming any such continuity in the revolutionary process. It may be that the constitutional revolution made possible the success of the nationalist revolution of 1916–23; it may be that it made some such revolution inevitable. But even if this is so, even if the constitutional revolution necessarily carried with it the dissolution of the legislative union, it was nevertheless complete in itself, and it remains the greatest monument of the union period.[50]

This explanation, even if not accepted in its entirety, directed historians' attention towards an important aspect of the 1916 Rising and its aftermath: the lack of any deep or significant social revolution. The leader of the rising certainly had in mind some important changes in the way in which Irish society would work after their revolution; it would be a land where greed and selfishness would play no part in social relationships, indeed it would be revolution that would release the Irish (Catholic) people from the slavery of the intensely competitive, intensely individualistic modern world. This would be a social revolution, in a sense, but one that would not touch the basis of property and ownership, but would make property and ownership open their eyes to their responsibilities to the nation: in short, Catholic social teaching written into a proclamation of rebellion, not overtly, but nonetheless implicitly and deeply.

The place of the rising in the broader perspective of Irish history was discussed by F.X. Martin in his *Leaders and Men* volume: was 1916 a case of 'revolution or evolution'? Martin drew attention to the importance of the British imprint on Ireland before 1916, an Ireland which on the eve of the rising 'still bore something of the splendour of one of His Majesty's prosperous dominions'. It was ruled by a kind of imperial 'triumvirate', and yet this triumvirate 'accepted the fact that they were on their way out and that the Irish Nationalists under Redmond were to take over the government of the country . . . Already an Irish triumvirate – Redmond, Dillon and Devlin – were in the wings, waiting to step on the stage at the appropriate moment'. He too posed the question: 'Did the armed revolt in 1916 represent a revolution, a complete discarding of the existing political forces in the country, or did Clarke, Pearse and their companions merely complete – though in dramatic fashion – the last stage of the work of Redmond and the parliamentarians?'[51] And in Desmond Williams' volume *The Irish Struggle*, Patrick Lynch asked 'Why did the rising of 1916 fail to produce also a social revolution of corresponding significance and consequence? What happened to avert it? Was it betrayed?', answering his own question by posing other questions, or at least other ways of looking at the same question:

> Such questions ignore many circumstances. They disregard, for instance, the fact that by 1916 most agricultural holdings had been purchased by their occupiers, subject to land annuities, which were not then a matter of contention. The tenant had become a proprietor, the owner of his land . . . Moreover, rural Ireland had profited from the introduction of the Old Age Pension. In addition, high prices during the Great War were bringing unprecedented prosperity to Irish agriculture, from which, of course, the bigger farmers benefited most.[52]

Lynch also took a longer view: middle-class leadership in Ireland had been firmly established by Daniel O'Connell. James Connolly, for his part, made little impression on rural areas, with a few exceptions. After 1916 national solidarity was the only issue, and Connolly's death in 1916 killed social militancy anyway. 'Gradually the middle classes generally moved towards Sinn Féin and this naturally tended to introduce into Sinn Féin an element of conservatism'. Sinn Féin was determined not to confuse the political struggle by becoming involved directly in any clash of social interests that might divide the growing numbers of mixed supporters it had gathered to itself; and its task was made easier by Labour's decision not to participate in the 1918 general election.[53]

These interpretations, however tentative, at least widened the discussion, and drew attention to the essentially conservative character of the rising, Connolly's presence there notwithstanding. As Owen Dudley Edwards put it, in certain aspects, notably the economic, the course of Irish history was 'surprisingly unaffected' by the rising. Politically, an 'alternative national group' to the Redmondites emerged; while in the cultural sphere, 'to describe as revolutionary a process which operated through a linguistic text is to give a very wide meaning indeed to the term revolution. Anyone could learn Irish'.[54]

But the rising could not thereby be dismissed merely as a kind of 'putsch'; it did establish itself in the Irish Nationalist tradition, and it did set an agenda for Irish politics and political ideas, even if it had no answers to offer to the chronic problems of the Irish economy and society, to the drain of Ireland's young people through emigration, to the backwardness of the rural economy. The rising was a sacrifice, even if it had originally been intended to be a success. It must now be seen in the perspective of Irish political thought, for it is here that it exercised, and perhaps continues to exercise, its greatest influence.

IV

On the occasion of the fiftieth anniversary of the rising, Eamon de Valera, by now the undisputed father of his nation, explained what the rising meant to him. Political freedom, he declared, was not the ultimate goal. It was to be the 'enabling condition for the gradual building up of a community in which an ever increased number of its members, relieved from the pressure of exacting economic demands, would be free to devote themselves more and more to the mind and spirit'. Thus 'our nation would then become again, as it was for centuries in the past, a great intellectual and missionary centre from which would go forth the satisfying saving truths of Divine Revelation, as well as the fruits of ripest secular knowledge'. De Valera wrote of his hopes, still, of a new 'national resurgence' such as followed 1916:

> We can have our people united as a family – a nation of brothers – each working in industrial harmony, not for himself only, but for the good of all. We could then march forward confidently to the exaltation of our nation amongst the nations to which the men of 1916 pledged themselves.

In this, the national language must play a 'vital role' for language was 'the chief characteristic of nationhood. We of this generation must see to it that our language lives, that would be the resolve of the men and women of 1916. Will it not be the resolve of the young men and women of 1966?'[55]

The latter question can now fairly be said to have been answered, and in the negative. But in the same year that de Valera wrote his version of what 1916 stood for, Father Francis Shaw, SJ, despatched an article to the journal *Studies* in which he delineated a very different version of the impact of Easter 1916.[56] Shaw challenged what he called the 'canon of Irish history' which 'stamps the generation of 1916 as nationally degenerate, a generation in need of redemption by the shedding of blood', condemning those who did not profess extremist nationalist doctrine as anti-Irish.[57] But the bulk of Father Shaw's essay was devoted to an attack on the ideas and beliefs of Patrick Pearse, and in particular Pearse's equation of the patriot and the patriot–people with Christ, and his misuse of Christian words and imagery to create a cult of violence in Ireland. Pearse glorified war, and Father Shaw was careful to note that, when Pearse wrote his speeches, war in Europe was regarded as a glorious affair. 'Nonetheless, one must admit that, for a man of obviously gentle and sensitive disposition, the writer Pearse is very bloody-minded'. The gospel of Irish nationalism, as interpreted by Pearse, was 'essentially a gospel of hate'.[58] Pearse's description of his warrior hero Cuchulainn, was sentimental and historically wrong.[59] Ireland in 1916 was not, Shaw declared, a suffering country, but one in which the people were already socially more advanced than at any time since the Union, and were moving towards the goal of independence in their own way and at their own pace.[60] The sword, Shaw concluded, 'is never as clean a weapon as we are sometimes led to believe. Wounds may often fester for a long time'. Pearse's sword inflicted 'three grave wounds on the body of the unity of Ireland': partition, for 1916 closed the door to a peaceful resolution of that question; the civil war of 1922–3, since the teaching of 1916 was that no compromise could be brooked, and that it was a separate republic or nothing; and the refusal of Ireland to honour those of her dead who fought in the Great War for the honour and freedom of their country. Shaw concluded that 'there can surely be no more criminal disservice to Ireland than the determination to keep the fire of hatred burning'.[61]

Shaw's essay was not published by *Studies* until 1972, on the grounds that, as Shaw himself later wrote, 'it was judged very understandably, that a critical study of this kind might be thought to be untimely and even inappropriate in what was in effect a commemorative issue.' The editor noted that it was not written as a 'tract for the times', for the troubled condition of Ireland in 1972; indeed in 1966 'it seemed likely that a new chapter was opening in relations between Ireland and England, with special reference to the unity of this country'.[62]

But, whatever its motives, and however questionable some of its historical judgements might be, Father Shaw's essay threw light on the dilemma that 1916 posed for Irish political ideas, with its mixture of high romantic endeavour and destructive violence, its self-sacrifice and its infliction of death on others. Above all, 1916 posed questions for the future of democratic government in Ireland.

The rising very quickly inspired a popular literature that depicted it, as the editor of the *Catholic Bulletin*, J.J. O'Kelly, put it, as the latest in a long struggle for 'faith and Fatherland'. The *Wolfe Tone Annual* placed it alongside other risings, and in 1966 the son of Brian O'Higgins, a volunteer of 1916, described the risings as a 'spiritual victory over selfishness, expedience and compromise and materialism'. The connection between religion and republicanism, F.X. Martin pointed out, was revealed in the diaries of Sean South and Fergal Hanlon, killed in an IRA raid on Brookeborough RUC Station in January 1957.[63] But the rising posed questions for the Irish Free State in other, more significant ways: could it claim to be the inheritor of the mantle of the men of 1916? Had it not betrayed their ideals? This appeared to pose no difficulties for de Valera and his Fianna Fáil party, described by Sean Lemass, a future Taoiseach of Ireland, as republican and 'slightly constitutional'. Yet, there again, the issue arose: if Fianna Fáil won power by democratic means, but did not fulfil the legacy of the rebels (a separate republic, a united Ireland) then their legitimacy too would be questioned, and armed force could be used against them. In 1934 de Valera warned republicans that there was 'no way today in which the arms of any section of the people can be used from the point of view of general national defence except under the control of the duly elected government'. The young men of Ireland must not be 'led away by the glamour attached to the name IRA'.[64]

This careful distinction between legitimate violence and non-legitimate violence, and yet the state's need to acknowledge the men of 1916 and their role in its foundation, called for a careful choosing of words by Ireland's political leaders. In 1966 Garret Fitzgerald, leader of Fine Gael whose founders had signed the Anglo-Irish Treaty of 1921 and thus, in the eyes of many, had 'betrayed' the rising, saluted the rebels for their having halted the process by which Ireland was becoming 'absorbed' into the United Kingdom 'like Scotland'. Before 1914 there had been a Home Rule, British Ireland in the making; after 1916 there was a 'separatist, anti-British Ireland'. The 'bridge across the chasm is strewn with the bodies of those who died in Easter week'. Fitzgerald noted that the political and social ideas of the rebels were 'fairly limited and naive, even by the standards of the time', and he deplored the erection of these sayings into political dogma. He acknowledges the revulsion against physical force in the 'advanced cultures of the world, our own included'.[65] But the rising had made a new Ireland possible, without which he asked

> would Ireland ever have become a largely self-reliant country, seeking to run its own affairs in its own way, or would it have shrunk like Northern Ireland into dependent provincialism, too concerned about its share of British agricultural subsidies or social welfare reinsurance policies to want ever to become a sovereign state?[66]

Would 1916 be seen as a 'psychological basis' for Ireland taking her place in the 'European super-State'?[67]

Sean Lemass, speaking for the Fianna Fáil party, recalled some of the goals of 1916, but referred to them in equally guarded language. The leaders of 1916 would 'see very clearly the implications of the continuation of Partition and the campaign to restore the Irish language. They would represent to them unfinished national tasks as, indeed, they are regarded today'. But at the same time, Lemass continued, they would have 'no illusions of the magnitude of these tasks'. So what had the men of 1916 pointed out to succeeding generations? Here Lemass shifted his ground to argue that Pearse's message to the present generation was to 'consolidate the economic foundations which supported our political institutions'.[68] The editor of the volume in which Lemass's speech was printed, M. O'Duohghaill, admitted that those who saw 'political freedom' as a still unrealised goal were 'logical on certain widely-accepted premises', but warned that this led to the 'tragic conclusion of the IRA "war" in occupied Ireland. And it is the awareness among intelligent people that the IRA position is both assured and in its way logical, that led to a questioning, awakening a number of people from dogmatic slumbers'.[69]

Absurdity and logic; these, far from constituting weaknesses in Irish Republicanism, gave it strength. In 1979 the centenary of Patrick Pearse's birth was handled with delicacy by the Irish political establishment. The tendency now was to stress Pearse's progressive views on education, rather than his romantic, mythologically inspired hopes for the nation. Charles Haughey preferred to concentrate on the iniquities of partition, insisting that Pearse would not have accepted it, but adding quickly that Pearse stood for Theobald Wolfe Tone's idea of a unity of Catholic, Protestant and Dissenter, and that when Pearse spoke of war, he was at one with his generation in thinking of war in chivalrous terms. Then Haughey moved on to Pearse the educational reformer and defender of the rights of women, urging that if Pearse were alive now his chief interest would be in the role of government in promoting the welfare of the people. His political philosophy was 'liberal, tolerant and progressive'. The President of Ireland, Dr Patrick Hillery, on the occasion of the opening of the Pearse family museum in Pearse's old school, St Enda's, Rathfarnham, County Dublin, contented himself with reasonable platitudes, stressing again Pearse the educationalist ('a bright light in the history of Irish education'), recalling the whole family's sense of service to their country, and ending with the hope that St Enda's might 'inspire all who come here as it has inspired so many in the past'. But he carefully refrained from defining or explaining precisely what that inspiration would be.[70] Clearly it was not Pearse's affirmation of the 'strength and . . . peace of mind of those who never compromise'.[71]

For Irish socialists, as much as for Irish Nationalists, 1916 posed as many questions as answers. Irish Labour after 1916 was pragmatic, non-revolutionary and willing to bargain within the existing economic system. But those socialists who were attracted to Connolly as the hero of 1916 opened up a different path. R.M. Fox, whose *History of the Irish Citizen Army* was published in 1943, praised Connolly for finding himself closer to Pearse's spiritual nation than to James Larkin's call for bread to be put on the table: 'both Pearse and Connolly asked the crucial question:

What shall it profit a man if he gain the whole world and lose his soul?'[72] Connolly, in pushing Labour towards 1916 had to 'fight on more than one front'. The trade unions 'represented the purely "hours and wages, bread and butter"' trade union viewpoint. They were afraid of the consequences to the Union of standing with the Citizen Army.

> Between this limited conception and Connolly's own views . . . that Labour had a big part to play and a stand to make on every question affecting the social and national life of the people, there was no compatibility. One view of the workers is that they are interested only in a larger trough and a bigger feed while the other takes them as men and women, citizens with ideas and aspirations, with something distinctive to contribute to the civilization of the world.[73]

Pearse could hardly have put it better. 'Thereafter', as one modern historian of Connolly's socialism has written, 'Marxian socialism in Ireland was to be a subordinate left wing of republicanism rather than an independent working-class party.'[74]

V

The seventy-fifth anniversary of the Easter Rising was less important in historical terms than the fiftieth had been. No new significant studies of the rising were published, although there was a keen historical and political debate. This anniversary, moreover, fell when the troubles in the North were in their twentieth year, and once again commentaries tended to become, not surprisingly, tracts for the times. But nothing much had changed, in that the central questions posed by the rising for Irish political thought: legitimacy of the state; the use of political violence; the relationship of violence to democratic government; Catholicism and republicanism – all still exercised the political imagination in Ireland, even if, in the south, they can hardly be said to have had much direct political impact, or exercised unduly the general public (through some 'alternative' celebrations were held in order to counteract the muted official response).[75] *Revising the Rising*, a publication of the Field Day Theatre Company, contained essays of varying quality and interest, but all of them addressed the enduring themes of 1916. Some booklets were published, attacking 'neo-Unionist "revisionist historians"' (sic), denouncing the way in which 1916 had been made to 'embellish the present regime' in the south, thus obscuring 'partition and the facts of neo-colonialism'.[76]

But most commentators were less combative. Declan Kiberd praised the bravery of the rebels, but denied that they provided any inspiration for the modern IRA,[77] a theme echoed by Tom Garvin, who set out to demonstrate that separatist Nationalism and constitutional Nationalism alike always stood for the most 'anti-sectarian' Irish political tradition.[78] These claims were not necessarily invalid, but they revealed how anxious southern Irish scholars were not to let contemporary, violent northern Republicanism capture the 1916 tradition even when, as Kiberd claimed, their inspiration was 'the bleak sectarian realities of life' in Northern Ireland.[79] Arthur Aughey, from a Unionist perspective, argued that it was precisely the logic of 1916 that

> In Northern Ireland, republicanism means armed struggle. It is characterised by a contempt for all political reform. It demands the sacrifice of the present generation for the salvation of future generations. It is committed to completing the unfinished business for the national revolution. It claims fidelity to the 'true' ideal of 1916, which gives it legitimacy that transcends any current institutional form. This ideological throwback is an acute discomfort to the republican state, whose legitimacy now transcends the 'true' ideal of 1916; and its citizens can well understand the distinction between a rebellion against the rule of a foreign power (as 1916 is currently interpreted in the Republic) and the use of the gun to force one million people to accept a destiny they have consistently denied.[80]

This debate, as Geriod O Crulaoich remarked in the Field Day anthology, showed that F.X. Martin's idea, first expressed in 1967, of establishing an institute for the study of the rising could not (however much information it accumulated) tell the whole story of the event. It could not be 'fixed', as to were, in its own time; it could not lose its sense of mystery[81] (at least, for some). Thus an analysis of the meaning of the Easter Rising cannot be confined to what is usually regarded as history, but must be analysed as an influence in the political history *and* ideas of Ireland.

VI

And how much space do the men and women of 1916 merit in the context of British history? For it would be one of the most disappointing (if perhaps unsurprising) aspects of the research done on the rising in the last twenty years if its findings failed to gain a fresh hearing, or more space, in modern British history textbooks. T.O. Lloyd in his *Empire to Welfare State* (1993 edn) dedicated only a paragraph or two to the event which destroyed the unity of the United Kingdom,[82] while Robert Blake in his *The Decline of Power* (1985) ventured the remark that 'modern Eire dates from Easter Monday 1916',[83] certainly an arguable position, but one which must have left its less well informed readers casting around for reasons why. A more hopeful sign is the brief, but intelligent, discussion of the rising under the heading 'Controversy: Easter 1916', which Malcolm Pearce and Geoffrey Stewart include in their textbook on British political history since 1867. Different interpretations are offered, and extracts from various authors, from the ranks of politicians as well as historians, are printed. They conclude – and it is difficult to disagree – that 'it is hardly surprising that the Irish question remains intractable both for historians and politicians'.[84] Thus it can at least be said that revisionism shows signs of breaking out of the narrow furrows of academic and political controversy, and into the wider fields of general historical discussion.

NOTES

1 F.X. Martin, 'Eoin MacNeill on the 1916 Rising', in *Irish Historical Studies*, vol. XI (1916), pp. 226–71.
2 *Ibid.*, pp. 234–6.
3 *Ibid.*, pp. 239–40.
4 *Ibid.*, p. 245, fn. 20.
5 F.X. Martin (ed.), *Leaders and Men of the Easter Rising: Dublin, 1916* (London, 1966).
6 *Ibid.*, p. 240.
7 J.C. Beckett, 'Carson: Unionist and Rebel', *ibid.*, p. 92.
8 David Thornley, 'Patrick Pearse: The Evolution of a Republican', *ibid.*, p. 151.
9 Edward MacLysaght, 'Larkin, Connolly and the Labour Movement', *ibid.*, p. 132.
10 Roger McHugh, 'Casement and German Help', *ibid.*, pp. 186–7.
11 T. Desmond Williams (ed.), *The Irish Struggle, 1916–1926* (London, 1966), W.I. Thompson, *The Imagination of an Insurrection: Dublin, 1916* (London, 1967). For a recent exposition of this latter, and other works on Pearse, see Sean Farrell Moran, *Patrick Pearse and the Politics of Redemption: The Mind of the Easter Rising, 1916* (Washington DC, 1994), ch. 1.
12 Owen Dudley Edwards and Fergus Pyle (eds), *1916: The Easter Rising* (London, 1968).
13 Kevin B. Nowlan (ed.), *The Making of 1916: Studies in the History of the Rising* (Dublin, 1969).
14 Maureen Wall, 'Partition: The Ulster Question, 1916–26', in Desmond Williams (ed.), *The Irish Struggle*, p. 79.
15 Father Francis Shaw, SJ, 'The Canon of Irish History: a Challenge', in *Studies*, vol. LXI (summer 1972), pp. 113–53.
16 Ruth Dudley Edwards, *Patrick Pearse: The Triumph of Failure* (London, 1977, New York, 1978), preface.
17 *Ibid.*, p. 183.
18 *Ibid.*, pp. 253–8.
19 *Ibid.*, p. 252.
20 *Ibid.*, p. 339.
21 *Ibid.*, p. 214.
22 For a rather myopic earlier assessment of Connolly's writings, see Edward MacLysaght, in F.X. Martin (ed.), *Leaders and Men*, ch. 10.
23 Austen Morgan, *James Connolly: a Political Biography* (Manchester University Press, 1988).
24 Austen Morgan, 'What is Revisionism?' Draft paper delivered at the University of North London, 24 February 1993, p. 9.
25 Austen Morgan, *James Connolly*, p. 10.
26 *Ibid.*, p. 133. For an example of Connolly's pro-German stance see Desmond

Ryan (ed.), *Socialism and Nationalism; a Selection from the Writing of James Connolly* (Dublin, 1948), pp. 136–42.

27 Morgan, *James Connolly*, p. 135.

28 *Ibid.*, p. 197.

29 *Ibid.*, pp. 199, 202–3.

30 See e.g., John Newsinger, 'As Catholic as the Pope: James Connolly and the Roman Catholic Church in Ireland', in *Saother* (The Journal of Irish Labour History), vol. 11 (1986), pp. 7–18; 'James Connolly, the German Empire and the Great War', in *Irish Sword*, vol. 65 (1986), pp. 272–83; 'James Connolly and the Easter Rising', in *Science and Society*, vol. 47 (1983) pp. 152–77.

31 D.G. Boyce, *Nationalism in Ireland* (London, 1992), pp. 263–5.

32 For an example of the modernist interpretation, see R.F. Foster, *Modern Ireland, 1600–1972* (London, 1988), pp. 471–84.

33 D.G. Boyce, '"One Last Burial" Culture, Counter-revolution and revolution in Ireland 1886–1916', in Boyce (ed.) *The Revolution in Ireland, 1879–1923* (London, 1988), pp. 115–38. See also the subtle interpretation offered by Donal McCartney, 'Gaelic Ideological Origins of 1916', in *Irish Times Review of the Easter Rising*, 7 April 1966, p. 11.

34 For a recent printing see Michael Hughes, *Ireland Divided: The Roots of the Modern Irish Problem* (Cardiff, 1994), pp. 97–8.

35 Maureen Wall, 'The Plans and the Countermand: the Country and Dublin', in Kevin B. Nowlan (ed.), *The Making of 1916*, pp. 157–9.

36 *Ibid.*, pp. 168–9, 226–7. See also F.X. Martin, 'The 1916 Rising: A Coup d'état or a "Bloody Protest"', in *Studia Hibernica*, vol. 8 (1968), pp. 117–18.

37 Ruth Dudley Edwards, *Patrick Pearse*, pp. 266–74.

38 Maureen Wall, 'The Plans and the Countermand', in K.B. Nowlan (ed.), *The Making of 1916*, p. 181.

39 G.A. Hayes-McCoy, 'A Military History of the 1916 Rising', in Nowlan, *op. cit.*, p. 287.

40 Newsinger, 'As Catholic as the Pope', in *Soathar*, vol. 11 (1986), pp. 15–16.

41 David Fitzpatrick, 'De Valera in 1917: the Undoing of the Easter Rising', in John P. O'Carroll and John A. Murphy (eds), *De Valera and his Times* (Cork, 1986), p. 101.

42 Austen Morgan, *James Connolly*, pp. 200–1. B. Mac Giolla Choille, *Intelligence Notes, 1913–1916*, (Dublin, State Paper Office, 1966), pp. 199–220, gives a convincing picture of the impact of the rising on the public. Attempts to revise this, and to suggest that opinion was initially much more favourable than is usually supposed, lack detailed research. See, for example, Joseph Lee, *Ireland, 1912–85: Politics and Society* (Cambridge, 1990), pp. 29–36.

43 Paul Bew, '1916: The Easter Rising: Lost Leaders and Lost Opportunities', in *The Irish Review*, vol. 11 (winter 1991–2), p. 12.

44 D.G. Boyce, 'British Opinion, Ireland and the War', in *Historical Journal*, vol. 17, no. 3 (1974), pp. 575–93, esp. pp. 578–9.

45 *Ibid.*, pp. 579–84; see also John Kendle, *Walter Long, Ireland and the Union, 1905–1920* (Kingston and Montreal, 1992), ch. 4.

46 David Fitzpatrick, *Politics and Irish Life, 1913–1921: Provincial Experience of War and Revolution* (Dublin, 1977), p. 131.

47 *Ibid.*, pp. 147–8; D.G. Boyce, *Nationalism in Ireland*, pp. 315–19.

48 For an analysis of the 1918 election see Brian Walker, *Parliamentary Election Results in Ireland, 1918–1992* (Belfast, 1992).

49 J.C. Beckett, 'Ireland under the Union', *Topic, 13* (Washington, PA, 1967), reprinted in Beckett, *Confrontations* (London, 1972), pp. 142–5. All references are to this latter edition.

50 *Ibid.*, p. 149.
51 F.X. Martin, *Leaders and Men*, pp. 239–52. See also Owen Dudley Edwards, 'The Achievement of 1916', in Edwards and Pyle, *1916: The Easter Rising*, pp. 210, 218–19.
52 Patrick Lynch 'The Social Revolution that never was', in Desmond Williams, *The Irish Struggle*, pp. 41–51, at p. 41.
53 *Ibid.*, p. 45.
54 Owen Dudley Edwards, 'The Achievement of 1916', in Edwards and Pyle, *op. cit.*, pp. 210–19, at pp. 210–11, 219.
55 Eamon de Valera, foreword to *The Irish Uprising, 1916–1922* (A CBS Legacy Collection Book, New York, 1966), p. v.
56 Father Francis Shaw, SJ, 'The Canon of Irish History: a Challenge', in *Studies*, vol. 61 (1972), pp. 113–53.
57 *Ibid.*, pp. 117–18.
58 *Ibid.*, pp. 121–5.
59 *Ibid.*, pp. 130–3.
60 *Ibid.*, pp. 145–6.
61 *Ibid.*, pp. 151–3.
62 *Ibid.*, pp. 113–14.
63 F.X. Martin, 'The Evolution of a Myth: the Easter Rising, Dublin, 1916', in E. Kamenka (ed.), *Nationalism: The Nature and Evolution of an Idea* (Canberra, 1973), pp. 66–8.
64 D.G. Boyce, *Nationalism in Ireland*, pp. 345–6.
65 Garrett FitzGerald, 'The Significance of 1916', in *Studies*, vol. LV (1966), pp. 29–37.
66 *Ibid.*, p. 35.
67 *Ibid.*, p. 37. By 1991 Fitzgerald was answering these questions in the affirmative; see his articles in the *Irish Times*, 13, 15, 16, 17 and 18 July 1991, especially his claim that 'it was in Irish membership of the European Community that Ireland's movement for national independence . . . was to find its ultimate justification' (13 July 1991).
68 Sean Lemass, in M.O Dubghaill, *Insurrection Fires at Eastertide* (Cork, 1966), p. vi.
69 *Ibid.*, p. 334.
70 *Irish Times*, 12 November 1979, p. 7. See also the article by Seamus Ó Buachalla, and comments by various Irish luminaries in the *Irish Press*, 10 November 1979.
71 Richard English, 'Irish Republican Solipsism in the 1930's', in *Irish Historical Studies*, vol. XXVIII, no. 112 (November 1993), p. 438.
72 R.M. Fox, *History of the Irish Citizen Army* (Dublin, 1943), pp. 123–4.
73 *Ibid.*, p. 126.
74 John Newsinger, 'The Easter Rebellion: Defeat or Victory?' in *Monthly Review*, vol. 34, no. 7 (1982), p. 40.
75 Declan Kiberd, 'The Elephant of Revolutionary Forgetfulness', in Máirín ni Dhonnchadha and Theo Dorgan (eds), *Revising the Rising* (Field Day, Derry, 1991), pp. 1–20, at pp. 1–5.
76 C. Desmond Greaves, *1916 as History: The Myth of the Blood Sacrifice* (Dublin, 1991), p. 38. See also the articles by Brendan Bradshaw and Ruth Dudley Edwards in the *Irish Times*, 1 April 1991, and by John McGahern, 3 April 1991.
77 Kiberd, in *Revising the Rising*, pp. 12–13, 17, 19.
78 Tom Garvin, 'The Rising and Irish Democracy', in *Revising the Rising*, pp. 21–8.
79 Kiberd, in *Revising the Rising*, p. 13.

80 Arthur Aughey, 'What is Living and what is Dead in the Ireland of 1916', in *Revising the Rising*, pp. 71–90, at p. 88.

81 Gearóid Ó Crualaoich, 'Responding to the Rising', in *Revising the Rising*, pp. 50–70, at pp. 50–51.

82 T.O. Lloyd, *Empire to Welfare State: English History, 1906–1992* (Oxford, 1992), pp. 72–3.

83 Robert Blake, *The Decline of Power, 1915–1964* (London, 1985), p. 39.

84 Malcolm Pearce and Geoffrey Stewart, *British Political History, 1867–1990: Democracy and Decline* (London, 1992), pp. 129–30 and pp. 132–5.

10

REVISING THE DIASPORA*

Alan O'Day

The race that lives in these ruinous cottages, behind broken windows mended with oilskin, sprung doors and rotten door-posts or in dark, wet cellars, in measureless filth and stench, in this atmosphere penned in as if with a purpose, this race must really have reached the lowest stage of humanity.

Frederick Engels, *The Condition of the Working-Class in England*, 1844[1]

INTRODUCTION

Frederick Engels' description of 'Little Irelands' in Manchester in the 1840s also depicts Famine era refugees to Boston and Montreal. Images of wretched refugees encrusted in poverty cling to the Irish diaspora. Popular memory also recalls other, usually less than flattering, visions. The Irish are often portrayed as given to excesses of drink and crime, as corrupt political fixers, as strike-breakers, as superstitious and pious, and as the witless but good-humoured stage Paddy.

In common with other aspects of Irish history, the experience of the diaspora has undergone a revaluation but this writing differs from mainstream 'revisionism' in two major ways – it is not alleged to be part of a contemporary anti-Nationalist project and this work is mostly the product of scholarship outside Ireland. With a few notable exceptions, such as David Doyle and David Fitzpatrick, one educated in America and the other an Australian, scholars in Ireland have given scant attention to the emigrants. Yet studies of the diaspora have remarkable parallels with other areas of Irish historiography without, it seems, raising any notable public anguish or academic finger-pointing. The object of the chapter is to trace the thematic development of the literature concerning the Irish abroad during the nineteenth century and to discuss its relationship to 'revisionism'. Examination of the diaspora confirms the wider pattern of skills-based historical techniques replacing the older politically inspired approaches; also in common with writings on other areas of Irish historiography, modern scholarship of the diaspora emphasises the fragmented nature of the past.

THE DIASPORA

Demographic material provides the essential raw data for interpreting the diaspora. That information is a cornerstone for re-interpretations of Irish migration and constitutes a form of 'revisionism', though until recently a sort that has not interacted intimately with mainstream Irish historiography. Some of these sources are imprecise but the volume of information available has increased greatly in recent years. Statistics, especially census information accumulated by governments, continue to be vital for establishing the demographic pattern. The Irish had one of the greatest proportionate propensities to emigrate of any people in Europe. In the seventeenth and eighteenth centuries the country as a whole, but especially Ulster, experienced considerable outflows of population. This pattern was interrupted during the Napoleonic Wars but resumed with a vengeance after 1815, peaking in the years 1846–55 when approximately two and a half million souls emigrated.[2] Between 1855 and 1914 a further four and a half to five million departed though at an uneven pace. Towards the close of the nineteenth century only some sixty per cent of people born in Ireland were still there. While the United States received almost two-thirds of the exiles, other destinations were also popular. Pre-Confederation Canada received nearly half a million between 1840 and 1855; approximately another 150,000 went there between 1867 and 1919.[3] In 1861 there were 177,405 Irish-born in Australia reaching a peak of 229,156 in 1891.[4] New Zealand received several thousand more. In 1870 the Irish were relatively more numerous in Scotland, Ontario, New Brunswick, New Zealand and Australia than in the United States. Great Britain was second only to America as a destination. Before the Famine influx over 400,000 Irish-born already lived in Great Britain and that number expanded to around 805,000 in 1861.[5] Additionally, although largely overlooked, a considerable troop of Irish settled in non-English speaking territories as well.

Emigration was dominated by the young of both sexes. Before the Famine about two-thirds of those going to North America were under thirty-five years old; between 1855 and 1914 most men and women making the journey were under thirty. Except during the Famine decade few emigrated in family groups. Women and men left Ireland in nearly equal numbers during the nineteenth century, although there was an imbalance in gender settlement preferences. At a macro level the differences were considerable. For Australia and New Zealand combined, for instance, the ratio of women immigrants to men never exceeded 87:100 and fell to as low as 52:100 in the later Edwardian years. However, between 1852 and 1921 the ratio for Great Britain was 92.6 women:100 men but this varied substantially over time, being as low as 80.9:100 for the years 1861–70 but achieving a female average of over 100 between 1891 and 1921.[6] Transatlantic migration had similar tendencies. Until the late 1830s men predominated; between 1840 and 1893 there was a rough balance; and in the years 1894–1905 females were the more numerous of the immigrant cohort.[7] Of those choosing South Africa, women were always a minority only reaching near parity in the years immediately before and following the First World War.[8] Micro analysis is in many ways even more telling. In Greenock, Scotland, males dominated Irish settlement in the late 1880s but in Dundee in 1871 there were two Irish women to every Irish man in the town. For Butte, Montana men outnumbered women by 5,200 to 2,400 in 1900 and by 4,900 to 2,900 in 1910.[9]

Only a minority left Ireland with capital or economic skills. At most periods three-quarters or more were classified as labourers or domestic servants but again there are important distinctions over time and by destination. Passenger lists for the American-bound confirm the density of male labourers in the immigrant cohort. Between 1851 and 1905 approximately four out of five fit this category. But not all were labourers and the proportions of farmers and others of higher occupational status varied from 75 per cent in 1820 to 9 per cent in 1900 with an overall average of about 25 per cent during the period.[10] Female migrants to Great Britain between 1877 and 1920 were overwhelmingly domestic servants, being 95.7 per cent of the total between 1881 and 1891 and only declining to a still high 85.6 per cent in the years 1911 to 1920.[11]

Motivation for striking out on the emigrant trail varied. Nationalist tradition insisted that the prime cause was the British misgovernment of Ireland. John Mitchel declaimed that they left Ireland 'only because of insufferable political tyranny which has made their native land uninhabitable to them'.[12] Thomas D'Arcy McGee expressed a similar opinion though he alluded to the compelling attractions of the new lands as well:

> whether we may wish it or not, one half of Ireland is here. We grieve that these laborious and obedient men were not possessed of a land of their own; you may regret that they possess already too much of yours. But whether we would alter it, or not, they are here. Here, by the immediate action of British misrule, here by the primal authority of man's first charter – 'Go forth, and fill the earth and subdue it'.[13]

Modern authorities have been more impressed by the allure of better prospects overseas. Robert Kennedy's sociological account suggests that despite the higher death rate for Irish immigrants in American and British cities than in Famine-struck rural Ireland, the 'pull' of the richer lands was compelling.[14] He postulates that even if there had been no Famine, emigration would have risen to approximately the same levels in the face of modernisation of Ireland's agriculture. Brenda Collins adopts a similar view of immigration to Scotland.[15]

Poorer regions over the long haul contributed disproportionately to the tide of emigration and there were distinct 'streams' or patterns for the relocation of the exiles. Yet, even this impression is tempered by modern research that reveals the pre-1870s wave of emigrants leaving not the most destitute regions but more often vacating places a notch or two up the economic scale. Direct emigration to the United States between 1876 and 1914 showed a propensity to be from the west while Canadian-bound Irish were apt to come from Ulster. Scotland received its immigrants from the North-east. From the early 1880s over 80 per cent originated in Ulster and between 1880 and 1910 Antrim (including Belfast) alone accounted for over 30 per cent, rising to more than 40 per cent for fifteen of this thirty-year span.[16] The Irish who chose England often were from the eastern and southern coastal regions. Australian Irish frequently originated from the South-west and North Midlands; many of those going to New Zealand were drawn from Ulster. Other links include Waterford and Newfoundland, Wexford and Argentina, Clare and Australia, Kerry and New Zealand, Derry and Philadelphia. Australia received a disproportionate number of immigrations from the contiguous districts of Kilkenny, Tipperary, East Limerick, east Clare and north Cork while those going to America were drawn more evenly from all parts of the island, though David Fitzpatrick cautions that localised nexuses were swamped statistically by the total numbers. Selection of destination undoubtedly was influenced by the comparative cost of passage. This was certainly true for North America where fares to Canada were lower than those to the United States thus attracting a higher proportion of family migrants. Fares and the availability of assisted passages certainly had a bearing on the flow of Irish settlers to Australia and New Zealand. Usually, it is assumed that Great Britain was chosen by people who had fewer means; it was resorted to by those intending to use this as a stepping-stone to re-migration overseas, or was the choice of the Irish who saw emigration as a short-term strategy and hoped to return home even if this usually was not realised. While there are certainly reasons to uphold portions of this hypothesis, its general value is by no means certain for there is evidence suggesting that Great Britain was preferred by many with skills suited to the local market.[17] To date there is little firm statistical support for the argument that migrants to Great Britain were financially poorer than their American-bound compatriots. There is a universal consensus, though, that the problem of re-migration bedevils estimates of immigration.

Fitzpatrick observes that regionalisation of settlement means that the immigrants displayed different characteristics in their various new destinations, something borne out in the case of the Irish from a small district of Cork who went to Butte, Montana (1,138 of the approximately 1,700 who emigrated to America from the parish of Eyeries in western-most County Cork went there) and also by those who participated in the political movements like the American Land League.[18] Arrivals in Britain often had urban roots while the America Irish who settled in towns frequently came from the surplus rural population of the West. The Australian Irish were more likely to be semi-skilled farm workers. Though only a small proportion of the immigrants anywhere returned permanently to Ireland they did not remain static in their new homes. Evidence from many places shows high geographical mobility through-out the nineteenth century. One modern observer notes of Boston that the Irish-born were as transient as Yankees and that 'even where there were highly segregated ethnic neighbourhoods there was little continuity of the *individuals* who composed them over time'.[19] High residential mobility was also characteristic of Philadelphia and similar findings for Newcastle upon Tyne and Stafford in England, among other towns, point towards this being the norm.[20]

Although the new arrivals followed no single mode of settlement and employment in their adopted lands, they adjusted to conditions impress-ively and 'often comprised a highly mobile proletariat, acutely responsive to fluctuations in demand and unusually adept at securing the best of the worst jobs',[21] Donald Akenson draws attention to the large numbers entering farming in Canada, speculating that some of these moved on to become agriculturists subsequently in the United States, and Fitzpatrick notes the diversity of patterns.[22] According to Fitzpatrick, while urban concentration was typical of Great Britain and America, diffusion was characteristic of Australia's Irish, who were not only evenly distributed between colonies but within them, seemingly confirming his and others' assessment that these people were highly responsive to economic oppor-tunity, a conclusion which incidentally, corresponds to modern views about the Irish at home. The Irish in New Zealand were distributed between urban and rural pursuits in the same proportion, Maoris excepted, as the rest of the population. As the United States received more of Ireland's people in the nineteenth century than everywhere else com-bined, it is not beside the point to note that the Catholic Irish did congre-gate in cities there. William V. Shannon observes 'the Irishness of the Irish in America is founded on a paradox. The Irish were a rural people in Ireland and became a city people in the United States'.[23] In 1890 only two per cent of Irish-born immigrants were engaged in agriculture. Britain's picture was similar. Not all of those choosing the United States took shelter along the East Coast, though many of the tidal wave of Famine refugees did. By 1850 the Irish-born in New York were 26 per cent of the population, reaching 34 per cent in 1855.[24] People of Irish extraction were one-third of the total numbers in New York and Brooklyn at the outset of the Gay Nineties. In Newburyport, Massachusetts, between 1850 and 1880 two-thirds of the labouring class were born outside America and nearly all of these were Irish.[25] Yet, by 1900 fewer than one-fifth of the Irish-born and their children lived in New England, 30 per cent were in the middle west and plains states, 12 per cent in the inland regions of the mid-Atlantic, 30 per cent in the mid-Atlantic area, and some 10 per cent planted themselves in the south, mountain states and west coast.[26] Occupational structures, too, shifted over time though the Irish-born tended to be over-represented among labourers. In England the census of 1891 noted that the Irish-born of Liverpool were 'engaged in the rougher kind of unskilled labour, the proportions of artisans and of dealers of all kinds and grades being very small'.[27] However, there were notable differences between places. A survey of the Irish in England in 1872 points out some of the discrepancies in migration preferences and employment possibilities.[28] As early as 1872 the second generation Irish enjoyed a measure of upward mobility in some places. London attracted professionals and other middle-class people. Philadelphia, likewise, witnessed a good deal of upward occupational mobility with the Irish drifting towards the better-paid jobs as the century progressed.[29] Detroit's Hibernians were to be found in a range of occupations while those who settled in Butte, Montana in copper mining enjoyed a relatively secure and remunerative employment.[30] San Francisco contained fewer Irish-born labourers as a proportion of the ethnic cohort than did eastern cities.[31] Similarly, few Irish labourers chose South Africa; immigration there contained an exceptionally high proportion of those classified as middle-class.[32]

An image of the Irish huddled together in ethnic ghettos permeates much earlier writing. This, too, has been re-evaluated in recent years and largely found wanting. Though the immigrants tended to cluster in certain districts, exclusively Irish streets, much more whole neighbourhoods, were rare. Even the most notorious areas of New York and Liverpool were not exclusively Irish and the larger pattern seems to be one of relative concentration and dispersal simultaneously as was true in Philadelphia and also of Liverpool.[33] Yet, in Butte, Montana where they were so significant a proportion of the population and heavily represented in mining, they lived in fairly mono-ethnic neighbourhoods.[34] Both tendencies had profound implications for the development of ethnic and religious institutions as it did also for the prospects of integration and assimilation.

Emigrants' religious profession influenced choices of destination as well. Both Protestants and Catholics fled their homeland but the latter certainly predominated numerically from the 1840s. A majority of Irish emigrants to Canada were Protestant.[35] They made up around two-thirds of the Irish in Ontario and were plentiful in New Brunswick and Nova Scotia though Catholics were the largest element in Newfoundland, Prince Edward Island and Quebec. Protestants were well represented among those going to New Zealand, Pennsylvania and Scotland also. Inadequate religious statistics make impossible a systematic enumeration of Protestants leaving Ireland or of their settlement overseas, except, in part, for Canada, where records are more complete. The Canadian census asked for religious affiliation whereas the American counterpart did not. Donald Akenson points out the important cross-border flow of Canadian Irish Protestants into the United States arguing that this is one of the reasons why '*the bulk of the Irish ethnic group in the United States is at present, and probably always has been, Protestant*'.[36] According to Akenson, 'this is in spite of the fact that the overwhelming bulk of the historical literature of the last fifty years deals almost entirely with Roman Catholics and, in many cases, states that the Irish in the United States were, and are, almost entirely Catholic'.

'Protestant' is an inclusive term that disguises important variations in religious allegiance. Denominational features of the Irish population in Canada in 1871 illustrate the point.[37] Then nearly 31 per cent of the ethnic Irish in Ontario were Catholic. Anglicans were 25 per cent of the ethnic cohort, Methodists 22.6 per cent and Presbyterians only 16.4 per cent (16.7 per cent of the Irish-born). Quebec reveals a different pattern. There Catholics were 60.5 per cent of the ancestral-Irish and 65.3 per cent of the Irish-born respectively, Quebec Anglicans totalled 19.9 per cent of the ethnic group, Methodists 9.2 per cent and Presbyterians merely 7.2 per cent, both among the Irish-born and also of the ancestral group as a whole. Despite heavy Protestant immigration to New Brunswick and Nova Scotia, Catholics were 41.9 per cent of the Irish-born and 49 per cent of the ancestral-Irish while Presbyterians totalled 15.8 per cent and 20 per cent respectively. In Australia Catholics were 71.3 per cent of the Irish-born.[38] Of the remaining 28.7 per cent, Anglicans were 14.1 per cent and Presbyterians 8.7 per cent. 'Protestants', as Akenson, Doyle, Fitzpatrick and O'Farrell among others observe, have been largely squeezed out of histories of the diaspora except when as in the west of Scotland, Liverpool or Ontario they played some part in ritualised anti-Catholicism or established Orange Lodges.[39] There is, for example, only limited study of Protestant immigrants into England, and they remain shadowy figures in standard accounts of the Irish in the United States generally faring only marginally better to date in work on Australia, New Zealand, Scotland and the American South. Canada forms a partial exception. Akenson, Bruce Elliott, Cecil Houston and William Smyth, for instance, enlarge understanding of this segment of the Irish diaspora considerably; their researches tend to further fragment the picture thus making simplistic generalisations less tenable.[40]

Construction of an exact profile of the Irish emigrant is impossible. For many areas tangible evidence is scanty, in others only partly complete or reliable, and relatively few places possess satisfactory material. The United Kingdom census recorded country of birth alone, thus giving no firm means to ascertain the size of an ethnic community that includes children born in Britain of Irish parents; furthermore the census does not provide evidence for the county or region of origin for the immigrants. American data suffer from the same omissions. Thus, the two largest receivers of Irish people have some of the least thorough documentation. Neither country included religious profession in its census returns, and enumeration of denominational affiliation depends on estimates of the sects themselves, a tabulation that commands limited confidence. Yet, there is universal agreement on the fundamental importance of religion in the lives of the Irish abroad. Even when formal religious observance was low or erratic, Catholicism as a cultural identity survived. Despite low levels of participation in some parts of Scotland, 'the Irish Catholic response to the experience of prejudice and discrimination was to identify with the Catholic Church'.[41] Canadian statistics for ethnicity and religion rather than simply of Irish birth compiled between 1871 and 1961 afford a better glimpse of the overall strength of the group.[42] Ethnic numbers in 1871 for the Atlantic provinces were 163,494 or 19.3 per cent of the entire population expanding to 192,766 (20.2 per cent) in 1881 but therefore slowly contracting to 148,714 (14.2 per cent) in 1911. For Quebec the ethnic Irish reached 123,478 (14.6 per cent) in 1871 but fell to 103,148 (11.6 per cent) in 1911; Ontario's figures were 559,442 (66.1 per cent) in 1871 and 608,139 (57.2 per cent) in 1911. In Australia the Irish portion of the population excluding aboriginal people was 25.5 per cent in 1861 while for New Zealand the ethnic proportion exclusive of Maoris was 13.1 per cent in the same year and then peaking at over 18 per cent between 1867 and the Great War.

Marriage and baptismal records offer some useful clues but tell little about intra-confessional unions when these took place outside a church and do not reveal the extent of wastage from the various faiths. Australian evidence suggests that exogamous marriages were considerable. In Victoria in the decade after 1851 between 33 and 50 per cent of Catholic women married in Protestant churches.[43] Evidence collected for the whole country shows that in 1911, 26.10 per cent of women and 17.73 per cent of Catholic men married outside their confession. Yet, three out of four Catholic wives were living with Catholic husbands and four-fifths of Catholic husbands had spouses who shared their faith. Collins hints at the importance of out-marriage in Scotland.[44] American evidence is ambiguous. Patrick Blessing points to the high levels of inter-communal unions even in Los Angeles; Jo Ellen Vinyard for Detroit and David Emmons' study of Butte, Montana claims that more than 90 per cent of marriages took place within the group. Emmons even notes a strong preference for marriages between partners from the same part of Ireland.[45] Comparative analysis of the Irish Catholic and also the Protestant experience in different locales is in its infancy. Doyle, for instance, posits a claim that the Catholic Church is a constant feature in both America and Britain but served differing purposes in the two countries.[46] Despite considerable work in recent decades on the diaspora, the map still has many gaps and the raw facts are not established to the same degree as is the case for many parts of Ireland's past. Basic spadework remains undone; indeed this effort will be essential before something like a convincing picture is available.

Statistics cannot properly recreate the variations of individual experience. But this material forms the basic starting-point for coming to grips with the diaspora. It also represents an attempt of modern scholarship to provide a fuller description of Irish communities. Such work thus far is not consistent in its findings and is sometimes controversial. It is certainly 'revisionist' to the extent of making dents in received notions of Irish emigration and confirms the triumph of skills-based historical methods. Still, the legend of Grosse Isle, the final resting place along the St Lawrence for many a Famine refugee, continues to dominate the popular imagination. Demographic investigations are reshaping thinking in several vital areas. It shows the importance of 'pull' factors in the decision to emigrate and choice of location. Furthermore, the myth that the Irish either left Ireland in large numbers because of political considerations or selected their destination for these reasons is dispelled. Additionally, the emigration pattern is now seen as a Protestant as well as a Catholic phenomenon. Such work demonstrates the variety and richness of immigration and forms the starting point for re-interpretation of other aspects of the diaspora. But demography exposes no more than the tip of the iceberg. To date only a limited amount is known about how immigration influenced the shape of the receiving societies and even less is known of the impact of emigration on Ireland. Comparative studies are still rare and Oliver MacDonagh's suggestion that though many more Irish went to America they were only 10 per cent of its newcomers, while in Australia, though fewer in number they represented a quarter of total immigration and thus had a more profound influence on the host community, is yet to be investigated in detail.[47] Brenda Collins makes a similar case for Scotland, arguing that the persistence of emigration to it 'added undiluted peasant elements to partly assimilated groups of descendants of earlier Irish immigrants and together they formed a major force in modern Scottish society' while John F. McCaffrey notes that Irish involvement in Scotland was part of a 'dynamic, evolutionary process'.[48]

These and other hypotheses demand further testing for the work done to date is only opening up new vistas.

INTERPRETATIONS

Interestingly, despite a huge literature on Irish migration, there is no standard account of the diaspora as a whole. Irish immigrants did not go unobserved anywhere, indeed, they usually became objects of derision. Anti-Catholic demonstrations were a sign of the fear these invaders evoked. Writing in the field was left to polemicists of an anti-Irish disposition or to Irishmen intent upon telling a story of perseverance and heroism. John Denvir's *The Irish in Britain* (1892), typifies such writings. His conclusion is a paean to Irish success, to immigrants' attachment to faith and fatherland despite the corrupting influences of their hostile and 'alien' environments:

> But, like the children of Israel in bondage, we have, despite persecution and innumerable proselytising influences, increased and multiplied, and become a mighty power, that statesmen must reckon with; permeating, in numerous ways, the religious, social and political life of Britain.[49]

Older general surveys of American and even more especially of British history usually allotted the immigrants only passing notice. This neglect is curious in view of the supposed importance the exiles played in providing cheap unskilled labour for rapid industrialisation, their part in bolstering successive Nationalist movements, and as the stalking-horse of Catholicism.

Yet, if an over-arching interpretation of the diaspora is absent, the field has spawned innumerable accounts of the Irish in certain places or countries. Not surprisingly, the literature on the American dimension is most voluminous and sets the pace for interpreting the immigration experience. More than 5,000 entries grace a recent bibliography, giving a ratio of something like 5:1 over a similar compilation for the Irish in Britain.[50] Indeed, despite many recent works on the Irish elsewhere, notably in Canada and Australia, the literature on the United States dimension greatly outdistances the outpourings for everywhere else combined. The writing owes much to the size and importance of America's Irish. In 1870 they were the largest first generation group in twenty-seven of the nation's forty-three most populous cities and second in the rest.[51] Emphasis upon the American aspect, particularly on the Irish-born who settled in eastern cities, has a distorting effect, for it seems that they were more Catholic and also more likely to originate from the rural impoverished West of Ireland than those who settled elsewhere, though even these entrenched certainties can no longer be taken as read.[52]

It seems as well that the reception newcomers received in these eastern American cities was a good deal less inviting than they often encountered elsewhere. In much of the older literature there was a tendency to equate the Irish patterns of Boston and New York with the whole of the diaspora; consequently, some 'revisionism' is merely a widening of the case studies thereby uncovering more complex and varied sets of experiences or, as seen in the previous section, an elaboration of the demographic profile.

Patrick O'Sullivan borrows from feminist studies an explanatory framework of oppression, compensation and contribution for analysis of Irish settlement overseas.[53] He believes that nearly all the literature can be encompassed within these headings – most making use of the whole gamut. O'Sullivan cites R.A. Burchell's study of the San Francisco Irish as an illustration of all three themes running in tandem in the same account. O'Sullivan's categorisation does not suit present purposes because it fails to discriminate sufficiently between types of writings. Instead, an alternative grouping is employed. The four categories used here are 'nativist' or anti-immigrant, 'patriotic' or Nationalist, 'history from below', and 'internalisation', that is to say that innate characteristics affected adaptation to new environments. These categories have been derived from the late John Whyte's classification of the literature on the present-day 'troubles' in Northern Ireland.[54] His categories are 'traditional Unionist', 'traditional Nationalist', 'Marxist', and 'internal conflict'. Many writings cross boundaries, particularly modern works that employ both 'history below' and 'internalisation' simultaneously. Nevertheless, this is not a survey of the literature but an attempt to account for the role of 'revisionism' and the framework affords a means of dissecting work on the diaspora and relating it to developments in Irish historiography generally.

American writing is an obvious point of departure due to its volume, influence, and also because of the early introduction of the Germanic Ph.D. The academic doctorate introduced 'objective' or 'value-free' skills-based methods in place of the old polemical approach to historical writing. Conditions in American society added to interest in immigration studies as well. Between 1840 and 1920 the new nation was deluged by waves of immigrants. Thus, it is scarcely surprising that Americans would be at the forefront in attempting to diagram immigration and its impact upon their culture. This obvious concern was coupled with the rise of sociology and investigations of local communities developed by the Chicago School. Yet, despite an obvious rationale for examining the Irish specifically, the Hibernian influx received surprising little systematic attention, and it usually was absorbed in general accounts of immigration. Irish immigrants scarcely featured on the Chicago School's agenda despite the ample raw material on the doorstep. The Irish community did not fill the void by initiating careful study of its past.

The American census of 1890 proclaimed that the frontier had closed thereby inspiring Frederick Jackson Turner to explore the implications of the announcement. Writing in the midst of the tidal wave of immigration, Turner asserted that the unique character of America was a product of the West, of a frontier, where the spirit of equality and co-operation, the absence of old European notions of hierarchy, class, and deference, enabled an egalitarian democratic spirit to flourish. Americans, then, were predominantly of Old World stock, but were no longer Europeans. Turner was an 'environmentalist' who focused on the adaptive character of Americans. But he wondered aloud whether the closure of the frontier would adversely affect the country in the future and lead to diminution of its unique virtue. His and others' concerns were heightened by the urban political machines of which the Irish-dominated Tammany Hall was symptomatic. These corrupt machines seemed a singular Irish contribution to urban life in late nineteenth-century America. His challenging intervention, for present purposes labelled 'nativist', soon found an echo in sociology. Generations of scholars tested the 'frontier' or 'Turner' thesis and its mutations. Within sociology the outcome was a debate between proponents of the 'melting pot' and 'pluralism' theses as the explanation for the character of American society. The Chicago School played a central role in the debate, emphasising problems in the transition from traditional to modern culture. American society, 'pluralists' maintained, functions as a series of accommodations and compromises between separate competing groups and interests, though some 'pluralists' pause to speculate on the completeness and success of the experiment. Irish–American fates played only a supporting role in the debate. Canadians have assumed that the American pattern of Irish immigration fitted them as well. It was the abiding imagery of the Famine generation that haunted all writings. Similarly, other major receivers of peoples, including Australia, spawned only modest investigations of Irish immigration. Concern about the fate of the exiles did not have a high priority anywhere. This record was often left in the hands of the diaspora itself; most of its chroniclers had a polemical purpose.

Thomas D'Arcy McGee's series of popular lectures first delivered in Boston was issued under the title, *A History of Irish Settlers in North America from the Earliest Period to the Census of 1850* (1855). His aim was to show how his compatriots had triumphed over adversity. However, D'Arcy McGee wanted to stress that the Irish were in North America to stay and must accommodate themselves to the adopted land. He was anxious to blunt Irish support for slavery and he urged the Federal Union, then racked by the strains of the 'peculiar institution', be upheld. John F. Maguire, *The Irish in America* (1868), also falls into the 'patriotic' mode. Maguire was a Nationalist member of the British Parliament and his objects were to examine the political and religious fidelity of the immigrants. As he observes,

I desired to learn if, as had been confidentially and repeatedly asserted, Irish Catholics lost their faith, or became indifferent to religion, the moment they landed in America; or whether as it had been asserted in their defence, they were at once the pioneers and the pillars of their faith. In this enquiry I was mainly influenced by the conviction that loss of faith or indifference to religion would be the most terrible of all calamities to Irish Catholics; that the necessary result of that loss of faith, or that indifference to religion, would be fatal to their material progress, would disastrously interfere with the proper performance of their duties as citizens, and would be certain to turn the public opinion of America against them.[55]

Predictably, Maguire found that the Irish largely adhered to faith and fatherland and he looks forward to their playing a part in helping the old country obtain self-government. Fr Stephen Byrne's 'patriotic' volume, *Irish Emigration to the United States* (1873), professes to warn intending emigrants about the dangers of British and American cities but is, in fact, a manual about the comparative virtues of locations for settlement. Nicholas Flood Davin's *The Irishman in Canada* (1877) sets out to show how 'the Irishman has played so large a part in Canada that his history could not be written without, to some extent, writing the history of Canada . . . '.[56] John Denvir's *The Irish in Britain* (1892) is another account in the 'patriotic' or Nationalist tradition meant to provide a record of the exiles in Britain but mainly directed at assessing their political potential for the Home Rule cause. J.F. Hogan, *The Irish in Australia* (1887), and P.S. Cleary, *Australia's Debt to the Irish Nation Builders* (1933), are 'patriotic' treatments of the Irish down under. These books were an antidote to anti-Irish literature but this work was neither systematic nor analytical. The authors cite official and religious data, note the growing successes of Irishmen abroad, and laud the prospects for the future. They lacked academic pretensions; most were journalists, politicians or priests.

The diaspora continued to receive notice from American writers, but serious study really began in the inter-war years paralleling advances in the historical craft in Ireland. Restrictions on immigration introduced after the First World War brought an era to an end. As one writer observes, 'it seems especially appropriate to review the whole history of immigration in its broadest political, economic, and cultural implications'.[57] Interest flowered just as the Roaring Twenties gave way to the trauma of the Great Depression which bit deep into the American dream of endless opportunity. In the 1920s Edith Abbott, working within the Chicago School, captured portions of immigrant life stressing the difficulties many experienced in the course of transference from a traditional to a modern environment.[58] She was only partly concerned with the Irish, however. William Forbes Adams, in *Ireland and Irish Emigration from 1815 to the Famine* (1932), deals mainly with the first cycle of immigration. Yet his dense study makes extensive use of census and official materials and, along with Abbott's collection of documents, marks an important stage in the understanding of immigration. Similarly, Carl Wittke's several studies, especially *We Who Built America: The Saga of the Immigrant* (1939) amplifies numerous themes and as the title suggests, defends the value of immigrants. Wittke, like Abbott, notes Irish problems adjusting to American life but credits to their favour their role in modifying the Puritan heritage of America.[59] Marcus Hansen's *The Immigrant in American History* (1942) added to the growing interest in, and professionalisation of, the literature.

The defining analyses for the next generation, however, is Oscar Handlin's *Boston's Immigrants, 1790–1865: A Study in Acculturation* (1941), a published version of his Harvard Ph.D. His theme is reprised in *The Uprooted* (1951). Handlin's mental world was stamped by a Brooklyn Jewish boyhood in the cauldron of immigrant America and late teen years marred by the trauma of the Great Depression. After taking a degree at Brooklyn College, a staging-post for the children of Jewish immigrants anxious to climb the ladder to success in America, he entered Harvard as a graduate student. Harvard in the 1930s was still a citadel of cultured, Anglo-Saxon Americans and unfriendly to Jewish students. The young man from Brooklyn undoubtedly felt a profound sense of social distance, if not alienation. Handlin's research on the Boston Irish went beyond the then normal preoccupation with demography, religion and politics, exploring instead the immigrant experience from below. His aim was to examine the 'internal constitution of the social *milieu*'.[60] Rather than the typical success story of the 'melting pot' or even of 'pluralism' he saw the Boston Irish as a socially and psychologically distraught group torn from their moorings in the Old World. He maintains that 'only among the Irish did the motives and circumstances of emigration necessitate settlement under the unfavourable conditions dictated by Boston's economic and social structure'.[61] For him emigration was not a story of triumph but one of social and psychological dislocation. In Handlin's estimation, group isolation and solidarity were enforced by Irish alienation from the host society on the one hand and was also the outcome of native hostility to them on the other. He notes,

> though the Irish acquired a secure place in the community, they remained distinct as a group. Prejudice against them lingered for many years. They never merged with the other elements in the city and consistently retained the characteristics originally segregating them from other Bostonians.[62]

His gloomy prognosis of Irish fortunes, 'revisionist' at the time, countered the rosy picture of immigration and struck at the heart of the 'melting pot' thesis. Handlin's influence spread widely. Armed with this new insight a bevy of researchers set out to explore immigration from the 'bottom up'. Demography, politics and religion were not forgotten, but the social and psychological dimensions of immigration usually had pride of place. Handlin's research was done independently of academic or political currents in Great Britain or Ireland. His formative ideas came from Brooklyn, Boston and Harvard. His intellectual mentor at a distance was Arthur Lovejoy's *Great Chain of Being*, and the research tools he employed, the attempt to establish an 'objective' framework, were common to his generation imbued in the Germanic approach to the historical craft. Handlin and his disciples contributed to debates swirling through American academe about their own society – issues dear to the heart of Ireland's intelligentsia were not part of the remit.

The Second World War was thought to have speeded up regional and class mobility, to have broken down old barriers inhibiting assimilation in America thus making ethnic or 'hyphenated-Americans', disdained by Woodrow Wilson a generation earlier, redundant. Similar factors are alleged to have broken down the sectarianism of Glasgow and Liverpool as well.[63] Edwin O'Connor's novel, *The Last Hurrah* (1956) offers a nostalgic farewell to the Irish ethnicity that had delineated Boston politics. Following the then current view, O'Connor suggests that the New Deal reforms rendered a social service Irish Catholic political machine irrelevant; the bars of prejudice that had held together the Irish were collapsing and they no longer required the mediation of a Boss. Prosperity and mobility had, it seems, made ethnicity passé even on Handlin's turf. Paradoxically, the supposed end of 'ethnicity' in the 1950s, much as the cessation of unlimited immigration in 1920, vitalised academic interest in the fates of the newcomers. A transitional study, Robert Ernst's *Immigrant Life in New York City 1825–1863* (1949) examines the newcomers' experiences in the metropolis. Ernst's treatment explores the fortunes of ethnic groups and concludes 'though the foreign born might rarely venture beyond New York's ghettos, their children grew more like the Americans, and their children's children became an integral part of America'.[64] His analysis of employment patterns provides statistical confirmation that the Irish were unevenly spread among occupations. This study partly restored the credibility of the 'melting pot', drawing an all-important distinction between successive generations within the ethnic cohort. Arnold Schrier's neglected *Ireland and the American Emigration 1850–1900* (1958) returns the discussion to the mental world of the immigrant, giving extensive attention to their letters sent back to Ireland and, like Ernst, represents a bridge between the pre-war generation and the wave of scholarship beginning in the 1960s. James Handley's *The Irish in Scotland 1798–1845* (1945), and a successor volume, *The Irish in Modern Scotland* (1947) , although undertaken within a 'patriotic' perspective, are considerably more systematic than earlier writings in this tradition. Important research on the geographical distribution of the immigrants in Great Britain by Richard Lawton and John Archer Jackson's sociological treatment, *The Irish in Britain* (1963), also stood between the old and new generation of historians. Lawton and Jackson note differentiation in location decision based on place of origin in Ireland and additionally stress the varieties of experience these newcomers had in the adopted land.[65] These scholars and their writings occupy a position similar to the early students of T.W. Moody and R. Dudley Edwards in pushing forward the boundaries of Irish history during the initial post-war wave of 'revisionism'.

Publication of works on the diaspora are more numerous and varied since the 1960s. Some of this research is spurred by the expansion of higher education and opportunities for an academic career. However, in America the election of John F. Kennedy to the Presidency in 1960, the first Catholic to reach the White House, invigorated interest in ethnicity, particularly of the Irish. A journalist, William V. Shannon, capitalised on this mood in *The American Irish* (1963) providing a readable popular treatment. He predictably gives attention to Irish-American politics. Two students of Handlin's shortly afterwards published innovative contributions. Stephan Thernstrom's *Poverty and Progress: Social Mobility in a Nineteenth Century City* (1964) explores the quest for Irish social mobility in Newburyport, Massachusetts, and, like Handlin, he offers a snapshot of Irish life from below. He uses a quantitative approach to test the occupational mobility of unskilled manual labourers and their families over the period 1850–80. His conclusion is less pessimistic than his mentor's for though finding the record to be one of modest social gains, Thernstrom notes 'yet *in their eyes* these accomplishments must have loomed large'.[66] For the Irish, he notes that some mobility for the better-off came through politics. In a further quantitative study, *The Other Bostonians: Poverty and Progress in the American Metropolis, 1880–1970* (1973), he explores social structure for the years after 1880. Thernstrom observes that the Irish moved ahead only sluggishly and erratically. He believes they were in much the same position everywhere in the latter half of the nineteenth century. Immigrants generally, he notes, fared better in South Bend, Indiana, than in Boston and he speculates that the reason for this was because the Irish and Italians were a lower proportion of the foreign-born who settled in the inland city. Thernstrom postulates that this imbalance in immigrant socio-economic performance operated across the country. As in the earlier volume, he observes that 'cultural expectations about mobility may prove as important as objective rates and patterns'.[67] Again, the author's investigation is driven by a desire to test assumptions about social progress in American society noting that 'the promise of mobility has been a key theme in American life because it mediates between the competing values of equality and inequality. . . . It is not equality of *condition* but equality of *opportunity* that Americans have celebrated'.[68] Though introducing a 'revisionism' within American historiography, Thernstrom confirms Ernst's earlier findings and he raises questions about why the Irish fared relatively poorly in the race for the bounty of the New World.

Thomas N. Brown's *Irish–American Nationalism, 1870–90* (1966), also brought important new insights about Irish character to the fore. This book extends the model of Handlin's mental world and is influenced by the Chicago School's concern for the transition from rural to modern society. His study is adumbrated in learned periodicals and the main themes already adopted by Daniel P. Moynihan's *Beyond the Melting Pot: The Negroes, Puerto Ricans, Italians, and Irish of New York City* (1963). Brown suggests that Irish–American nationalism 'was something more than an Irish export'.[69] He goes on,

> it sprang also from the experience of life in the United States. First of all, the Irish, like all immigrants were afflicted with loneliness. To quiet its pangs, the immigrants came together in social clubs and gatherings, places of many kinds: fire fighting brigades, literary clubs, militia companies, corner saloons. All afforded Irishmen the comforts of fraternity, and some of them opportunities not available in parochial Ireland, to intermingle with Irishmen from all parts of their native land. In that way loneliness encouraged a sense of nationality.

For Brown, 'immigrant nationalism thus had as one of its sources the all too human melancholia and sense of loss suffered by those who have irrevocably broken with the past that nurtured them'.[70] He asserts that the claims of Irishness extracted a heavy psychological toll. According to Brown,

> the formation of an Irish–American community at odds with the larger American community had profound consequences. Thereafter, most American Irish would find it difficult to live their lives solely as individuals, without reference to the Irish–American community . . . they would be made to feel the pull of the Irish–American community and the demands it made for their loyalties. Those demands placed a heavy burden upon the spirit.[71]

Partly contradicting himself, Brown finds that the leadership of Nationalism came not from the new arrivals but the second generation who 'were fiercely active in the cause. They wanted to be respected as Americans and this . . . gave immigrant nationalism its dynamic thrust'.[72] Brown, then, challenges the whole Nationalist project in America arguing that

Irish–American nationalism was riddled with ambiguities. An independent Ireland was the goal it pursued. But this was, after all, a remote possibility, a dream. Irish–American societies dedicated to this dream however, were not at all remote. They were living realities, of consequence in American life. To all they offered companionship and to some business and political opportunities. They could transform a nobody into a somebody. In the minds of their members, therefore, these organisations tended to assume a greater importance than the pursuit of Irish freedom. Ends and means got confused.[73]

Irish–American nationalism took on a radicalised character, Brown insists, as a consequence of the depression of 1873 for that 'redirected the thrust of Irish hatreds. Many aspects of American life now came under Irish fire, and disaffection for American plutocracy became a new Irish passion. No longer did England seem unique in cruelty. Nevertheless John Bull remained the most compelling symbol of Irish frustration'.[74] Certainly, this was 'revisionist'; Irish–American Nationalism receded into a personal and collective response to insecurity and blocked mobility in the United States. Brown was among the first to make substantial use of Irish as well as American source material, but he does not challenge the orthodoxy in Ireland about indigenous Nationalism. T.W. Moody's extended review of the book observes that it 'calls for so much revision of accepted views'.[75] 'Conventional treatment of the Irish–Americans in Irish politics has been uncritically Irish-oriented and to have substituted for it a thoroughly critical and illuminating American-oriented interpretation', is a major innovation, he observes. Moody is especially interested in Brown's evidence that Michael Davitt's ideas about Irish land were formed not while in prison, as previously believed, but forged on the anvil of Irish–American radicalism during his trip in 1878. Strangely, though, the doyen of Trinity historians does not comment on the potential implications of Brown's internalised and psychological insight for Nationalism in Ireland.

Thernstrom and Brown shift discussion of the diaspora towards cultural factors inside the Irish community producing frustrations and blockages to their advancement. As noted already, Moynihan's influential study reproduces the core of Brown's thesis. He observes that 'for the Irish Nationalism gave a structure to working-class resentments that in other groups produced political radicalism'.[76] Edward M. Levine's *The Irish and Irish Politicians: A Study of Cultural and Social Alienation* (1966) arises from the author's experience working for the Kennedy presidential campaign in Chicago in 1960 and as the subtitle indicates, employs the framework originated by Handlin and refined by Thernstrom and Brown while a subsequent study of Chicago politics Michael F. Funchion's *Chicago's Irish*

Nationalists 1881–1890 (1976) borrows Brown's concepts. David Ward's *Cities and Immigrants: A Geography of Change in Nineteenth-Century America* (1971) looks at immigration residential concentrations identifying these with patterns of industrialisation and other employment; similar investigations emanating from the Department of Geography at the University of Liverpool soon yielded comparable results.[77] Kennedy's sociological investigation already cited went back to the Irish roots to establish why so many chose to leave home and arrives at essentially economic explanations. Meanwhile a rash of books on the Irish in various American cities began to appear. Dennis Clark's *The Irish in Philadelphia: Ten Generations of Urban Experience* (1973) is a good example, for while employing the 'history from below' perspective, he comments on differences between Irish experiences in the Quaker City and Boston. Clark, in a theme he develops further subsequently, sees relative Irish impotence in Philadelphia as a consequence of a residential mobility that enervated their ability to extract concessions through politics.[78] Emphasis on the 'internal' factors within the diaspora became the orthodoxy by the mid-1970s. Andrew Greeley and William C. McCready, for example, note the Irish penchant for 'fatalism', and as a foretaste of the'revisionism' of the 1980s observe that it is 'very difficult to understand the present behaviour of American immigrant groups without knowing something of the cultural heritage from which they came'.[79] They contend that it is essential to see 'how the interaction between Old World culture and the New World experience shaped the phenomenon of American ethnic group cultures'.

Fr Brendan Bradshaw who sees 'revisionism' becoming more aggressive and iconoclastic from the late 1970s is partly sustained by an examination of writings on the diaspora. Seeing the emigrant experience in terms of its own 'internal' constraints reached an apogee in the publications of Kerby Miller, including a collaboration with Bruce Boling and David Doyle.[80] This work had the virtue of attempting to establish an over-arching explanation of the diaspora, something largely missing in the earlier literature and certainly in retreat since the studies of different American cities revealed disparate outcomes. Building upon earlier perspectives they seek to establish how the Irish looked upon emigration, to discover the controlling ideas or world-view which affect attitudes to leaving Ireland, and to assess how the mental outlook shaped actual experiences. According to them, the Irish regarded emigration as exile. This attitude led to a series of interactions between culture and historical experience and their effect on Irish character. In turn this caused Irish emigrants to interpret their own experiences in ways which were often distorted and even alienating with the consequence of making them receptive to Irish–American nationalism. Much of the argument hinges on the assertion that 'the way of handling the strains of modernisation via nationalist self-assertion seems to have been rooted in similar tension in both Ireland and Irish America, and trans-Atlantically reinforced from Fenian times onward by letters and communal rhetoric'.[81] 'Modern nationalism,' from this perspective, 'merely gave form to old fears/resentments about emigration deep in Gaelic culture'. The comparatively poor economic performance of American immigrants is explained by a Catholic communal culture that is more dependent, fatalistic and inclined to accept conditions passively. By comparison with Protestant culture, it is seen as less individualistic, independent, optimistic and pre-modern. 'Thus', the authors contend, 'we see Gaelic culture as three interlocking sub-systems (secular, religious and linguistic) supporting a world-view which valued conservatism, collective behaviour, and dependence, and limited responsibility in broad areas'.[82] 'Revisionism' in the contemporary sense runs through this interpretation especially in the assertion that Nationalism rather than being a modern and modernising force, was, in fact, a carrier of old culture.[83] Miller later reprises the theme in *Emigrants and Exiles: Ireland and the Irish Exodus to North America* (1985). In this extended account he maintains,

> that Irish–American homesickness, alienation, and nationalism were rooted ultimately in a traditional Irish Catholic worldview which predisposed Irish emigrants to perceive or at least justify themselves not as voluntary, ambitious emigrants but as involuntary, nonresponsible 'exiles', compelled to leave home by forces beyond individual control, particularly by British and landlord oppression. In premodern times Gaelic culture's secular, religious, and linguistic aspects expressed or reinforced a worldview which de-emphasised and even condemned individualistic and innovative actions such as emigration. Although Gaelic Ireland withered from the blasts of conquest and change, not only did certain real continuities remain to justify the retention of archaic attitudes and behaviour patterns but in fact those institutions – family, church and nationalism – which dominated modern Catholic Ireland strove to perpetuate old outlooks which both minimised the demoralising impacts of change and cemented communal loyalties in the face of internal conflicts and external enemies. Thus, tradition and expediency merged, and emigration remained forced banishment – demanding political redress and the emigrants' continued fealty to sorrowing Mother Ireland.[84]

His theme is buttressed by immigrant letters home which Miller insists is the most reliable source for understanding the mentality of the diaspora. It is a claim that bears comparison with the assertion of A.B. Cooke and J.R. Vincent that only private diaries and letters provide satisfactory evidence for the inner motivations of political leaders.[85] This work brings 'revisionist' writings on Nationalism and the diaspora into an interface not often present earlier. The history of Ireland and of the Irish overseas at last had a sort of unity, perhaps even coherence.

This overarching interpretation has not stood unchallenged. Impressive studies of New Orleans, Detroit and San Francisco, to name but three, had emphasised the diversity of Irish experience already.[86] Hasia Diner's intriguing *Erin's Daughters in America: Irish Immigrant Women in the Nineteenth Century* (1983) adds to that diversity pointing out the success of the transplanation for most women. She argues, also, that they 'migrated not as depressed survivors of Famine, but in the main they made the journey with optimism . . . ', a view endorsed by Janet Nolan and in the case of Scotland by Brenda Collins as well. Nolan, in particular, counters Miller's gloomy outlook with the assertion that 'their emigration must be seen not as an exile but rather as an unprecedented opportunity'.[87] Fitzpatrick supports their view though with both genders in mind and politely suggests that Miller's reading of immigrant letters is too selective, pointing out that these 'illustrate eagerness and reluctance to emigrate in roughly equal measure'[88] Patrick O'Farrell's *The Irish in Australia* (1986) proposes an almost Turner-like thesis for the immigrants down-under. According to O'Farrell, the unique character of Australia was the outcome of the contest between and Irish minority and the English majority. 'It was the Irish minority that was compelled to entertain the matter of an Australian nationalism which would repudiate the extremes of Tory Britain, hierarchical, conservative, rigorist'.[89] Richard Davis' *Irish Issues in New Zealand Politics 1868–1922* (1974) hints at a comparable role for the Irish in New Zealand. A volume on Chicago adds to the doubts about the Miller perspective.[90] Additionally, Brian C. Mitchell's *The Paddy Camps: The Irish of Lowell 1821–61* (1988) though employing a Handlin perspective, suggests that external rather than internal factors were decisive in shaping the Irish experience. However, Donald Akenson's *Small Differences: Irish Catholics and Irish Protestants 1815–1922* (1988) affords the first compelling evidence (or in his estimation, its absence) of any stark difference between Catholics and Protestants in Ireland confounding not only Miller but long-held and cherished assumptions about the diaspora. Still, Miller has not been wholly without followers. David Emmons' *The Butte Irish: Class and Ethnicity in an American Mining Town 1875–1925* (1989) perhaps the most satisfying of the studies of individual communities published to date, accepts his premises. Yet, these and other interjections do not take the literature back to the halcyon days of Handlin or even Brown though most of the writing now starts from the perspectives pioneered by Handlin and his students.

Work on Irish immigration to Great Britain has been slower to emerge. Specific attention to the diaspora in Britain was no doubt inhibited by the comparatively slender representation of academics of Irish origin. Some studies did treat the Irish presence but generally these considered them within the context of British industrialisation and the labour market though investigations of religious developments note their role in the spread of post-1850 Catholicism. Post-war interest in the British working class also sometimes has had an Irish dimension. Many of these authors were Marxists and almost all were supporters of the political left. Britain's Irish were, of course, a notable part of the working-class. Few of those specialising in working-class history were from Irish ancestry and the diaspora presents an inconvenient ideological difficulty. On the one hand, they, like Karl Marx, recognise the important and sometimes divisive role of the Irish and Catholicism in working-class organisation; on the other, they were reluctant to separate the immigrant experience from that of the native downtrodden. E.P. Thompson's *The Making of the English Working Class* (1963) tries to identify linkages between the Irish and other working-class people, to minimise competition and strife, as part of a thesis articulating the cohesion of the labouring poor during industrialisation. Thompson's perspectives excited a generation of largely middle-class historians who mostly skirt the problem of accommodating the Irish immigrants into their vision of labouring life.[91]

Real advances in exploring the diaspora and particularly the richness of the Irish life in Britain began intensively in the 1970s. Several of these begin from a Handlin perspective, notably Lynn Hollen Lees, *Exiles of Erin: Irish Migrants in Victorian London* (1979) and M.A.G. Ó Tuathaigh's 'The Irish in Nineteenth-Century Britain: Problems of Integration' first published in *Transactions of the Royal Historical Society* (1981).[92] Studies of religious observance and politics have entered caveats about the Handlin/Brown approach for Great Britain.[93] Much of the work is part of the ongoing mapping of the exile experience and seeks out the variations in the pattern of Irish integration. Publications by Graham Davis, Stephen Fielding, Ruth-Ann-Harris, Sheridan Gilley, David Fitzpatrick, William Lowe and Roger Swift to name a few are of no small importance in this exercise. Yet, neither these nor published works on the Irish in other countries offer a significant new framework of analysis or stake out a 'revisionism' relevant to the present controversy. The difference that has been emerging centres on whether the Irish retained a distinctive sense of identity over several generations or if, for most, it dissolved on an individual basis within a comparatively brief span of time. Irish political activities in Britain have featured less prominently in post-1965 writings but there yet may be something to be learned about ethnicity and immigrant adaptation to new environments from closer examination of these. David Doyle, for instance, suggests that the Irish in Britain were proportionately more preoccupied with Nationalism and separatism than their American cousins but some recent research casts doubt on the level of widespread intensity of involvement in these in Great Britain.[94] Whether this is indicative of integration or alienation is not worked out in detail.

CONCLUSION

As noted at the outset, this is not a survey of writings on the diaspora but an attempt to place this theme in the context of the 'revisionism' controversy. First, it is evident that the literature is vast, is diverse thematically, and is the product of numerous cultures and, the outcome of varied influences. There has never been an acknowledged standard interpretation of the diaspora, indeed none was attempted prior to Kerby Miller's work which has an American slant. Second, it is also apparent that very little of the literature owes anything to the agenda of the founding fathers of modern Ireland's historical fraternity, or to conditions good or ill in any portion of contemporary Ireland. Indeed, with the exception of the study by an American, William J. Lowe, *The Irish in Mid-Victorian Lancashire: The Shaping of a Working Class Community* (1989), none of the research has been done under the guidance of academics in Ireland. Despite differences of origin, the chronology and methodology bears a remarkable similarity to other areas of Irish history. This convergence is not to be explained by any agreed project or shared bias but by the universality of the development of history as a skills-based, not politically motivated, discipline; by an academic approach pioneered initially in Germany that has since come to dominate intellectual life throughout the western world. Proliferation of research has widened the boundaries for understanding the diaspora and in all areas – demography, religion, politics, socio-economic performance, culture, the mental world – the outcome is to see complexities and variety in the migrants' experiences.

Although the volume of writings on the diaspora greatly exceeds those from all other areas of Irish history, it is evident that the field has not spawned a consensus view. Indeed, in many areas the history of the Irish overseas is still to be established. To date American writings dominate the field in terms of volume, methodology and influence though recent work on Australia, Britain and Canada suggests that this pre-eminence is under threat. Whether this wider interest leads to a different framework or perspective for analysing the diaspora remains to be seen. To date, research has not been much influenced by the arguments and conceptual framework developed for the studies of American ethnicity though these possibly have much to contribute to further evaluations of the Irish.[95] Unfortunately, these works, though voluminous, give little systematic attention to the Irish. What can be stated with some confidence is that more research on Irish communities is sure to add to the diversity, and no doubt emphasise the richness, of Irish culture but to these must be added some of the conceptual insights developed for analysis of ethnicity and race generally if the field is to reach a higher plateau.

NOTES

* I wish to acknowledge the assistance Frederick Bode, George Boyce, Miles Bradbury, Mike Bromley, Dennis Dean, Barbara Gauntt, Sheridan Gilley, Jonathan Moore, R.J. Scally and Roger Swift. Portions of this work were begun as part of the project Comparative Studies on Governments and Non-Dominant Ethnic Groups in Europe, 1850–1940 sponsored by the European Science Foundation (Strasbourg, France). I wish to express my continued appreciation to the Foundation for support to also to Christoph Mühlberg and Geneviéve Schauinger.

1 Karl Marx and Frederick Engels, *Ireland and the Irish Question* (reprinted Moscow, 1986), p. 40.

2 See David Fitzpatrick, *Irish Emigration 1801–1921* (Dundalk, 1984); David A. Wilson, *The Irish in Canada* (Ottawa, 1989).

3 Cecil J. Houston and William J. Smyth, *Irish Emigration and Canadian Settlement: Patterns, Links, & Letters* (Toronto, 1990), pp. 20–31.

4 Donald Harman Akenson, *The Irish Diaspora: A Primer* (Belfast, 1993), pp. 59–122.

5 John Archer Jackson, *The Irish in Britain* (London, 1963), pp. 1–23.

6 *Ibid.*, p. 192; Akenson, *op. cit.* pp. 105, 157–87.

7 Patrick J. Blessing, 'Irish Emigration to the United States, 1800–1920: An Overview' in P.J. Drudy (ed.), *Irish Studies 4: The Irish in America: Emigration, Assimilation and Impact* (Cambridge, 1985), p. 19.

8 Akenson, *op. cit.*, p. 123.

9 Brenda Collins, 'The Origins of Irish Immigration to Scotland in the Nineteenth and Twentieth Centuries' in T.M. Devine (ed.), *Irish Immigrants and Scottish Society in the Nineteenth and Twentieth Centuries* (Edinburgh, 1991), p. 11; David M. Emmons, *The Butte Irish: Class and Ethnicity in an American Mining Town 1875–1925* (Urbana and Chicago, 1989), pp. 70–1.

10 Blessing, *op. cit.*, p. 20; see Deirdre M. Magean, 'Nineteenth-Century Irish Emigration: A Case Study Using Passenger Lists' in O'Sullivan, *op. cit.*, pp. 39–61.

11 Jackson, *op. cit.*, p. 192.

12 Quoted in Kerby Miller with Bruce Boling and David N. Doyle, 'Emigration and Exiles: Irish Cultures and Irish Emigration to North America, 1790–1922', *Irish Historical Studies*, xxii, September 1980, p. 100.

13 Thomas D'Arcy McGee, *A History of Irish Settlers in North America from the Earliest Period to the Census of 1850* (Boston, 1855), p. 195.

14 Robert E. Kennedy Jr, *The Irish: Emigration, Marriage, and Fertility* (Berkeley, Los Angeles, and London, 1972), p. 207.

15 Collins, *op. cit.*, pp. 1–16.

16 *Ibid.*, pp. 14–16; Oliver MacDonagh, 'The Irish in Australia: A General View' in Oliver MacDonagh and W.F. Mandle, *Ireland and Irish-Australia: Studies in Cultural and Political History* (London, Sydney, and Wolfeboro, NH, 1986), p. 160; Fitzpatrick, *op. cit.*, p. 11; Emmons, *op. cit.*, p. 15.

17 Ruth-Ann M. Harris , *The Nearest Place That Wasn't Ireland: Early Nineteenth-Century Irish Labor Migration* (Ames, IO, 1995), pp. 9–10, 24, 99, and 129.

18 David M. Emmons, 'Faction Fights: The Irish Worlds of Butt, Montana, 1875–1917' in Patrick O'Sullivan (ed.), *The Irish World Wide: Volume One: The Irish in the New Communities* (London, 1992), pp. 82–98; Victor A. Walsh, 'Irish Nationalism and Land Reform: The Role of the Irish in America' in Drudy (ed.), *op. cit.*, pp. 254–69.

19 Stephan Thernstrom, *The Other Bostonians: Poverty and Progress in the American Metropolis, 1880–1970* (Cambridge, MA and London, 1973), p. 232.

20 John Herson, 'Irish Migration and Settlement in Victorian Britain: A Small-Town Perspective' in Roger Swift and Sheridan Gilley (eds), *The Irish in Britain 1815–1939* (London, 1989), pp. 84–103; R.J. Cooter, 'The Irish in County Durham and Newcastle, c. 1840–1880', M.A., University of Durham (1973); Dale B. Light Jr., 'The Role of Irish-American Organisations in Assimilation and Community Formation' in Drudy (ed.), *op. cit.*, p. 116.

21 David Fitzpatrick, 'Irish Emigration in the Later Nineteenth Century', *Irish Historical Studies*, xxii, September 1980, p. 134.

22 Akenson, *op. cit.*, pp. 217–69; and 'The Historiography of the Irish in the United States', in Patrick O'Sullivan (ed.), *The Irish World Wide: Volume Two: The Irish in the New Communities* (London, 1992), pp. 99–127; Fitzpatrick, 'Irish Emigration in the Later Nineteenth Century', p. 136; also *Oceans of Consolation: Personal Accounts of Irish Migration to Australia* (Ithaca, NY and London, 1994), p. 16.

23 William V. Shannon, *The American Irish* (New York and London, 1963), p. 27.

24 Daniel P. Moynihan, 'The Irish' in Nathan Glazer and Daniel Moynihan, *Beyond the Melting Pot: The Negroes, Puerto Ricans, Jews, Italians, and Irish of New York City* (Cambridge, MA, 1963), pp. 219–20.

25 Stephan Thernstrom, *Poverty and Progress: Social Mobility in a Nineteenth Century City* (Cambridge, MA, 1964), p. 27.

26 David N. Doyle, 'The Regional Bibliography of Irish America, 1800–1939: A Review and Addendum', *Irish Historical Studies*, xxiii, May 1983, p. 256.

27 Quoted in Kenneth Inglis, *Churches and the Working Classes in Victorian Britain* (London, 1963), p. 193.

28 Alan O'Day (ed.), *A Survey of the Irish in England (1872)* (London, 1990).

29 Light, *op. cit*, p. 117.

30 See, Emmons, *The Butte Irish*; Jo Ellen Vinyard, *The Irish on the Urban Frontier: Nineteenth Century Detroit, 1850–1880* (New York, 1976).

31 R.S. Burchell, *The San Francisco Irish 1848–1880* (Manchester, 1979), pp. 52–72.

32 Akenson, *The Irish Diaspora*, pp. 123–39.

33 Light, *op. cit.*, pp. 123–4; Colin G. Pooley, 'Segregation or Integration? The Residential Experience of the Irish in Mid-Victorian Britain' in Roger Swift and Sheridan Gilley (eds), *The Irish in Britain 1815–1939* (London, 1989), pp. 60–83; Frank Neal, *Sectarian Violence: The Liverpool Experience, 1819–1914* (Manchester, 1988), pp. 11–15.

34 Emmons, *The Butte Irish*, p. 77.

35 Houston and Smyth, *op. cit.*, pp. 67–78.

36 Akenson, *The Irish Diaspora*, p. 219.

37 Houston and Smyth, *op. cit.*, p. 229.

38 Akenson, *The Irish Diaspora*, p. 106.

39 See Cecil J. Houston and William J. Smyth, *The Sash Canada Wore: A Historical Geography of the Orange Order in Canada* (Toronto, 1980); Hereward Senior, 'Orangemen on the Frontier: The Prairies and British Columbia' in Robert O'Driscoll and Lorna Reynolds (eds), *The Untold Story, the Irish in Canada* (Toronto, 1988), II, pp. 417–22; Donald M. MacRaild, 'William Murphy, the Orange Order and Communal Violence: The Irish in West Cumberland, 1871–84' in Panikos Panayi (ed.), *Racial Violence in Britain 1840–1950* (Leicester and London, 1993), pp. 44–64; Akenson, *The Irish Diaspora*, p. 106.

40 Akenson, *The Irish in Ontario: A Study in Rural History* (Kingston and Montreal, 1984); Bruce S. Elliott, *Irish Migrants in the Canadas* (Kingston and Montreal, 1988). Also, see Graham Walker, 'The Protestant Irish in Scotland' in Devine (ed.), *op. cit.*, pp. 44–66.

41 William Sloan, 'Religious Affiliation and the Immigrant Experience: Catholic Irish and Protestant Highlanders in Glasgow, 1830–1850', in Devine (ed.), *op. cit.* p. 78.

42 Akenson, *The Irish Diaspora*, pp. 69, 113, 262, 267.

43 *Ibid.*, pp. 184–5; Fitzpatrick, *Oceans of Consolation*, p. 18.

44 Collins, *op. cit.*, p. 11.

45 Blessing, *op. cit.*, pp. 25–6; Vinyard, *op. cit., passim*; Emmons, *The Butte Irish*, p. 82.

46 David N. Doyle, 'Small Differences? The Study of the Irish in the United States and Britain', *Irish Historical Studies*, xxix, May 1994, p. 119.

47 MacDonagh, *op. cit.*, p. 159.

48 Collins, *op. cit.*, p. 1; John F. McCaffrey, 'Irish Issues in the Nineteenth and Twentieth Century' in Devine (ed.), *op. cit.*, p. 135.

49 John Denvir, *The Irish in Britain* (2nd edn, London, 1894), p. 462.

50 Patrick J. Blessing, *The Irish in America: A Guide to the Literature and the Manuscript Collections* (Washington, DC, 1992); Doyle, 'Small Differences? The Study of the Irish in the United States and Britain', p. 119.

51 Alun Muslow, 'A "Bigger, Better and Busier Boston" The Pursuit of Political Legitimacy in America: The Boston Irish, 1890–1920' in O'Sullivan (ed.), *op. cit.*, vol. 1, p. 128.

52 Note especially the work of Akenson and Fitzpatrick.

53 O'Sullivan (ed.), *op. cit.*, vol. 1, pp. xviii–xx.

54 John Whyte, *Interpreting Northern Ireland* (Oxford, 1990).

55 John Francis Maguire, *The Irish in America* (reprinted New York, 1969), pp. viii–ix.

56 Nicholas Flood Davin, *The Irishman in Canada* (Limerick, 1969), p. ix.

57 Carl Wittke, *We Who Built America: The Saga of the Immigrant* (New York, 1939), p. xvii.

58 Edith Abbott (ed.), *Historical Aspects of the Immigration Problem: Select Documents* (Chicago, 1926).

59 Wittke, *op. cit.*, p. 186.

60 Oscar Handlin, *Boston's Immigrants 1790–1865: A Study in Acculturation* (Cambridge, MA, 1941), p. vii.

61 *Ibid.*, p. 58.

62 *Ibid.*, p. 221.

63 See Tom Gallagher, *Glasgow – The Uneasy Peace* (Manchester, 1987); Scotland, Britain and Conflict in Ireland' in Yonah Alexander and Alan O'Day (eds), *Terrorism in Ireland* (London, 1984), pp. 53–72; Iain McLean, *The Legend of Red Clydeside* (Edinburgh, 1983).

64 Robert Ernst, *Immigrant Life in New York City 1825–1863* (New York, 1949), p. 184.

65 Richard Lawton, 'Irish Migration to England and Wales in the Mid-Nineteenth Century', *Irish Geography*, 4, 1959, pp. 35–54.

66 Thernstrom, *Poverty and Progress*, pp. 164–5.

67 Thernstrom, *The Other Bostonians: Poverty and Progress in the American Metropolis, 1880–1970* (Cambridge, MA and London, 1973), p. 259; but, Vinyard, *op. cit.*, offers some comparison between the Irish and other groups in Detroit, notably the Germans, that cast doubt on Thernstrom's assertion, *passim*.

68 *Ibid.*, p. 256.

69 Thomas N. Brown, *Irish-American Nationalism, 1870–1890* (Philadelphia and New York, 1966), p. 20.

70 *Ibid.*, p. 21.

71 *Ibid.*, pp. 24–5.

72 *Ibid.*, p. 24.

73 *Ibid.*, p. 38.

74 *Ibid.*, p. 63.

75 T.W. Moody, 'Irish-American Nationalism', *Irish Historical Studies*, xv, September 1967, pp. 438–45. For useful critiques of Brown, see Walsh, *op. cit.*, pp. 253–69; Emmons, *The Butte Irish*, pp. 292–332.

76 Moynihan, *op. cit.*, p. 241.

77 See, Colin G. Poole, 'The Irish in Liverpool circa 1850–1940' in Max Engman, Francis W. Carter, A.C. Hepburn and Colin G. Pooley (eds), *Comparative Studies on Governments and Non-Dominant Ethnic Groups in Europe, 1850–1940: Volume VIII: Ethnic Identity in Urban Europe* (Aldershot and New York, 1992), pp. 71–97.

78 Dennis Clark, *The Irish in Philadelphia: Ten Generations of Urban Experience* (Philadelphia, 1973), pp. 165–83; *The Irish Relations: Trials of an Immigrant Tradition* (Rutherford, Madison and Teanock, 1982); *Hibernia America: The Irish and Regional Cultures* (New York, Westport, CT, and London, 1986); *Erin's Heirs: Irish Bonds of Community* (Lexington, KY, 1991).

79 Andrew Greeley and William C. McCready, 'The Transmission of Cultural Heritage: The Case of the Irish and Italians' in Nathan Glazer and Daniel P. Moynihan (eds), *Ethnicity: Theory and Experience* (Cambridge, MA, 1975), p. 229.

80 Miller, Boling and Doyle, *op. cit.*.

81 *Ibid.*, p. 102.

82 *Ibid.*, p. 113.

83 *Ibid.*, p. 114.

84 Kerby A. Miller, *Emigrants and Exiles: Ireland and the Irish Exodus to North America* (New York and Oxford, 1985), p. 556. It should be noted that Houston and Smyth along with O'Farrell above make extensive use of immigrant letters without reaching Miller's conclusion; also, see, David Fitzpatrick (ed.), *Home Or Away: Immigrants in Colonial Australia* (Canberra, 1992) for a measured use of this source and, also, his impressive *Oceans of Consolation*. An implicit critique of Miller's assessment is, Karen P. Corrigan, '"I gcuntas De Muin Bearla do na Leanbhain Eisimirce Aqus an Ghaeilge sa Naou Aois Deag"', in O'Sullivan (ed.), *op. cit.*, vol. 2, pp. 143–61. She suggests that the chief reason for the decline of Gaelic was calculated choice, a modernising understanding 'rooted in the Irish psyche, which had come to perceive the acquisition of English as a prerequisite of social and economic advancement in an expanding and increasingly urbanised world' (pp. 155–6).

85 A.B. Cooke and J.R. Vincent, *The Governing Passion: Cabinet Government and Party Politics in Britain 1885–86* (Brighton, 1974).

86 Burchell, *op. cit.*; Vinyard, *op. cit.*; Earl F. Niehaus, *The Irish in New Orleans, 1800–1860* (Baton Rouge, LA, 1965).

87 Hasia Diner, *Erin's Daughters in America: Irish Immigrant Women in the Nineteenth Century* (Baltimore and London, 1983), p. 42; Janet Nolan, *Ourselves Alone: Women's Emigration from Ireland 1885–1920* (Lexington, KY, 1989), pp. 94–5; Collins, *op. cit.*, p. 14.

88 Fitzpatrick, *Oceans of Consolation*, pp. 25, 517 and 610; see Emmons, *The Butte Irish*, p. 3; see Robert J. Scally, *The End of Hidden Ireland: Rebellion, Famine and Emigration* (New York and Oxford, 1995).

89 Patrick O'Farrell, *The Irish in Australia*, (Sydney, 1986), pp. 11–12.

90 Lawrence J. McCaffrey, Ellen Skerrett, Michael F. Funchion and Charles Fannon, *The Irish in Chicago* (Urbana and Chicago, 1987).

91 E.P. Thompson, *The Making of the English Working Class* (Harmondsworth, 1968), p. 480; for an exception see Neville Kirk, *The Growth of Working Class Reformism in Mid-Victorian England* (London, 1985), pp. 310–48.
92 Also see Gallagher, *op. cit.*, pp. 25–8; Alan O'Day, *The English Face of Irish Nationalism: Parnellite Involvement in British Politics 1880–86* (Dublin, 1977; reprinted Aldershot, 1994), pp. 108–24.
93 See Gerard Connolly, 'Irish and Catholic: Myth Or Reality?: Another Sort of Irish and the Renewal of the Clerical Profession Among Catholics in England, 1791–1918' in Roger Swift and Sheridan Gilley (eds), *The Irish in the Victorian City* (London, 1985), pp. 225–54; Alan O'Day, 'The Political Representation of the Irish in Great Britain, 1850–1940' in Geoffrey Alderman, John Leslie and Klaus Erich Pollmann (eds), *Comparative Studies on Governments and Non-Dominant Ethnic Groups in Europe, 1850–1940: Vol. IV: Governments, Ethnic Groups and Political Representation* (Aldershot and New York, 1993), pp. 31–83.
94 Doyle, 'Small Differences? The Study of the Irish in the United States and Britain', p. 117.
95 Russell A. Kazal, 'Reevisiting Assimilation: The Rise, Fall, and Reappraisal of a Concept in American Ethnic History', *American Historical Review*, April 1995, pp. 437–71. This interesting essay appeared when the present article had reached proof stage and, therefore, it has been impossible to give adequate recognition to its implications. However, the article makes little direct reference to the Irish.

11

PAST AND PRESENT REVISIONISM AND THE NORTHERN IRELAND TROUBLES

D. George Boyce

> I took pains to determine the flight of crook-taloned birds, marking
> which were of the right by nature, and which of the left, and what
> were their ways of living, each after his own kind, and the enmities
> and affections that were between them: and how they consorted
> together.

> Aeschylus, quoted in Julia Namier, *Lewis Namier:*
> *A Biography* (London, 1971), p. 192

In 1985 a young historian published what was avowedly a 'revisionist tract' which 'ventures to sound a note of dissent from the methodological conventions which I have come to realise are almost universally shared by a particular cohort of scholars who have worked in the field in recent decades, the heirs of the "Whig interpretation of history"'. He warned against the 'common process by which the polemics of one generation provide the historical categories for the next', and claimed that nineteenth-century values of political and religious progress had coloured inter-pretations of the institutions and values of the world before 1832. Moreover, the words of one historian were a caution against 'the current search for a "usable past"' which only impelled scholars 'towards histori-cal subjects that resemble contemporary problems'. This, the young historian alleged, caused even scholars of eminence to pay little attention to writers who argued against those ideas which did not appeal to the 'present minded', because 'the future lay not with them'.[1]

The young revisionist was J.C.D. Clark, who was not (or at least not primarily) an Irish historian, but an historian of eighteenth-century England. What appears, or what has been taken, as unique to Irish history turns out after all to be part of the wider world of historical interpretation; and the danger which Clark singled out – what he called 'present mind-edness' – was epitomised by Professor Lawrence Stone's description of

his witnessing the events in Paris in May 1968, and of his active participation in the subsequent crisis at Princeton University in protest against
the Vietnam War, which, he claimed, taught him about 'the nature and
process of revolutions'.[2] The Irish historical/political equivalent would
be to participate in the Bogside riots of the summer of 1969 in order to feel
what it was like to be in the siege of Derry in 1689.

And yet there is a sense in which these events do connect in some way:
even words such as 'siege', 'resistance', 'Protestant', 'Catholic', have a
special meaning when they are placed in the context of history. In 1689
the Catholics besieged the Protestant resisters; in 1969 the Protestant-
dominated Royal Ulster Constabulary besieged the Catholic resisters; but
there was a real sense in which 'Taig' met 'Prod' yet again. The present is
so clearly the result of the past that historians cannot ignore the historical
dimension of the Ulster troubles. But they must also be aware of the
danger of writing history teleologically; and they would not want to say
that Irish history must be seen in the light of the Bogside confrontation of
1969.

It is hard, then, for the historian not to be present minded; hard for the
historian to clear the mind of the world around him or her. The hasty
revision of books written about modern German history (let alone
modern Russian history) following the extraordinary events of 1989 bear
witness to the link between present and past. No historian will ever write
about Germany, east-central Europe or the USSR in quite the same way,
or from the same perspective. Economic determinism has had a deep
shock; cultural and nationalistic factors have had a revival. But this differs
from the kind of teleological writing that even such a distinguished
historian as A.J.P. Taylor was guilty of when he wrote his book, *The
Course of German History*, and came near to saying that the Germany of
1933–45 was implicit in the Germany or Germanies that had preceded it.
Yet when Taylor described the origins of the Second World War in highly
contingent terms, employing a very different methodology, he was
attacked for having underestimated the philosophy of the Third Reich,
and its drive towards conquest and war.[3]

Contingency and yet the story told; the end product known, and yet
the historian's need to put this knowledge under his pillow, behind his
back, and in some degree at least out of his reckoning. These dual needs,
central to the historian's dilemma, are not unique to the writing of any
country's history. Indeed, it is not without significance that J.C.D. Clark
wrote his revisionist work in the 1980s, and thus might stand accused of
reflecting the reaction against the liberal, progressive values that had
pervaded English social and political thinking since at least the 1960s. If
J.H. Plumb was the intellectual child of Clement Attlee,[4] then might not
Clark be the scion of the House of Margaret Thatcher?

History is in one sense a complete story: the historian knows the outcome, and therefore must, in a sense, work backwards from that knowledge. Yet in another sense he must deny that he knows the story; or, rather, he must try to tell the story from the perspective of contemporaries who, for example, did not know that they were living in what we later called the 'Middle Ages', or did not know that the First World War would break out in August 1914. There is, quite simply, no escape either from this dilemma, nor is there any necessity to do so. The historian knows the 'future' that past generations did not even dream of; yet the historian must not ignore those with whom the future, as we now know, did not lie. The process is more important than the conclusion.

The danger of present-mindedness is perhaps most evident in the case of Ireland, which for the past twenty-five years has experienced civil and political turmoil on a scale unprecedented in its modern history, or at least in its history after the 'Troubles' of 1916–23. Yet present-mindedness, if it is tempered with an awareness of the contingencies of the past, can open up new perspectives, and prove fruitful, as new generations of historians find their attention drawn to previously neglected or under-rated issues. As one of the new generation of historians has written,

> While the founding fathers of Irish revisionism wrote against the background of a relatively peaceful Ireland, in the late 1960s a second wave of revisionism emerged in very different historical circumstances. The old sectarianism was brutally in evidence once again and it challenged the scholar with the imperative to understand how unresolved historical problems still linger today.[5]

This chapter does not address the question of how the Northern Ireland problem has been interpreted, a subject already dealt with in John Whyte's *Interpreting Northern Ireland*; nor does it suggest ways in which the problem might be resolved, which has been considered in hundreds of books and articles.[6] It is focused on the narrower, and yet at the same time wider question of the light that the interaction of history and politics throws on how historical research is conducted as new perspectives merge, and old issues regain a significance for the historian. This, in turn, throws light on the historian's approach to interpreting other periods, and on the relationship between past and present in historical thinking.

Two kinds of publications are under consideration here. Those which have directly addressed the troubles, that is, those of a recent history or political science character; and those which, while not confined to contemporary events, still reflect resonances of the present discontents. An early example of the former is Owen Dudley Edwards' passionate and forceful *The Sins of Our Fathers: The Roots of Conflict in Northern Ireland* (1970) and Conor Cruise O'Brien's equally absorbing *States of Ireland* (1972),[7] which has been described by O'Brien's biographer, Donald H. Akenson, as 'the most influential book about Irish Nationalism and Irish politics written in the second half of the twentieth century', which, 'unlike most works of history . . . was intended to influence the real world'.[8] Professor T.W. Moody's *The Ulster Question, 1603–1973* (1974) presents the best example of the latter.[9] Here was a book by one of Ireland's most rigorous professional historians which distorted the history of Ulster in the light of the present crisis. The book was described as tracing 'the history of community conflict in Ulster since the early seventeenth century when the British and protestant colony was planted in a province that had been a Gaelic and Catholic stronghold. Intended to establish British power in Ulster on a basis of economic and cultural supremacy over the expropriated native population, the colony by its very success created the polarised society that still characterises Northern Ireland'. But the book covered a wide period, and compressed the relationships within Ulster, and the relationship between Ulster and the rest of Ireland, into a single theme. There was no 'Ulster Question' in the eighteenth century, or, if there was one, it was concerned with Ulster radical Presbyterians, with little to do with the troubles of post-1968. Moody's concern to trace a direct line from the seventeenth century to the present day is not wholly misconceived; clearly, without the plantation of Ulster in the seventeenth century, there would have been hardly any British or protestant population in the north of Ireland. But he drew the lines too sharply, and ignored the fact that a special local characteristic may rise and fall in importance; and that, moreover, the character of that region's politics developed different trends according to the wider circumstances of the time. As Brian Walker pointed out in his book, *Ulster Politics*, 'the formative years' were 1885–6, when the first Home Rule bill produced a dramatic and lasting realignment of Ulster politics on sectarian lines.[10] Moody's direct political interest was spelt out in his concluding sentences, when he offered his own formula for resolving the crisis – and one, interestingly, not far removed from the political framework now (in 1995), on offer.[11] His book may have distorted history, but it was meant to be a contribution to the political debate, and thus its telescoped sections and shorthand judgements were those of a committed and earnest citizen of Ireland seeking to come out of his ivory tower.

Moody made his purpose more explicit in his valedictory lecture at Trinity College, Dublin, in 1977. Here he identified nine popular myths that needed demolition by historians, myths being defined as 'received views' which combined 'elements of fact and fiction'. Amongst these were the 'dogma that the true Irishman was both Catholic and Gaelic', and the Anglican myth that the Church of Ireland was descended from the Celtic Church of St Patrick. But Moody singled out for special attention the notion that there was a kind of Irish predestiny that linked past and present, and that saw the only valid theme in Irish history as the struggle, the long, enduring struggle, between Ireland and England. This was to telescope Irish History; and few would disagree. But Moody was particularly anxious because this myth was used by the Provisional Irish Republican Army as the primary justification of its 'irredentist war to abolish partition'.[12]

This is perhaps an unusually obvious example, by a man who loved his country, and who wrote in an effort to contribute to its better settlement. But the shifts and movements of Northern politics since then drew similar responses from other scholars as well. Paul Bew, Peter Gibbon and Henry Patterson, in their original and provocative book, *The State in Northern Ireland, 1921–1972*, made the point that the Unionist working man was hardly given the chance to be other than Unionist, in the circumstances of the state's foundation and its continued obsession with the border and survival.[13] This, while not directly politically-inspired, clearly had political implications for the current troubles, since the Nationalist criticism of the northern state, and its attempt to alter that state's structures, and especially its relation to the Republic of Ireland, must have a similar impact on the Unionist working classes, who were caught yet again in the old dilemma of having to place the constitutional issue before all others. More directly, Bew ended his study of the Redmondite era with a direct reference to the 1985 Anglo-Irish agreement, when he commented:

> Two generations were to pass before mainstream Irish nationalism was again to show signs of grasping the importance of Parnell's advocacy of conciliation; even then it was often to be combined with the arguably less sophisticated assumption that it was the duty of the British state to manufacture Irish Unionist consent to the arrangements for a 'new Ireland'.[14]

Certainly, the historian did not have to work hard to find parallels between the past and the present. Bew, again, was the first to draw attention to the similarity between what the Anglo-Irish Agreement had created – what he brilliantly called 'direct rule with a green tinge', – and what Redmond was closest to getting in the pre-war Home Rule crisis of 1912–14: a southern state, a northern region governed from London, but administered from Dublin.[15] The crisis of Nationalism in the early twentieth century was then not all that different from the crisis of Nationalism in the last decade of the century.

D.G. Boyce was similarly influenced in his study of British public opinion and government policy in Ireland between 1918 and 1922. His thesis, written before the troubles gained serious proportions, differed from his book in historical detail – new material, a reworking of the text to free it from its thesis constrictions. But in his book, published in 1972, after the troubles had involved the British government directly, and at a time when the British government and public was already regretting that involvement, he wrote

But whether or not England could ignore Irish questions depended ultimately upon the degree of political stability in the partitioned island. And when that stability was seriously threatened, as it began once more to be threatened in October 1968, British public opinion found itself unable to ignore its Irish responsibilities. These responsibilities stem directly from the treaty settlement of 1921, which left Northern Ireland an integral part of the United Kingdom; but, in effect, British influence over Ireland extends beyond the boundary of the six counties, England's wealth, her proximity to Ireland and her power, have made her, whether she likes it or not, the arbiter of Ireland's political destiny. Very often England has supplied the wrong answer: but she has never, to this day, been able to avoid confronting Irish questions.[16]

Was this an historical judgement alone, or a shot across the bows of the already gathering 'troops out' movement, 'Ulster, Time to Quit' lobby?

If the latter, then historians were, to use Tom Paulin's phrase, carnivores rather than Brahmins.[17] Their engagement with the present was not unconnected with the way they saw the past; their writing about the past was to a degree present-orientated. If they had not the future in their bones, then they certainly had the present in their minds; if they were not predicting, they were warning. History was engaged with politics.

The Ulster troubles had the impact of drawing historians' attention to issues which, while by no means neglected, had not been given the prominence at one time that they now began to enjoy. The very existence of an Ulster question could hardly be denied, long before 1969; there was an Ulster Question as long as there had been a Home Rule question, and the foundation of the Northern state only changed the form but not the substance, of that question. But the troubles gave a new awareness to the deep dimensions of the Ulster problem. They caused historians to look again at its significance, and to research it from a different perspective. Conor Cruise O'Brien, for example, in his study of *Parnell and his Party*, first published in 1957, discussed the Ulster question as it presented itself to Parnell. In 1957 O'Brien mused on the great conundrum

Whether that policy, backed as it was by a great English party, and a great Irish party, and by the combined prestige of Gladstone and Parnell, could have succeeded in bringing all Ulster without serious bloodshed, within the framework of home rule, can obviously never be known. It may be said, however, that no subsequent policy, and no subsequent combination of leaders, offered such good grounds for hope of a united and self-governing Ireland – or of real and well-founded friendship between England and Ireland.

But by 1978, after a decade of the Ulster troubles, the same writer, as

Professor Paul Bew noted, commented on the issue of Ulster and Ireland in a very different tone:

> He could not . . . ever have 'won Home Rule' because Home Rule was simply not winnable. Parnell, though a Protestant, was speaking for the Catholics of Ireland, not – as he and his followers appeared to take for granted – for an Irish nation that included the Ulster Protestants.

F.S.L. Lyons underwent a similar conversion. In his biography of John Dillon he remarked that the 'obstinate . . . resistance of Ulster and English Unionists to the extremely moderate self-government which Parnell, Redmond and Dillon were originally prepared to accept will always remain one of the strangest mysteries of politics'. By 1977 he acknowledged that Parnell 'never seems to have asked himself what he meant by an "Irish nation" or "Irish race" which he claimed to lead, and the idea that Ireland might possibly contain two nations, not one, apparently never entered his head'.[18]

Moody's book, discussed above, was another example of an historian who had written about the 'Ulster question' of the seventeenth century – in his magisterial book, *The Londonderry Plantation* (1939),[19] but he had not traced the theme, and not in such a direct way. Now the Ulster question was *the* question, and not merely one that was a sideshow to the broader, and more important issue, of Anglo-Irish relations. F.S.L. Lyons, in his *Culture and Anarchy in Ireland, 1890–1939*, first published in 1979, was so concerned to address the essentials of the Ulster question that he declared that the reason why British and Irish governments had failed to find a way out, or even to make progress, was because they had misdiagnosed the problem. The problem, in his view, was not merely political, but was one of a clash of cultures. He identified three different cultures in the north of Ireland: the Gaelic, the Anglican and the Presbyterian – and he urged the government to recognise these as well, for only when it did so could it hope to construct a political settlement.

He concluded

> That is why the Ulster situation can only be understood, however dimly, in its historical context. To seek to lay bare the historical roots of difference will not necessarily lead us to a solution. But the recognition of difference, especially by Irishmen themselves, is a prerequisite for peaceful coexistence. Such recognition, if it did nothing else, might at least bring us one stage further towards that sympathetic insight which is what the problem has always demanded but too seldom received.[20]

Peter Brooke, in a book based on his Ph.D thesis, *Ulster Presbyterianism*, ended with a plea for the British state to recognise that 'The progressive –

that is, British – development of the Ulster Protestants has been cut off by the British themselves. The community is forced back on its own resources'. 'If Northern Ireland continues to be suspended in a limbo between Catholic Ireland and secular Britain, if it continues to be excluded from the wider politics of the British state, then "bigotry" will have a long future before it.'[21]

There was another, more strictly historical, dimension to the growing recognition of the special nature of the Ulster question. The troubles forced historians to admit that they had spent very little time researching the Ulster region and its politics in the first place. Patrick Buckland's pioneering research on southern Irish Unionism, following directly on from his earlier work on the Irish question in British politics between 1910 and 1914, came from an English student working originally in a British university, Birmingham. He confronted ignorance and apathy, and found that few in Ireland had even heard of southern Unionism (which many people confused with trade unionism). But his work on Ulster Unionism was published at the suggestion of Gill and MacMillan,[22] and was clearly inspired by the need in the early 1970s to provide some coherent account of another, this time dangerously neglected subject. It must be said that the hostile reaction in some quarters to the serious study of Unionism was hardly likely to induce any young researchers to follow Buckland's lead. And it was again from a British university, this time Oxford, that a young Northern Irish academic began his attempt to set right what he regarded as the caricaturing of Irish, and especially Ulster, Unionism.[23] But the prevalence of Loyalist violence from the 1970s, though its character was intermittent, tended to distract attention from mainstream constitutional Unionism. Indeed, the only important study of the Ulster Unionist party published in 1972, almost eschewed any study of its ideological motivation altogether.[24] Unionism suffered from two skewed perceptions; either that it could be fully characterised by reference to its most extreme manifestation; or that (short of that extreme dimension) it had no discernible set of ideas at all, and therefore, no justification in politics. Moreover, the fragmented nature of Irish historical scholarship was reflected in the fact that historians from the south of Ireland largely ignored these Ulster political movements and ideologies. It would be to push the point too far to suggest that the existence of the border had resulted in the growth of a kind of academic partitionism among historians, thus giving them a southern-centred perspective on the north. Certainly, the disappointingly short shrift given to Ulster Unionism, and the character of the language used to describe it, in Joseph Lee's *Ireland, 1912–1985* seemed to bear this out.[25] For whatever the reasons, the north was to most southern Irish historians what Africa had been to the Victorians: a largely blank map, with few guiding features, and inhabited by unknown, and possibly unknowable, beings. But ignorance was soon followed by a realisation that here was new work to be done, and a new item to be added to the historical agenda.

A second major issue now highlighted by the troubles was political violence. The violence in the north was so severe, brutal and prolonged that it would hardly be ignored by anyone involved in Northern Ireland. The violence, moreover, was not (to use the common expression) mindless; on the contrary it was very mindful, and directly linked to the men whose military acts founded the Irish State in 1916, and whose Republicanism inspired their deeds in the war of independence of 1919–21 and the civil war of 1922–3. This placed some earlier political judgements at risk. Thus T.W. Moody's sense of scientific history once again deserted him when he finally came to write up his long-gestating biography of the Fenian and Land Leaguer Michael Davitt. Moody began by seeing Davitt in an essentially secular and socialist light. His early writings on Davitt stressed this side of his subject, and his connection with the British labour movement. But when Moody encountered a letter written by Davitt in 1880, in which Davitt rejoiced in the reflection that the people were arming themselves, and that violence was likely, and certainly very necessary, Moody, clearly embarrassed by his subject (but too scrupulous a scholar to ignore it), sought to attribute Davitt's mood to 'the state of excessive mental stimulation and physical exertion in which he was living and from which he was only to be rescued by renewed imprisonment.[26] Some might take a less psychological explanation, and see in this the resonances of the young Fenian who, while he had never fired a shot in anger, engaged in collecting and distributing arms for those who did. It was hard for historians, in truth, to view Irish political violence with any kind of Brahmin-like detachment any more. This had implications for their professional behaviour. Thus in 1986 Irish historians were criticised for declining an invitation to participate in the Terence MacSwiney memorial lectures in (of all places) London, through their doubts about the use to which such attendance would be put by the organisers.[27]

But, once again, violence stimulated historical writing of a non-political kind. Moreover, this was not confined to the study of Republican violence. This in itself contradicted the anti-revisionist claim that revisionist history was specifically directed against Republicans, and especially those in Northern Ireland, who, to use Desmond Fennell's phrase, were engaged in a rebellion 'which, in the 1980s, has led to an Anglo-Irish Agreement that some revisionists, like most people, regard as a good thing'. Fennell claimed that revisionists were mistaken in their belief (as he saw it) that the IRA in the North sit 'cowering in their burrows and trenches fearful of some new blast of revisionism from University College Dublin' (sic).[28] But this was to miss the point of the new interest shown in political violence, the study of which began, once again, in universities outside Ireland. Charles Townshend in Keele University, and

Alan O'Day in the University of North London, led the way in opening up a forum on political violence which adopted historical, sociological, religious, and economic methodology to explain why violence was used, what form it took and why it was, or was not, successful in attaining its supporters' and perpetrators' aims.[29] Paul Bew and Henry Patterson examined the role of violence in the establishment of the Northern Ireland state.[30] Bryan Follis placed the state's foundation and subsequent character in the context of the use of force both to defend and attack it.[31] Earlier, Patrick Buckland had explained that relations between Catholics and Protestants in the North were not bound to deteriorate in some historically determined form, but were soured by the state's use of law and order powers and special legislation to deal with IRA attacks, and to assure Unionists that the state would rally to the defence of its own people above all other considerations.[32] The role of the Great War in encouraging the use of force as a political weapon was illuminated, and the whole question of the origins, nature and significance of the 'cult of armed men' was made the subject of a panel as the American Historical Association Annual Conference in Chicago in January 1995. Thus the special relationship between state and people, between state force and paramilitary activity, and between paramilitary groups, together with an explanation of the historical roots of political violence, were all given a more critical, and deeply analytical assessment. Moreover, the relationship between violence and constitutionalism, hitherto seen as opposites, was now revealed in more subtle light. In particular, the contrast between the southern state's success in accommodating the undemocratic coup d'état of the Easter Rising to its democratic politics and the failure of the Northern Ireland state to effect a similar transition to full democracy prompted D.G. Boyce to muse on the connections between sectarianism and democracy in Ireland, and to invite scholars to investigate the very different outcomes of the making of the two states of Ireland between 1919 and 1923.[33]

The centrality of Irish Nationalism in the politics of the North was in contrast to the political context in which the rest of Ireland now found itself. There, the increasingly important context of the European Union and its implications for national sovereignty seemed to call in question the whole purpose of the founders of the modern Irish state. This was essentially a problem for Ireland's politicians to manage. But a younger generation of scholars now began to reassess the character and role of Nationalism in Irish history and politics. This was approached from several different angles. Tom Garvin adopted a sociological approach, both in his analysis of the Nationalist movement and especially of the revolutionary generation who benefited from the Great War and its impact on the Redmondite parliamentary party. Garvin advanced the study of radical Nationalism from the world of politics into the personal family and generational status of the individuals who made the Irish revolution of 1916–23.[34] His at times irreverent style drew criticism upon his head, and he seemed inclined to modify his views to suggest that the 1916 Rising was a direct response to what he called a lack of democracy in Ireland. He attributed the Rising to the behaviour of the British Government, which was by no means an untenable position, but one that needed more than mere assertion to make its point.[35]

This was nothing to the obloquy that fell upon those who looked critically at the life and times of the hitherto heroic figure of James Connolly. Connolly's socialism had at one time placed him above criticism; he was the harbinger of a Marxist Ireland in which Protestant and Catholic working men could combine in their mutual class interests. His writings were supposed to give inspiration to all those who longed for a secular socialist Ireland. Now new studies of Connolly stressed his nationalism rather than his socialism, indicated his prejudice against the Protestant working man of the north, and exposed his failure to grapple with the relationship between Irish nationalism and the Roman Catholic religion. Indeed, Connolly seemed not to want to make this distinction at all, but, rather, to accept and reinforce the connection between the two. His acceptance of the need for solidarity was confirmed in a short article in the new, popular Irish history journal, *History, Ireland*, which brought the fruits of the latest research to a wider audience, and which could claim to be one of the most exciting initiatives in Irish historical publishing in the last twenty-five years. Patrick Maume, in characteristically incisive style, explained how Connolly not only insisted upon dying a Roman Catholic, for the sake of maintaining what W.B. Yeats called 'hearts with one purpose alone'; he also troubled the living stream by insisting that his wife and family become Catholics as well.[36]

But perhaps the most vigorous and sustained criticism of Irish nationalism, and one linked directly to the Northern predicament, was made by Clare O'Halloran in her powerfully argued work, *Partition and the Limits of Irish Nationalism: An Ideology under Stress* (1987).[37] O'Halloran pointed out that, for all nationalism's rhetoric about partition, the fact remained that no-one had any idea of how to resolve the problem. Some hoped that economic improvement would align the two states, and encourage unification; others hoped that the sheer illogicality of partition on a small, 'natural' political unit, the island of Ireland, would reveal itself in the end; but mainly partition was an irritation; and one of the most important aspects of the revision of Irish nationalism lay in the discovery that nationalists in the south of Ireland were as baffled and annoyed as much by nationalists in the north as they were by Unionists (a feeling reciprocated by Ulster Unionists who, as Dennis Kennedy revealed in his book *The Widening Gulf*, found themselves increasingly out of sympathy with southern Unionists).[38] Indeed, Nationalism in Northern Ireland remained, until very recently, a neglected subject, and one left to be discovered and researched by authors from the north.[39] Not surprisingly, the greatest nationalist leader of twentieth-century Ireland, Eamon de Valera, came in for particular attention. De Valera, like Patrick Pearse, represented, or seemed to represent, the ideological dimension of Irish nationalism. Now his combination of pragmatism and caution on the Ulster question was revealed by the careful researches of John Bowman, Dierdre McMahon, and John P. O'Carroll and Joseph Lee,[40] while the strongly republican T.P. Coogan found it in his heart to declare, in his revisionist biography of de Valera, that he 'showed a consistently ungenerous spirit towards the Protestants of Northern Ireland'[41] (whom, however, he compared to the Afrikaaners in their own ungenerosity and bigotry).

It must be stressed that there was no incompatibility between thoroughly-researched historical scholarship, and the practice of drawing attention to the implications of this scholarship for the contemporary political predicament. Indeed, it would have been odd if historians had exercised some kind of self-denying ordinance, and shrugged off their responsibilities to their own generation. Thus Professor Marianne Elliott, in her magisterial biography of one of the greatest heroes of Irish nationalism, and especially Republicanism, Theobald Wolfe Tone, traced what she called the 'cult of Tone', attributing this to Tone's own *Life* which 'in its style and intimacy was "ageless"' and was 'packaged over the years to reach the widest audience'. Tone's desire to 'break the connection with England, the never failing source of all our political evils, and to assert the independence of my country', and his hope of substituting the 'common name of Irishman, in the place of the denominations of Protestant, Catholic and Dissenter' became, as Elliott observed 'the most quoted passage of Irish history'. But she showed that, whatever its appeal, it was essentially a construct, one re-launched in the nineteenth century, and culminating in the writings and deeds of Patrick Pearse in the 1916 Rising. Critics of Tone received 'short shrift'; in 1981 the Sinn Féin spokesman, Danny Morrison, told the gathering at Tone's grave in Bodenstown about 'men of property, who spend hours swivelling in their leather chairs, their judgement tempered and chosen by their own affluence, concocting distortions of republican history to berate us . . . [and] to support their contention about just how different the Republican Movement today is supposedly from the Republican Movement of the past'. But Elliott pointed out that those who rejected Tone for his anti-Englishness and his takeover by Catholic Republicans and those who cited him in support for armed revolt were, up to a point, right. But only up to a point. Tone's movement even before he died in 1798 had already developed characteristics which he could hardly approve of: 'His ideas were of an age which had already passed, and one suspects that his own militant republicanism might not have outlived that recognition. For his reputation as nationalist hero, his death was perhaps timely'.[42]

The life, and equally timely death, of Tone's canonizer, Patrick Pearse, must also move to the centre of historical as well as contemporary discussion. Not only because of his central role in the 1916 Rising and the martyrdom of the rebels; but also because he catalogued for his – and subsequent – generations, the pantheon of Irish nationalist thinkers, from Tone to Parnell. Pearse's nationalism was of particular relevance to the Northern troubles, because it was postulated on the idea that Ireland was a nation, rather than on the idea that she had yet to be made into one. In an article in *Studies*, John Coakley wrote that 'Tone recognised that an Irish nation . . . did not exist: his object was to create one'. He went on

> The mistaken assumption that Tone's ideal has been realized has contributed towards undermining the approach of southern Irish political leaders towards the attainment of unity. A number of false political positions flow from the assumption that Northern Irish Protestants are part of the 'Irish nation'.

Coakley argued that the failure to apprehend the ideology of Ulster Unionism, or even to accept that there was such a thing, was traceable to the enduring myth of the Irish nation. Pearse's views on Irish nationalism had acquired 'an unquestioned orthodoxy not only through the efforts of informal socialisation agencies but also through a deliberate policy of political education promoted by the Department of Education'.[43]

Coakley's article was of special interest, because he placed himself neither in the revisionist camp, nor in the ranks of those who regarded Pearse's ideas and influence uncritically. Thus, Coakley showed how the need to address the past anew, because of its influence upon the present, need not fall into the trap of a new polemicism. His article carefully analysed Pearse's ideas in philosophical terms, tracing the influence of the German thinker, J.G. Herder, on Pearse's concept of the nation as sharing a collective 'soul' which manifests itself in a characteristic language, literature, culture and institutions. He showed how this differed from Tone's rationalist French tradition of the late eighteenth century, which was itself not a stage in the evolution of Irish nationalist tradition, but rather was better understood in 'synchronic than in diachronic terms: as related to a great European or "Atlantic" movement of the late eighteenth century'. Tone's main objection to the British connection was that it acted as a prop to a corrupt ruling oligarchy. Coakley went on to demonstrate that Tone's nationalism differed radically from that of Thomas Davis, who belonged to the romantic tradition of early nineteenth-century Europe, seeing the nation as a historically-evolved, spiritual entity. Fintan Lalor, the next in Pearse's pantheon, was more akin to Tone than Davis, in that he was influenced by French and

American ideas. Moreover, he saw the redress of economic grievances, not spirituality, as the goal.[44]

Finally, Coakley addressed the Ulster Question head on. He showed how Pearse took uncritically Davis' assertion that

He who fancies some intrinsic objection to our nationality to lie in the co-existence of two languages, three of four great sects, and a dozen different races in Ireland, will learn that in Hungary, Switzerland, Belgium and America, different languages, creeds and races flourish kindly side by side, and he will seek in English intrigues the real well of the bitter woes of Ireland.

Pearse accepted that there was one nation, that any divisions were of a vague, medieval kind, and that differences were spurious. A trawl through Davis's 'kindly nations' revealed that, either they were held together by practical politics, as in Belgium, linguistic assimilation, as in America, or that Davis was mistaken, as in Canada, where French and English were at odds. But while Coakley denied the existence of 'one nation' he refused to follow the apparent logic of the argument that led to the acceptance of two nations. He argued that each community had its distinct version of history; that defeats for one were victories for the other. But Coakley pointed out that the Ulster Protestants had not developed a National theory; they had not created a coherent, positive version of the history of the protestant people of Ulster, nor had they developed a national political programme. They were hedged about by uncertainties.[45]

But the non-existence of an Irish nation did not entail the non-existence of Irish nationalists.[46] This seems an obvious point; but Coakley reinforced it by maintaining that not only did Protestants refuse to give their loyalty to the 'Irish people' who were assumed to constitute the nation; most Catholics did not give their primary loyalty to it either. An all-embracing territorial nationalism was, paradoxically, embraced by members of the southern Protestant minority; it was soon to fall victim to the narrower nationalism of the majority, which grew in strength as mass political mobilisation progressed. The Irish nation was, after all, only twenty per cent greater than the Catholic population; it was hardly surprising that the wider nation was easily identified with the narrower one. Thus the terms 'Irish' and 'Ireland' were used formally and informally by Catholics as a description of themselves. This forced many northern Protestants to deny their Irishness. 'This is an irony on which few southern Irish people pause to ponder when they criticise loyalist appropriations of the term "Ulster"; yet the latter usage arises from a similar lexical deficiency'.[47] Pearse's nationalism belonged to the narrower type. Pearse used history as a lawyer uses it: 'if it produces victory it has served its purpose'.[48] The victory, Coakley concluded, was bought at a high price; 'unity was sacrificed to independence, mobilisation of Hibernian nationalism having contributed to a further undermining of pan-nationalist sentiment'.[49]

Thus the northern troubles, though they inspired a closer look at the Irish past, and the interpretation of that past, did not fall victim to the idea that the past must become a slave of present concerns. This had important implications for those who argued that Irish history must attend to the needs of both communities, must satisfy them and support them. But the need to divorce the political imperative from the historical study of the past was not easily or readily accepted. Brian Murphy in an article on 'The Canon of Irish Cultural History: Some Questions',[50] challenged two assumptions prevalent in the writing of Irish history: first, that Catholic periodicals such as the *Catholic Bulletin* and the *Irish Monthly* were sources for quotes to 'prove that there was a nation of blind fools'; second, that national myths which 'emancipated' ought to be discriminated from those which 'incarcerated'. Tradition could and should be a positive force for shaping an Irish culture of the future.[51] Murphy argued that Catholic intellectual life had been portrayed at an unfairly low level at the turn of the century.[52] He also criticised the view that liberating influences were to be found in the heritage of such thinkers as George Russell and Sir Horace Plunkett, whose ideas were in turn rooted in the spirit of Swift and Berkeley.[53] When the writing of all these were set in their historical context and examined critically they were shown to be far from liberating, but rather, were reflecting the prejudices and politics of the time. They contributed to the 'two nations' theory, Murphy argued, in that they endorsed the view, later promulgated by F.S.L. Lyons, that there were in Ireland 'two irreconcilable cultures'.[54]

Murphy sought to rescue the Catholic intellectual tradition from what he regarded as its misrepresentation. But his main purpose was to challenge what he regarded as the political implications of those historians who emphasised the divisions, the irreconcilable divisions, of the Irish past. In a second essay Murphy claimed that the constitutional nationalism's possibility of overcoming dissensions in Irish society in the early twentieth century had been overlooked. By 'projecting a revolutionary dimension on Irish nationalism', he argued, 'it becomes reasonable for Unionists to distance themselves from the nationalist movement. An argument for separation and partition is again advanced.' He declared that Roy Foster's 'final verdict on Irish nationalism', that it was prepared to incorporate Unionists into a vision of an independent Ireland, whether they liked it or not, was 'revealed not only as partial history, but a highly political statement'. Murphy singled out the Australian historian Patrick O'Farrell for particular criticism, alleging that his work, which Foster acknowledged as deeply influencing *Modern Ireland*, was flawed, and showed a bias against Irish nationalism that Foster had all too willingly adopted. Murphy's attack upon Foster and O'Farrell for allegedly arguing the necessity of partition hardly did justice to the complexity of their work; and it did not go unanswered.

Peter Murray, in an analysis of the Gaelic League through the letters exchanged between its founder, Douglas Hyde, and the Reverend James Owen Hannay (George Birmingham) concluded that they revealed 'the difficulty of sustaining non-sectarian action in a country where politico-religious division runs as deep as it does in Ireland'; he criticised both the 'broad brush' of Foster and the 'more careful strokes' of Murphy, because 'the appropriate colour for such a study is surely grey'. [56] Patrick O'Farrell's reply was in interesting contrast. Whereas Murray explained the nuances that must be teased out to comprehend the ideas and realities of the Gaelic League, O'Farrell was more concerned with the attack that he felt that Murphy had made upon his integrity as an historian. His point was that the quotations he made in his book (which he claimed Murphy wrongly ascribed as *Ireland's English Question*, instead of his *England and Ireland Since 1800*, which Foster had in fact used), were clear and unmistakable, and could not be ascribed to any political desire to support Unionism or partitionism. He accused Murphy of 'railing against the real past', of seeking for a non-existent 'brilliant, unifying and ecumenical Catholic intelligentsia in Ireland at the end of the nineteenth century and the beginning of this'. Murphy wanted '1916 not to have been revolutionary, to have embraced and represented all Irish traditions and aspirations, but yet to have been "native Irish"'. Murphy had 'established his day-dream and then has moved back to bring the past into line'.[57]

O'Farrell used his rejoinder to raise a further criticism of Irish historians in their professional lives: that they were unable 'to perceive needs for initiative or response to change – or even in some cases, unawareness of the existence of material which might raise such questions'.[58] Were Irish historians resistant to change? Reluctant to read new material or even to search for it? Here again the question of the relationship between politics and history surfaced. Reluctance to change was, after all, another way of saying that Irish historians were content to accept received opinion, not to challenge it, and not to search for material that would challenge it. This in turn raised questions about the kind of political world they inhabited: one that was not conducive to liberal, critical analysis. Thus they still turned out what O'Farrell called 'pious (if hard headed) mythology, as distinct from professional history'.[59] There may be some force in this criticism, though the evidence suggests otherwise. But the most striking aspect of the last twenty-five years of historical research, which coincided with the northern troubles, is how new areas of interest have been defined, new problems identified, and new perspectives sought. This has been of uneven value, and some books have hardly done more than reinforce, or commend, traditional political values. Most have not. But while most historians have avoided writing political tracts, they have been unable to escape the consequences of the impact of politics upon history. This in fact was not ideological; it was methodological. In *The Unresolved Question*, Nicholas Mansergh ended a lifetime's writing about Irish history by commenting upon the Unionist state in the following terms:[60]

> in perspectives other than that of Ulster Unionists and possibly even in theirs, the sequel to Stormont has left an imprint of overall failure so bleak as to suggest that the explanation must needs be sought against a wider background and at a deeper level.

As Mansergh admitted, judged in terms of what Unionists wanted and needed, the devolution experiment might be assessed as an uneven rather than an altogether discouraging failure. Now the verdict had changed: 'bleak' failure is another way of summarising the politics of Northern Unionists since the late 1960s; it might indeed provoke a different kind of research into the history of Northern Ireland. If Irish historians are as complacent as Professor O'Farrell maintains then, again, it might not thus provoke them. But if they are provoked, then their history of Northern Ireland will bear a very different imprint from that of, say, the young Mansergh, or Reginald Lawrence, both of whom discussed the government of Northern Ireland in straightforward functional terms.[61]

This chapter has been concerned with the relationship between the past and the present. It has not addressed the question of how far the more public and directly political stance of some historians has had an impact on the making of the present, that is, upon the policy-making process itself. Historians, as F.S.L. Lyons remarked in 1973, have in some cases placed themselves on the side of what Lyons called 'the interest of enlightenment', by which he meant the need for historians not to wash their hands of contemporary history,

> For if professionals ignore those years, others will not. The books about Ulster or the IRA will not cease to roll from the presses merely because the historians have deliberately washed their hands of these subjects.[62]

Thus prominent historians have served on such bodies as the Opsahl commission, which investigated a wide range of opinion in Northern Ireland, or the Cadogan Group, which sought to influence government thinking about a political settlement in the North.[63] Clearly, then, the eruption of violence in the north has stirred the conscience of historians, and has caused some of them at least to seek to avoid the accusation that they are engaging in a *trahison des clercs*, a retreat from the political problems of the day.

Professor Ronan Fanning has suggested that the troubles may even have encouraged the enthusiasm for socio-economic, at the expense of political history. Social and economic historians, he suggests, are more immune to the paralysis of pessimism induced by the savage violence of the past and present, because 'their subject does not impose the same necessity to grapple with the use of myth in political ideology that confronts political historians.[64] There is evidence for this. In his *The Study of Local History as an Agent of Reconciliation* W.A. Maguire wrote

> The proper study of local history (as distinct from the history of a nation or a movement) can, I believe, do much to further reconciliation. For one thing the smaller scale of local history in itself enables more of us to get closer to the real complexity of events in the lives of our forefathers than history of a wider scope may do. More than that, the variety of history, the number of different strands – political, religious, social, economic, technological, and the sometimes harmonious, sometimes conflicting connections between the one and another – is literally brought home to members of a local history society, in a way that is for many people convincing because it is related to their own neighbourhood. There is a good chance that such a society will be all-embracing in its interests, inclusive rather than exclusive in its outlook, so that its members will educate each other.[65]

This development reflects the notion, held since the Second World War, that the historian plays an important functional role in modern society; and that historical research has a responsibility to set right, or at least to modify, chauvinism and myth.[66] This may be an over-ambitious strategy; and it may be the case that groups in conflict will always seek justification for their actions in a version of history, quite untroubled by the scepticism and doubt that are the hallmark of the professional historian. Yet patriotic history has declined in western Europe since 1945, partly through the experience of the two world wars, partly through the changing role of the university, which produced trained historians, rather than practitioners of *belles lettres*, or apologists for commonly held myths. History, as Professor Paul Kennedy has remarked, is 'not a static study, concerned merely with the accumulation of facts about the past, but a fluid one, reflecting the ever-changing world in which we live and one which, while rejecting relativism, is searching for a less biased, more objective understanding of man and society and the past'. This, as he goes on to say, makes history an imperfect discipline, striving after the two unattainable goals of impartiality and finality; and one point that may be made against revisionism is that, at times, it has displayed some of the less welcome characteristics of the chauvinism it seeks to undermine.[67]

But this is a less important question than the issue of how the present and the past stand in relation to each other. If thought and knowledge are the products of culture, then our thoughts and knowledge about the past are inevitably shaped by our culture.[68] We are therefore deeply influenced by our standards for explaining action. The presentness of the past can be illustrated in this way. In his *The Making of Modern Ireland*, J.C. Beckett wrote of the settlement of 1921 that, though it left 'a legacy of bitterness issuing occasionally in local and sporadic disturbances', yet 'it inaugurated for Ireland a longer period of general tranquillity than she had known since the first half of the eighteenth century'. Professor Fanning drew attention to these words, commenting that 'today such a statement might well provoke incredulity if not, indeed, derision – at least among non-historians'. But, as he pointed out, the sentence in the second, revised edition of the book, published in 1981, read: 'But the settlement, whatever its final outcome, did at least inaugurate for Ireland a longer period of general tranquillity than she had known since the first half of the eighteenth century'.[69] This is an example of how the historian, writing in the present, revises the generalisations which he brings to the study of the past. But this is not the same as saying that the historian simply builds up his explanatory categories from 'personal experience of actions done in his own day and then applies these to his study of the past'. Historians proceed by rules of how to do their research; and they accumulate concepts 'built up over the generations'; at the same time, our explanatory categories are those which we first learn to use in application to the present:[70] thus, if we talk about 'political power', and study its working in ninth-century institutions, then we are using a concept that we understand today. But we do not use it without reservation or caution: the Anglo-Saxon Witanagemot is not the nineteenth-century parliament. And yet there is what one scholar has called an 'export-import relationship' between our present-day understanding of actions and our understanding of actions done in the past'.[71]

Past and present are, as Professor Rex Martin points out, relative terms. 'What has been present becomes past and the past has been studied by many different presents'.[72] But the historian is not a participant in the past; he or she is an investigator, working by agreed research rules.[73] This is what distinguishes the work of a Buckland or a Fanning from that of a Desmond Fennell or a C. Desmond Greaves.[74] At the same time the student of revisionism in Irish, or any other history, is well advised to follow E.H. Carr's dictum that 'before you study the historian, study his historical and social environment'.[75] This is at least part of the reason why the outlook of historians changes from generation to generation, and why, for example, Fritz Fischer's book on Germany's aims in the First World War differs from those written in the 1930s, and why, in British history we can understand and appreciate the different perspectives of a J.H. Plumb and a J.C.D. Clark, or, for that matter, of those historians who saw the Norman conquest of Anglo-Saxon England as a positive gain or a deep cultural and political loss.[76]

The impact of the Northern Ireland crisis on historical thinking and research is, then, a more complex business than it first appears. It is not merely a personal response to a troubled political environment; rather, it has encouraged the historian to use his or her special skills in ways that help us interpret and understand modern Irish history: thus, a reappraisal of broad-based Ulster Unionism and Ulster Nationalism is now on the agenda. It has also added to our existing stock of historical concepts, through the 'export–import relationship' involved in our understanding of actions done in the past. The present in which the historian lives influences the choice of subject and the way in which it is analysed. But this is different from the 'usable' past as deployed by political propagandists or politicians, or their supporters: W.A. Maguire's plea for local history may be influenced by the 'Troubles'; but a local history based on sound archival research has much to offer. Historians work by the rules of their discipline, and apply their professional skills to what they are doing. They are probably nearer today to understanding each other's methods than ever they have been before; they are probably closer to adopting each other's skills than ever they were before. The revolution in Irish historical work is therefore a product of a wider, cross-national movement in historical scholarship, confronting all the difficulties and possibilities that the historian in his or her social and political context must confront, and, to the best of his or her ability, try to resolve. In the end, what seems to be the most parochial aspect of the study of modern Irish history, the last twenty-five years of political instability and their impact on historical thinking, turns out to be of the most general significance for the historian of whatever country who wants to be self-conscious about the methodology of the discipline.

NOTES

1 J.C.D. Clark, *English Society, 1688–1832: Ideology, Social Structure and Political Practice during the Ancien Regime* (Cambridge, 1985), pp. 1, 4, 10, 12.
2 *Ibid.*, p. 10.
3 A.J.P. Taylor, *The Course of German History* (London, 1945); *The Origins of the Second World War* (London, 1961). For a review article of the latter, which considers its methodological implications, see F.W. Hinsley in *Historical Journal* vol. 4 (1961), pp. 222–9.
4 Clark, *op. cit.*, p. 1.
5 Kathleen Nutt, 'Irish Identity and the Writing of History', in *Eire/Ireland*, vol. XXIX, 2 (summer 1994), pp. 160–72, at p. 168.
6 John Whyte, *Interpreting Northern Ireland* (Oxford, 1990).
7 Owen Dudley Edwards, *The Sins of Our Fathers: The Roots of Conflict in Northern Ireland* (Dublin, 1970). Conor Cruise O'Brien, *States of Ireland* (London, 1971).
8 Donald H. Akenson, *Conor: A Biography of Conor Cruise O'Brien* (Montreal and Kingston, 1994), p. 378.
9 T.W. Moody, *The Ulster Question, 1603–1973* (Cork, 1974).

10 B.M. Walker, *Ulster Politics: the Formative Years, 1868–86* (Belfast, 1989).

11 Moody, *op. cit.*, p. 101.

12 L.P. Curtis Jr, 'The Greening of Irish History', in *Eire/Ireland*, vol. XXIX, 2 (summer 1994), pp. 7–28, at pp. 7–8.

13 Paul Bew, Peter Gibbon and Henry Patterson, *The State in Northern Ireland: 1921–72: Political Forces and Social Classes* (Manchester, 1979).

14 Paul Bew, *Conflict and Conciliation in Ireland, 1890–1910: Parnellites and Radical Agrarians* (Oxford, 1987), p. 222.

15 Paul Bew, 'The Easter Rising: Lost Leaders and Lost Opportunities', in *The Irish Review*, 11 (winter 1991/92), pp. 9–13, at p. 13. See also his *Ideology and the Irish Question: Ulster Unionism and Irish Nationalism, 1912–1916* (Oxford, 1994), pp. 158–60.

16 D. George Boyce, *Englishmen and Irish Troubles: British Public Opinion and the Making of Irish Policy, 1918–1922* (London, 1972), p. 186.

17 Tom Paulin, *Ireland and the English Crisis* (Newcastle upon Tyne, 1984), p. 155.

18 D. George Boyce, '"The Portrait of the King is the King": The Biographers of Charles Stewart Parnell', in D. George Boyce and Alan O'Day (eds), *Parnell in Perspective* (London, 1991), pp. 284–306, at pp. 304–5.

19 T.W. Moody, *The Londonderry Plantation, 1609–1641* (Belfast, 1939).

20 F.S.L. Lyons, *Culture and Anarchy in Ireland, 1890–1939* (Oxford, 1979), p. 145.

21 Peter Brooke, *Ulster Presbyterianism: The Historical Perspective, 1610–1970* (Dublin, 1987), pp. 213–14.

22 Patrick Buckland, *Irish Unionism II: Ulster Unionism and the Origins of Northern Ireland, 1886–1922* (Dublin, 1973).

23 Alvin Jackson, *The Ulster Party: Irish Unionists in the House of Commons, 1884–1911* (Oxford, 1989).

24 John F. Harbinson, *The Ulster Unionist Party 1882–1973* (Belfast, 1973); Harbinson devotes only about four pages to what he calls 'certain recurring themes' in Ulster Unionist 'political attitudes'.

25 Joseph Lee, *Ireland, 1912–1985: Politics and Society* (Cambridge, 1990); for a criticism of Lee's treatment of Unionism see Graham Walker, 'Old History: Protestant Ulster in Lee's Ireland', in *The Irish Review*, 12 (spring/summer 1992) pp. 65–71.

26 T.W. Moody, *Michael Davitt and Irish Revolution, 1846–82* (Oxford, 1981), pp. 440–2.

27 M.A. G. Ó Tuathaigh, 'Irish Historical "Revisionism": State of the Art or Ideological Project', in Ciaran Brady (ed.), *Interpreting Irish History: The Debate on Historical Revisionism, 1938–1994* (Dublin, 1994), pp. 306, fn. 1.

28 Desmond Fennell, 'Against Revisionism', *ibid.*, p. 189.

29 For example, Charles Townshend, *The British Campaign in Ireland, 1919–1921: The Development of Political and Military Policies* (Oxford, 1975); *Political Violence in Ireland* (Oxford, 1983), Alan O'Day and Yonah Alexander (eds), *Terrorism in Ireland* (London and New York, 1984); and *Ireland's Terrorist Dilemma* (Dordrecht, 1986).

30 Bew, Gibbon and Patterson, *The State in Northern Ireland*, pp. 50–70.

31 Bryan A. Follis, *A State under Siege: the Establishment of Northern Ireland, 1920–1925* (Oxford, 1995).

32 Patrick Buckland, *The Factory of Grievances: Devolved Government in Northern Ireland, 1921–39* (Dublin, 1979), pp. 179–205.

33 D. George Boyce, *Ireland 1828–1923: From Ascendancy to Democracy* (Oxford, 1992), pp. 109–11.

34 Tom Garvin, *The Evolution of Irish Nationalist Politics* (Dublin, 1981); *Nationalist Revolutionaries in Ireland, 1858–1928* (Oxford, 1987).

35 Tom Garvin, 'The Rising and Irish Democracy', in Mairin Ó Dhonnchadha and Theo Dorgan (eds), *Revising the Rising* (Derry, 1991), pp. 21–8.
36 Patrick Maume, 'Lily Connolly's Conversion', in *History Ireland*, vol. 2, 3 (autumn 1994), pp. 30–1.
37 Clare O'Halloran, *Partition and the Limits of Irish Nationalism: An Ideology under Stress* (Dublin, 1987).
38 Dennis Kennedy, *The Widening Gulf: Northern Attitudes to the Independent Irish State, 1919–1949* (Belfast, 1988).
39 Notably Eamonn Phoenix, *Northern Nationalism: Nationalist Politics, Partition and the Catholic Minority in Northern Ireland, 1890–1940* (Belfast, 1994).
40 John Bowman, *De Valera and the Ulster Question, 1917–73* (Oxford, 1980); Deirdre McMahon, *Republicans and Imperialists: Anglo-Irish Relations in the 1930s* (New Haven and London, 1984); John P. O'Carroll and John A. Murphy, *De Valera and his Times* (Cork, 1983), J. Lee and G. Ó Tuathaigh, *The Age of de Valera* (Dublin, 1982).
41 T.P. Coogan, *De Valera: Long Fellow, Long Shadow* (London, 1993) p. 695.
42 Marianne Elliott, *Wolfe Tone: Prophet of Irish Independence* (New Haven and London, 1989), pp. 411–19.
43 John Coakley, 'Patrick Pearse and the "Noble Lie" of Irish Nationalism', in *Studies*, vol. LXXII, 286 (summer 1983), pp. 119–36, at p. 120.
44 Coakley, *op. cit.*, pp. 121–6.
45 *Ibid.*, pp. 126–9.
46 *Ibid.*, p. 129.
47 *Ibid.*, pp. 130–1.
48 *Ibid.*, pp. 132–3.
49 *Ibid.*, p. 133.
50 Brian Murphy, 'The Canon of Irish Cultural History: Some Questions', in *Studies*, vol. 77, 305 (spring 1988), pp. 68–83.
51 *Ibid.*, p. 68.
52 *Ibid.*, p. 69.
53 *Ibid.*, pp. 72–3.
54 *Ibid.*, pp. 77–9.
55 Brian Murphy, 'The Canon of Irish Cultural History: Some Questions concerning Roy Foster's *Modern Ireland*', in *Studies*, vol. 82, 326 (summer 1993) pp. 178–9.
56 Peter Murray, 'A Sectarian Skeleton in the Gaelic League's Cupboard? Roy Foster, Brian Murphy and the case of George A. Birmingham', in *Studies*, vol. 82 (winter 1993), pp. 481–6.
57 Patrick O'Farrell, 'The Canon of Irish Cultural History: A Reply to Brian Murphy', in *op. cit.*, pp. 487–98.
58 *Ibid.*, pp. 496–7, fn. 2.
59 *Ibid.*, p. 498, fn. 9.
60 Nicholas Mansergh, *The Unresolved Question: the Anglo-Irish Settlement and its Undoing* (New Haven and London, 1991), p. 351. See also his revised *The Irish Question, 1840–1921* (London, 1975), p. 19.
61 Nicholas Mansergh, *The Government of Northern Ireland: a study in devolution* (London, 1936); R.J. Lawrence, *The Government of Northern Ireland: Public Finance and Public Services* (Oxford, 1965). For an example of the 'deeper level' approach see A.T.Q. Stewart, *The Narrow Ground: Aspects of Ulster, 1609–1969* (London, 1977).
62 F.S.L. Lyons, 'The Dilemma of the Irish Contemporary Historian', in *Hermathena*, no. CXV (summer 1973), pp. 45–56, at p. 55.

63 See Andy Pollack (ed.), *The Opsahl Report on Northern Ireland: A Citizens' Inquiry* (Belfast, 1993); The Cadogan Group, *Blurred Vision: Joint Authority and the Northern Ireland Problem* (Belfast, 1994). John Whyte noted that, although 'it is quite possible that, in proportion to size, Northern Ireland is the most heavily researched area on earth', research on the problem had not been effective in influencing the course of events (Whyte, *Interpreting Northern Ireland* (Oxford, 1990), pp. viii, 246–50; see also his inaugural lecture, *Is Research on the Northern Ireland Problem Worth While?* (Belfast, 1983). For an example of practical research see John McGarry and Brendan O'Leary (eds), *The Future of Northern Ireland* (Oxford, 1990).

64 Ronan Fanning, '"The Great Enchantment": Uses and Abuses of Modern Irish History', in Ciaran Brady (ed.), *Interpreting Irish History*, p. 156. See also Kathleen Nutt, 'Irish Identity and the Writing of History', in *Eire/Ireland*, vol. XXIX, 2, p. 163.

65 Quoted in Edward O'Donnell, 'History Lessons', in *Studies*, vol. LXXII (winter 1984), p. 270.

66 Paul M. Kennedy, 'The Decline of Nationalistic History in the West, 1900–1970', in *Journal of Contemporary History*, vol. 8, 1 (January 1973), pp. 77–100, at p. 99.

67 *Ibid.*, pp. 99–100.

68 For a discussion of these issues see Rex Martin, *Historical Explanation: Re-enactment and Practical Inference* (Ithaca, NY, 1977), esp. pp. 216–17.

69 Fanning, 'The Great Enchantment', pp. 148–9, and fn. 7.

70 Martin, *op. cit.*, pp. 228–30.

71 *Ibid.*, pp. 230–1.

72 *Ibid.*, p. 232.

73 *Ibid.*, pp. 232–40.

74 For examples of Greaves' work see *1916 as History: The Myth of the Blood Sacrifice* (Dublin, 1991), and for Fennell see *The Revision of Irish History* (Dublin, 1989).

75 Kennedy, 'Decline of Nationalistic History', p. 77.

76 Norman F. Cantor, *Inventing the Middle Ages: The Lives, Works, and Ideas of the Great Medievalists of the Twentieth Century* (Cambridge, 1992), pp. 276–7.

INDEX

This index attempts to bring together scattered information and draw attention to less obvious themes. An index entry to a concept is not meant to validate that concept.